Sliding Mask

Exam Tips:

1. Read each question carefully before looking at the possible answers.

2. After formulating an answer, determine which of the choices most nearly corresponds with that answer. It should completely answer the question.

3. Answer each question according to the latest regulations and procedures. You will receive credit if the regulations or procedures have changed. Computerized exams may be updated as regulations and procedures change.

4. There is only one answer that is correct and complete. The other answers are either incomplete or are derived from popular misconceptions.

5. If you do not know the answer to a question, try not to spend too much time on it. Continue with those you can answer. Then, return to the unanswered or difficult questions.

6. Unanswered questions will be counted as incorrect.

7. On calculator problems, select the answer nearest your solution. If you have solved it correctly, your answer will be closer to the correct answer than the other choices.

D1636124

POWERPLANT TECHNICIAN
TEST GUIDE WITH ORAL AND
PRACTICAL STUDY GUIDE

The charts, tables, and graphs used in this publication are for illustration purposes only and cannot be used for navigation or to determine actual aircraft performance.

ISBN: 978-0-88487-194-1

Cover: 787 Engine Fan Close Up Courtesy of Boeing

Jeppesen
55 Inverness Dr. East
Englewood, CO 80112-5498
Web Site: www.jeppesen.com
Email: Captain@jeppesen.com
Copyright © Jeppesen
All Rights Reserved. Published 2004 - 2011, 2016
Printed in the United States of America

10002001-006

WELCOME TO THE JEPPESEN AVIATION MAINTENANCE TECHNICIAN INTEGRATED TRAINING SYSTEM

Our general, airframe, and powerplant mechanic course materials are fully integrated, providing a complete and systematic training program. Textbooks and test guides are written in a simple to understand format, delivering all Lhe necessary information for you to obtain yom aircraft maintenance certificate and ratings. Cow-se materials are organized into the same chapter and section formats to integrate study as you progress through each subject area. FAA Learnfog Statement Code topics are f-t11ly covered and cross-referenced in test guide materials.

TEXTBOOKS

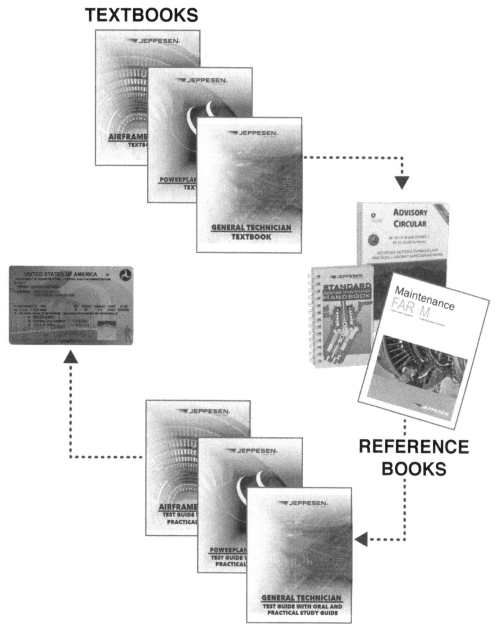

REFERENCE BOOKS

TEST GUIDES
WITH ORAL AND PRACTICAL
STUDY GUIDES

JEPPESEN INTEGRATED TRAINING SYSTEM

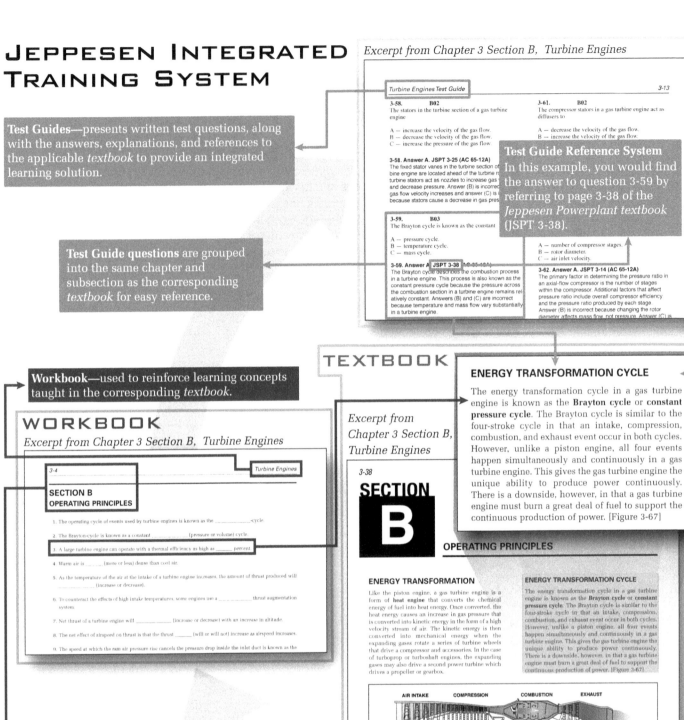

Test Guides—presents written test questions, along with the answers, explanations, and references to the applicable *textbook* to provide an integrated learning solution.

Test Guide questions are grouped into the same chapter and subsection as the corresponding *textbook* for easy reference.

Excerpt from Chapter 3 Section B, Turbine Engines

Turbine Engines Test Guide
3-13

3-58.   B02
The stators in the turbine section of a gas turbine engine

A — increase the velocity of the gas flow.
B — decrease the velocity of the gas flow.
C — increase the pressure of the gas flow.

3-58. Answer A. JSPT 3-25 (AC 65-12A)
The fixed stator vanes in the turbine section of a gas turbine engine are located ahead of the turbine rotor. The turbine stators act as nozzles to increase gas velocity and decrease pressure. Answer (B) is incorrect because gas flow velocity increases and answer (C) is incorrect because stators cause a decrease in gas pressure.

3-59.   B03
The Brayton cycle is known as the constant

A — pressure cycle.
B — temperature cycle.
C — mass cycle.

3-59. Answer A. JSPT 3-38 (AC 65-12A)
The Brayton cycle describes the combustion process in a turbine engine. This process is also known as the constant pressure cycle because the pressure across the combustion section in a turbine engine remains relatively constant. Answers (B) and (C) are incorrect because temperature and mass flow vary substantially in a turbine engine.

3-61.   B02
The compressor stators in a gas turbine engine act as diffusers to

A — decrease the velocity of the gas flow.
B — increase the velocity of the gas flow.

A — number of compressor stages.
B — rotor diameter.
C — air inlet velocity.

3-62. Answer A. JSPT 3-14 (AC 65-12A)
The primary factor in determining the pressure ratio in an axial-flow compressor is the number of stages within the compressor. Additional factors that affect pressure ratio include overall compressor efficiency and the pressure ratio produced by each stage. Answer (B) is incorrect because changing the rotor diameter affects mass flow, not pressure. Answer (C) is

Test Guide Reference System
In this example, you would find the answer to question 3-59 by referring to page 3-38 of the *Jeppesen Powerplant* textbook (JSPT 3-38).

TEXTBOOK

Workbook—used to reinforce learning concepts taught in the corresponding *textbook*.

WORKBOOK

Excerpt from Chapter 3 Section B, Turbine Engines

3-4
Turbine Engines

SECTION B
OPERATING PRINCIPLES

1. The operating cycle of events used by turbine engines is known as the _____ cycle.

2. The Brayton-cycle is known as a constant _____ (pressure or volume) cycle.

3. A large turbine engine can operate with a thermal efficiency as high as _____ percent.

4. Warm air is _____ (more or less) dense than cool air.

5. As the temperature of the air at the intake of a turbine engine increases, the amount of thrust produced will _____ (increase or decrease).

6. To counteract the effects of high intake temperatures, some engines use a _____ thrust augmentation system.

7. Net thrust of a turbine engine will _____ (increase or decrease) with an increase in altitude.

8. The net effect of airspeed on thrust is that the thrust _____ (will or will not) increase as airspeed increases.

9. The speed at which the ram air pressure rise cancels the pressure drop inside the inlet duct is known as the

Workbook questions are grouped into the same chapter and subsection as the corresponding *textbook* for easy reference.

Excerpt from Chapter 3 Section B, Turbine Engines

3-38

SECTION B

OPERATING PRINCIPLES

ENERGY TRANSFORMATION

Like the piston engine, a gas turbine engine is a form of **heat engine** that converts the chemical energy of fuel into heat energy. Once converted, the heat energy causes an increase in gas pressure that is converted into kinetic energy in the form of a high velocity stream of air. The kinetic energy is then converted into mechanical energy when the expanding gases rotate a series of turbine wheels that drive a compressor and accessories. In the case of turboprop or turboshaft engines, the expanding gases may also drive a second power turbine which drives a propeller or gearbox.

ENERGY TRANSFORMATION CYCLE

The energy transformation cycle in a gas turbine engine is known as the **Brayton cycle** or **constant pressure cycle**. The Brayton cycle is similar to the four-stroke cycle in that an intake, compression, combustion, and exhaust event occur in both cycles. However, unlike a piston engine, all four events happen simultaneously and continuously in a gas turbine engine. This gives the gas turbine engine the unique ability to produce power continuously. There is a downside, however, in that a gas turbine engine must burn a great deal of fuel to support the continuous production of power. [Figure 3-67]

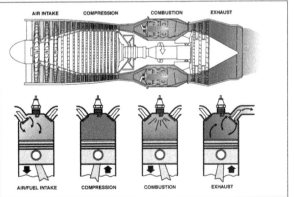

Figure 3-67. In a gas turbine engine, air is taken in through an air inlet, compressed in the compressor, mixed with fuel and ignited in the combustors, then exhausted through the turbines and exhaust nozzle. This allows a gas turbine engine to perform the same functions as a cylinder and piston in a reciprocating engine except that, in a turbine engine, the events happen continuously.

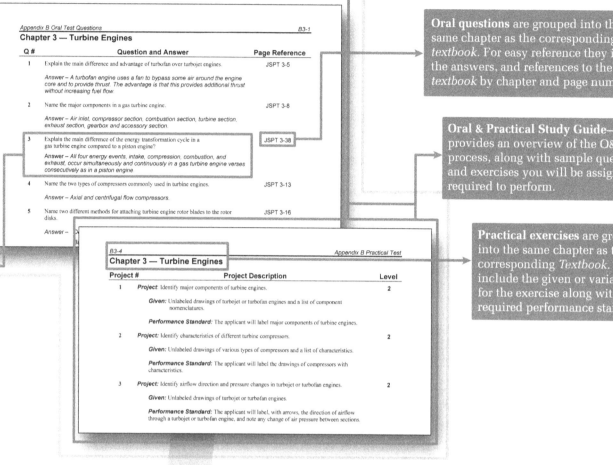

Oral questions are grouped into the same chapter as the corresponding *textbook*. For easy reference they include the answers, and references to the *textbook* by chapter and page number.

Oral & Practical Study Guide— provides an overview of the O&P process, along with sample questions and exercises you will be assigned and required to perform.

Practical exercises are grouped into the same chapter as the corresponding *Textbook*. They include the given or variables for the exercise along with the required performance standard.

...fers back to Jeppesen ...ining system.

...bject matter knowledge codes—can be ...ed to reference *Jeppesen's training system.*

...sing "B03" as an example, to find information ... the installation of turbine engines, look up ... subject "turbine engine installation" in the ...ppesen index and it will refer you to the ...propriate chapter and page in the ...owerplant textbook.

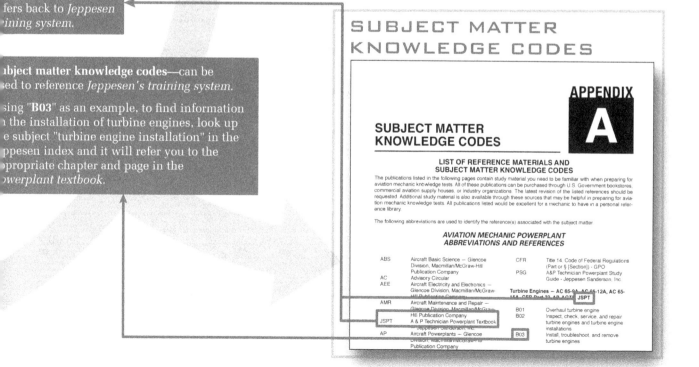

Within the first cropped image (Appendix B Oral Test Questions):

Appendix B Oral Test Questions — B3-1

Chapter 3 — Turbine Engines

Q #	Question and Answer	Page Reference
1	Explain the main difference and advantage of turbofan over turbojet engines.	JSPT 3-5
	Answer – A turbofan engine uses a fan to bypass some air around the engine core and to provide thrust. The advantage is that this provides additional thrust without increasing fuel flow.	
2	Name the major components in a gas turbine engine.	JSPT 3-8
	Answer – Air inlet, compressor section, combustion section, turbine section, exhaust section, gearbox and accessory section.	
3	Explain the main difference of the energy transformation cycle in a gas turbine engine compared to a piston engine?	JSPT 3-38
	Answer – All four energy events, intake, compression, combustion, and exhaust, occur simultaneously and continuously in a gas turbine engine verses consecutively as in a piston engine.	
4	Name the two types of compressors commonly used in turbine engines.	JSPT 3-13
	Answer – Axial and centrifugal flow compressors.	
5	Name two different methods for attaching turbine engine rotor blades to the rotor disks.	JSPT 3-16
	Answer –	

B3-4 — Appendix B Practical Test

Chapter 3 — Turbine Engines

Project #	Project Description	Level
1	**Project**: Identify major components of turbine engines.	2
	Given: Unlabeled drawings of turbojet or turbofan engines and a list of component nomenclatures.	
	Performance Standard: The applicant will label major components of turbine engines.	
2	**Project**: Identify characteristics of different turbine compressors.	2
	Given: Unlabeled drawings of various types of compressors and a list of characteristics.	
	Performance Standard: The applicant will label the drawings of compressors with characteristics.	
3	**Project**: Identify airflow direction and pressure changes in turbojet or turbofan engines.	2
	Given: Unlabeled drawings of turbojet or turbofan engines.	
	Performance Standard: The applicant will label, with arrows, the direction of airflow through a turbojet or turbofan engine, and note any change of air pressure between sections.	

Within the second cropped image (Subject Matter Knowledge Codes):

SUBJECT MATTER KNOWLEDGE CODES

SUBJECT MATTER KNOWLEDGE CODES

APPENDIX A

LIST OF REFERENCE MATERIALS AND SUBJECT MATTER KNOWLEDGE CODES

The publications listed in the following pages contain study material you need to be familiar with when preparing for aviation mechanic knowledge tests. All of these publications can be purchased through U.S. Government bookstores, commercial aviation supply houses, or industry organizations. The latest revision of the listed references should be requested. Additional study material is also available through these sources that may be helpful in preparing for aviation mechanic knowledge tests. All publications listed would be excellent for a mechanic to have in a personal reference library.

The following abbreviations are used to identify the reference(s) associated with the subject matter.

AVIATION MECHANIC POWERPLANT ABBREVIATIONS AND REFERENCES

ABS	Aircraft Basic Science — Glencoe Division, Macmillan/McGraw-Hill Publication Company	CFR	Title 14, Code of Federal Regulations (Part or § [Section]) - GPO
AC	Advisory Circular	PSG	A&P Technician Powerplant Study Guide - Jeppesen Sanderson, Inc
AEE	Aircraft Electricity and Electronics — Glencoe Division, Macmillan/McGraw-Hill Publication Company		Turbine Engines — AC 65-9A, AC 65-12A, AC 65-15A, CFR Part 33, AP, ACTE, **JSPT**
AMR	Aircraft Maintenance and Repair — Glencoe Division, Macmillan/McGraw-Hill Publication Company	B01	Overhaul turbine engine
JSPT	A & P Technician Powerplant Textbook - Jeppesen Sanderson, Inc	B02	Inspect, check, service, and repair turbine engines and turbine engine installations
AP	Aircraft Powerplants — Glencoe Division, Macmillan/McGraw-Hill Publication Company	B03	Install, troubleshoot, and remove turbine engines

TABLE OF CONTENTS

PREFACE

Thank you for purchasing this Powerplant Technician Test Guide. This Test Guide will help you understand the answers to the test questions so you can take the FAA Computerized Knowledge, Oral, and Practical exams with confidence. It includes FAA Aviation Mechanic Powerplant Knowledge test questions, sample oral test questions, and samples of typical practical projects that an FAA Designated Examiner may assign during the Practical exam. For the Computerized Knowledge Exam portion of the Test Guide, the correct answers are included with explanations, along with study references. Explanations of why the other choices are wrong have been included where appropriate. Questions are organized by topic with explanations conveniently located following each question. Figures identical to those on the FAA test are included.

The material for the Powerplant Technician Oral and Practical exams is included in Appendix B of the Test Guide. Since the Oral and Practical exam questions are not public domain information, our questions may not reflect the exact questions that you will be asked during your test. However, we feel confident that if you can answer the sample oral questions and perform the practical projects that we present in this Test Guide, you should have no difficulty passing your FAA exams. Our sample questions and projects reflect the most current information that the FAA requires Designated Mechanic Examiners to use during testing. Please note that this Test Guide is intended to be a supplement to your instructor-led maintenance training, not a stand-alone learning tool.

Refer to the diagram of the Jeppesen Integrated Training System on the following pages to see how the various training materials complement each other. This diagram shows the integrated features of the Textbooks, Workbooks and Test Guides in detail.

If you would like to find out more about career opportunities in aviation maintenance and how you can get started, you can email your specific career and/or training questions to:

trainingservices@jeppesen.com

Also use this address for comments/questions regarding technical content of Jeppesen maintenance materials.

INTRODUCTION

The Powerplant Technician Test Guide is designed to help you prepare for the FAA Aviation Mechanic Powerplant Knowledge computerized test. It covers FAA exam material that applies to powerplant knowledge related to aircraft maintenance.

We recommend that you use this Test Guide in conjunction with the Jeppesen Powerplant Technician Textbook. The Test Guide is organized along the same lines as the Powerplant Textbook, with 14 chapters and distinctive sections within most chapters. Questions are covered in the Test Guide in the same sequence as the material in the textbook. References to applicable chapters and pages in the various textbooks are included along with the answers.

Within the chapters, the FAA exam questions and answers appear side by side. The first line of the explanation for each question contains the correct answer and the page reference if the question is covered in the Powerplant Technician Textbook. There is also an abbreviation for an FAA or other authoritative source document, if appropriate.

Example:Answer B. JSPT 8E

Next is a brief explanation of the correct answer. An explanation of why the other answers are incorrect is sometimes included. In cases where no page reference or authoritative source document is given, consider the explanation as a supplement to the textbook.

Abbreviations used in the Test Guide are as follows:

AC — Advisory Circular

ASTM — American Society for Testing and Materials

FA 150 — Airborne Digital Logic Principles

FAH — FAA Airframe Handbook (AC 65-15A until it is superseded by FAA-H-8083-32)

FAR — Federal Aviation Regulation

FGH — FAA General Handbook (previously AC 65-9A; now FAA-H-8083-30)

FPH — FAA Powerplant Handbook (AC 65-12A until it is superseded by FAA-H-8083-31)

JSAB — Jeppesen Aircraft Batteries

JSAD — The Aviation Dictionary

JSAT — Jeppesen Airframe Textbook

JSGT — Jeppesen General Textbook

JSHM — Helicopter Maintenance

JSHS — Aircraft Hydraulic Systems

JSPT — Jeppesen Powerplant Textbook

JSTS — Transport Category Aircraft Systems (TCAS)

JSTT — Aircraft Tires and Tubes

JSWB — Aircraft Weight and Balance

MMM — Manufacturer's Maintenance Manual

PHB — Pilot's Handbook of Aeronautical Knowledge (FAA-H-8083-25)

TEP2 — Aircraft Gas Turbine Powerplants

TSO — Technical Standard Order

WBH — FAA Aircraft Weight and Balance Handbook (FAA-H-8083-1)

Since the FAA does not provide answers with their test questions, the answers in this Test Guide are based on official reference documents and, in our judgment, are the best choice of the available answers. Some questions which were valid when the FAA Computerized Test was originally released may no longer be appropriate due to changes in regulations or official operating procedures. However, with the computer test format, timely updating and validation ofquestions is anticipated. Therefore, when taking the FAA test, it is important to answer the questions according to the latest regulations or official operating procedures.

Appendix A includes Learning Statement Codes from the FAA test materials. Learning Statement Codes have replaced the subject matter knowledge codes previously used on FAA knowledge tests. Appendix B is a listing by chapter of sample questions and suggested answers that may be asked during the Oral and Practical Tests.

Figures and figure numbers in the Test Guide are the same as those used in the FAA Computerized Testing Supplement. These figures, which are referred to in many of the questions, are placed throughout the Test Guide as close as practical to the applicable questions.

While good study material is beneficial, it is important to realize that to become a safe, competent technician, you need more than just the academic knowledge required to pass a written test. A certified Airframe and Powerplant Mechanic's school will give you the practical shop skills that are indispensable to mechanics working in the field.

WHO CAN TAKE THE TEST

The Aviation Mechanic Powerplant Exam is sometimes taken in conjunction with the General exam. When you are ready to take these tests, you must present to the FAA, either a graduation certificate or certificate of completion from a certificated aviation maintenance technician school, or documentary evidence of practical work experience. The work experience for a single rating must show that you have had at least 18 months of practical experience with the procedures, practices, and equipment generally used in constructing, maintaining, or altering airframes or powerplants. To test for both ratings, you must show at least 30 months of practical experience concurrently performing the duties appropriate to both the airframe and powerplant ratings. Documentary evidence of practical experience must be satisfactory to the administrator.

You must also provide evidence of a permanent mailing address, appropriate identification, and proof of your age. The identification must include a current photograph, your signature, and your residential address, if different from your mailing address. You may present this information in more than one form of identification, such as a driver's license, government identification card, passport, alien residency (green) card, or a military identification card.

Once the FAA is satisfied that you meet the eligibility requirements for an aircraft mechanic's certificate, you will be given two FAA Form 8610-2 forms to complete. Once filled out, an FAA inspector will review the forms for accuracy and completeness, and then sign them, authorizing you to take the required FAA tests. DO NOT LOSE THESE FORMS. You will be required to present them to FAA designated testing personnel to show evidence of eligibility to take the Airman Knowledge, Oral and Practical Exams.

HOW TO PREPARE FOR THE FAA TEST

It is important to realize that to become a safe, competent mechanic, you need more than just the academic knowledge required to pass a test. For a comprehensive training program, we recommend a structured maintenance school with qualified instructors. An organized course of instruction will help you complete the course in a timely manner, and you will be able to have your questions answered.

Regardless of whether or not you are in a structured training program, you will find that this Test Guide is an excellent training aid to help you prepare for the FAA tests. The guide contains all of the FAA questions as they are presented in the FAA computerized test format. By reviewing the questions and studying the Jeppesen Sanderson Maintenance Training materials, you should be well equipped to take the test.

You will also benefit more from your study if you test yourself as you proceed through the Test Guide. Cover the answers in the right-hand column, read each question, and choose what you consider the best answer. You may want to mark the questions you miss for further study and review prior to taking the exam.

The sooner you take the exam after you complete your study, the better. This way, the information will be fresh in your mind, and you will be more confident when you actually take the FAA test.

GENERAL INFORMATION—FAA COMPUTERIZED TEST

Detailed information on FAA computer testing is contained in FAA Order 8080.6, Conduct of Airmen Knowledge Tests Via The Computer Medium. This FAA order provides guidance for Flight Standards District Offices (FSDOs) and personnelxii
associated with organizations that are participating in, or are seeking to participate in, the FAA Computer-Assisted Airmen Knowledge Testing Program You may also refer to FAA Order 8300.1, Airworthiness Inspector's Handbook, for guidance on computer testing by FAR Part 147 maintenance training schools that hold examining authority.

As a test applicant, you don't need all of the details contained in FAA Orders, but you may be interested in some of the general information about computer testing facilities. A Computer Testing Designee (CTD) is an organization authorized by the FAA to administer FAA airmen knowledge tests via the computer medium. A Computer Testing Manager (CTM) is a person selected by the CTD to serve as manager of its national computer testing program. A Testing Center Supervisor (TCS) is a person selected by the CTM, with FAA approval, to administer FAA airmen knowledge tests at approved testing centers. The TCS is responsible for the operation of the testing center.

CTDs are selected by the FAA's Flight Standards Service. Those selected may include companies, schools, universities, or other organizations that meet specific requirements. For example, they must clearly demonstrate competence in computer technology, centralized database management, national communications network operation and maintenance, national facilities management, software maintenance and support, and technical training and customer support. They must provide computer-assisted testing, test administration, and data transfer service on a national scale. This means they must maintain a minimum of 20 operational testing centers geographically dispersed throughout the United States. In addition, CTD's must offer operational hours that are convenient to the public. An acceptable plan for test security is also required.

WHAT TO EXPECT ON THE COMPUTERIZED TEST

Computer testing centers are required to have an acceptable method for the 'on-line' registration of test applicants during normal business hours. They must provide a dual method for answering questions, such as keyboard, touch screen, or mouse. Features that must be provided also include an introductory lesson to familiarize you with computer testing procedures, the ability to return to a test question previously answered (for the purpose of review or answer changes), and a suitable display of multiple-choice and other question types on the computer screen in one frame. Other required features include a display of the time remaining for the completion of the test, a 'HELP' function which permits you to review test questions and optional responses, and provisions for your test score on an Airmen Computer Test Report.

On the computerized tests, the selection of questions is done for you, and you will answer the questions that appear on the screen. You will be given a specific amount of time to complete the test, which is based on past experience with others who have taken the exam. If you are prepared, you should have plenty of time to complete the test. After you begin the test, the screen will show you the time remaining for completion. When taking the test, keep the following points in mind:

1. Answer each question in accordance with the latest regulations and procedures. If the regulation or procedure has recently changed, and you answer according to the recent change, you will receive credit for the affected question. However, these questions will normally be deleted or updated on the FAA computerized tests.

2. Read each question carefully before looking at the possible answers. You should clearly understand the problem before attempting to solve it.

3. After formulating an answer, determine which of the alternatives most nearly corresponds with that answer. The answer chosen should completely resolve the problem.

4. From the answers given, it may appear that there is more than one possible answer; however, there is only one answer that is correct and complete. The other answers are either incomplete or are derived from popular misconceptions.

5. Make sure you select an answer for each question. Questions left unanswered will be counted as incorrect.

6. If a certain question is difficult for you, it is best to proceed to other questions. After you answer the less difficult questions, return to those which were unanswered. The computerized test format helps you identify unanswered questions, as well as those questions you wish to review.

7. When solving a calculator problem, select the answer nearest your solution. The problem has been checked with various types of calculators; therefore, if you have solved it correctly, your answer will be closer to the correct answer than the other choices.

8. Generally, the test results will be available almost immediately. Your score will be recorded on an Airmen Computer Test Report form, which includes learning statement codes for incorrect answers. To determine the knowledge area in which a particular question was incorrectly answered, compare the learning statement codes on this report to Appendix A, in this book.

TEST MATERIALS, REFERENCE MATERIALS, AND AIDS

You are allowed to use an electronic calculator for this test. Simple programmable memories, which allow addition to, subtraction from, or retrieval of one number from the memory, are acceptable. Simple functions such as square root or percent keys are also acceptable.

In addition, you may use any reference materials provided with the test. You will find that these reference materials are the same as those in this book.

RETESTING

As stated in FAR section 65.19, an applicant who fails a test may not apply for retesting until 30 days after the date the test was failed. However, the applicant may apply for retesting before the 30 days have expired provided the applicant presents a signed statement from an airman holding the certificate and rating sought by the applicant. The statement must indicate that the airman has given the applicant additional instruction in each of the subjects failed and that the airman considers the applicant ready for retesting.

WHERE TO TAKE THE TEST

Testing is administered via computer at FAA-designated test centers. As indicated, these CTDs are located throughout the U.S. You can expect to pay a fee and the cost varies at different locations. The following are approved testing designees at the time of publication of this test guide. You may want to check with your local FSDO for changes.

Computer Assisted Testing Services
(CATS aka Aviation Business Services)
1-800-947-4228
Outside U.S. (650) 259-8550

PSI/LaserGrade Computer Testing
1-800-211-2754
Outside U.S. (360) 896-9111

RECIPROCATING ENGINES

SECTION A — DESIGN AND CONSTRUCTION

Section A of Chapter 1 contains information related to the design, construction, and basic maintenance practices for radial and horizontally opposed reciprocating engines.

1-1 AMP056

Which statement is true regarding bearings used in high-powered reciprocating aircraft engines?

A– The outer race of a single-row, self-aligning ball bearing will always have a radius equal to the radius of the balls.

B– There is less rolling friction when ball bearings are used than when roller bearings are employed.

C– Crankshaft bearings are generally of the ball-type due to their ability to withstand extreme loads without overheating.

1-1. Answer B. JSPT 1A, FPH

Both ball bearings and roller bearings are used in aircraft engines. However, since the steel balls in a ball bearing offer less surface contact than the rollers of a roller bearing, ball bearings produce less rolling friction. Therefore, ball bearings are generally used in high-powered reciprocating engines to keep friction to a minimum.

1-2 AMP053

What is the principal advantage of using propeller reduction gears?

A– To enable the propeller RPM to be increased without an accompanying increase in engine RPM.

B– To enable the engine RPM to be increased with an accompanying increase in power and allow the propeller to remain at a lower, more efficient RPM.

C– To enable the engine RPM to be increased with an accompanying increase in propeller RPM.

1-2. Answer B. JSPT 1A, JSPT 12D, FPH

The amount of horsepower an engine produces is directly related to the engine's RPM. Therefore, most aircraft engines must run at a speed in excess of 2,000 RPM to develop sufficient power. However, propeller efficiency at these speeds decreases rapidly. Therefore, in order to maintain an acceptable level of propeller efficiency a reduction gear is used. A reduction gear allows an engine to run at the high rpm needed to produce more horsepower while at the same time, allow the propeller to rotate at a lower, more efficient RPM.

1-3   AMP054

Which of the following is a characteristic of a thrust bearing used in most radial engines?

A– Tapered roller

B– Double-row ball

C– Deep-groove ball

1-3. Answer C. JSPT 1A, FPH

Special deep-groove ball bearings are used as thrust bearings in most radial engines. This type of bearing generates the least amount of friction of all the types of bearings listed while still being able to withstand both the thrust and radial loads. Although tapered roller bearings and double-row ball bearings are capable of withstanding both thrust and radial loads, they produce more friction than a deep-groove ball bearing.

1-4   AMP056

Which bearing is least likely to be a roller or ball bearing?

A– Rocker arm bearing (overhead valve engine)

B– Master rod bearing (radial engine)

C– Crankshaft main bearing (radial engine)

1-4. Answer B. JSPT 1A, FPH

The question asks for the least likely use of a roller or ball bearing. Master rod bearings on radial engines are generally subjected to radial loads only and, therefore, plain bearings are used. Therefore, Master rod bearing (radial engine) is correct.

1-5   AMP054

The operating temperature valve clearance of a radial engine as compared to cold valve clearance is

A– greater.

B– less.

C– the same.

1-5. Answer A. JSPT 1A, FPH

As a radial engine warms up, the aluminum alloy cylinder heads expand causing the rocker arm in the head to move away from the crankcase. At the same time, the pushrod also expands but at a lesser rate than the cylinder head. The difference in expansion amounts between the cylinder head and pushrod effectively increases the space between the valve stem and rocker arm (valve clearance). Therefore, greater is correct.

1-6   AMP056

Which statement is correct regarding engine crankshafts?

A– Moveable counterweights serve to reduce the torsional vibrations in an aircraft reciprocating engine.

B– Moveable counterweights serve to reduce the dynamic vibrations in an aircraft reciprocating engine.

C– Moveable counterweights are designed to resonate at the natural frequency of the crankshaft.

1-6. Answer B. JSPT 1A, FPH

Each time a cylinder on an engine fires, a pulse of energy is transferred to the crankshaft. Since the power stroke occurs out of line with the throw of the crank, dynamic vibrations occur. To dampen these vibrations, moveable counterweights, or dynamic dampers, align to dampen out the vibrations.

1-7   AMP056

Master rod bearings are generally what type?

A– Plain

B– Roller

C– Ball

1-7. Answer A. JSPT 1A, FPH

The master rod in a radial engine is subjected to radial loads only and, therefore, plain bearings are typically used as master rod bearings.

1-8   AMP056

Cam-ground pistons are installed in some aircraft engines to

A– provide a better fit at operating temperatures.

B– act as a compensating feature so that a compensated magneto is not required.

C– equalize the wear on all pistons.

1-8. Answer A. JSPT 1A, FPH

A cam-ground piston is constructed with a slightly oval cross-section. In other words, the piston's diameter perpendicular to the piston pin is slightly larger than the diameter parallel to the piston pin. This oval shape holds the piston square in the cylinder when an engine is cold and allows the greater mass of the piston pin bosses to expand more freely at operating temperatures. Once expanded, camground pistons provide a better fit within the cylinder.

1-9   AMP056

Some aircraft engine manufacturers equip their product with choked or taper-ground cylinders in order to

A– provide a straight cylinder bore at operating temperatures.

B– flex the rings slightly during operation and reduce the possibility of the rings sticking in the grooves.

C– increase the compression pressure for starting purposes.

1-9. Answer A. JSPT 1A

Most cylinders have a certain degree of choke, or taper. This means that the cylinder barrel is slightly narrower at the cylinder head than at the cylinder skirt. A choked cylinder allows for cylinder expansion resulting from the higher operating temperatures near the head. Once a choked cylinder reaches operating temperature, the choked area expands to match the bore at the skirt, and the entire bore becomes straight.

1-10   AMP056

An aircraft reciprocating engine using hydraulic valve lifters is observed to have no clearance in its valve-operating mechanism after the minimum inlet oil and cylinder head temperatures for takeoff have been reached. When can this condition be expected?

A– During normal operation

B– When the lifters become deflated

C– As a result of carbon and sludge becoming trapped in the lifter and restricting its motion

1-10. Answer A. JSPT 1A, FPH

In a zero-lash or zero-clearance hydraulic valve lifter, oil pressure forces the lifter outward until all clearance between the rocker arm and the valve stem is removed. This condition in an engine is normal.

1-11   AMP056

Some cylinder barrels are hardened by

A– nitriding.

B– shot peening.

C– tempering.

1-11. Answer A. JSPT 1A, FPH

The cylinder barrel of a reciprocating engine is made of a steel alloy forging with its inner surface hardened to resist wear. One method used to harden cylinders is nitriding. In the nitriding process, the cylinder is heated and exposed to ammonia or cyanide gas. Nitrogen from the gas is absorbed by the steel causing iron nitrides to form on the steel's surface.

1-12   AMP056

What is the purpose of the safety circlet installed on some valve stems?

A— To hold the valve guide in position

B— To hold the valve spring retaining washer in position

C— To prevent valves from falling into the combustion chamber

1-12. Answer C. JSPT 1A, FPH

The stems of some valves have a narrow groove cut in them just below the lock ring groove that allows for the installation of safety circlets or spring rings. The circlets are designed to prevent the valves from falling into the combustion chamber should the valve tip break during engine operation.

1-13   AMP056

The valve clearance of an engine using hydraulic lifters, when the lifters are completely flat, or empty, should not exceed

A— a specified amount below zero.

B— a specified amount above zero.

C— 0.00 inch.

1-13. Answer B. JSPT 1A, FPH

When operating properly, an engine equipped with hydraulic lifters will have a valve clearance of zero. However, when the lifters are flat or empty, the lifter must have a specified clearance greater than zero in order to provide the proper operating range.

1-14   AMP056

Full-floating piston pins are those which allow motion between the pin and

A— the piston.

B— both the piston and the large end of the connecting rod.

C— both the piston and the small end of the connecting rod.

1-14. Answer C. JSPT 1A, FPH

A full-floating piston pin gets its name from the fact that the pin is free to rotate in both the piston and in the small end of the connecting rod.

1-15   AMP008

If the hot clearance is used to set the valves when the engine is cold, what will occur during operation of the engine?

A— The valves will open early and close early.

B— The valves will open late and close early.

C— The valves will open early and close late.

1-15. Answer B. FPH

When an engine is hot, the clearance between the rocker arm and the valve stem is greater than when the engine is cold. Therefore, if the valves are set to hot clearances when the engine is cold, the overall valve clearance will be excessive and the valves will open late and close early.

1-16   AMP056

The purpose of two or more valve springs in aircraft engines is to

A– equalize side pressure on the valve stems.

B– eliminate valve spring surge.

C– equalize valve face loading.

1-16. Answer B. JSPT 1A, FPH

Each valve on a reciprocating engine is closed by two or three helical-coiled springs. If only a single spring were used to close a valve, the spring would vibrate or surge at certain speeds. However, with multiple springs, each spring vibrates at a different engine speed resulting in rapid dampening of all spring surge vibrations.

1-17   AMP007

What special procedure must be followed when adjusting the valves of an engine equipped with a floating cam ring?

A– Adjust valves when the engine is hot.

B– Adjust all exhaust valves before intake valves.

C– Eliminate cam bearing clearance when making valve adjustment.

1-17. Answer C. JSPT 1A, FPH

When adjusting the valves on a radial engine with a floating cam ring, the clearance between the cam ring and cam bearing must be eliminated so the cam is in a definite position prior to adjusting the valve clearance. To do this, specific valves must be depressed and released simultaneously to remove the spring tension from the side positions on the cam. This permits the cam to slide away from the valves you are adjusting.

1-18   AMP056

What is an advantage of using metallic-sodium filled exhaust valves in aircraft reciprocating engines?

A– Increased strength and resistance to cracking

B– Reduced valve operating temperatures

C– Greater resistance to deterioration at high valve temperatures

1-18. Answer B. JSPT 1A, FPH

Metallic-sodium is used in some valves because it is an excellent heat conductor. In a metallic-sodium filled valve, the sodium melts at approximately 208°F. When this happens, the reciprocating motion of the valve circulates the liquid sodium enabling it to carry away excess heat, thereby reducing valve operating temperatures.

1-19   AMP056

Valve clearance changes on opposed-type engines using hydraulic lifters are accomplished by

A– rocker arm adjustment.

B– rocker arm replacement.

C– push rod replacement.

1-19. Answer C. JSPT 1A, FPH

The only way to adjust the valve clearance on an engine using hydraulic lifters is to insert a different sized push rod.

1-20   AMP056
What could cause excessive pressure buildup in the crankcase of a reciprocating engine?

A– Plugged crankcase breather

B– Improper warm-up operation

C– An excessive quantity of oil

1-20. Answer A. FPH
All piston rings let some combustion chamber pressure into the engine crankcase. This pressure is vented to the atmosphere through a crankcase breather. Therefore, if a crankcase breather becomes plugged, pressure will build up inside the crankcase.

1-21   AMP049
How is the oil collected by the piston oil ring returned to the crankcase?

A– Down vertical slots cut in the piston wall between the piston oil ring groove and the piston skirt

B– Through holes drilled in the piston oil ring groove

C– Through holes drilled in the piston pin recess

1-21. Answer B. JSPT 1A, FPH
Oil control rings regulate the oil film thickness on the cylinder wall. Excess oil that collects on oil control rings as a cylinder moves is routed back to the crankcase through holes that are drilled in the piston ring grooves or in the lands next to these grooves.

1-22   AMP050
Oil accumulation in the cylinders of an inverted in-line engine and in the lower cylinders of a radial engine is normally reduced or prevented by

A– reversed oil control rings.

B– routing the valve-operating mechanism lubricating oil to a separate scavenger pump.

C– extended cylinder skirts.

1-22. Answer C. FPH
Some radial engine cylinders and all cylinders in an inverted engine are located at the bottom of the engine. To prevent these cylinders from being flooded with oil and suffering hydraulic lock, extended cylinder skirts are often installed. With these extended skirts, oil that falls into the cylinders is immediately thrown back into the crankcase.

1-23   AMP030
Where are sludge chambers, when used in aircraft engine lubrication systems, usually located?

A– In the crankshaft throws

B– Adjacent to the scavenger pumps

C– In the oil storage tank

1-23. Answer A. JSPT 1A, FPH
Some crankshafts are manufactured with hollow crankpins that serve as sludge removers, or chambers. On a crankshaft with sludge chambers, centrifugal motion forces sludge and other foreign material into the sludge chambers during engine operation. This sludge remains in the sludge chamber until the engine is overhauled.

1-24   AMP056

Excessive oil is prevented from accumulating on the cylinder walls of a reciprocating engine by

A– the design shape of the piston skirt.

B– internal engine pressure bleeding past the ring grooves.

C– oil control rings on the pistons.

1-24. Answer C. JSPT 1A, FPH

Oil control rings regulate the oil film thickness on the cylinder wall by removing excess oil and allowing it to return to the crankcase. Although extended piston skirts can help keep oil from accumulating in the lower cylinders of radial engines, piston skirt shape does not prevent excessive oil buildup on cylinder walls.

1-25   AMP030

The valve assemblies of opposed reciprocating engines are lubricated by means of a

A– gravity feed system.

B– splash and spray system.

C– pressure system.

1-25. Answer C. JSPT 1A, FPH

The overhead valve assemblies of opposed engines used in helicopters and airplanes are lubricated by a pressure system. In this type of system, pressurized oil flows through the hydraulic tappet body and through hollow pushrods to the rocker arm where it lubricates the rocker arm bearing and the valve stem.

1-26   AMP030

How are the piston pins of most aircraft engines lubricated?

A– By pressure oil through a drilled passageway in the heavy web portion of the connecting rod

B– By oil which is sprayed or thrown by the master or connecting rods

C– By the action of the oil control ring and the series of holes drilled in the ring groove directing oil to the pin and piston pin boss

1-26. Answer B. FPH

The piston pins on most reciprocating engines are lubricated by oil which is sprayed or thrown from the master or connecting rod.

1-27   AMP030

Which of the following bearing types must be continuously lubricated by pressure oil?

A– Ball

B– Roller

C– Plain

1-27. Answer C. JSPT 1A, FPH

All bearings require lubrication. However, plain bearings must have oil supplied to them under pressure to prevent metal-to-metal contact.

1-28   AMP056

The undersides of pistons are frequently finned. The principal reason is to

A— provide sludge chambers and sediment traps.

B— provide for greater heat transfer to the engine oil.

C— support ring grooves and piston pins.

1-28. Answer B. FPH

The majority of aircraft engine pistons are machined from aluminum alloy forgings. On some pistons, cooling fins are provided on the underside of the piston to facilitate the transfer of heat to the engine oil.

1-29   AMP056

Sodium-filled valves are advantageous to an aviation engine because they

A— are lighter.

B— dampen valve impact shocks.

C— dissipate heat well.

1-29. Answer C. JSPT 1A, FPH

Metallic sodium is used in some valves because it is an excellent heat conductor. In a metallic sodium valve, the sodium melts at approximately 208 degrees Fahrenheit. When this happens, the reciprocating motion of the valve circulates the liquid sodium enabling it to carry away excess heat and reduce valve operating temperatures.

1-30   AMP056

At what speed must a crankshaft turn if each cylinder of a four-stroke cycle engine is to be fired 200 times a minute?

A— 800 RPM

B— 1,600 RPM

C— 400 RPM

1-30. Answer C. JSPT 1A, FPH

In a four-stroke engine, each cylinder fires once every two crankshaft revolutions. Therefore, in order for a cylinder to fire 200 times a minute, the crankshaft must rotate at a speed of 400 RPM (200 x 2 = 400).

1-31   AMP007

You are performing a 100-hour inspection on an R985-22 aircraft engine. What does the "985" indicate?

A— The total piston displacement of the engine

B— The pistons will pump a maximum of 985 cubic inches of air per crankshaft revolution

C— The total piston displacement of one cylinder

1-31. Answer A. JSPT 1A, FPH

In the designation for an engine R985-22, the 985 indicates the total piston displacement of the engine in cubic inches.

SECTION B — OPERATING PRINCIPLES

Section B of Chapter 1 contains information related to reciprocating engine operating theory.

1-32   AMP056

Which of the following will decrease volumetric efficiency in a reciprocating engine?

1. Full throttle operation

2. Low cylinder head temperatures

3. Improper valve timing

4. Sharp bends in the induction system

5. High carburetor air temperatures

A– 2, 4, and 5

B– 1, 2, 3, and 4

C– 3, 4, and 5

1-32. Answer C. JSPT 1B, FPH

Volumetric efficiency is a comparison of the volume of? a fuel/air charge inducted into all cylinders to the total? piston displacement. Factors that reduce volumetric? efficiency include part-throttle operation, long, small? diameter intake pipes, sharp bends in the induction? system, excessive carburetor air temperatures,? excessive cylinder head temperatures, incomplete? scavenging, and improper valve timing. Of the five? choices given in the question only #3, #4, and #5 affect? volumetric efficiency.

1-33   AMP056

A nine-cylinder engine with a bore of 5.5 inches and a stroke of 6 inches will have a total piston displacement of

A– 740 cubic inches.

B– 1,425 cubic inches.

C– 1,283 cubic inches.

1-33. Answer C. JSPT 1B, FPH

The total piston displacement of an engine is equal to the displacement, or volume of one cylinder multiplied by the total number of cylinders. The volume of a cylinder is calculated using the formula $V = \pi (r)^2 h$, where (V) is the volume, (r) is the radius of the cylinder, and (h) is the height, or stroke of the piston. The displacement of each cylinder is 142.55 cubic inches ($3.1416 \times (2.75)^2 \times 6 = 142.55$). To determine the displacement of the entire engine, multiply the displacement of each cylinder by the total number of cylinders. The total engine displacement is 1,282.95 cubic inches ($142.55 \times 9 = 1,282.95$). 1,283 cubic inches is the closest.

1-34   AMP056

The five events of a four-stroke cycle engine in the order of their occurrence are

A— intake, ignition, compression, power, exhaust.

B— intake, power, compression, ignition, exhaust.

C— intake, compression, ignition, power, exhaust.

1-34. Answer C. JSPT 1B, FPH

The four-stroke cycle begins when the piston starts? moving down in the cylinder on the intake stroke.? When the piston reaches bottom center it reverses? direction and starts moving up on the compression? stroke. Near the top of the compression stroke, the? spark plug fires causing ignition of the fuel/air mixture.? As soon as the fuel/air mixture begins to burn, the? piston is forced down in the power stroke. As the piston? approaches bottom center, the exhaust valve opens? and the piston reverses direction to begin the exhaust? stroke. Therefore, the five events of a four stroke? engine are intake, compression, ignition, power, and? exhaust.

1-35   AMP056

The primary concern in establishing the firing order for an opposed engine is to

A— provide for balance and eliminate vibration to the greatest extent possible.

B— keep power impulses on adjacent cylinders as far apart as possible in order to obtain the greatest mechanical efficiency.

C— keep the power impulses on adjacent cylinders as close as possible in order to obtain the greatest mechanical efficiency.

1-35. Answer A. JSPT 1B, FPH

The firing order within an engine is designed to provide for balance and to eliminate vibration to the greatest extent possible.

1-36   AMP056

If fuel/air ratio is proper and ignition timing is correct, the combustion process should be completed

A— 20° to 30° before top center at the end of the compression stroke.

B— when the exhaust valve opens at the end of the power stroke.

C— just after top center at the beginning of the power stroke.

1-36. Answer C. JSPT 1B, FPH

Combustion is the third event in the cycle of a four stroke engine. The combustion process begins as the piston reaches the top of the compression stroke and the fuel/air charge is ignited by means of an electric spark. The time of ignition varies from 20 to 35 degrees before top dead center to ensure complete combustion by the time the piston is slightly past the top dead center position.

1-37 AMP056

On which strokes are both valves on a four-stroke cycle reciprocating engine open?

A– Power and exhaust

B– Intake and compression

C– Exhaust and intake

1-37. Answer C. JSPT 1B, FPH

For a reciprocating engine to operate properly, each valve must open at the proper time, stay open for a specific length of time, and close at the proper time. In a typical reciprocating engine, the intake valve opens just before the piston reaches top dead center on the exhaust stroke and remains open into the intake stroke. On the other hand, the exhaust valve is open throughout the exhaust stroke and remains open after top dead center when the piston begins the intake stroke. Therefore, at the end of the exhaust stroke and the beginning of the intake stroke both valves are open at the same time.

1-38 AMP056

The actual power delivered to the propeller of an aircraft engine is called

A– friction horsepower.

B– brake horsepower.

C– indicated horsepower.

1-38. Answer B. JSPT 1B, FPH

Brake horsepower is the horsepower that is delivered to the propeller shaft. One way to determine an engine's brake horsepower is to subtract an engine's friction horsepower from its indicated horsepower.

1-39 AMP056

Using the following information, determine how many degrees the crankshaft will rotate with both the intake and exhaust valves seated. Intake opens 15° BTDC. Exhaust opens 70° BBDC. Intake closes 45° ABDC. Exhaust closes 10° ATDC.

A– 290°

B– 245°

C– 25°

1-39. Answer B. JSPT 1B, FPH

One complete revolution of a crankshaft and piston takes 360 degrees, with top dead center (TDC) being 0 degrees and bottom dead center (BDC) 180 degrees. The only time both valves are closed in a four-stroke engine is during a portion of the compression and combustion strokes. This question indicates that the intake valve closes 45 degrees after bottom dead center, or 135 degrees before top dead center (180 - 45 = 135). The exhaust valve, on the other hand, opens 70 degrees before bottom dead center, or 110 degrees after top dead center (180 - 70 = 110). Therefore the number of degrees both valves are seated is 245 degrees (135 + 110 = 245).

1-40   AMP056

If an engine with a stroke of 6 inches is operated at 2,000 RPM, the piston movement within the cylinder will be

A– at maximum velocity around TDC.

B– constant during the entire 360° of crankshaft travel.

C– at maximum velocity 90° after TDC.

1-40. Answer C. JSPT 1B, FPH

As a piston leaves top dead center (TDC) and bottom dead center (BDC), it accelerates and attains its maximum speed at 90 degrees after TDC and 90 degrees after BDC.

1-41   AMP056

Which statement is correct regarding a four-stroke cycle aircraft engine?

A– The intake valve closes on the compression stroke.

B– The exhaust valve opens on the exhaust stroke.

C– The intake valve closes on the intake stroke.

1-41. Answer A. JSPT 1B, FPH

Depending upon the specific engine, an intake valve is timed to open prior to the piston reaching top dead center on the exhaust stroke and to close about 50 to 75 degrees past bottom dead center on the compression stroke. This allows the momentum of the incoming gases to charge the cylinder more completely. The exhaust valve, on the other hand, typically opens around 70 degrees before bottom dead center on the power stroke and closes at approximately 15 degrees after top dead center on the intake stroke.

1-42   AMP056

When is the fuel/air mixture ignited in a conventional reciprocating engine?

A– When the piston has reached top dead center of the intake stroke

B– Shortly before the piston reaches the top of the compression stroke

C– When the piston reaches top dead center on the compression stroke

1-42. Answer B. JSPT 1B, FPH

In a reciprocating engine, the fuel/air charge is fired by means of an electric spark shortly before the piston reaches top dead center on the compression stroke. The time of ignition varies from 20 degrees to 35 degrees before top dead center, depending upon the engine requirements. By igniting the fuel/air charge before the piston reaches top dead center, complete combustion is ensured by the time the piston is slightly past top dead center and maximum power is delivered to the crankshaft.

1-43   AMP056

Ignition occurs at 28° BTDC on a certain four-stroke cycle engine, and the intake valve opens at 15° BTDC.

How many degrees of crankshaft travel after ignition does the intake valve open? (Consider one cylinder only.)

A– 707°

B– 373°

C– 347°

1-43. Answer B. JSPT 1B, FPH

Ignition occurs at 28 degrees before top dead center. Therefore, the piston will travel 28 degrees to complete the stroke. As the piston moves from top to bottom dead center on the power stroke, the crankshaft turns another 180 degrees. According to the question, the intake valve opens 15 degrees before top dead center of the exhaust stroke, or 165 degrees after bottom dead center. Therefore, total crankshaft travel is 373 degrees (28 + 180 + 165 = 373).

1-44   AMP056

Valve overlap is defined as the number of degrees of crankshaft travel

A– during which both valves are off their seats.

B– between the closing of the intake valve and the opening of the exhaust valve.

C– during which both valves are on their seats.

1-44. Answer A. JPST 1B, FPH

Valve overlap represents the degree of crankshaft travel in which both the intake valve and exhaust valve are open (off their seat). On most reciprocating engines, the intake valve opens before top dead center on the exhaust stroke, while the exhaust valve closes after the piston has passed TDC and started the intake stroke. This results in a valve overlap of anywhere from 40 to 75 degrees.

1-45   AMP056

If the exhaust valve of a four-stroke cycle engine is closed and the intake valve is just closed, the piston is on the

A– intake stroke.

B– power stroke.

C– compression stroke.

1-45. Answer C. JSPT 1B, FPH

The intake valve of a reciprocating engine is timed to close about 50 to 75 degrees past bottom dead center on the compression stroke. After the intake valve closes, the continued upward travel of the piston compresses the fuel/air mixture to obtain the desired burning and expansion characteristics.

1-46   AMP056

How many of the following are factors in establishing the maximum compression ratio limitations of an aircraft engine?

1. Detonation characteristics of the fuel used

2. Design limitations of the engine

3. Degree of supercharging

4. Spark plug reach

A– Four

B– Two

C– Three

1-46. Answer C. JSPT 1B, FPH

An engine's compression ratio is the controlling factor in determining the amount of horsepower an engine develops. Some of the factors that must be considered when establishing a maximum compression ratio include the detonation characteristics of the fuel used, the engine's design limitations, and the degree of supercharging. Spark plug reach does not limit an engine's compression ratio. Based on this, three of the four factors listed are valid limitations.

1-47   AMP056

The primary purpose in setting proper valve timing and overlap is to

A– permit the best possible charge of fuel/air mixture into the cylinders.

B– gain more thorough exhaust gas scavenging.

C– obtain the best volumetric efficiency and lower cylinder operating temperatures.

1-47. Answer C. JSPT 1B, FPH

Reciprocating engines are timed so that both the intake and exhaust valves are open near the end of the exhaust stroke and into the beginning of the intake stroke. This valve overlap allows a larger quantity of the fuel/air charge to be drawn into the cylinder which, in return, increases volumetric efficiency. Furthermore, overlap helps to expel the exhaust gases from the previous power stroke and lower operating temperatures.

1-48   AMP056

Compression ratio is the ratio between the

A– piston travel on the compression stroke and on the intake stroke.

B– combustion chamber pressure on the combustion stroke and on the exhaust stroke.

C– cylinder volume with piston at bottom dead center and at top dead center.

1-48. Answer C. JSPT 1B, FPH

The compression ratio of an engine is a comparison of the volume of a cylinder when the piston is at the bottom of a stroke to the volume of the same cylinder when the piston is at the top of a stroke.

1-49   AMP056

What does valve overlap promote?

A– Lower intake manifold pressure and temperatures.

B– A backflow of gases across the cylinder.

C– Better scavenging and cooling characteristics.

1-49. Answer C. JSPT 1B, FPH

Valve overlap represents the number of degrees that both the exhaust and intake valves are open. Two benefits of valve overlap are improved scavenging and cooling characteristics and increased volumetric efficiency.

1-50   AMP056

The horsepower developed in the cylinders of a reciprocating engine is known as the

A– shaft horsepower.

B– indicated horsepower.

C– brake horsepower.

1-50. Answer B. JSPT 1B, FPH

The horsepower developed in the combustion chambers without considering friction is referred to as indicated horsepower.

1-51   AMP056

When does valve overlap occur in the operation of an aircraft reciprocating engine?

A– At the end of the exhaust stroke and the beginning of the intake stroke.

B– At the end of the power stroke and the beginning of the exhaust stroke.

C– At the end of the compression stroke and the beginning of the power stroke.

1-51. Answer A. JSPT 1B, FPH

Valve overlap identifies the period when both the intake and exhaust valves are open in a cylinder. The only time valve overlap occurs is at the end of the exhaust stroke and the beginning of the intake stroke.

1-52   AMP056

An increase in manifold pressure with a constant RPM will cause the bearing load in an engine to

A– decrease.

B– remain relatively constant.

C– increase.

1-52. Answer C. JSPT 1B, FPH

Manifold pressure represents the absolute pressure of the fuel/air mixture prior to entering the cylinders. Therefore, an increase in manifold pressure for a given RPM represents a higher pressure fuel/air mixture entering the cylinders. This higher pressure produces a corresponding increase in brake mean effective pressure and power output. Any time the brake mean effective pressure or power output is increased, additional force is transmitted through the pistons to the crankshaft and bearing load increases.

1-53   AMP056

Reduced air density at high altitude has a decided effect on carburetion, resulting in a reduction of engine power by

A– excessively enriching the air/fuel mixture.

B– excessively leaning the air/fuel mixture.

C– reducing fuel vaporization.

1-53. Answer A. JSPT 1B, FPH

A combustion engine relies on a specific air/fuel mixture to produce a given amount of power. Any deviation from this mixture affects power output.

As an aircraft climbs, air density decreases thereby decreasing the amount of air in the fuel/air mixture. This results in an excessively rich air/fuel mixture which causes a reduction in engine power.

1-54   AMP056

An unsupercharged aircraft reciprocating engine, operated at full throttle from sea level to 10,000 feet, provided the RPM is unchanged, will

A– lose power due to the reduced volume of air drawn into the cylinders.

B– produce constant power due to the same volume of air drawn into the cylinders.

C– lose power due to the reduced density of the air drawn into the cylinders.

1-54. Answer C. JSPT 1B, FPH

As a rule, an unsupercharged reciprocating engine operated at altitude produces less power than it does at sea level. This is because, at higher altitudes, less dense air is drawn into the cylinders resulting in a less potent fuel/air charge.

1-55   AMP056

Which of these conditions will cause an engine to have an increased tendency to detonate?

1. High manifold pressure.

2. High intake air temperature.

3. Engine overheated.

4. Late ignition timing.

A– 1 and 4.

B– 1, 2, and 3.

C– 1, 2, 3, and 4.

1-55. Answer B. JSPT 1B, FPH

Detonation is the uncontrolled burning of the fuel/air mixture. Typical causes of detonation include use of fuel with too low an octane rating, high manifold pressure, high intake air pressure, and engine overheating. Of the conditions provided, only numbers 1, 2, and 3 are correct.

1-56   AMP008

Excessive valve clearance in a piston engine

A– increases valve overlap.

B– increases valve opening time.

C– decreases valve overlap.

1-56. Answer C. FPH

Valve overlap represents the time when both the intake and exhaust valves are open simultaneously. When there is too much valve clearance, the valves do not open as wide or remain open as long as they should. If the valves are not open as long, the amount of overlap decreases.

1-57   AMP056

Which of the following results in a decrease in volumetric efficiency?

A– Cylinder head temperature too low

B– Part-throttle operation

C– Short intake pipes of large diameter

1-57. Answer B. JSPT 1B, FPH

Volumetric efficiency is the ratio of the volume of the fuel/air charge drawn into a cylinder to the actual volume of the cylinder. Therefore, anything that limits airflow through an engine's induction system will cause a decrease in volumetric efficiency. At part throttle operation, the partially closed throttle valve restricts airflow to the cylinders and, therefore, causes a decrease in volumetric efficiency.

1-58   AMP056

Increased engine heat will cause volumetric efficiency to

A– remain the same.

B– decrease.

C– increase.

1-58. Answer B. JSPT 1B, FPH

Volumetric efficiency is the ratio of the volume of the fuel/air charge drawn into a cylinder to the actual volume of the cylinder. With high engine temperatures the air entering an engine heats up and becomes less dense before it enters the cylinders. Because of this, less oxygen reaches the engine's cylinders and volumetric efficiency decreases.

1-59   AMP056

Why does the smoothness of operation of an engine increase with a greater number of cylinders?

A– The power impulses are spaced closer together.

B– The power impulses are spaced farther apart.

C– The engine has larger counterbalance weights.

1-59. Answer A. JSPT 1B, FPH

The more cylinders an engine has, the closer together the power impulses occur and the smoother the engine operates.

SECTION C — DIESEL ENGINE TECHNOLOGY

Section C of Chapter 1 provides an introduction to diesel engine technology. Diesel engines are gaining popularity among many aircraft manufacturers. As the technology expands, diesel engines will likely become common in civil aviation. At this time, however, the FAA does not require an AMT to demonstrate knowledge with regard to diesel engines.

RECIPROCATING ENGINE OPERATION, INSTRUMENTS, MAINTENANCE, AND OVERHAUL

CHAPTER 2

SECTION A — ENGINE OPERATION, INSTRUMENTS, AND MAINTENANCE

The first section of Chapter 2 covers information related to reciprocating engine operations and maintenance practices. Reciprocating engine instrument systems are also covered in this section.

2-1   AMP056

Which unit most accurately indicates fuel consumption of a reciprocating engine?

A– Fuel flowmeter

B– Fuel pressure gauge

C– Electronic fuel quantity indicator

2-1. Answer A. JSGT 2A, FPH

Electronic fuel flowmeters (vane-type or mass-flow type) are what many modern aircraft use to measure the amount of fuel consumed by an engine. Fuel flowmeters monitor the amount of fuel that flows past a given point and display this flow rate in the cockpit as pounds of fuel consumed per hour.

2-2   AMP054

A condition that can occur in radial engines but is unlikely to occur in horizontally opposed engines is

A– valve overlap.

B– zero valve clearance.

C– hydraulic lock.

2-2. Answer C. JSPT 2A, FGH

Before starting a radial engine that has been shutdown for more than 30 minutes, the propeller should be pulled through by hand in the direction of normal rotation to detect hydraulic lock. Hydraulic lock is more likely to occur in radial engines because the inverted lower cylinders may allow oil to collect in the combustion chambers.

2-3   AMP056

If the intake valve is opened too early in the cycle of operation of a four-stroke cycle engine, it may result in

A– improper scavenging of exhaust gases.

B– engine kickback.

C– backfiring into the induction system.

2-3. Answer C. JSPT 2A, FPH

The distance an intake valve may be opened before TDC is limited by several factors. For example, if the intake valve opens too early hot gases remaining in the cylinder may flash back into the intake pipe and induction system causing a backfire.

2-4   AMP057

What is the purpose of a power check on a reciprocating engine?

A– To check magneto drop

B– To determine satisfactory performance

C– To determine if the fuel/air mixture is adequate

2-4. Answer B. JSPT 2A, FPH

The basic principle behind doing a power check is to measure the performance of an engine against an established standard and determine if the engine is performing satisfactorily.

2-5   AMP056

Which of the following will be caused by excessive valve clearance of a cylinder on a reciprocating aircraft engine?

A– Reduced valve overlap period

B– Intake and exhaust valves will open early and close late

C– A power increase by shortening the exhaust event

2-5. Answer A. JSPT 2A, FPH

When valve clearance is excessive, the valves will not open as wide or remain open as long as they should. Therefore, both the intake and exhaust valves will open late and close early resulting in a reduced valve overlap period.

2-6   AMP057

As the pressure is applied during a reciprocating engine compression check using a differential pressure tester, what would a movement of the propeller in the direction of engine rotation indicate?

A– The piston was on compression stroke.

B– The piston was on exhaust stroke.

C– The piston was positioned past top dead center.

2-6. Answer C. JSPT 2A, FPH

When a differential compression test is being performed on an aircraft engine, the piston should be at top dead center when the air pressure is introduced into the cylinder. If the piston is past top dead center, the air pressure will force the piston to the bottom of the cylinder causing the propeller to rotate in the normal direction of rotation.

2-7   AMP008

Excessive valve clearance results in the valves opening

A– late and closing early.

B– early and closing late.

C– late and closing late.

2-7. Answer A. JSPT 2A, FPH

Excessive valve clearance describes a condition where there is too much clearance between a rocker arm and the end of a valve stem. The excessive clearance results in the valve opening late due to the time required for the rocker arm to contact the valve stem. Furthermore, the valve will close early due to the decreased dwell time.

2-8   AMP031

If the oil pressure gauge fluctuates over a wide range from zero to normal operating pressure, the most likely cause is

A– low oil supply.

B– broken or weak pressure relief valve spring.

C– air lock in the scavenge pump intake.

2-8. Answer A. JSPT 2A, FPH

The most likely cause of oil pressure fluctuating between zero and normal oil pressure is a low oil supply. If you have an engine with a low oil supply, the oil pressure will be normal as long as the oil is being picked up by the pump. However, momentary losses of oil pick-up will cause the oil pressure to drop to zero.

2-9   AMP056

Excessive valve clearances will cause the duration of valve opening to

A– increase for both intake and exhaust valves.

B– decrease for both intake and exhaust valves.

C– decrease for intake valves and increase for exhaust valves.

2-9. Answer B. JSPT 2A, FPH

When there is excessive clearance between the valve stem and rocker arm (valve clearance), the valves will not open as wide or remain open as long during engine operation. This reduces the overlap period and the cylinder's volumetric efficiency.

2-10   AMP054

Before attempting to start a radial engine that has been shut down for more than 30 minutes,

A– turn the propeller by hand three or four revolutions in the opposite direction of normal rotation to check for liquid lock.

B– turn the ignition switch on before energizing the starter.

C– turn the propeller by hand three to four revolutions in the normal direction of rotation to check for liquid lock.

2-10. Answer C. JSPT 2A, FPH

Whenever a radial engine remains shut down for more than 30 minutes, oil and fuel may drain into the combustion chambers of the lower cylinders or accumulate in the lower intake pipes. These fluids can cause a liquid lock, or hydraulic lock, which can damage the engine if a start is attempted. To check for a liquid lock, the propeller should be turned by hand in the normal direction of rotation a minimum of two complete revolutions.

2-11   AMP057

A hissing sound from the exhaust stacks when the propeller is being pulled through manually indicates

A– a cracked exhaust stack.

B– exhaust valve blow-by.

C– worn piston rings.

2-11. Answer B. JSPT 2A, FPH

Exhaust valve blow-by occurs when the exhaust valve does not seat properly, allowing a portion of the fuel/air charge to escape before combustion takes place. Exhaust valve blow-by is identified by a hissing or whistling sound coming from the exhaust stacks.

2-12   AMP056

Which of the following is most likely to occur if an overhead valve engine is operated with inadequate valve clearances?

A– The valve will not seat positively during start and engine warm-up.

B– The further decrease in valve clearance that occurs as engine temperatures increase will cause damage to the valve-operating mechanism.

C– The valves will remain closed for longer periods than specified by the engine manufacturer.

2-12. Answer A. JSPT 2A, FPH

When the valve clearance on a reciprocating engine is inadequate, the push rods open the valves earlier and close them late. In addition, as the engine warms-up, the valve clearances tend to increase as the cylinders expand. The valves will not remain seated as long during engine starting and warm-up.

2-13   AMP057

If air is heard coming from the crankcase breather or oil filler during a differential compression check, what is this an indication of?

A– Exhaust valve leakage

B– Intake valve leakage

C– Piston ring leakage

2-13. Answer C. JSPT 2A, FPH

Excessive leakage past the piston rings can be detected by the sound of escaping air at the engine breather tube or oil filler cap.

2-14   AMP062

Standard sea level pressure is

A– 29.00 in. Hg.

B– 29.29 in. Hg.

C– 29.92 in. Hg.

2-14. Answer C. JSGT 2C, FPH

A standard day is defined by a sea level pressure of 29.92 inches of mercury, or 14.7 PSI.

2-15   AMP012
Using standard atmospheric conditions, the standard sea level temperature is

A– 59°F.

B– 59°C.

C– 29°C.

2-15. Answer A. JSGT 2C, FPH
A standard day is defined by an atmospheric pressure of 29.92 inches of mercury, or 14.7 PSI, and a temperature of 59°F or 15°C.

2-16   AMP020
Newton's First Law of Motion, generally termed the Law of Inertia, states:

A– To every action there is an equal and opposite reaction.

B– Force is proportional to the product of mass and acceleration.

C– Every body persists in its state of rest, or of motion in a straight line, unless acted upon by some outside force.

2-16. Answer C. JSGT 2B, FGH
Newton's First Law of Motion states that any body at rest will remain at rest and any body in motion will remain in a straight line motion, unless acted upon by some outside force.

2-17   AMP007
What section in the instructions for continued airworthiness is FAA approved?

A– Engine maintenance manual or section

B– Engine overhaul manual or section

C– Airworthiness limitations section

2-17. Answer C. JSGT 14A, Part 33, Appendix A
According to FAR Part 33 Appendix A, the Instructions for Continued Airworthiness must contain a section titled Airworthiness Limitations that is segregated and clearly distinguishable from the rest of the document. This section is FAA approved and must list the mandatory replacement time, inspection interval, and related procedures required for certification.

2-18   AMP041
The fuel flow meter used with a continuous-fuel injection system installed on an aircraft horizontally opposed reciprocating engine measures the fuel pressure drop across the

A– manifold valve.

B– fuel nozzles.

C– metering valve.

2-18. Answer B. JSPT 2A
Most light aircraft equipped with continuous-fuel injection systems utilize a fuel flow indication system that measures the pressure drop across the injection nozzles to determine fuel flow. With this type of system, a higher fuel flow results in a greater pressure drop and a corresponding increase in fuel flow is indicated in the cockpit.

2-19   AMP041

The principle fault in the pressure type fuel flow meter indicating system, installed on a horizontally opposed continuous-flow fuel injected aircraft reciprocating engine, is that a plugged fuel injection nozzle will cause a

A– normal operation indication.

B– lower than normal fuel flow indication.

C– higher than normal fuel flow indication.

2-19. Answer C. JSPT 2A

Most light aircraft equipped with continuous-fuel injection systems utilize a fuel flow indication system that measures the pressure drop across the injection nozzles to determine fuel flow. With this type of system, a higher fuel flow results in a greater pressure drop and a corresponding increase in fuel flow is indicated in the cockpit. However, if an injector nozzle becomes restricted, the pressure drop across the nozzle becomes greater and produces a false or high fuel flow reading.

2-20   AMP026

Motor driven impeller and turbine fuel flow transmitters are designed to transmit data

A– using aircraft electrical system power.

B– mechanically.

C– by fuel pressure.

2-20. Answer A. JSPT 2A, FAH

In an autosyn system installed in the fuel system of turbine engine aircraft, fuel-flow data are transmitted using the aircraft's electrical system.

2-21   AMP009

The fuel-flow indicator rotor and needle for a motor-impeller and turbine indicating system is driven by

A– an electrical signal.

B– direct coupling to the motor shaft.

C– a mechanical gear train.

2-21. Answer A. JSPT 2A, FAH

The only fuel flow indicating system that utilizes an impeller and turbine is the synchronous mass flow system. In this type of system both the indicator rotor and needle are driven by an electrical signal.

2-22   AMP057

On a twin-engine aircraft with fuel-injected reciprocating engines, one fuel-flow indicator reads considerably higher than the other in all engine operating configurations. What is the probable cause of this indication?

A– Carburetor icing

B– One or more fuel nozzles are clogged

C– Alternate air door stuck open

2-22. Answer B. JSPT 2A

Most light twin-engine aircraft utilize a fuel flow indication system that measures the pressure drop across the injection nozzles to determine fuel flow. With this type of system, a higher fuel flow results in a greater pressure drop and a corresponding increase in fuel flow is indicated in the cockpit. However, if an injector nozzle becomes restricted, the pressure drop across the nozzle becomes greater and produces a false or high fuel flow reading.

2-23   AMP041

The fuel-flow indication system used with many fuel-injected opposed engine airplanes utilizes a measure of

A– fuel flow volume.

B– fuel pressure.

C– fuel flow mass.

2-23. Answer B. JSPT 2A, FAH

The fuel flow indication used for fuel injected opposed engines is actually a measure of the pressure drop across the fuel injection nozzles. With this type of system, a higher fuel flow creates a greater pressure drop and a corresponding increase in the indicated fuel flow.

2-24   AMP009

In addition to fuel quantity, a computerized fuel system (CFS) with a totalizer-indicator provides indication of how many of the following?

 1. Fuel flow rate

 2. Fuel used since reset or initial start-up.

 3. Fuel time remaining at current power setting

 4. Fuel temperature

A– Two

B– Three

C– Four

2-24. Answer B. JSPT 2A

A computerized fuel system (CFS) utilizes a transducer mounted in the fuel line leading to the engine to provide fuel flow in gallons or pounds per hour, gallons or pounds remaining, time remaining for flight at the current power setting, and gallons used since startup or reset. Of the four items listed, three are provided by a CFS.

2-25   AMP041

The fuel-flow indication data sent from motor driven impeller and turbine, and motorless type fuel flow transmitters is a measure of

A– fuel mass-flow.

B– fuel volume-flow.

C– engine burner pressure drop.

2-25. Answer A. JSPT 2A, FGH

In both a motor driven impeller and turbine, and a motorless fuel flow indication system a flow meter transmitter converts the fuel's mass-flow rate into electronic signals that produce a fuel flow indication in the cockpit.

2-26   AMP009

In an aircraft equipped with a pressure-drop type fuel-flow indicating system, if one of the injector nozzles becomes restricted, this would cause a decrease in fuel flow with

A– a decreased fuel flow indication on the gauge.

B– an increased fuel flow indication on the gauge.

C– no change in fuel flow indication on the gauge.

2-26. Answer B. JSPT 2A

If an injector nozzle becomes restricted in an aircraft equipped with a pressure-drop type fuel flow indicating system the pressure drop across the nozzle increases and produces a false or high fuel flow indication.

2-27   AMP009

A manifold pressure gauge is designed to

A– maintain constant pressure in the intake manifold.

B– indicate differential pressure between the intake manifold and atmospheric pressure.

C– indicate absolute pressure in the intake manifold.

2-27. Answer C. JSPT 2A, FPH

A manifold pressure gauge measures the absolute pressure in the induction system of a piston engine.

2-28   AMP057

The purpose of an exhaust gas analyzer is to indicate the

A– brake specific fuel consumption.

B– fuel/air ratio being burned in the cylinders.

C– temperature of the exhaust gases in the exhaust manifold.

2-28. Answer B. JSPT 2A

The purpose of an exhaust gas analyzer is to indicate the fuel/air ratio being burned in the cylinders. It identifies cylinders that are running too rich or too lean, and can be used to fine tune the fuel metering system.

2-29   AMP009
Which of the following types of electric motors are commonly used in electric tachometers?

A– Direct current, series-wound motors

B– Synchronous motors

C– Direct current, shunt-wound motors

2-29. Answer B. JSPT 2A, FAH
A typical electric tachometer consists of a three-phase generator mounted to the engine that is connected electrically to a three-phase synchronous motor in the tachometer instrument. The engine-mounted generator produces a three-phase current that is sent to the synchronous motor where a rotating field is produced in the stator. The rotating field causes the rotor to turn which, in turn, moves the tachometer's indicating needle.

2-30   AMP009
Where are the hot and cold junctions located in an engine cylinder temperature indicating system?

A– Both junctions are located at the instrument.

B– Both junctions are located at the cylinder.

C– The hot junction is located at the cylinder and the cold junction is located at the instrument.

2-30. Answer C. JSPT 2A, FAH
A thermocouple is a circuit of two dissimilar metals connected together at two junctions to form a loop. When there is a temperature difference between the two junctions an electromotive force is produced which can be measured with a galvanometer. Therefore, when a thermocouple temperature indicating system is used on a reciprocating engine, the thermocouple's hot junction is placed at the cylinder whereas the system's cold junction is at the instrument.

2-31   AMP009
Basically, the indicator of a tachometer system is responsive to change in

A– current flow.

B– frequency.

C– voltage.

2-31. Answer B. JSPT 2A, FAH
The typical electric tachometer system utilizes a three-phase AC generator coupled to the aircraft engine and connected electrically to a synchronous motor indicator mounted to the instrument panel.

The generator transmits three-phase power to the synchronous motor at a frequency that is proportional to the engine speed. The exact frequency determines the motor speed which, in turn, produces the instrument indication.

2-32   AMP012

Which statement is correct concerning a thermocouple-type temperature indicating instrument system?

A– It is a balanced-type, variable resistor circuit.

B– It requires no external power source.

C– It usually contains a balancing circuit in the instrument case to prevent fluctuations of the system voltage from affecting the temperature reading.

2-32. Answer B. JSPT 2A, FAH

Because a thermocouple produces its own milli-amp current flow, a temperature indicating system using thermocouples does not require any external power. However, most systems do use external power and an amplifier to improve the response.

2-33   AMP066

Which statement is true regarding a thermocouple-type cylinder head temperature measuring system?

A– The resistance required for cylinder head temperature indicators is measured in farads.

B– The voltage output of a thermocouple system is determined by the temperature difference between the two ends of the thermocouple.

C– When the master switch is turned on, a thermocouple indicator will move off-scale to the low side.

2-33. Answer B. JSPT 2A, FAH

A thermocouple is a circuit of two dissimilar metals connected together at two junctions to form a loop. When there is a temperature difference between the two junctions an electromotive force is produced which can be measured with a galvanometer. The greater the temperature difference the greater the voltage produced.

2-34   AMP009

What basic meter is used to indicate cylinder head temperature in most aircraft?

A– Electrodynamometer.

B– Galvanometer.

C– Thermocouple-type meter.

2-34. Answer B. JSPT 2A, FAH

A thermocouple is a circuit of two dissimilar metals connected together at two junctions to form a loop. When there is a temperature difference between the two junctions an electromotive force is produced which can be measured with a galvanometer.

2-35   AMP009

Which of the following is a primary engine instrument?

A– Tachometer

B– Fuel flowmeter

C– Airspeed indicator

2-35. Answer A. JSPT 2A, FAR 91.205

On both reciprocating and turbine powered aircraft, the tachometer is the primary engine instrument. On turboprop and turboshaft powered aircraft that utilize a torque meter gauge, it also becomes a primary engine instrument.

2-36   AMP009

A complete break in the line between the manifold pressure gauge and the induction system will be indicated by the gauge registering

A– prevailing atmospheric pressure.

B– zero.

C– lower than normal for conditions prevailing.

2-36. Answer A. JSPT 2A, FPH

A manifold pressure gauge measures the absolute pressure within an engine's intake manifold. However, if a break exists in the line between the manifold pressure gauge and the manifold, the gauge will only be able to display the prevailing atmospheric pressure.

2-37   AMP009

Engine oil temperature gauges indicate the temperature of the oil

A– entering the oil cooler.

B– entering the engine.

C– in the oil storage tank.

2-37. Answer B. JSPT 2A, FPH

In both wet and dry-sump lubricating systems, the oil temperature bulb is located somewhere in the oil inlet line between the supply tank and the engine.

This means the oil temperature gauge in the cockpit indicates the temperature of the oil entering the engine.

2-38   AMP009

Why do helicopters require a minimum of two synchronous tachometer systems?

A– One indicates engine RPM and the other tail rotor RPM.

B– One indicates main rotor RPM and the other tail rotor RPM.

C– One indicates engine RPM and the other main rotor RPM.

2-38. Answer C. JSPT 2A, FAH

Helicopters require a minimum of two tachometers to monitor both the engine rpm and the rotor RPM.

2-39   AMP066

If the thermocouple leads were inadvertently crossed at installation, what would the cylinder temperature gauge pointer indicate?

A— Normal temperature for prevailing condition

B— Moves off-scale on the zero side of the meter

C— Moves off-scale on the high side of the meter

2-39. Answer B. JSPT 2A, FAH

A thermocouple type of temperature indicating system produces a current flow in one direction when there is a difference in temperature between the hot junction and the cold junction. Therefore, if the leads to the temperature gauge are reversed, the temperature gauge pointer movement will reverse and the needle will peg out at the meter's zero side.

2-40   AMP009

A common type of electrically operated oil temperature gauge utilizes

A— either a Wheatstone bridge or ratiometer circuit.

B— a thermocouple type circuit.

C— vapor pressure and pressure switches.

2-40. Answer A. JSPT 2A, FAH

The two types of circuits typically used in electrically operated oil temperature gauges are the Wheatstone bridge circuit and the ratiometer circuit.

2-41   AMP066

The indication on a thermocouple-type cylinder head temperature indicator is produced by

A— resistance changes in two dissimilar metals.

B— a difference in the voltage between two dissimilar metals.

C— a current generated by the temperature difference between dissimilar metal hot and cold junctions.

2-41. Answer C. JSPT 2A, FPH

A thermocouple is a circuit of two dissimilar metals connected together at two junctions to form a loop. When there is a temperature difference between the two junctions an electromotive force is produced which can be measured with a galvanometer. The greater the temperature difference the greater the voltage produced.

2-42   AMP009

Thermocouple leads

A– may be installed with either lead to either post of the indicator.

B– are designed for a specific installation and may not be altered.

C– may be repaired using solderless connectors.

2-42. Answer B. JSPT 2A, FAH

Thermocouple leads are designed for a specific installation. For example, in order to function properly there must be a specific amount of resistance in the thermocouple circuit. Thus, their length or cross sectional size cannot be altered unless some compensation is made for the change in total resistance. A thermocouple system for a typical turbine engine, for example, has eight ohms of resistance.

2-43   AMP009

What unit in a tachometer system sends information to the indicator?

A– The three-phase AC generator

B– The two-phase AC generator

C– The synchronous motor

2-43. Answer A. JSPT 2A, FAH

The typical electric tachometer system uses a three-phase AC generator coupled to the engine to send information to an AC synchronous motor that is attached to the indicator.

2-44   AMP059

Which of the following instrument discrepancies require replacement of the instrument?

1. Red line missing from glass

2. Glass cracked

3. Case paint chipped

4. Will not zero out

5. Pointer loose on shaft

6. Mounting screw loose

7. Leaking at line B nut

4. Fogged

A– 2, 3, 7, and 8

B– 2, 4, 5, and 8

C– 1, 2, 4, and 7

2-44. Answer B. JSPT 2A, FAH

Items 2, 4, 5 and 8 cannot be repaired by a maintenance technician and, therefore, the instrument must be removed from the aircraft and sent to a certified instrument repair station. The remaining items (items 1, 3, 6, and 7) can be repaired by an aviation technician and do not require the removal and replacement of the instrument.

2-45   AMP012

A Bourdon-tube instrument may be used to indicate

1. pressure.

2. temperature.

3. position.

4. quantity.

A– 1 and 2

B– 1 and 3

C– 2 and 4

2-45. Answer A. JSPT 2A, FAH

A Bourdon tube is a metal tube that is formed in a circular shape with an oval or flattened cross section and is used to measure both pressure and temperature. When air or liquid pressure enters the open end of a Bourdon tube, the tube has a tendency to straighten out. By the same token, if a Bourdon tube is filled with a gas and sealed at both ends, changes in temperature will cause the sealed gas to expand and contract thereby causing the tube to move. Through a series of gears, this movement is then used to move an indicating needle.

2-46   AMP012

Which of the following instrument conditions is acceptable and does NOT require immediate correction?

1. Red line missing

2. Pointer loose on shaft

3. Glass cracked

4. Mounting screws loose

5. Case paint chipped

6. Leaking at line B nut

7. Will not zero out

4. Fogged

A– 1

B– 4

C– 5

2-46. Answer C. JSPT 2A, FAH

Chipped paint on an instrument case has no effect on an instrument's operational condition and, therefore, no immediate corrective action is required.

2-47   AMP012

Instruments that provide readings of low or negative pressure, such as manifold pressure gauges, are usually what type?

A– Vane with calibrated spring

B– Bourdon tube

C– Diaphragm or bellows

2-47. Answer C. JSPT 2A, FAH

Typically, instruments that provide low or negative pressure readings utilize a sensitive diaphragm or bellows that expands and contracts to drive an indicator needle.

2-48   AMP012

Instruments that measure relatively high fluid pressures, such as oil pressure gauges, are usually what type?

A– Vane with calibrated spring

B– Bourdon tube

C– Diaphragm or bellows

2-48. Answer B. JSPT 2A, FAH

Oil pressure gauges typically utilize a Bourdon tube type indicator. A Bourdon tube is a metal tube that is formed in a circular shape with an oval or flattened cross section. When air or liquid pressure enters the open end of a Bourdon tube, the tube has a tendency to straighten out. Through a series of gears, this movement is used to move an indicating needle.

2-49   AMP012

The RPM indication of a synchronous AC motor-tachometer is governed by the generator

A– voltage.

B– current.

C– frequency.

2-49. Answer C. JSPT 2A

Modern AC tachometers utilize a three-phase AC generator coupled to an engine and connected electrically to an indicator mounted in the instrument panel. As an engine runs, the three-phase generator transmits a frequency that is proportional to the engine speed of a synchronous motor mounted to the indicator.

The transmitted frequency causes the synchronous motor to turn at a specific RPM and provide a specific indication

2-50   AMP012

A red triangle, dot, or diamond mark on an engine instrument face or glass indicates

A– the maximum operating limit for all normal operations.

B– the maximum limit for high transients such as starting.

C– a restricted operating range.

2-50. Answer B. JSPT 2A, AC 20-88A

A red mark on an instrument face designates the maximum limit for a high transient condition.

2-51   AMP056

The EGT gauge used with reciprocating engines is primarily used to furnish temperature readings in order to

A— obtain the best mixture setting for fuel efficiency.

B— obtain the best mixture setting for engine cooling.

C— prevent engine overtemperature.

2-51. Answer A. JSPT 2A, FAH

The exhaust gas temperature (EGT) gauge provides a pilot with a means of properly adjusting the fuel/air mixture for efficient operation.

2-52   AMP066

Thermocouples are usually inserted or installed on the

A— front cylinder of the engine.

B— rear cylinder of the engine.

C— hottest cylinder of the engine.

2-52. Answer C. JSPT 2A, FPH

A thermocouple-type indicating device is typically used to indicate the cylinder head temperature on a reciprocating engine. To help ensure that none of the cylinders are hotter than the temperature indicated in the cockpit, cylinder head temperature readings are usually taken from the hottest cylinder.

2-53   AMP026

When an electric primer is used, fuel pressure is built up by the

A— internal pump in the primer solenoid.

B— suction at the main discharge nozzle.

C— booster pump.

2-53. Answer C. JSPT 2A, FGH

One of the many purposes of a boost pump is to supply fuel under pressure for priming prior to starting an engine.

2-54   AMP065

If a fire starts in the induction system during the engine starting procedure, what should the operator do?

A— Turn off the fuel switches to stop the fuel.

B— Continue cranking the engine.

C— Turn off all switches.

2-54. Answer B. JSPT 2A, FGH

If a fire breaks out in a reciprocating engine's induction system during a start attempt, you should continue to crank the engine to try and draw the fire into the engine. If the fire does not go out, the fuel selector valve and ignition should be shut off, the mixture placed in the idle cutoff position, and a fire extinguisher used to put out the fire.

2-55   AMP056

An engine becomes overheated due to excessive taxiing or improper ground run-up. Prior to shutdown, operation must continue until cylinders have cooled, by running engine at

A– low RPM with oil dilution system activated.

B– idle RPM.

C– high RPM with mixture control in rich position.

2-55. Answer B. JSPT 2A, FPH

After a flight and a few minutes of taxiing, an engine typically will not become excessively warm and, therefore, can be shut down almost immediately. However, if an engine becomes excessively hot as indicated by the cylinder head temperature gauge and the oil temperature gauge, you should allow the engine to cool at idle speed for a short time before shutdown.

2-56   AMP056

High cylinder head temperatures are likely to result from

A– a very lean mixture at high power settings.

B– fouled spark plugs.

C– a very rich mixture at high power settings.

2-56. Answer A. JSPT 2A, FPH

At higher power settings, a very lean mixture does not allow any excess fuel into the engine to aid in cooling and, therefore, high cylinder temperatures typically result.

2-57   AMP057

What will be the likely result if the piston ring gaps happen to be aligned when performing a differential-pressure compression check on a cylinder?

A– Little or no effect.

B– The rings will not be seated.

C– A worn or defective ring(s) indication.

2-57. Answer C. JSPT 2A, FPH

If all the ring gaps happen to be aligned when performing a differential pressure compression check they will allow air to escape from the cylinder and give the same indication as if the rings were defective or worn. To remedy this problem, run the engine for a period of time so the ring gaps have a chance to shift.

2-58   AMP057

Which of the following would indicate a general weak-engine condition when operated with a fixed-pitch propeller or test club?

A– Lower than normal static RPM, full throttle operation

B– Manifold pressure lower at idle RPM than at static RPM

C– Lower than normal manifold pressure for any given RPM

2-58. Answer A. JSPT 2A, FPH

When performing a power check on a reciprocating engine, it should be noted that with a constant air density, a given propeller and blade angle will always turn at the same RPM for a given horsepower. Therefore, if an engine is producing a lower than normal rpm at a full throttle setting, the engine may be weak.

2-59   AMP056

Engine operating flexibility is the ability of the engine to

A– deliver maximum horsepower at a specific altitude.

B– meet exacting requirements of efficiency and low weight per horsepower ratio.

C– run smoothly and give the desired performance at all speeds.

2-59. Answer C. JSPT 2A, FPH

Operating flexibility is defined as the ability of an engine to run smoothly and give desired performance at all engine speeds.

2-60   AMP056

In a reciprocating engine oil system, the temperature bulb senses oil temperature

A– at a point after the oil has passed through the oil cooler.

B– while the oil is in the hottest area of the engine.

C– immediately before the oil enters the oil cooler.

2-60. Answer A. JSPT 2A, FPH

In wet sump engines, the oil temperature bulb is located after the oil cooler. This allows the sensing bulb to measure the temperature of the oil entering the engine.

SECTION B — ENGINE REMOVAL AND OVERHAUL

Section B of Chapter 2 includes information related to engine removal and overhaul operations for reciprocating engines, including overhaul terminology.

2-61   AMP056

On which part of the cylinder walls of a normally operating engine will the greatest amount of wear occur?

A– Near the center of the cylinder where piston velocity is greatest

B– Near the top of the cylinder

C– Wear is normally evenly distributed

2-61. Answer B. JSPT 2B, FPH

At the top of a stroke, a piston is subjected to extreme heat, pressure, and a more erosive environment than at the bottom of a stroke. These factors tend to cause greater piston movement at the top of a cylinder. Therefore, cylinder walls tend to wear more at the top than at the bottom.

2-62   AMP057

During overhaul, reciprocating engine exhaust valves are checked for stretch

A– with a suitable inside spring caliper.

B– with a contour or radius gauge.

C– by placing the valve on a surface plate and measuring its length with a vernier height gauge.

2-62. Answer B. JSPT 2B, FPH

Intake and exhaust valves can be checked for stretch by one of two methods. One involves checking the diameter of the valve stem near the neck of the valve with a micrometer. If the diameter is smaller than normal, the valve has been stretched. The second method involves checking the valve with a radius or contour gauge. The contour gauge is designed to fit along the underside of the valve head. If the contour of the gauge and that of the valve do not match, it indicates that the valve has been stretched.

2-63   AMP007

During overhaul, the disassembled parts of an engine are usually degreased with some form of mineral spirits solvent rather than water-mixed degreasers primarily because

A– solvent degreasers are much more effective.

B– water-mixed degreaser residues may cause engine oil contamination in the overhauled engine.

C– water-mixed degreasers cause corrosion.

2-63. Answer B. JSPT 2B, FPH

Water-mixed degreasing compounds usually contain some form of alkali. If allowed to remain in the pores of metal engine parts when the engine is returned to service, the alkali will contaminate the oil and cause oil foaming.

2-64   AMP049

1. Cast iron piston rings may be used in chrome-plated cylinders.

2. Chrome-plated rings may be used in plain steel cylinders.

Regarding the above statements,

A– only No.1 is true.

B– neither No.1 nor No. 2 is true.

C– both No.1 and No. 2 are true.

2-64. Answer C. JSPT 2B, FPH
Both statements (1) and (2) are true. As a general rule, chrome rings should never be used in a chrome cylinder. However, it is extremely important that only approved piston ring and cylinder combinations be used. If approved combinations are not used, excessive cylinder and/or piston ring wear could result.

2-65   AMP007
When cleaning aluminum and magnesium engine parts, it is inadvisable to soak them in solutions containing soap because

A– some of the soap will become impregnated in the surface of the material and subsequently cause engine oil contamination and foaming.

B– the soap can chemically alter the metals causing them to become more susceptible to corrosion.

C– the parts can be destroyed by dissimilar metal electrolytic action if they are placed together in the solution for more than a few minutes.

2-65. Answer A. JSPT 2B, FPH
Water-mixed degreasing compounds usually contain alkali or soap which, if allowed to remain in the pores of the metal, will react with hot oil and cause foaming.

2-66   AMP056
Grinding the valves of a reciprocating engine to a feather edge is likely to result in

A– normal operation and long life.

B– excessive valve clearance.

C– preignition and burned valves.

2-66. Answer C. JSPT 2B, FPH
A thin edge on a poppet valve is called a feather edge. Valves with a feather edge are likely to overheat and burn away in a short period of time. Both of these conditions can lead to preignition.

2-67   AMP007

During routine inspection of a reciprocating engine, a deposit of small, bright, metallic particles which do not cling to the magnetic drain plug is discovered in the oil sump and on the surface of the oil filter. This condition

A— may be a result of abnormal plain type bearing wear and is cause for further investigation.

B— is probably a result of ring and cylinder wall wear and is cause for engine removal and/or overhaul.

C— is normal in engines utilizing plain type bearings and aluminum pistons and is not cause for alarm.

2-67. Answer A. JSPT 2B, FPH

Plain bearings used in aircraft engines are usually made of nonferrous metals, such as silver, bronze, aluminum, and various alloys of copper, tin, or lead. If this type of material is found in the oil sump of an engine and on the surface of the oil filter, it is an indication that the bearings may be experiencing abnormal wear.

2-68   AMP008

A characteristic of dyna-focal engine mounts as applied to aircraft reciprocating engines is that the

A— shock mounts eliminate the torsional flexing of the power plant.

B— engine attaches to the shock mounts at the engine's center of gravity.

C— shock mounts point toward the engine's center of gravity.

2-68. Answer C. JSPT 2B, FPH

One characteristic of dyna-focal engine mounts is that the shock mounts point toward the engine's center of gravity. This design feature helps prevent vibration from being transmitted to the airframe. The shock mounts consist of a piece of rubber inside a round metal mount. The rubber within the mount helps absorb vibration and allows some torsional flexing.

2-69   AMP007

If metallic particles are found in the oil filter during an inspection,

A— it is an indication of normal engine wear unless the particles are nonferrous.

B— the cause should be identified and corrected before the aircraft is released for flight.

C— it is an indication of normal engine wear unless the deposit exceeds a specified amount.

2-69. Answer B. JSPT 2B, FPH

Metal particles on engine oil screens or magnetic sump plugs are generally an indication of partial internal engine failure. However, due to the construction of aircraft oil systems, it is possible that metal particles could have collected in the oil system sludge at the time of a previous engine failure. At any rate, the cause or source of the particles should be determined before the engine is returned to service.

2-70   AMP057

Engine crankshaft runout is usually checked

1. during engine overhaul.

2. during annual inspection.

3. after a "prop strike" or sudden engine stoppage.

4. during 100-hour inspection.

A– 1, 3, and 4

B– 1 and 3

C– 1, 2, and 3

2-70. Answer B. JSPT 2B, FPH

Engine crankshaft runout is typically checked when the crankshaft is separated from the engine. Therefore, crankshaft runout is usually checked during an engine overhaul. Furthermore, manufacturers generally require runout checks after sudden stoppage or a sudden reduction in speed, such as a prop strike.

2-71   AMP056

Standard aircraft cylinder oversizes usually range from 0.010 inch to 0.030 inch. Oversize on automobile engine cylinders may range up to 0.100 inch. This is because aircraft engine cylinders

A– have more limited cooling capacity.

B– have relatively thin walls and may be nitrided.

C– operate at high temperatures.

2-71. Answer B. JSPT 2B, FPH

Generally, standard aircraft cylinder oversizes are 0.010 inch, 0.015 inch, 0.020 inch, or 0.030 inch. The reason aircraft cylinders cannot be oversized as much as automobile cylinders is because aircraft cylinders have relatively thin walls and may have a nitrided surface.

2-72   AMP021

Direct mechanical push-pull carburetor heat control linkages should normally be adjusted so that the stop located on the diverter valve will be contacted

A– before the stop at the control lever is reached in both HOT and COLD positions.

B– before the stop at the control lever is reached in the HOT position and after the stop at the control lever is reached in the COLD position.

C– after the stop at the control lever is reached in both HOT and COLD positions.

2-72. Answer A. JSPT 2B, FPH

When rigging any carburetor control linkage, the component being moved must contact its stop prior to the stop in the cockpit is reached. This ensures full control travel.

2-73   AMP057

Which of the following engine servicing operations generally requires engine pre-oiling prior to starting the engine?

A– Engine oil and filter change

B– Engine installation

C– Replacement of oil lines

2-73. Answer B. JSPT 2B, FPH

After an engine is installed it should be pre-oiled prior to starting. Pre-oiling helps prevent excessive wear or failure of the engine bearings.

2-74   AMP007

During the inspection of an engine control system in which push-pull control rods are used, the threaded rod ends should

A– not be adjusted in length for rigging purposes because the rod ends have been properly positioned and staked during manufacture.

B– be checked for thread engagement of at least two threads but not more than four threads.

C– be checked for the amount of thread engagement by means of the inspection holes.

2-74. Answer C. JSPT 2B, FPH

After a push/pull control rod has been adjusted you should check the number of threads engaging the rod end. To check for the proper amount of engagement, an inspection hole is typically provided in which a piece of safety wire is inserted. If the safety wire can pass through the hole, there is insufficient thread engagement.

2-75   AMP057

How may it be determined that a reciprocating engine with a dry sump is pre-oiled sufficiently?

A– The engine oil pressure gauge will indicate normal oil pressure.

B– Oil will flow from the engine return line or indicator port.

C– When the quantity of oil specified by the manufacturer has been pumped into the engine.

2-75. Answer B. JSPT 2B, FPH

When an engine is being pre-oiled, a line from the inlet side of the engine-driven oil pump must be disconnected to permit the pre-oiler tank to be connected. Then, a line near the nose of the engine is disconnected to allow oil to flow out. Once oil flows out of the engine pre-oiling is complete.

2-76   AMP007

The breaking loose of small pieces of metal from coated surfaces, usually caused by defective plating or excessive loads, is called

A– flaking.

B– chafing.

C– brinelling.

2-76. Answer A. JSPT 2B, FPH

Flaking is defined as the breaking loose of small pieces of metal from coated surfaces. It is usually caused by defective plating or excessive loading.

2-77   AMP007

A severe condition of chafing or fretting in which a transfer of metal from one part to another occurs is called

A– scoring.

B– burning.

C– galling.

2-77. Answer C. JSPT 2B, FPH

Galling is defined as a severe condition of chafing or fretting in which a transfer of metal from one part to another occurs. It is usually caused by a slight movement of mated parts under high loads and having limited relative motion.

2-78   AMP007

Indentations on bearing races caused by high static loads are known as

A– fretting.

B– brinelling.

C– galling.

2-78. Answer B. JSPT 2B, FPH

Brinelling is defined as one or more indentations on bearing races, usually caused by high loads or the application of force during installation or removal. The indentations are rounded or spherical due to the impression left by the contacting ball or roller bearings.

2-79   AMP048

A ground incident that results in propeller sudden stoppage may require a crankshaft runout inspection.

What publication would be used to obtain crankshaft runout tolerance?

A– Current Manufacturer's maintenance instructions

B– Type Certificate Data Sheet

C– AC 43.13-1A, Acceptable Methods, Techniques, and Practices Aircraft Inspection and Repair

2-79. Answer A. JSPT 2B, AC 43.13-1B

When an engine has been subjected to a sudden stoppage requiring a crankshaft run-out check, it should be done in accordance with the manufacturer's technical data. Therefore, the manufacturer's maintenance instructions would typically be used.

2-80   AMP057

How is proper end-gap clearance on new piston rings assured during the overhaul of an engine?

A– By accurately measuring and matching the outside diameter of the rings with the inside diameter of the cylinders

B– By using rings specified by the engine manufacturer

C– By placing the rings in the cylinder and measuring the end-gap with a feeler gauge

2-80. Answer C. JSPT 2B, FPH

The end gap clearance of piston rings is checked by placing a piston ring in the cylinder and inserting a thickness, or feeler gauge, between the two ring ends to determine the amount of clearance.

2-81   AMP057

If an engine cylinder is to be removed, at what position in the cylinder should the piston be?

A– Bottom dead center

B– Top dead center

C– Halfway between top and bottom dead center

2-81. Answer B. JSPT 2B, FPH

Before removing a cylinder from an engine, the piston should be at top dead center on the compression stroke. Having the piston in this position helps prevent damage to the cylinder, piston, and valves and helps relieve pressure on both the intake and exhaust rocker arms.

2-82   AMP057

If the crankshaft runout readings on the dial indicator are plus .002 inch and minus .003 inch, the runout is

A– .005 inch.

B– plus .001 inch.

C– minus .001 inch.

2-82. Answer A. JSGT 9B, FPH

The total indicator reading for runout on a crankshaft is the sum of the plus (+) and minus (-) readings. In this case, the runout is .005 in. (.002 + .003 = .005).

2-83   AMP008

Straightening nitrided crankshafts is

A– recommended.

B– not recommended.

C– approved by the manufacturer.

2-83. Answer B. JSPT 2B, FPH

Crankshaft surfaces that are nitrided are extremely brittle. Any attempt to straighten surfaces deformed from being bent can rupture the surface finish.

TURBINE ENGINES

SECTION A — DESIGN AND CONSTRUCTION

Section A of Chapter 3 contains information related to the design, construction, and basic maintenance practices of turbine engines, including turbine-powered auxiliary power units.

3-1   AMP019
At what point in an axial-flow turbojet engine will the highest gas pressures occur?

A– At the turbine entrance

B– Within the burner section

C– At the compressor outlet

3-1. Answer C. JSPT 3A, FPH
The highest gas pressure in an axial-flow turbojet engine occurs at the exit of the diffuser section, which is between the compressor outlet and combustion (burner) section. Of the answer choices in this question, the compressor outlet has the highest gas pressure, although this pressure is only slightly higher than those in the burner section or at the inlet to the turbine section.

3-2   AMP068
One function of the nozzle diaphragm in a turbine engine is to

A– decrease the velocity of exhaust gases.

B– center the fuel spray in the combustion chamber.

C– direct the flow of gases to strike the turbine blades at a desired angle.

3-2. Answer C. JSPT 3A, FPH
When high energy gases leave the combustion section of a turbine engine, they enter the turbine section. The turbine section is made up of stationary and rotating airfoils, or vanes. The stationary vanes, sometimes called a nozzle diaphragm, direct the high energy gases leaving the combustor into the rotating turbine blades. The nozzle diaphragm also increases the velocity of the gases.

3-3   AMP068
What is the profile of a turbine engine compressor blade?

A– The leading edge of the blade

B– A cutout that reduces blade tip thickness

C– The curvature of the blade root

3-3. Answer B. JSPT 3A, FPH
When looking at the profile of a compressor blade you will see that the tip of each blade is cut out to reduce tip thickness. This shape allows the blade to wear rather than break if the blade tip should come in contact with the case.

3-4   AMP019

The fan rotational speed of a dual axial compressor forward fan engine is the same as the

A– low-pressure compressor.

B– forward turbine wheel.

C– high-pressure compressor.

3-4. Answer A. JSPT 3A, FPH

On a dual axial or dual spool turbofan engine, the forward fan is typically bolted to the first compressor making the fan part of the low-pressure compressor. On some turbofan engines, the fan is mounted aft of the turbine wheel but never forward of it.

3-5   AMP068

What turbine engine section provides for proper mixing of the fuel and air?

A– Combustion section

B– Compressor section

C– Diffuser section

3-5. Answer A. JSPT 3A, FPH

The combustion section of a turbine engine is where the fuel and air are mixed and then burned. The compressor section compresses the inlet air and the diffuser section directs the compressed air to the burner cans.

3-6   AMP068

In a gas turbine engine, combustion occurs at a constant

A– volume.

B– pressure.

C– density.

3-6. Answer B. TEP2, FPH

During the combustion process in a turbine engine, burning fuel provides heat to expand the compressed air coming from the compressor. Throughout this process the pressure remains relatively constant.

3-7   AMP068

Some high-volume turboprop and turbojet engines are equipped with two-spool or split compressors. When these engines are operated at high altitudes, the

A– low-pressure rotor will increase in speed as the compressor load decreases in the lower density air.

B– throttle must be retarded to prevent overspeeding of the high-pressure rotor due to the lower density air.

C– low-pressure rotor will decrease in speed as the compressor load decreases in the lower density air.

3-7. Answer A. JSPT 3A, FPH

A two-spool or dual spool turbine engine is one in which there are two independently rotating units.

The front compressor is called the low-pressure compressor, and the rear compressor is called the high-pressure compressor. This type of engine has more operating flexibility than a single spool engine because the two compressors are free to find their own optimum RPM. This allows the low pressure compressor to increase in RPM at altitude because of the reduction in drag caused by the decrease in air density.

3-8   AMP068

Turbine nozzle diaphragms located on the upstream side of each turbine wheel are used in the gas turbine engine to

A– decrease the velocity of the heated gases flowing past this point.

B– direct the flow of gases parallel to the vertical line of the turbine blades.

C– increase the velocity of the heated gases flowing past this point.

3-8. Answer C. JSPT 3A, FPH

When high energy gases leave the combustion section of a turbine engine, they enter the turbine section. The turbine section is made up of stationary and rotating airfoils, or vanes. The stationary vanes are grouped together to form a nozzle which increases the velocity of the gases and directs the high energy gases leaving the combustor into the turbine's rotating blades.

3-9   AMP068

Where is the highest gas pressure in a turbojet engine?

A– At the outlet of the tailpipe section

B– At the entrance of the turbine section

C– In the entrance of the burner section

3-9. Answer C. JSPT 3A, FPH

The gas pressure in a turbine engine reaches its highest value as compressed air leaves the compressor and enters the burner. Once in the burner section, the air expands due to the heat produced by the burning fuel. From here, the gases pass through a nozzle diaphragm where they are accelerated prior to entering the turbine blades. This increase in gas speed results in a corresponding decrease in gas pressure in both the turbine section and tailpipe section.

3-10   AMP068

An exhaust cone placed aft of the turbine in a jet engine will cause the pressure in the first part of the exhaust duct to

A– increase and the velocity to decrease.

B– increase and the velocity to increase.

C– decrease and the velocity to increase.

3-10. Answer A. JSPT 3A, FPH

A jet engine exhaust cone collects the exhaust gases discharged from the turbine buckets and gradually converts them into a steady stream. In doing this, the divergent shape of the exhaust cone causes the velocity to decrease and the pressure to increase.

3-11   AMP019

What is the function of the stator vane assembly at the discharge end of a typical axial-flow compressor?

A– To straighten airflow to eliminate turbulence

B– To direct the flow of gases into the combustion chambers

C– To increase air swirling motion into the combustion chambers

3-11. Answer A. JSPT 3A, FPH

As air passes through the compressor section of a typical axial-flow compressor, it becomes extremely turbulent. To help prevent turbulent air from flowing into the combustion section, the air passes through a stator vane which straightens airflow and eliminates turbulence.

3-12   AMP008

The turbine section of a jet engine

A– increases air velocity to generate thrust forces.

B– utilizes heat energy to expand and accelerate the incoming gas flow.

C– drives the compressor section.

3-12. Answer C. JSPT 3A, FPH

In all turbine engines the turbine transforms a portion of the kinetic energy of the exhaust gases into mechanical energy to drive the compressor section.

3-13   AMP019

In the dual axial-flow or twin spool compressor system, the first stage turbine drives the

A– N1 and N2 compressors.

B– N2 compressor.

C– N1 compressor.

3-13. Answer B. JSPT 3A, FPH

In a twin spool axial-flow compressor system the first compressor (N1) is driven by the second stage turbine while the second compressor (N2) is driven by the first stage turbine.

3-14   AMP068

What are the two basic elements of the turbine section in a turbine engine?

A– Impeller and diffuser

B– Hot and cold

C– Stator and rotor

3-14. Answer C. JSPT 3A, FPH

The two basic turbine section elements are the stator and the rotor. The stator includes the stationary vanes located in front of the rotor that make up the turbine nozzle or nozzle diaphragm. The rotor includes the rotating vanes, or turbine blades.

3-15   AMP068

The function of the exhaust cone assembly of a turbine engine is to

A– collect the exhaust gases and act as a noise suppressor.

B– swirl and collect the exhaust gases into a single exhaust jet.

C– straighten and collect the exhaust gases into a solid exhaust jet.

3-15. Answer C. JSPT 3A, FPH

A jet engine exhaust cone collects the exhaust gases discharged from the turbine buckets and gradually converts them into a relatively straight and solid stream.

3-16   AMP068

What are the two functional elements in a centrifugal compressor?

A– Turbine and compressor

B– Bucket and expander

C– Impeller and diffuser

3-16. Answer C. JSPT 3A, FPH

The two parts that make up a centrifugal compressor are the impeller and the diffuser. The impeller accelerates the flow of air to the diffuser which is designed to direct the flow of air to the manifold at an angle that returns the maximum amount of energy.

3-17   AMP068

Some engine manufacturers of twin spool gas turbine engines identify turbine discharge pressure in their maintenance manuals as

A– Pt7.

B– Pt2.

C– Tt7.

3-17. Answer A. JSPT 3A, FPH

Turbine discharge pressure is identified in service manuals and on engine instruments by the standardized abbreviation Pt7.

3-18   AMP068

Main bearing oil seals used with turbine engines are usually what type(s)?

A– Labyrinth and/or carbon rubbing

B– Teflon and synthetic rubber

C– Labyrinth and/or silicone rubber

3-18. Answer A. JSPT 3A, FPH

Turbine main bearing oil seals are generally either the labyrinth or carbon rubbing (carbon ring) type. The labyrinth seal relies on pressure to prevent oil from leaking along the compressor shaft. Carbon rubbing seals, on the other hand, are usually spring loaded and are similar in material and application to the carbon brushes used in electrical motors. These seals rest against the surface provided and create a sealed bearing cavity or void that prevents oil leakage.

3-19   AMP019

How does a dual axial-flow compressor improve the efficiency of a turbojet engine?

A— More turbine wheels can be used.

B— Higher compression ratios can be obtained.

C— The velocity of the air entering the combustion chamber is increased.

3-19. Answer B. JSPT 3A, FPH

One of the advantages of a dual spool axial compressor over a single spool is the ability to have two separate compressors rotate at their own optimum RPM. By having two compressors rotate at different speeds, higher compression ratios are obtained.

3-20   AMP068

Three types of turbine blades are

A— reaction, converging, and diverging.

B— impulse, reaction, and impulse-reaction.

C— impulse, vector, and impulse-vector.

3-20. Answer B. JSPT 3A

Turbine blades are classified as impulse, reaction, or a combination impulse-reaction type. Most engines incorporate a blade design utilizing an impulse-reaction combination.

3-21   AMP008

Which statements are true regarding aircraft engine propulsion?

1. An engine driven propeller imparts a relatively small amount of acceleration to a large mass of air.

2. Turbojet and turbofan engines impart a relatively large amount of acceleration to a smaller mass of air.

3. In modern turboprop engines, nearly 50 percent of the exhaust gas energy is extracted by turbines to drive the propeller and compressor with the rest providing exhaust thrust.

A— 1, 2, and 3

B— 1 and 2

C— 1 and 3

3-21. Answer B. JSPT 3A, FPH

A propeller generates thrust by imparting a relatively small amount of acceleration to a large quantity of air. Turbojet and turbofan engines, on the other hand, generate thrust by imparting a relatively large amount of acceleration to a smaller quantity of air. Based on this, statements 1 and 2 are correct.

3-22   AMP019

An advantage of the axial-flow compressor is its

A– low starting power requirements.

B– low weight.

C– high peak efficiency.

3-22. Answer C. JSPT 3A, FPH

Although an axial-flow compressor does not give as high a compression rise per stage as a centrifugal compressor, its multiple stages and ability to take advantage of ram air pressure allow it to produce higher peak pressures.

3-23   AMP068

What is one purpose of the stator blades in the compressor section of a turbine engine?

A– Stabilize the pressure of the airflow

B– Control the direction of the airflow

C– Increase the velocity of the airflow

3-23. Answer B. JSPT 3A, FPH

In an axial-flow compressor, the stator blades are fixed airfoils that are placed at the discharge end of each compressor stage. Their purpose is to control the direction of airflow into the next compressor stage or combustion section and eliminate turbulence. The stationary airfoils in the axial flow compressor are most appropriately called stator vanes.

3-24   AMP068

What is the purpose of the diffuser section in a turbine engine?

A– To increase pressure and reduce velocity

B– To convert pressure to velocity

C– To reduce pressure and increase velocity

3-24. Answer A. JSPT 3A, FPH

In a centrifugal-flow compressor, the diffuser is placed at the outlet of the compressor. The purpose of the diffuser is to reduce the velocity of the gases and to increase their pressure. This prepares the air for entry into the burner cans at low velocity so combustion can occur with a flame that will not blow out.

3-25   AMP068

In which type of turbine engine combustion chamber is the case and liner removed and installed as one unit during routine maintenance?

A– Can

B– Can annular

C– Annular

3-25. Answer A. JSPT 3A, FPH

Both the case and liner of can-type combustion chambers are self-contained and placed externally around the circumference of an engine. These features allow the individual chambers to be removed and installed as one unit during routine maintenance operations.

3-26   AMP068

The diffuser section of a jet engine is located between

A– the burner section and the turbine section.

B– station No.7 and station No.8.

C– the compressor section and the burner section.

3-26. Answer C. JSPT 3A, FPH

The diffuser section of a centrifugal-flow compressor is located between the outlet of the compressor section and the inlet of the burner section. The purpose of the diffuser is to reduce the velocity of the air exiting the compressor, thereby increasing air pressure. This prepares the air for entry into the burner cans.

3-27   AMP068

Reduced blade vibration and improved airflow characteristics in gas turbines are brought about by

A– fir-tree blade attachment.

B– impulse type blades.

C– shrouded turbine rotor blades.

3-27. Answer C. JSPT 3A, FPH

The use of shrouded turbine rotor blades reduces blade vibration and improves turbine efficiency. With shrouded blades the blade tips contact each other and provide additional support. This added support reduces vibration substantially. The shrouds also prevent air from escaping over the blade tips making the entire turbine more efficient. Although the type of blade used and the means of attaching a blade can affect a blade's vibration characteristics, neither has the degree of impact that using shrouded blades does.

3-28   AMP068

The highest heat-to-metal contact in a jet engine is the

A– burner cans.

B– turbine inlet guide vanes.

C– turbine blades.

3-28. Answer B. JSPT 3A, FPH

The highest heat-to-metal contact in a turbine engine occurs as the heated gases leave the combustion section and enter the turbine inlet vanes. Although the highest temperatures occur in the middle of the flame zone within the burner can, the high temperature is shielded from heat-to-metal contact by an insulating blanket of air.

3-29   AMP019

Which two elements make up the axial-flow compressor assembly?

A– Rotor and stator

B– Compressor and manifold

C– Stator and diffuser

3-29. Answer A. JSPT 3A, FPH

An axial-flow compressor assembly is made up of two principle elements, the rotor and the stator. The rotor consists of a set of blades installed on a spindle that rotates at a high speed and impels intake air through a series of stages. The stator blades, on the other hand, act as diffusers at each stage, changing high velocity to pressure.

3-30   AMP068

The two types of centrifugal compressor impellers are

A– single entry and double entry.

B– rotor and stator.

C– impeller and diffuser.

3-30. Answer A. JSPT 3A, FPH

The two types of centrifugal-flow compressor impellers are the single entry and the double entry. The single entry has vanes on only one side of the impeller, while the double entry has vanes on both sides of the impeller.

3-31   AMP068

Between each row of rotating blades in a turbine engine compressor, there is a row of stationary blades which act to diffuse the air. These stationary blades are called

A– buckets.

B– rotors.

C– stators.

3-31. Answer C. JSPT 3A, FPH

Between each row of rotating blades in an axial-flow compressor there is a set of stationary airfoils called stator vanes. The stator vanes direct the air between stages and diffuse, or slow down the air causing pressure to increase.

3-32   AMP019

In an axial-flow compressor, one purpose of the stator vanes at the discharge end of the compressor is to

A– straighten the airflow and eliminate turbulence.

B– increase the velocity and prevent swirling and eddying.

C– decrease the velocity, prevent swirling, and decrease pressure.

3-32. Answer A. JSPT 3A, FPH

At the discharge end of an axial-flow compressor, the air is extremely turbulent. To help eliminate this turbulence, as well as slow the air flow, stator vanes are installed. These vanes are sometimes called straightening vanes or the outlet vane assembly.

3-33   AMP019

A purpose of the shrouds on the turbine blades of an axial-flow engine is to

A– reduce vibration.

B– increase tip speed.

C– reduce air entrance.

3-33. Answer A. JSPT 3A, FPH

The use of shrouded turbine rotor blades reduces blade vibration and improves turbine efficiency. With shrouded blades, the tips of the blades contact each other and provide support. This added support reduces vibration substantially. The shrouds also prevent air from escaping over the blade tips making the turbine more efficient.

3-34   AMP019

In a dual axial-flow compressor, the first stage turbine drives

A– A–N2 compressor.

B– B–N1 compressor.

C– C–low pressure compressor.

3-34. Answer A. JSPT 3A, FPH

In a dual spool axial-flow compressor the first compressor (N1) is driven by the second turbine, while the second compressor (N2) is driven by the first turbine.

3-35   AMP068

A weak fuel to air mixture along with normal airflow through a turbine engine may result in

A– A–a rich flameout.

B– B–a lean die-out.

C– C–high EGT.

3-35. Answer B. JSPT 3A, FPH

If you operate a turbine engine with a weak or lean fuel to air mixture, you risk encountering what is known as a lean die-out. In other words, the amount of fuel supplied is insufficient to support combustion.

3-36   AMP068

What is used in turbine engines to aid in stabilization of compressor airflow during low thrust engine operation?

A– A–Stator vanes and rotor vanes

B– B–Variable guide vanes and/or compressor bleed valves

C– C–Pressurization and dump valves

3-36. Answer B. JSPT 3A, TEP2

Airflow through some turbine engines during low thrust operations must be stabilized to prevent the compressor from stalling. To do this, variable inlet guide vanes or compressor bleed valves are used. Variable guide vanes rotate to maintain the correct angle of attack relationship between inlet air flow and compressor speed. Compressor bleed valves, on the other hand, dump away unwanted air.

3-37   AMP068

In a turbine engine with a dual-spool compressor, the low speed compressor

A– A–always turns at the same speed as the high speed compressor.

B– B–is connected directly to the high speed compressor.

C– C–seeks its own best operating speed.

3-37. Answer C. JSPT 3A, FPH

Most modern gas turbine engines use a dual-spool compressor that utilizes two axial-flow rotors or one axial and one centrifugal-flow rotor. An advantage of the dual-spool compressor is the ability of the first compressor (N1) to seek its own best operating speed. Therefore, when the engine is operated at altitude where the air is less dense, the reduced drag on the first stage compressor allows the compressor to speed up thereby increasing efficiency.

3-38   AMP019

What is the function of the inlet guide vane assembly on an axial-flow compressor?

A– Directs the air into the first stage rotor blades at the proper angle

B– Converts velocity energy into pressure energy

C– Converts pressure energy into velocity energy

3-38. Answer A. JSPT 3A, FPH
The guide vanes direct the airflow into the first stage rotor blades at the proper angle.

3-39   AMP019

The stator vanes in an axial-flow compressor

A– convert velocity energy into pressure energy.

B– convert pressure energy into velocity energy.

C– direct air into the first stage rotor vanes at the proper angle.

3-39. Answer A. JSPT 3A, FPH
Each set of rotor blades within an axial-flow compressor has a corresponding set of stator vanes. The stator vanes direct the airflow to the next set of rotor blades at the proper angle and partially convert velocity energy to pressure energy.

3-40   AMP019

What is the primary advantage of an axial-flow compressor over a centrifugal compressor?

A– High frontal area

B– Less expensive

C– Greater pressure ratio

3-40. Answer C. JSPT 3A, FPH
Although an axial-flow compressor does not provide a high pressure rise per stage, it is capable of greater peak pressure ratios. The higher peak ratios are made possible by increasing the number of stages.

3-41   AMP068

What is meant by a double entry centrifugal compressor?

A– A compressor that has two intakes

B– A two-stage compressor independently connected to the main shaft

C– A compressor with vanes on both sides of the impeller

3-41. Answer C. JSPT 3A, FPH
A double entry centrifugal compressor is one that has vanes on both sides of the impeller.

3-42   AMP068

What is the major function of the turbine assembly in a turbojet engine?

A– Directs the gases in the proper direction to the tailpipe

B– Supplies the power to turn the compressor

C– Increases the temperature of the exhaust gases

3-42. Answer B. JSPT 3A, FPH

The purpose of the turbine section in a gas turbine engine is to extract energy from the gases coming off the combustor. The energy extracted drives the turbine which, in turn, drives the compressor and all accessories.

3-43   AMP019

Stator blades in the compressor section of an axial-flow turbine engine

A– increase the air velocity and prevent swirling.

B– straighten the airflow and accelerate it.

C– decrease the air velocity and prevent swirling.

3-43. Answer C. JSPT 3A, FPH

Each set of rotor blades within an axial-flow compressor has a corresponding set of stator vanes. The stator vanes help prevent swirling as they direct airflow to the next set of rotor blades and decrease air velocity by converting velocity energy to pressure energy.

3-44   AMP068

A gas turbine engine comprises which three main sections?

A– Compressor, diffuser, and stator

B– Turbine, combustion, and stator

C– Turbine, compressor, and combustion

3-44. Answer C. JSPT 3A, FPH

The three main sections of a gas turbine engine are the compressor, combustor, and turbine.

3-45   AMP068

What type of turbine blade is most commonly used in

aircraft jet engines?

A– Reaction.

B– Impulse.

C– Impulse-reaction.

3-45. Answer C. JSPT 3A

The most common type of turbine blade used in jet engines is the impulse-reaction type. This type of blade is constructed with an impulse section at its base and a reaction section at its tip. This design distributes the workload evenly along the blade's length.

3-46   AMP019

The non-rotating axial-flow compressor airfoils in an

aircraft gas turbine engine are called

A– pressurization vanes.

B– stator vanes.

C– bleed vanes.

3-46. Answer B. JSPT 3A, FPH

The two main elements of an axial-flow compressor are the rotor and stator. The rotor blades are attached to a rotating spindle while the stator vanes are fixed and act as diffusers at each stage.

3-47   AMP019

1. In a turbine engine axial-flow compressor, each consecutive pair of rotor and stator blades constitutes a pressure stage.

2. In a turbine engine axial-flow compressor, the number of rows of stages is determined by the amount of air and total pressure rise required.

Regarding the above statements,

A– only No.1 is true.

B– only No.2 is true.

C– both No.1 and No.2 are true.

3-47. Answer C. JSPT 3A, FPH

Both statements (1) and (2) are correct. Each consecutive pair of rotor and stator blades constitutes a single pressure stage that produces a given pressure rise. Therefore, the total amount of air and pressure rise required dictates the number of rows or stages needed in a particular engine.

3-48   AMP008

The air passing through the combustion chamber of a turbine engine is

A– used to support combustion and to cool the engine.

B– entirely combined with fuel and burned.

C– speeded up and heated by the action of the turbines.

3-48. Answer A. JSPT 3A, FPH

As air leaves the compressor and enters the combustion section it is divided into a primary and secondary path. The primary path consists of approximately 25 to 35 percent of the total airflow and is routed to the area around the fuel nozzle to support combustion. The secondary path consists of the remaining 65 to 75 percent of the total airflow and is used to form an air blanket on either side of the combustion liner that cools the engine and centers the flames so they do not contact any metal.

3-49   AMP068

The stators in the turbine section of a gas turbine engine

A– increase the velocity of the gas flow.

B– decrease the velocity of the gas flow.

C– increase the pressure of the gas flow.

3-49. Answer A. JSPT 3A, FPH

The fixed stator vanes in the turbine section of a gas turbine engine are located ahead of the turbine rotor. The turbine stators act as nozzles to increase gas velocity and decrease pressure.

3-50   AMP068

The compressor stators in a gas turbine engine act as diffusers to

A– decrease the velocity of the gas flow.

B– increase the velocity of the gas flow.

C– increase the velocity and decrease the pressure of the gas.

3-50. Answer A. JSPT 3A, FPH

A set of stator blades is placed immediately behind each set of rotor blades in an axial-flow compressor. The stators act as diffusers to decrease air velocity and increase pressure before the airflow is allowed to continue to the next stage or to the burners.

3-51   AMP068

The compression ratio of an axial-flow compressor is a function of the

A– number of compressor stages.

B– rotor diameter.

C– air inlet velocity.

3-51. Answer A. JSPT 3A, FPH

The primary factor in determining the pressure ratio in an axial-flow compressor is the number of stages within the compressor. Additional factors that affect pressure ratio include overall compressor efficiency and the pressure ratio produced by each stage.

3-52   AMP068

Why do some turbine engines have more than one turbine wheel attached to a single shaft?

A– To facilitate balancing of the turbine assembly

B– To help stabilize the pressure between the compressor and the turbine

C– To extract more power from the exhaust gases than a single wheel can absorb

3-52. Answer C. JSPT 3A, FPH

The number of turbine wheels used in a gas turbine engine is determined by the amount of energy that must be extracted to drive the compressor and all accessories. Both turbofan and turboprop engines require more turbine wheels than a turbojet, because more energy is required to drive the fan or prop.

3-53   AMP068

Which of the following types of combustion sections are used in aircraft turbine engines?

A– Annular, variable, and cascade vane

B– Can, multiple-can, and variable

C– Multiple-can, annular, and can-annular

3-53. Answer C. JSPT 3A, FPH

The three types of combustion chambers used in gas turbine engines are the multiple-can, annular, and can-annular. In modern day engines, the annular is the most popular.

3-54   AMP068

What is meant by a shrouded turbine?

A– The turbine blades are shaped so that their ends form a band or shroud.

B– The turbine wheel is enclosed by a protective shroud to contain the blades in case of failure.

C– The turbine wheel has a shroud or duct which provides cooling air to the turbine blades.

3-54. Answer A. JSPT 3A, FPH

The term shrouded turbine refers to a gas turbine engine that uses shrouded turbine blades. The use of shrouded turbine rotor blades reduces blade vibration and improves turbine efficiency. With shrouded blades the tips of the blades contact each other, thereby providing support. This added support reduces vibration substantially. The shrouds also prevent air from escaping over the blade tips making the turbine more efficient.

3-55   AMP068

At what stage in a turbine engine are gas pressures the greatest?

A– Compressor inlet

B– Turbine outlet

C– Compressor outlet

3-55. Answer C. JSPT 3A, FPH

The highest gas pressure in an axial-flow turbojet engine occurs at the exit of the diffuser section, which is between the compressor outlet and combustion (burner) section. Of the answer choices in this question, the compressor outlet has the highest gas pressure.

3-56   AMP071

In what section of a turbojet engine is the jet nozzle located?

A– Combustion

B– Turbine

C– Exhaust

3-56. Answer C. JSPT 3A, FPH

The jet nozzle of a gas turbine engine is attached to the rear of the tailpipe or rear flange of the exhaust duct and represents the last component the exhaust gases pass through. Therefore, the jet nozzle is part of the exhaust section.

3-57   AMP068

Compressor stall is caused by

A– a low angle of attack airflow through the first stages of compression.

B– a high angle of attack airflow through the first stages of compression.

C– rapid engine deceleration.

3-57. Answer B. JSPT 3A, TEP2

A compressor stall occurs when the inlet airflow strikes the compressor blades at an excessive angle of attack causing the blades to momentarily lose the ability to compress inlet air.

3-58   AMP033

1. Engine pressure ratio (EPR) is a ratio of the exhaust gas pressure to the engine inlet air pressure, and indicates the thrust produced.

2. Engine pressure ratio (EPR) is a ratio of the exhaust gas pressure to the engine inlet air pressure, and indicates volumetric efficiency.

Regarding the above statements,

A– only No.1 is true.

B– only No.2 is true.

C– both No.1 and No.2 are true.

3-58. Answer A. JSPT 3A, FPH

Only statement number (1) is correct. By definition, engine pressure ratio (EPR) is the ratio of the total turbine discharge pressure to the total compressor inlet pressure and indicates the thrust being produced. The EPR reading is displayed in the cockpit on the EPR gauge and is used by the pilot to set the power levers.

3-59   AMP033

Engine pressure ratio is determined by

A– multiplying engine inlet total pressure by turbine outlet total pressure.

B– dividing turbine outlet total pressure by engine inlet total pressure.

C– dividing engine inlet total pressure by turbine outlet total pressure.

3-59. Answer B. JSPT 3A, FPH

Engine pressure ratio (EPR) is the ratio of the total pressure leaving the turbine to the total pressure entering the engine and indicates the amount of thrust produced by an engine. EPR is calculated by dividing the total turbine outlet pressure by the total compressor inlet pressure.

3-60   AMP068

In a turbine engine, where is the turbine discharge pressure indicator sensor located?

A– At the aft end of the compressor section

B– At a location in the exhaust cone that is determined to be subjected to the highest pressures

C– Immediately aft of the last turbine stage

3-60. Answer C. JSPT 3A, FPH

In a gas turbine engine, the turbine discharge pressure sensor is located immediately aft of the last turbine stage. The readings taken from this sensor and the compressor inlet pressure sensor are used to determine the engine pressure ratio.

3-61   AMP068

The oil dampened main bearing utilized in some turbine engines is used to

A– provide lubrication of bearings from the beginning of starting rotation until normal oil pressure is established.

B– provide an oil film between the outer race and the bearing housing in order to reduce vibration tendencies in the rotor system, and to allow for slight misalignment.

C– dampen surges in oil pressure to the bearings.

3-61. Answer B. TEP2

The oil dampened main bearings used in some turbine engines contain oil dampening compartments that provide space for an oil film to build between the outer race and the bearing housing. This oil film reduces vibration tendencies in the rotor system and allows for slight misalignment.

3-62   AMP019

In an axial-flow turbine engine, compressor bleed air is sometimes used to aid in cooling the

A– fuel.

B– inlet guide vanes.

C– turbine, vanes, blades, and bearings.

3-62. Answer C. JSPT 3A, FPH

In some axial-flow turbine engines, compressor bleed air is used to aid in cooling the turbine section, including the turbine vanes, blades, and bearings.

3-63   AMP068

The purpose of directing bleed air to the outer turbine case on some engines is to

A– provide optimum turbine blade tip clearance by controlling thermal expansion.

B– provide up to 100 percent kinetic energy extraction from the flowing gases.

C– allow operation in a thermal environment 600 to 800°F above the temperature limits of turbine blade and vane alloys.

3-63. Answer A. JSPT 3A, TEP2

Active turbine blade tip clearance control is accomplished by varying the amount of bleed air that is let into the turbine case to control the thermal expansion of the outer turbine case. This, in turn, keeps efficiency losses at the blade tips to a minimum at all power settings.

3-64   AMP068

The vortex dissipators installed on some turbine-powered aircraft to prevent engine FOD utilize

A– variable inlet guide vanes (IGV) and/or variable first stage fan blades.

B– variable geometry inlet ducts.

C– a stream of engine bleed air blown toward the ground ahead of the engine.

3-64. Answer C. JSPT 3A, FPH

Vortex dissipators, sometimes called blow-away jets, destroy the low pressure vortex which forms between the ground and the engine inlet by blowing a stream of bleed air ahead of the engine during ground operations. By destroying this low pressure vortex, the engine is less likely to suck up and ingest foreign objects that can cause compressor blade damage.

3-65   AMP068

Vortex dissipator systems are generally activated by

A– a landing gear switch.

B– a fuel pressure switch anytime an engine is operating.

C– an engine inlet airflow sensor.

3-65. Answer A. JSPT 3A, FPH

Vortex dissipator systems, or blow-away jets, destroy the low pressure vortex which forms between the ground and the engine inlet by blowing a stream of bleed air ahead of the engine during ground operations. These systems are typically activated by a landing gear switch.

3-66   AMP068

The component(s) in a turbine engine that operate(s) at the highest temperatures is/ are the

A— first stage turbine nozzle guide vanes.

B— turbine disks.

C— exhaust cone.

3-66. Answer A. JSPT 3A

In a turbine engine, the fuel/air mixture is burned in the combustors, then flows into the first stage turbine nozzle guide vanes. Therefore, of the choices given, the guide vanes operate at the highest temperatures in a turbine engine.

3-67   AMP017

Frequently, an aircraft's auxiliary power unit (APU) generator

A— is identical to the engine-driven generators.

B— supplements the aircraft's engine-driven generators during peak loads.

C— has a higher load capacity than the engine- driven generators.

3-67. Answer A. JSPT 3A, JSTS 2-2

Depending on the aircraft, an auxiliary power unit drives one or two generators that are typically identical to the engine driven generators.

3-68   AMP017

Fuel is normally supplied to an APU from

A— its own independent fuel supply.

B— the airplane's reserve fuel supply.

C— the airplane's main fuel supply.

3-68. Answer C. JSPT 3A, JSTS 2-2

Fuel is normally supplied to the auxiliary power unit from one of the aircraft's main tanks.

3-69   AMP017

An APU is usually rotated during start by

A— a turbine impingement system.

B— a pneumatic starter.

C— an electric starter.

3-69. Answer C. JSPT 3A, JSTS 2-1

Due to the size and relatively low starting torque, virtually all gas turbine auxiliary power units use an electric starting motor. Neither turbine impingement systems nor pneumatic starters are commonly used to start auxiliary power units.

3-70   AMP017

The function of an APU air inlet plenum is to

A– increase the velocity of the air before entering the compressor.

B– decrease the pressure of the air before entering the compressor.

C– stabilize the pressure of the air before it enters the compressor.

3-70. Answer C. JSPT 3A, JSAD

A plenum is an enlargement in a duct or chamber in a turbine engine's induction system that helps eliminate pulsations and stabilize the pressure of the incoming air flow.

3-71   AMP017

When in operation, the speed of an APU

A– is controlled by a cockpit power lever.

B– remains at idle and automatically accelerates to rated speed when placed under load.

C– remains at or near rated speed regardless of the load condition.

3-71. Answer C. JSPT 3A, TEP2

After an auxiliary power unit is started it will accelerate to its rated speed and remain at that speed regardless of the load imposed. As pneumatic or electrical loads change, the APU fuel control automatically meters fuel to maintain the rated speed.

3-72   AMP017

Generally, when maximum APU shaft output power is being used in conjunction with pneumatic power

A– pneumatic loading will be automatically modulated to maintain a safe EGT.

B– electrical loading will be automatically modulated to maintain a safe EGT.

C– temperature limits and loads must be carefully monitored by the operator to maintain a safe EGT.

3-72. Answer A. JSPT 3A, JSTS

Pneumatic power requirements impose the greatest load on an operating auxiliary power unit. Therefore, when maximum shaft output is used in conjunction with pneumatic bleed air, the pneumatic loading will be automatically modulated to keep the APU's exhaust gas temperature within its limits.

3-73   AMP017

When necessary, APU engine cooling before shutdown may be accomplished by

A– unloading the generator(s).

B– closing the bleed air valve.

C– opening the bleed air valve.

3-73. Answer B. JSPT 3A

Providing bleed air for an aircraft's pneumatic system places the greatest load on an auxiliary power unit (APU). Therefore, if you close the bleed valve, most of the load on the APU will be removed and the APU will cool.

3-74   AMP017
Usually, most of the load placed on an APU occurs when

A– an electrical load is placed on the generator(s).

B– the bleed air valve is opened.

C– the bleed air valve is closed.

3-74. Answer B. JSPT 3A
Opening the pneumatic bleed valve places the greatest load on an auxiliary power unit and causes an almost immediate rise in the APU's exhaust gas temperature.

3-75   AMP017
Fuel scheduling during APU start and under varying pneumatic bleed and electrical loads is maintained

A– manually through power control lever position.

B– automatically by the APU fuel control system.

C– automatically by an aircraft main engine fuel control unit.

3-75. Answer B. JSPT 3A
Fuel scheduling for an auxiliary power unit is controlled automatically during start and under load by the APU fuel control system.

3-76   AMP061
If the RPM of an axial flow compressor remains constant, the angle of attack of the rotor blades can be changed by

A– changing the velocity of the airflow.

B– changing the compressor diameter.

C– increasing the pressure ratio.

3-76. Answer A. JSPT 3A, AFH
The angle of attack of the rotor blades is a result of inlet air velocity and the compressor's rotational velocity, or RPM. These two forces combine to form a vector, which defines the blades' angle of attack to the approaching inlet air. A compressor stall can occur if there is an imbalance between the inlet velocity and compressor rotational speed.

3-77   AMP017
On APU's equipped with a free turbine and load compressor, the primary function of the load compressor is to

A– provide air for combustion and cooling in the engine gas path.

B– provide bleed air for aircraft pneumatic systems.

C– supply the turning force for operation of the APU generator(s).

3-77. Answer B. JSPT 3A, JSTS
An auxiliary power unit consists of a gas turbine engine that drives an electrical generator to provide electrical power and a load compressor that provides bleed air for the aircraft's pneumatic systems.

SECTION B — OPERATING PRINCIPLES

Section B of Chapter 3 contains information related to turbine engine operating principles, including factors that affect thrust.

3-78   AMP068

Which statement is true regarding jet engines?

A— At the lower engine speeds, thrust increases rapidly with small increases in RPM.

B— At the higher engine speeds, thrust increases rapidly with small increases in RPM.

C— The thrust delivered per pound of air consumed is less at high altitude than at low altitude.

3-78. Answer B. JSPT 3B

In a typical turbine engine, a small increase in rpm produces a relatively proportional increase in thrust when operating at low engine speeds. However, at high engine speeds a small increase in RPM produces a large increase in thrust.

3-79   AMP068

The velocity of subsonic air as it flows through a convergent nozzle

A— increases.

B— decreases.

C— remains constant.

3-79. Answer A. JSPT 3B, FAH

According to Bernoulli's Principle, any time a fluid passes through a constriction at subsonic speeds pressure decreases while velocity increases. The diameter of a convergent nozzle decreases as the exhaust gases move aft. Therefore, as exhaust gases pass through a convergent nozzle the velocity of the gases increases while the pressure decreases.

3-80   AMP068

The pressure of subsonic air as it flows through a convergent nozzle

A— increases.

B— decreases.

C— remains constant.

3-80. Answer B. JSPT 3B, FAH

According to Bernoulli's Principle, any time a fluid passes through a constriction at subsonic speeds pressure decreases while velocity increases. The diameter of a convergent nozzle decreases, or constricts, as the exhaust gases move aft.Therefore, as exhaust gases pass through a convergent nozzle the velocity of the gases increases while the pressure decreases.

3-81   AMP068

The Brayton cycle is known as the constant

A– pressure cycle.

B– temperature cycle.

C– mass cycle.

3-81. Answer A. JSPT 3B, FPH

The Brayton cycle describes the combustion process in a turbine engine. This process is also known as the constant pressure cycle because the pressure across the combustion section in a turbine engine remains relatively constant.

3-82   AMP068

Which of the following variables affect the inlet air density of a turbine engine?

1. Speed of the aircraft

2. Compression ratio

3. Turbine inlet temperature

4. Altitude of the aircraft

5. Ambient temperature

6. Turbine and compressor efficiency

A– 1, 3, and 6

B– 1, 4, and 5

C– 4, 5, and 6

3-82. Answer B. JSPT 3B, FPH

The power produced by a turbine engine is directly proportional to the density of the air at the inlet. The factors which affect air density at the inlet are the speed of the aircraft, the altitude at which the aircraft is flying, and the ambient air temperature.

3-83   AMP068

Which of the following factors affect the thermal efficiency of a turbine engine?

1. Turbine inlet temperature

2. Compression ratio

3. Ambient temperature

4. Speed of the aircraft

5. Turbine and compressor efficiency

6. Altitude of the aircraft

A– 3, 4, and 6

B– 1, 2, and 5

C– 1, 2, and 6

3-83. Answer B. JSPT 3B, FPH

Thermal efficiency refers to the ratio of net work produced by a turbine engine to the chemical energy supplied in the form of fuel. The three most important factors affecting thermal efficiency are turbine inlet temperature, compression ratio, and the efficiency of the compressor and turbine.

TURBINE ENGINE OPERATION, MAINTENANCE, INSPECTION, AND OVERHAUL

SECTION A — OPERATION, INSTRUMENTS, AND MAINTENANCE

The first section of Chapter 4 covers information related to turbine engine operations and maintenance practices. Turbine engine instrument systems are also covered in this section.

4-1   AMP068

When starting a turbine engine, a hung start is indicated if the engine

A– exhaust gas temperature exceeds specified limits.

B– fails to reach idle RPM.

C– RPM exceeds specified operating speed.

4-1. Answer B. JSPT 4A, FGH

A hung start occurs if a turbine engine starts normally but the rpm remains at some low value rather than increasing to the normal idle RPM. Hung starts are generally a result of shutting off the starter too soon, or by insufficient starter power. In contrast, a hot start occurs if the exhaust gas temperature exceeds specified limits.

4-2   AMP068

When starting a turbine engine,

A– a hot start is indicated if the exhaust gas temperature exceeds specified limits.

B– an excessively lean mixture is likely to cause a hot start.

C– release the starter switch as soon as indication of light-off occurs.

4-2. Answer A. JSPT 4A, FGH

One of the critical factors to observe when starting a turbine engine is the exhaust gas temperature. A hot start is characterized by the exhaust gas temperature exceeding the specified limits during an attempted start and can cause substantial damage to the combustion and turbine sections.

4-3   AMP042

What must be done after the fuel control unit has been replaced on an aircraft gas turbine engine?

A– Perform a full power engine run to check fuel flow.

B– Recalibrate the fuel nozzles.

C– Retrim the engine.

4-3. Answer C. JSPT 4A, FPH

After a fuel control has been replaced on a turbine engine, it is often necessary to retrim the engine. Retrimming consists of adjusting both the idle and maximum speed. On some newer turbine engines, such as the GE T700, retrimming may not be necessary after the fuel control is replaced.

4-4   AMP068

What is the first engine instrument indication of a successful start of a turbine engine?

A– A rise in the engine fuel flow

B– A rise in oil pressure

C– A rise in the exhaust gas temperature

4-4. Answer C. JSPT 4A, FPH

The first indication in the cockpit that a successful start has occurred is an abrupt rise in temperature indicated on the exhaust gas temperature gauge. Although engine fuel flow and oil pressure will also rise, they will lag behind the exhaust gas temperature.

4-5   AMP069

Who establishes mandatory replacement times for critical components of turbine engines?

A– The FAA

B– The operator working in conjunction with the FAA.

C– The engine manufacturer

4-5. Answer C. JSPT 4A, 14 CFR Part 33, Appendix

Within a turbine engine, all critical components have mandatory replacement times that are established by the engine manufacturer and approved by the FAA.

4-6   AMP068

Which of the following is the ultimate limiting factor of turbine engine operation?

A– Compressor inlet air temperature

B– Turbine inlet temperature

C– Burner-can pressure

4-6. Answer B. JSPT 4A, FPH

The materials within the turbine section of an engine will deteriorate rapidly if exposed to extreme temperatures. Therefore, the turbine inlet temperature is the limiting factor for a turbine engine.

4-7   AMP068

Which of the following engine variables is the most critical during turbine engine operation?

A– Compressor inlet air temperature

B– Compressor RPM

C– Turbine inlet temperature

4-7. Answer C. JSPT 4A, FPH

The materials within the turbine section of an engine will deteriorate rapidly if exposed to extreme temperatures. Therefore, the turbine inlet temperature is the limiting factor for a turbine engine.

4-8   AMP069

Compressor field cleaning on turbine engines is performed primarily in order to

A— prevent engine oil contamination and subsequent engine bearing wear or damage.

B— facilitate flight line inspection of engine inlet and compressor areas for defects or FOD.

C— prevent engine performance degradation, increased fuel costs, and damage or corrosion to gas path surfaces.

4-8. Answer C. JSPT 4A, FPH

Accumulation of dirt on the compressor blades reduces the aerodynamic efficiency of the blades, with resultant deterioration in engine performance. Furthermore, dirt deposits can retain moisture and other chemicals that cause corrosion.

4-9   AMP068

What should be done initially if a turbine engine catches fire when starting?

A— Turn off the fuel and continue engine rotation with the starter.

B— Continue engine start rotation and discharge a fire extinguisher into the intake.

C— Continue starting attempt in order to blow out the fire.

4-9. Answer A. JSPT 4A, FPH

If a turbine engine catches fire during an attempted start, you should immediately turn off the fuel and continue to turn the engine with the starter. By continuing to rotate the engine, the fire is likely to be drawn into the engine and discharged out the tailpipe.

4-10   AMP068

What is the proper starting sequence for a turbojet engine?

A— Ignition, starter, fuel

B— Starter, ignition, fuel

C— Starter, fuel, ignition

4-10. Answer B. JSPT 4A, FPH

The first step in starting a typical turbine engine is to engage the starter. Once this is done, the ignition is turned on. Then, when the N1 compressor obtains a predetermined RPM, the fuel lever is moved to the idle position. Normal light off is indicated by a rise in the exhaust gas temperature (EGT).

4-11   AMP068

Generally, when starting a turbine engine, the starter should be disengaged

A— after the engine has reached self-accelerating speed.

B— only after the engine has reached full idle RPM.

C— when the ignition and fuel system are activated.

4-11. Answer A. JSPT 4A, FPH

When starting a turbine engine you should always follow the manufacturer's instructions. However, as a general guideline for a nonautomatic system, the starter is disengaged after the engine reaches its self-accelerating speed.

4-12   AMP069

The procedure for removing the accumulation of dirt deposits on compressor blades is called

A— the soak method.

B— field cleaning.

C— the purging process.

4-12. Answer B. JSPT 4A, TEP2

Compressor field cleaning is the process of removing an accumulation of contaminants from compressor blades. Dirty compressor blades reduce aerodynamic efficiency and engine performance. Two common methods used for removing dirt deposits are a fluid wash and an abrasive grit blast. The soak method and purging process do not refer to any known power plant cleaning process.

4-13   AMP068

Dirt particles in the air being introduced into the compressor of a turbine engine will form a coating on all but which of the following?

A— Turbine blades

B— Casings

C— Inlet guide vanes

4-13. Answer A. JSPT 4A, FPH

As air passes through a compressor, centrifugal force throws particles of dirt, oil, soot, and other foreign matter outward so that they build up on the casing, guide vanes, and compressor blades. However, because of the high temperatures present in the hot section, the turbine blades are not susceptible to this problem.

4-14   AMP069

If a turbine engine is unable to reach take-off EPR before its EGT limit is reached, this is an indication that the

A— fuel control must be replaced.

B— EGT controller is out of adjustment.

C— compressor may be contaminated or damaged.

4-14. Answer C. JSPT 4A, FPH

If the compressor blades of a turbine engine are dirty or damaged, the engine will run at a higher internal temperature. Whenever an engine's internal temperature increases, the corresponding exhaust gas temperature (EGT) also increases. Under these circumstances, an engine's EGT limits may be reached before its maximum or takeoff engine pressure ratio (EPR) is obtained.

4-15   AMP068
A cool-off period prior to shutdown of a turbine engine is accomplished in order to

A– allow the turbine wheel to cool before the case contracts around it.

B– prevent vapor lock in the fuel control and/or fuel lines.

C– prevent seizure of the engine bearings.

4-15. Answer A. JSPT 4A, FPH
Prior to shutting down some turbine engines, a cool-off period is required to allow the turbine wheel to cool and contract before the case contracts around it. Although the turbine case and turbine wheels operate at approximately the same temperature when the engine is running, the turbine wheels are relatively massive compared to the case and, therefore, cool and contract more slowly.

4-16   AMP068

1. Accumulation of contaminates in the compressor of a turbojet engine reduces aerodynamic efficiency of the blades.

2. Two common methods for removing dirt deposits from turbojet engine compressor blades are a fluid wash and an abrasive grit blast.

Regarding the above statements,

A– only No.1 is true.

B– only No.2 is true.

C– both No.1 and No.2 are true.

4-16. Answer C. JSPT 4A, FPH
Both statements (1) and (2) are correct. The accumulation of dirt, oil, and soot on compressor blades reduces the aerodynamic efficiency of the blades which, in turn, decreases engine performance. The two most common methods for removing dirt deposits are a fluid wash and an abrasive grit blast. The fluid cleaning procedure is accomplished by first spraying an emulsion type surface cleaner into the compressor as it is turning and then applying a rinse. Grit blasting, on the other hand, requires the injection of an abrasive grit into the engine operating at a selected power setting.

4-17   AMP068
Which of the following is used to monitor the mechanical integrity of the turbines, as well as to check engine operating conditions of a turbine engine?

A– Engine oil pressure

B– Exhaust gas temperature

C– Engine pressure ratio

4-17. Answer B. JSPT 4A, FPH
One of the most important indicators of how a turbine engine is performing as well as its mechanical integrity is exhaust gas temperature (EGT). If there is damage to the turbine section of an engine, it will show up as an increase in EGT.

4-18   AMP068

1. Generally, when a turbine engine indicates high EGT for a particular EPR (when there is no significant damage), it means that the engine is out of trim.

2. Some turbine-powered aircraft use RPM as the primary indicator of thrust produced, others use EPR as the primary indicator.

Regarding the above statements,

A– only No.1 is true.

B– only No.2 is true.

C– both No.1 and No.2 are true.

4-18. Answer C. JSPT 4A, FPH
Both statements (1) and (2) are correct. If a turbojet engine is undamaged and the turbine blades are clean a high exhaust gas temperature (EGT) for a given engine pressure ratio (EPR) identifies an out-of-trim condition. Furthermore, on turbine engines that utilize centrifugal flow compressors, compressor RPM is a direct indication of the thrust being produced. Therefore, on some turbine-powered aircraft, RPM is the primary indicator of the thrust produced.

4-19   AMP066
Jet engine thermocouples are usually constructed of

A– chromel-alumel.

B– iron-constantan.

C– alumel-constantan.

4-19. Answer A. JSPT 4A, FAH
The thermocouples used in turbine engines are usually constructed of Chromel® , a nickel/chromium alloy; and Alumel® , a nickel/aluminum alloy. These are dissimilar metals which produce a milliamp current flow when heated.

4-20   AMP068
What instrument on a gas turbine engine should be monitored to minimize the possibility of a "hot" start?

A– RPM indicator

B– Turbine inlet temperature

C– Torquemeter

4-20. Answer B. JSPT 4A, FPH
A "hot" start is a start in which the turbine temperature exceeds specific limits. To minimize the chance of a hot start the temperature at the turbine should always be monitored when starting a gas turbine engine. Depending on the aircraft, turbine temperature is monitored by watching the turbine inlet temperature, exhaust gas temperature, or interstage gas temperature.

4-21   AMP033
Engine pressure ratio is the total pressure ratio between the

A– aft end of the compressor and the aft end of the turbine.

B– front of the compressor and the rear of the turbine.

C– front of the engine inlet and the aft end of the compressor.

4-21. Answer B. JSPT 4A, FPH
By definition, engine pressure ratio is the ratio of the total pressure leaving the turbine to the total pressure entering the compressor.

4-22   AMP019
What is the primary purpose of the tachometer on an axial-compressor turbine engine?

A– Monitor engine RPM during cruise conditions.

B– It is the most accurate instrument for establishing thrust settings under all conditions.

C– Monitor engine RPM during starting and to indicate overspeed conditions.

4-22. Answer C. JSPT 4A, FPH
A tachometer on an axial-flow compressor turbine engine is used to monitor the engine during starting and during possible overspeed conditions. However, a tachometer on a centrifugal-flow compressor presents a direct indication of the amount of engine thrust being produced.

4-23   AMP033
The engine pressure ratio (EPR) indicator is a direct indication of

A– engine thrust being produced.

B– pressure ratio between the front and aft end of the compressor.

C– ratio of engine RPM to compressor pressure.

4-23. Answer A. JSPT 4A, FPH
The engine pressure ratio (EPR) indicator is, for the majority of turbine powered airplanes, the primary indicator of engine thrust. EPR represents the ratio of the total pressure aft of the turbines to the total pressure at the engine inlet.

4-24   AMP068

The exhaust gas temperature (EGT) indicator on a gas turbine engine provides a relative indication of the

A— exhaust temperature.

B— temperature of the exhaust gases as they pass the exhaust cone.

C— turbine inlet temperature.

4-24. Answer C. JSPT 4A, FPH

The exhaust gas temperature (EGT) indicator provides a relative indication of the turbine inlet temperature (TIT). Engineers who design an engine know how much heat energy the turbine section will absorb from the gases flowing through it. Therefore, TIT can be calculated as a function of EGT.

4-25   AMP068

What instrument indicates the thrust of a gas turbine engine?

A— Exhaust gas temperature indicator

B— Turbine inlet temperature indicator

C— Engine pressure ratio indicator

4-25. Answer C. JSPT 4A, FPH

The engine pressure ratio (EPR) indicator is, for the majority of turbine powered airplanes, the primary indicator of engine thrust. EPR represents the ratio of the total pressure aft of the turbines to the total pressure at the engine inlet. Answers (A) and (B) are wrong because temperature readings do not indicate thrust.

4-26   AMP009

In what units are turbine engine tachometers calibrated?

A— Percent of engine RPM

B— Actual engine RPM

C— Percent of engine pressure ratio

4-26. Answer A. JSPT 4A, FPH

Gas turbine engine tachometers are usually calibrated in percent RPM. This allows various types of engines to be operated on the same basis of comparison.

4-27   AMP068

What effect does high atmospheric humidity have on the operation of a jet engine?

A— Decreases engine pressure ratio

B— Decreases compressor and turbine RPM.

C— Has little or no effect.

4-27. Answer C. JSPT 4A, FPH

Of the air consumed by a turbine engine, only about 25 percent is used to support combustion. Because of this, high atmospheric humidity has very little effect on the thrust produced by a jet engine.

4-28   AMP069

The abbreviation P_{t7} used in turbine engine terminology means

A— the total inlet pressure.

B— pressure and temperature at station No. 7.

C— the total pressure at station No. 7.

4-28. Answer C. JSPT 4A, FPH

P_{t7} is the total pressure measured at station 7 in turbine discharge section of the engine. Pt_7 is the pressure part of the EPR equation.

SECTION B — ENGINE REMOVAL AND OVERHAUL

Section B of Chapter 4 includes information related to engine removal and overhaul operations for turbine engines, including overhaul terminology.

4-29   AMP069

The blending of blades and vanes in a turbine engine

A– is usually accomplished only at engine overhaul.

B– should be performed parallel to the length of the blade using smooth contours to minimize stress points.

C– may sometimes be accomplished with the engine installed, ordinarily using power tools.

4-29. Answer B. JSPT 4B, FPH

Minor damage to turbine engine blades and vanes can usually be repaired if the damage can be removed without exceeding the allowable limits established by the manufacturer. However, all repairs must be well blended so that the blade's surface is smooth. Blending is almost always done by hand using crocus cloth, fine files, and stones. Furthermore, whenever possible, blending is performed parallel to the length of the blade to minimize stress points. Cracks are normally not allowed, in any area.

4-30   AMP069

During inspection, turbine engine components exposed to high temperatures may only be marked with such materials as allowed by the manufacturer. These materials generally include

1. layout dye.

2. commercial felt tip marker.

3. wax or grease pencil.

4. chalk.

5. graphite lead pencil.

A– 1, 2, and 4.

B– 1, 3, and 4.

C– 2, 4, and 5.

4-30. Answer A. JSPT 4B, FPH

Certain materials may be used to mark combustion and turbine components during disassembly and assembly. For example, layout dye, chalk, and some commercial felt-tip markers are considered acceptable for use in marking parts that are directly exposed to an engine's gas path such as turbine blades and disks, turbine vanes, and combustion chamber liners.

4-31   AMP007

If, during inspection at engine overhaul, ball or roller bearings are found to have magnetism but otherwise have no defects, they

A– cannot be used again.

B– are in an acceptable service condition.

C– must be degaussed before use.

4-31. Answer C. JSPT 4B, FGH

If a bearing becomes magnetized, metal particles would be attracted to the bearing surfaces and cause premature wear. Therefore, if a bearing has magnetism present, it must be removed with a suitable degausser before the bearing can be reused.

4-32   AMP068

Who establishes the recommended operating time between overhauls (TBO) of a turbine engine used in general aviation?

A– The engine manufacturer.

B– The operator (utilizing manufacturer data and trend analysis) working in conjunction with the FAA.

C– The FAA.

4-32. Answer A. JSPT 4B, FPH

Engine manufacturers always establish an engine's recommended time between overhaul (TBO).

4-33   AMP069

1. Welding and straightening of turbine engine rotating airfoils does not require special equipment.

2. Welding and straightening of turbine engine rotating airfoils is commonly recommended by the manufacturer.

Regarding the above statements,

A– only No.1 is true.

B– only No.2 is true.

C– neither No.1 nor No.2 is true.

4-33. Answer C. JSPT 4B, FPH

Neither statement (1) nor (2) is correct. Welding and straightening of rotating airfoils typically requires very specialized equipment. Furthermore, only authorized overhaul facilities and manufacturer are typically authorized to weld or straighten a damaged rotating airfoil.

4-34   AMP069

Turbine engine components exposed to high temperatures generally may NOT be marked with

1. layout dye.

2. commercial felt tip marker.

3. wax or grease pencil.

4. chalk.

5. graphite lead pencil.

A– 1, 2, and 3.

B– 3 and 5.

C– 4 and 5.

4-34. Answer B. JSPT 4B, FPH

Only certain materials may be used to mark combustion and turbine components during assembly and disassembly. For example, layout dye, chalk, and some commercial felt tip markers are typically used to mark parts that are directly exposed to an engine's gas path such as turbine blades and disks, turbine vanes, and combustion chamber liners. However, the question asks what may NOT be used. Wax or grease pencils, when used on turbine engine components, can cause hot spots to occur, and graphite lead pencils can cause dissimilar metal corrosion.

4-35   AMP069

Where do stress rupture cracks usually appear on turbine blades?

A– Across the blade root, parallel to the fir tree.

B– Along the leading edge, parallel to the edge.

C– Across the leading or trailing edge at a right angle to the edge length.

4-35. Answer C. JSPT 4B, FPH

Stress rupture cracks on turbine blades usually appear as minute hairline cracks on or across the leading or trailing edge at a right angle to the edge length. Stress rupture cracks located on the first stage turbine indicate either an over-temperature condition or centrifugal loading.

4-36   AMP069

When the leading edge of a first-stage turbine blade is found to have stress rupture cracks, which of the following should be suspected?

A– Faulty cooling shield.

B– Over-temperature condition.

C– Overspeed condition.

4-36. Answer B. JSPT 4B, FPH

Stress rupture cracks on turbine blades usually appear as minute hairline cracks on or across the leading or trailing edge at a right angle to the edge length. Stress rupture cracks located on the first stage turbine indicate either an over-temperature condition or centrifugal loading.

4-37   AMP068

Turbine blades are generally more suscep-tible to operating damage than compressor blades because of

A– higher centrifugal loading.

B– exposure to high temperatures.

C– high pressure and high velocity gas flow.

4-37. Answer B. JSPT 4B, FPH

Turbine blades are usually inspected and cleaned in the same manner as compressor blades. However, because turbine blades are consistently exposed to extreme temperatures, they are more susceptible to damage.

4-38   AMP068

The recurrent ingestion of dust or other fine airborne particulates into a turbine engine can result in

A– foreign object damage to the compressor section.

B– the need for less frequent abrasive grit cleaning of the engine.

C– erosion damage to the compressor and turbine sections.

4-38. Answer C. JSPT 4B, FPH

The ingestion of dust and other fine particulates in a turbine engine causes erosion damage to compressor and turbine blades over a period of time.

4-39   AMP069

Jet engine turbine blades removed for de-tailed inspection must be reinstalled in

A– a specified slot 180° away.

B– a specified slot 90° away in the direction of rotation.

C– the same slot.

4-39. Answer C. JSPT 4B, FPH

In order to maintain the balance of the turbine assembly, when a turbine blade is removed for inspection, it must be reinstalled in the same slot.

4-40   AMP069

When aircraft turbine blades are subjected to excessive heat stress, what type of fail-ures would you expect?

A– Bending and torsion.

B– Torsion and tension.

C– Stress rupture.

4-40. Answer C. JSPT 4B, FPH

When turbine blades are subjected to excessive temperatures, stress rupture cracks are likely to develop. Stress rupture cracks usually appear as minute hairline cracks on or across the leading or trailing edge at a right angle to the edge length.

4-41   AMP069
Continued and/or excessive heat and centrifugal force on turbine engine rotor blades is likely to cause

A– profile.

B– creep.

C– galling.

4-41. Answer B. JSPT 4B, FPH
Creep, or growth, are terms used to describe the permanent elongation of rotating parts. Creep is most pronounced in turbine blades because they are continually subjected to extreme heat and centrifugal loads.

4-42   AMP069
What term is used to describe a permanent and cumulative deformation of the turbine blades of a turbojet engine?

A– Stretch.

B– Distortion.

C– Creep.

4-42. Answer C. JSPT 4B, FPH
Creep, or growth, are terms used to describe the permanent elongation and deformation of rotating parts. Creep is most pronounced in turbine blades because they continually must operate in extreme heat while being subjected to excessive centrifugal loads.

4-43   AMP069
Severe rubbing of turbine engine compressor blades will usually cause

A– bowing.

B– cracking.

C– galling.

4-43. Answer C. JSPT 4B, FPH
Galling is a transfer of metal from one surface to another usually caused by severe rubbing.

4-44   AMP069
Which of the following conditions is usually not acceptable to any extent in turbine blades?

A– Cracks.

B– Pits.

C– Dents.

4-44. Answer A. JSPT 4B, FPH
Any crack or sharp bend that may result in cracking is cause for rejection of a turbine blade.

4-45   AMP069

1. Serviceability limits for turbine blades are much more stringent than are those for turbine nozzle vanes.

2. A limited number of small nicks and dents can usually be permitted in any area of a turbine blade.

Regarding the above statements,

A– both No.1 and No. 2 are true.

B– neither No.1 nor No. 2 is true.

C– only No. 1 is true.

4-45. Answer C. JSPT 4B, FPH
Only statement number (1) is correct. Because the centrifugal stresses and gas temperatures imposed on turbine blades is greater than those imposed on turbine nozzle vanes, serviceability limits are more stringent for turbine blades than for nozzle vanes. Furthermore, any nicks or dents found in the root area of a turbine blade is cause for immediate replacement.

4-46   AMP048
What publication contains the mandatory replacement time for parts of a turbine engine?

A– Engine Manufacturer's service instructions.

B– Engine Manufacturer's maintenance manual.

C– Federal Aviation Regulation Part 43.

4-46. Answer A. JSPT 4B
Manufacturer's service instructions contain instructions for continued airworthiness information such as mandatory replacement times, inspection intervals and related procedures. You normally cannot find this information in the maintenance manual.

INDUCTION SYSTEMS

SECTION A — RECIPROCATING ENGINES

Section A of Chapter 5 contains information related to induction system theory, operation, and maintenance on reciprocating engines.

5-1   AMP056
When will small induction system air leaks have the most noticeable effect on engine operation?

A– At high RPM

B– At maximum continuous and takeoff power settings

C– At low RPM

5-1. Answer C. JSPT 5A, FPH
A small induction system air leak will have the most noticeable effect on engine operation at idle. The reason for this is that at low engine speeds the volume of air entering the induction system is small. Therefore, the additional air coming in through a crack will lean the fuel/air mixture appreciably.

5-2   AMP070
To what altitude will a turbo charged engine maintain sea level pressure?

A– Critical altitude

B– Service ceiling

C– Pressure altitude

5-2. Answer A. JSPT 5A, FPH
A reciprocating engine's critical altitude is that altitude at which the engine can maintain sea level power. Any increase above an engine's critical altitude results in a decrease in available horsepower. The critical altitude of a typical turbocharged engine is generally between 8,000 and 16,000 feet MSL. An aircraft's service ceiling represents the altitude at which an aircraft is able to maintain a maximum climb rate of 100 feet per minute. Pressure altitude represents the altitude read off the altimeter with 29.92 set in the barometric window.

5-3   AMP008
An indication of unregulated power changes that result in continual drift of manifold pressure indication on a turbosuper-charged aircraft engine is known as

A– Overshoot.

B– Waste gate fluctuation.

C– Bootstrapping.

5-3. Answer C. JSPT 5A, FPH
Bootstrapping occurs when a turbocharger system senses small changes in temperature or RPM and continually changes the turbocharger output in an attempt to establish an equilibrium. Bootstrapping typically occurs during part-throttle operation and is characterized by a continual drift of manifold pressure.

5-4   AMP003

During engine operation, if carburetor heat is applied, it will

A– increase air-to-fuel ratio.

B– increase engine RPM.

C– decrease the air density to the carburetor.

5-4. Answer C. JSPT 5A, FPH

When carburetor heat is applied, warm air is directed into the carburetor intake. Warm air is less dense than cool air and, therefore, the application of carburetor heat results in a richer fuel/air mixture.

5-5   AMP003

Carburetor icing is most severe at

A– air temperatures between 30 and 40°F.

B– high altitudes.

C– low engine temperatures.

5-5. Answer A. JSPT 5A, FGH

Normally aspirated engines using float-type carburetors are most susceptible to icing when operated in temperatures between 30 and 40 degrees Fahrenheit. The reason for this is that any time the air being brought into the carburetor is near freezing, the additional temperature drop created by the carburetor venturi can readily cause water vapor to condense and freeze. However, it is important to note that carburetor icing can occur when the outside temperature is as high as 70 degrees Fahrenheit.

5-6   AMP003

Into what part of a reciprocating engine induction system is deicing alcohol normally injected?

A– The supercharger or impeller section

B– The airstream ahead of the carburetor

C– The low-pressure area ahead of the throttle valve

5-6. Answer B. JSPT 5A, FPH

In addition to a carburetor heat system, some large reciprocating engines utilize an alcohol deicing system. This system allows the pilot to spray alcohol into the inlet of the carburetor to remove ice and assist the warm air in keeping the carburetor free of ice.

5-7   AMP003
Carburetor icing on an engine equipped with a constant-speed propeller can be detected by

A— a decrease in power output with no change in manifold pressure or RPM.

B— an increase in manifold pressure with a constant RPM.

C— a decrease in manifold pressure with a constant RPM.

5-7. Answer C. JSPT 5A, FPH
On engines equipped with constant speed propellers, the engine's power output is indicated on the manifold pressure gauge. Therefore, induction system icing is readily detected by a reduction in manifold pressure and no change in RPM.

5-8   AMP003
What part of an aircraft in flight will begin to accumulate ice before any other?

A— Wing leading edge

B— Propeller spinner or dome

C— Carburetor

5-8. Answer C. JSPT 5A, FPH
When the air temperature is above freezing and there is no visible moisture, a carburetor will be the first part of an aircraft to accumulate ice. The reason for this is that as fuel vaporizes and the air pressure drops in the venturi, the air temperature typically drops enough to cause water vapor to condense and freeze.

5-9   AMP003
Carburetor icing may be eliminated by which of the following methods?

A— Alcohol spray and electrically heated induction duct

B— Ethylene glycol spray and heated induction air

C— Alcohol spray and heated induction air

5-9. Answer C. JSPT 5A, FPH
Heating the air in the inlet duct and spraying alcohol in the carburetor inlet are the two primary methods of eliminating carburetor ice.

5-10   AMP003
Where would a carburetor air heater be located in a fuel injection system?

A— At the air intake entrance

B— None is required

C— Between the air intake and the venturi

5-10. Answer B. JSPT 5A, FPH
Because fuel injection systems inject fuel directly into an engine's intake manifold, there is no need for a carburetor. Therefore, no carburetor air heater is required.

5-11   AMP003

An increase in manifold pressure when carburetor heat is applied indicates

A– ice was forming in the carburetor.

B– mixture was too lean.

C– overheating of cylinder heads.

5-11. Answer A. JSPT 5A, FPH

On engines equipped with constant speed propellers, engine power output is indicated on the manifold pressure gauge. Therefore, the onset of induction system icing is indicated by a reduction in manifold pressure. Another indication of the presence of carburetor ice is when manifold pressure increases after carburetor heat is applied.

5-12   AMP056

During full power output of an unsupercharged engine equipped with a float-type carburetor, in which of the following areas will the highest pressure exist?

A– Venturi

B– Intake manifold

C– Carburetor air scoop

5-12. Answer C. JSPT 5A, FPH

In the induction system of an unsupercharged engine, the air pressure from the venturi to the intake valve is always less than atmospheric pressure when the engine is running. Therefore, of the options given, the highest pressure exists in the carburetor air scoop where ram air enters the induction system.

5-13   AMP003

The use of the carburetor air heater when it is not needed causes

A– a very lean mixture.

B– excessive increase in manifold pressure.

C– a decrease in power and possibly detonation.

5-13. Answer C. JSPT 5A, FPH

When carburetor heat is used, warm air is routed into the carburetor. Since warm air is not as dense as cool air, the application of carburetor heat when it is not needed results in a slight decrease in power and an increase in cylinder head temperature which could lead to detonation.

5-14   AMP056

As manifold pressure increases in a reciprocating engine, the

A– volume of air in the cylinder increases.

B– weight of the fuel/air charge decreases.

C– density of air in the cylinder increases.

5-14. Answer C. JSPT 5A, FPH

The pressure of a gas and its density are directly proportional to each other. In other words, as the pressure of a gas increases, its density also increases. Therefore, as an engine's manifold pressure increases, the density of the fuel/air charge going to the cylinders increases proportionally.

5-15   AMP056

Which of the following statements regarding volumetric efficiency of an engine is true?

A— The volumetric efficiency of an engine will remain the same regardless of the amount of throttle opening.

B— It is impossible to exceed 100 percent volumetric efficiency of any engine regardless of the type of supercharger used.

C— It is possible to exceed 100 percent volumetric efficiency of some engines by the use of superchargers of the proper type.

5-15. Answer C. JSPT 5A, FPH

The volumetric efficiency of an engine is the ratio of the volume of fuel/air charge drawn into the cylinders to the engine's total piston displacement. If an engine draws in a fuel/air charge that equals the piston's displacement, volumetric efficiency is 100 percent. All unsupercharged engines have volumetric efficiencies less than 100 percent. However, by using a supercharger, it is possible to force a fuel/air charge with a greater volume than that of the cylinder displacement into a cylinder and achieve a volumetric efficiency greater than 100 percent.

5-16   AMP070

Bootstrapping of a turbocharged engine is indicated by

A— a overboost condition of the engine on takeoff.

B— a transient increase in engine power.

C— a maximum increase in manifold pressure.

5-16. Answer B. JSPT 5A, FPH

Bootstrapping occurs when a turbocharger system senses small changes in temperature or RPM and continually changes the turbocharger output in an attempt to establish an equilibrium. Bootstrapping typically occurs during part-throttle operation and is characterized by a continual drift or transient increase in manifold pressure.

5-17   AMP021

Which of the following would be a factor in the failure of an engine to develop full power at takeoff?

A— Improper adjustment of carburetor heat valve control linkage

B— Excessively rich setting on the idle mixture adjustment

C— Failure of the economizer valve to remain closed at takeoff throttle setting

5-17. Answer A. JSPT 5A, FPH

When carburetor heat is used, warm, less dense air is let into the engine and a drop in engine power output results. In addition, the warmer intake air causes cylinder head temperatures to increase, which can lead to detonation, especially during high-power operations. Therefore, if the carburetor heat valve is improperly adjusted and warm air is allowed to enter the engine during takeoff, less than full power will be developed.

5-18   AMP070

If the turbocharger waste gate is completely closed,

A– none of the exhaust gases are directed through the turbine.

B– the turbocharger is in the OFF position.

C– all the exhaust gases are directed through the turbine.

5-18. Answer C. JSPT 5A, FPH

The waste gate in a turbocharging system controls the amount of exhaust gas that is routed to the turbocharger, which ultimately dictates the amount of air that is forced into the engine. When the waste gate is closed, all the exhaust gas is routed to the turbocharger. However, if the waste gate is completely open, no exhaust gases flow to the turbocharger.

5-19   AMP070

Boost manifold pressure is generally considered to be any manifold pressure above

A– 14.7 in. Hg.

B– 50 in. Hg.

C– 30 in. Hg.

5-19. Answer C. JSPT 5A

A boosted manifold pressure is any pressure that is higher than atmospheric pressure or 29.92 inches of mercury. For practical purposes, this is rounded to 30 inches of mercury.

5-20   AMP070

What is the purpose of the density controller in a turbocharger system?

A– Limits the maximum manifold pressure that can be produced at other than full throttle conditions.

B– Limits the maximum manifold pressure that can be produced by the turbocharger at full throttle.

C– Maintains constant air velocity at the carburetor inlet.

5-20. Answer B. JSPT 5A, FPH

A density controller contains a nitrogen-filled bellows that responds to changes in pressure and temperature to control the position of the waste gate and prevent an overboost condition. Therefore, the density controller in a turbocharger system limits the manifold pressure produced by the turbocharger at full throttle.

5-21   AMP070

What directly regulates the speed of a turbocharger?

A– Turbine

B– Waste gate

C– Throttle

5-21. Answer B. JSPT 5A, FPH

The speed of a turbocharger is most directly affected by the amount of exhaust gas entering the turbocharger. The component that controls the amount of exhaust gas that is allowed to flow through the turbine is the waste gate.

5-22   AMP056

What is the purpose of a turbocharger system for a small reciprocating aircraft engine?

A– Compresses the air to hold the cabin pressure constant after the aircraft has reached its critical altitude.

B– Maintains constant air velocity in the intake manifold.

C– Compresses air to maintain manifold pressure constant from sea level to the critical altitude of the engine.

5-22. Answer C. JSPT 5A, FPH

As an aircraft gains altitude, the decrease in air density causes a decrease in engine power output. One way to help maintain sea level pressure within an engine is to use a turbocharger to compress the air before it enters the engine, thereby maintaining sea level air density and manifold pressure up to the turbocharger's critical altitude.

5-23   AMP070

What are the three basic regulating components of a sea-level boosted turbocharger system?

1. Exhaust bypass assembly

2. Compressor assembly

3. Pump and bearing casing

4. Density controller

5. Differential pressure controller

A– 2, 3, and 4

B– 1, 4, and 5

C– 1, 2, and 3

5-23. Answer B. JSPT 5A, FPH

A typical sea-level boosted turbocharger system is automatically regulated by an exhaust bypass valve assembly, a density controller, and a differential pressure controller.

5-24   AMP070

The differential pressure controller in a turbocharger system

A– reduces bootstrapping during part-throttle operation.

B– positions the waste gate valve for maximum power.

C– provides a constant fuel-to-air ratio.

5-24. Answer A. JSPT 5A, FPH

A differential pressure controller senses air pressure upstream and downstream of the throttle valve and repositions the waste gate to smooth out pressure fluctuations, or bootstrapping.

5-25   AMP070
The purpose of a sonic venturi on a turbo-charged engine is to

A– limit the amount of air that can flow from the turbocharger into the cabin for pressurization.

B– increase the amount of air that can flow from the turbocharger into the cabin for pressurization.

C– increase the velocity of the fuel/air charge.

5-25. Answer A. JSPT 5A
In some aircraft, air for cabin pressurization is provided by the turbocharger. However, before it reaches the pressurization system it must first pass through a sonic venturi, which acts as a flow limiter. A sonic venturi accelerates air to the speed of sound, thereby creating a shock wave that limits the amount of airflow into the cabin. Since a sonic venturi limits airflow, it cannot increase the amount of air flowing from the turbocharger into the cabin.

5-26   AMP056
What is used to drive a supercharger?

A– Exhaust gasses

B– Gear train from the crankshaft

C– Belt drive through a pulley arrangement

5-26. Answer B. JSPT 5A, FPH
A supercharger is driven by the crankshaft through a gear train.

5-27   AMP003
If carburetor or induction system icing is not present when carburetor heat is applied with no change in the throttle setting, the

A– mixture will become richer.

B– manifold pressure will increase.

C– engine RPM will increase.

5-27. Answer A. JSPT 5A
When carburetor heat is turned on, warm, less dense air is drawn into the carburetor. Therefore, if the mixture is not adjusted, the same amount of fuel continues to mix with the air. The combination of less dense air with no change in the amount of fuel supplied produces a mixture that is richer than it was before carburetor heat was applied.

5-28   AMP003
When starting an engine equipped with a carburetor air heater, in what position should the heater be placed?

A– Hot

B– Cold

C– Neutral

5-28. Answer B. JSPT 5A, FPH
A carburetor air heater should be placed in the cold position when starting an engine. If placed in the hot position, damage to the carburetor heat air box could result if the engine backfires. Furthermore, since carburetor heat air is typically not filtered, starting an engine with the carburetor heat knob in the hot position increases the chance of ingesting dirt into the engine.

5-29   AMP003

The application of carburetor heat during engine operation will

A– decrease the weight of the fuel/air charge.

B– decrease the volume of air in the cylinder.

C– increase the density of air in the cylinder.

5-29. Answer A. JSPT 5A, FPH

When carburetor heat is turned on, warm, less dense air is drawn into the engine. Since air density is directly proportional to the weight of a given volume of air, less dense air decreases the weight of the fuel/air charge.

5-30   AMP003

The application of carburetor heat will have which of the following effects?

A– The manifold pressure will be increased.

B– The mixture will become leaner.

C– The mixture will become richer.

5-30. Answer C. JSPT 5A

When carburetor heat is turned on, warm, less dense air is drawn into the carburetor. Therefore, if the mixture is not adjusted, the same amount of fuel continues to mix with the air. The combination of less dense air with no change in the amount of fuel supplied produces a mixture that is richer than it was before carburetor heat was applied.

5-31   AMP056

In addition to causing accelerated wear, dust or sand ingested by a reciprocating engine may also cause

A– silicon fouling of spark plugs.

B– sludge formation.

C– acid formation.

5-31. Answer A. JSPT 5A

Silicon glazing occurs when sand or dust enters an engine's induction system and proceeds to the cylinders where the sand forms a glaze on the nose of spark plugs.

5-32   AMP056

In an airplane equipped with an alternate air system, if the main air duct air filter becomes blocked or clogged, the

A– system will automatically allow warm, unfiltered air to be drawn into the engine.

B– flow of air into the engine will be slowed or cut off unless alternate air is selected.

C– system will automatically allow warm, filtered alternate air to be drawn into the engine.

5-32. Answer A. JSPT 5A, FPH

There are two possible answers to this question. An alternate air system is commonly installed on engines that are equipped with a fuel injection system. As the air filter becomes blocked, warm, unfiltered air is drawn into the induction system through an alternate air door. In most modern aircraft this door is spring-loaded closed and automatically opens when sufficient engine vacuum is created due to the air filter blockage. However, some aircraft manufacturers provide a control inside the cockpit that must be manually positioned to open the alternate air door. If the door is not opened, the flow of air to the engine will be slowed or cut off.

5-33   AMP056

On small aircraft engines, fuel vaporization may be increased by

A– cooling the air before it enters the engine.

B– circulating the fuel and air mixture through passages in the oil sump.

C– heating the fuel before it enters the carburetor.

5-33. Answer B. JSPT 5A

Many horizontally opposed engines have their carburetors mounted on the oil sump so the induction pipes pass through the sump and allow the fuel/air mixture to be heated to aid fuel vaporization.

5-34   AMP056

The action of a carburetor air scoop is to supply air to the carburetor, but it may also

A– cool the engine.

B– keep fuel lines cool and prevent vapor lock.

C– increase the pressure of the incoming air by ram effect.

5-34. Answer C. JSPT 5A, FPH

In addition to supplying air to the carburetor, a typical air scoop is positioned to increase intake air pressure by utilizing the ram effect supplied by the slipstream.

5-35   AMP056

A carburetor air pre-heater is not generally used on takeoff unless absolutely necessary because of the

A— loss of power and possible detonation.

B— possibility of induction system overboost.

C— inability of the engine to supply enough heat to make a significant difference.

5-35. Answer A. JSPT 5A, FPH

The use of carburetor heat results in less dense air entering the engine. This less dense air causes a decrease in engine power and leads to increased cylinder head temperatures that can cause detonation. Therefore, carburetor heat should only be used on takeoff when absolutely necessary.

5-36   AMP070

The purpose of an intercooler when used with a turbocharger is to cool the

A— exhaust gases before they come in contact with the turbo drive.

B— turbocharger bearings.

C— air entering the carburetor from the turbocharger.

5-36. Answer C. JSPT 5A, FPH

When air is compressed, its temperature rises. Therefore, some turbocharger systems utilize an intercooler that cools the compressed air before it enters the carburetor.

5-37   AMP056

One source commonly used for carburetor air heat is

A— turbocharger heated air.

B— alternate air heat.

C— exhaust gases.

5-37. Answer C. JSPT 5A, FPH

Most light aircraft have a carburetor heat system that draws air from within the cowling and routes it through a shroud that surrounds the exhaust pipe. With this type of system, the hot exhaust gases provide a source of heat that adequately heats the intake air to prevent or remove carburetor ice.

SECTION B — TURBINE ENGINES

Section B of Chapter 5 contains information related to induction system theory, operation, and maintenance on turbine engines.

5-38   AMP068

The velocity of supersonic air as it flows through a divergent nozzle

A– increases.

B– decreases.

C– is inversely proportional to the temperature.

5-38. Answer A. JSPT 5B, FAH

A supersonic flow of air differs from a subsonic flow in that as a supersonic flow passes through an expanding tube its speed increases while pressure decreases. The diameter of a divergent nozzle increases, or expands, as exhaust gases move aft. Therefore, as supersonic gases pass through a divergent nozzle, gas velocity increases and pressure decreases.

5-39   AMP068

The pressure of supersonic air as it flows through a divergent nozzle

A– increases.

B– decreases.

C– is inversely proportional to the temperature.

5-39. Answer B. JSPT 5B, FAH

A supersonic flow of air differs from a subsonic flow in that as a supersonic flow passes through an expanding tube its speed increases while pressure decreases. The diameter of a divergent nozzle increases, or expands, as exhaust gases move aft. Therefore, as supersonic gases pass through a divergent nozzle, gas velocity increases and pressure decreases.

5-40   AMP016

Anti-icing of jet engine air inlets is commonly accomplished by

A– electrical heating elements inside the inlet guide vanes.

B– engine bleed air ducted through the critical areas.

C– electrical heating elements located within the engine air inlet cowling.

5-40. Answer B. JSPT 5B, FPH

Anti-icing of turbine engine inlets is typically accomplished by routing warm engine bleed air through the inside of the inlets. In fact, engine bleed air is used to accomplish a variety of things including: cabin pressurization and heating, deicing and antiicing, pneumatic starting, and powering auxiliary drive units, control-booster servo systems, and instruments. The exact location where the bleed air is taken from the engine depends on the pressure and temperature required for a particular job.

5-41   AMP016

On an aircraft turbine engine, operating at a constant power, the application of engine anti-icing will result in

A– noticeable shift in EPR.

B– a false EPR reading.

C– an increase in EPR.

5-41. Answer A. JSPT 5B, TEP2

Inlet anti-ice systems use compressor bleed air to prevent ice formation on inlet ducts. When air is bled off the compressor, less pressure is available at all stations downstream, and EPR drops. Therefore, the application of engine anti-ice will cause a noticeable shift in the EPR indication in the cockpit.

5-42   AMP013

The purpose of a bellmouth compressor inlet is to

A— provide an increased ram air effect at low airspeeds.

B— maximize the aerodynamic efficiency of the inlet.

C— provide an increased pressure drop in the inlet.

5-42. Answer B. JSPT 5B, FPH

A bellmouth inlet has smooth, rounded surfaces that create very little resistance to air flow. Because of this, bellmouth inlets are extremely efficient.

5-43   AMP050

What method(s) is/are used to provide clean air to the engines of helicopters and turboprop airplanes that have particle (sand and ice) separators installed?

A— Positive and negative charged areas to attract and/or repel particulates out of the airflow

B— Air/moisture separators, and "washing" the air clean utilizing water droplets

C— Sharp airflow directional change to take advantage of inertia and/or centrifugal force, and filters or engine inlet screens

5-43. Answer C. JSPT 5B, TEP2

Some aircraft utilize a variety of screens, inertia separators, or particle separators to remove foreign objects such as sand. One type of particle separator relies on sharp directional changes in airflow to keep foreign particles from entering the engine. The exact type of filter used depends on the airflow of the engine and the type of installation.

5-44   AMP068

When an engine with a subsonic divergent type inlet duct is running in place at high speed on the ground, the air pressure within the inlet is

A— positive.

B— negative.

C— ambient.

5-44. Answer B. JSPT 5B, TEP2

When a gas turbine engine with a divergent type inlet is operated in place on the ground, negative, or low pressure develops within its inlet because the engine inlet acts like a venturi and as the airflow accelerates through a venturi, air pressure decreases.

5-45   AMP068

What indications may shift when a turbo-fan engine anti-icing (bleed air) system is turned on?

1. Tachometer.

2. EGT.

3. EPR.

A– 1 and 2

B– 1, 2, and 3

C– 2 and 3

5-45. Answer B. JSPT 5B, TEP2

When an anti-ice system utilizing engine bleed air is turned on, an indicator light will illuminate in the cockpit and the EGT will rise slightly. Furthermore, both the engine pressure ratio (EPR) and compressor RPM will shift due to the momentary change in compression delivered to the combustor.

5-46   AMP016

The purpose of an engine/inlet anti-ice system is primarily to

A– remove ice from engine and/or inlet areas.

B– prevent ice formation in engine and/or inlet areas.

C– remove ice from engine and/or inlet areas and prevent ice formation in engine and/or inlet areas.

5-46. Answer B. JSPT 5B, TEP2

Anti-ice systems are used to prevent ice from forming, while de-ice systems remove ice that has already formed. Therefore, an engine/inlet anti-ice system is used to prevent ice formation in the engine and inlet areas. Using a turbine engine antiice system to de-ice the inlet could result in ice ingestion and compressor damage.

CHAPTER 6

EXHAUST SYSTEMS

SECTION A — RECIPROCATING ENGINES

Section A of Chapter 6 contains information related to exhaust system theory, operation, and maintenance on reciprocating engines.

6-1   AMP057

On a reciprocating engine aircraft using a shrouded exhaust muffler system as a source for cabin heat, the exhaust system should be

A– visually inspected for any indication of cracks or an operational carbon monoxide detection test should be done.

B– replaced at each reciprocating engine overhaul by a new or overhauled exhaust system or a hydrostatic test should be accomplished.

C– removed and the exhaust muffler checked for cracks by using magnetic particle inspection method or a hydrostatic test should be done on the exhaust muffler.

6-1. Answer A. JSPT 6A, FPH

Many piston engine powered aircraft use the engine exhaust as a source of cabin heat. This is done by installing a jacket, or shroud, around the exhaust system. With this type of system, air passes between the exhaust and the shroud and is heated by the exhaust manifold. When this type of system is used, it must be inspected on a regular basis to ensure that no leaks exist in the exhaust system. Furthermore, a carbon monoxide detection test should be performed periodically to verify that no exhaust fumes are entering the cabin area.

6-2   AMP056

Why is high nickel chromium steel used in many exhaust systems?

A– High heat conductivity and flexibility

B– Corrosion resistance and low expansion coefficient

C– Corrosion resistance and high heat conductivity

6-2. Answer B. JSPT 6A

Exhaust system parts are subjected to corrosive exhaust gases and large changes in temperature. Therefore, the metals used in these areas must be able to resist corroding and have a low expansion coefficient. One metal that possesses these properties is nickel chromium steel (stainless steel).

6-3   AMP056

Reciprocating engine exhaust system designs commonly used to provide for ease of installation and/or allow for expansion and contraction, may include the use of

1. spring loaded ball/flexible joints.

2. slip joints.

3. bellows.

4. flexible metal tubing.

A– 1, 2, 3, and/or 4.

B– 1, 2, and/or 4.

C– 1, 2, and/or 3.

6-3. Answer C. JSPT 6A

Spring loaded ball/flexible joints and slip joints are commonly used to correct slight misalignments, allow movement and expansion, and simplify installation. Bellows, on the other hand, allow the exhaust components to expand and contract without causing buckling.

6-4   AMP056

What is the purpose of a slip joint in an exhaust collector ring?

A– It aids in alignment and absorbs expansion.

B– It reduces vibration and increases cooling.

C– It permits the collector ring to be installed in one piece.

6-4. Answer A. JSPT 6A, FPH

As an exhaust system heats up, the various system components expand. One way to allow for this expansion so adjacent components do not start buckling against each other is to use slip joints to join different components.

6-5   AMP056

What type nuts are used to hold an exhaust system to the cylinders?

A– Brass or heat-resistant nuts

B– High-temperature fiber self-locking nuts

C– High-temperature aluminum self-locking nuts

6-5. Answer A. JSPT 6A, FPH

Engine manufacturers typically use brass or heatresistant nuts to fasten exhaust system components to cylinder heads. Neither high-temperature fiber self-locking nuts nor high-temperature aluminum self-locking nuts are designed to withstand the high temperatures encountered on exhaust system components.

6-6   AMP057
Repair of exhaust system components

A– is impossible because the material cannot be identified.

B– must be accomplished by the component manufacturer.

C– is not recommended to be accomplished in the field.

6-6. Answer C. JSPT 6A, FPH
Although repair of exhaust system components can be accomplished, it requires special equipment and techniques that are not typically available in the field. Therefore, it is recommended that exhaust stacks, mufflers, and tailpipes be replaced with new or reconditioned components rather than being repaired.

6-7   AMP057
On an aircraft that utilizes an exhaust heat exchanger as a source of cabin heat, how should the exhaust system be inspected?

A– X-rayed to detect any cracks

B– Hydrostatically tested

C– With the heater air shroud removed

6-7. Answer C. JSPT 6A, AC 43.13-1B
Most exhaust systems that use a heat exchanger as a source of cabin heat can be inspected visually once the heater air shroud is removed. Although Xray inspection can detect cracks in exhaust system components, these defects are more easily and economically found by frequent and thorough visual inspection.

6-8   AMP057
How should ceramic-coated exhaust components be cleaned?

A– With alkali

B– By degreasing

C– By mechanical means

6-8. Answer B. JSPT 6A, FPH
Ceramic coated stacks are typically cleaned using degreasing agents. However, you should always consult the manufacturer's specifications before using any cleaning agents.

6-9   AMP073
Select a characteristic of a good weld on exhaust stacks.

A– The weld should be built up 1/8 inch.

B– Porousness or projecting globules should show in the weld.

C– The weld should taper off smoothly into the base metal.

6-9. Answer C. JSPT 6A, AC 43.13-1B
When welding an exhaust stack, the completed weld should have a smooth seam of uniform thickness and the weld should taper smoothly into the base metal.

6-10   AMP057

How should corrosion-resistant steel parts such as exhaust collectors be blast cleaned?

A– Use steel grit which has not previously been used on soft iron

B– Use super fine granite grit

C– Use sand which has not previously been used on iron or steel

6-10. Answer C. JSPT 6A, FPH

To prevent dissimilar metal corrosion, corrosion-resistant steel parts should be blast cleaned using sand that has not previously been used on iron or steel.

6-11   AMP057

Reciprocating engine exhaust systems that have repairs or sloppy weld beads which protrude internally are unacceptable because they cause

A– base metal fatigue.

B– localized cracks.

C– local hot spots.

6-11. Answer C. JSPT 6A, FPH

Repairs or sloppy weld beads on exhaust components that protrude into the exhaust gas flow can restrict the exhaust gas flow and cause localized hot spots.

6-12   AMP057

Ball joints in reciprocating engine exhaust systems should be

A– tight enough to prevent any movement.

B– disassembled and the seals replaced every engine change.

C– loose enough to permit some movement.

6-12. Answer C. JSPT 6A, FPH

Flexible ball joints absorb movement between stationary and movable portions of an engine's exhaust system. Therefore, ball joints must be installed with a specified clearance to prevent binding when expanded by hot exhaust gas.

6-13   AMP057

All of the following are recommended markers for reciprocating engine exhaust systems except

A– India ink.

B– lead pencil.

C– Prussian blue.

6-13. Answer B. JSPT 6A, FPH

Exhaust system parts should never be marked with a lead pencil. The lead is absorbed by the metal when heated, creating a distinct change in the metal's molecular structure. This change softens the metal in the area of the mark.

6-14   AMP056
Augmenter tubes are part of which reciprocating engine system?

A– Induction

B– Exhaust

C– Fuel

6-14. Answer B. JSPT 6A, FPH
Augmenter tubes are exhaust system components that assist engine cooling and provide a source of heat for anti-icing and cabin heating.

6-15   AMP056
Dislodged internal muffler baffles on a small reciprocating engine can

A– obstruct the muffler outlet and cause excessive exhaust back pressure.

B– cause the engine to run excessively cool.

C– cause high fuel and oil consumption.

6-15. Answer A. JSPT 6A, AC 43.13-1B
Internal failures in a muffler, such as displaced baffles or diffusers, can restrict the flow of exhaust gases resulting in excessive exhaust back pressure that can lead to a partial or complete engine power loss.

6-16   AMP056
What is the purpose of an exhaust outlet guard on a small reciprocating engine?

A– To prevent dislodged muffler baffles from obstructing the muffler outlet

B– To reduce spark exit

C– To shield adjacent components from excessive heat

6-16. Answer A.
Engine power loss and excessive back

pressure caused by exhaust outlet blockage can be prevented by the installation of an exhaust outlet guard.

A typical exhaust outlet guard extends approximately two inches inside the muffler outlet port, thereby preventing any debris from blocking the outlet.

6-17   AMP056
What could be a result of undetected exhaust system leaks in a reciprocating engine powered airplane?

A– Pilot/passenger incapacitation caused by carbon monoxide entering the cabin

B– A rough-running engine with increased fuel consumption

C– Too low exhaust back pressure resulting in the desired power settings not being attained

6-17. Answer A. JSPT 6A, AC 43.13-1B
Cabin heat in most light aircraft is provided by a shroud that routes air over the exhaust system. Therefore, any exhaust system leakage should be regarded as a severe hazard. An undetected exhaust system leak can allow carbon monoxide to enter the cabin and incapacitate the pilot and passengers.

6-18   AMP057

How may reciprocating engine exhaust system leaks be detected?

A– An exhaust trail aft of the tailpipe on the airplane exterior

B– Fluctuating manifold pressure indication

C– Signs of exhaust soot inside cowling and on adjacent components

6-18. Answer C. JSPT 6A, AC 43.13-1B

Prior to any cleaning in an engine compartment, the exhaust system and surrounding areas should be thoroughly inspected. The cowling and nacelle areas adjacent to the exhaust system should be inspected for signs of heat damage or exhaust gas soot, indicating possible exhaust leaks.

6-19   AMP070

Compared to normally aspirated engines, turbocharged engine exhaust systems operate at

A– similar temperatures and higher pressures.

B– higher temperatures and higher pressures.

C– similar temperatures and pressures.

6-19. Answer B. JSPT 6A

Turbocharged engine exhaust systems extract energy from the exhaust gas flow to compress the intake air before it enters the cylinders. Any time a gas is compressed, its temperature increases. Therefore, turbocharged engine exhaust systems typically operate at higher temperatures and higher pressures than normally aspirated systems.

6-20   AMP057

Most exhaust system failures result from thermal fatigue cracking in the areas of stress concentration.

This condition is usually caused by

A– the drastic temperature change which is encountered at altitude.

B– improper welding techniques during manufacture.

C– the high temperatures at which the exhaust system operates.

6-20. Answer C. JSPT 6A, AC 43.13-1B

Approximately one half of all exhaust system failures are traced to cracks or ruptures in the heat exchanger surfaces used for cabin and carburetor air heat sources. The high temperature of the exhaust system components along with the vibration from the engine promotes thermal and vibration fatigue cracking in areas of stress concentration.

SECTION B — TURBINE ENGINES

Section B of Chapter 6 contains information related to exhaust system theory, operation, and maintenance on turbine engines.

6-21   AMP032

On turbojet powered airplanes, thrust reversers are capable of producing between?

A– 35 and 50 percent of the rated thrust in the reverse direction

B– 35 and 75 percent of the rated thrust in the reverse direction

C– 35 and 65 percent of the rated thrust in the reverse direction

6-21. Answer A. JSPT 6B, TEP2

To satisfy the minimum braking requirements after landing, a thrust reverser should be able to produce reverse thrust that is between 35 and 50 percent of the full forward thrust for which the engine is capable.

6-22   AMP032

Operating thrust reversers at low ground speeds can sometimes cause

1. sand or other foreign object ingestion.

2. hot gas re-ingestion.

3. compressor stalls.

A– 1, 2, and 3

B– 1 and 2

C– 2 and 3

6-22. Answer A. JSPT 6B, TEP2

Statements number (1), (2), and (3) are true. The operation of thrust reversers at low ground speeds or during power backs disrupts the air flow into the compressor, increasing the chance of compressor stall. Furthermore, exhaust gas from the thrust reversers can blow sand and other foreign objects into the compressor inlet, and cause hot exhaust gas to be re-ingested.

6-23   AMP032

Engines using cold stream, or both cold and hot stream reversing include

A– high bypass turbofans.

B– turbojets.

C– turbojets with afterburner.

6-23. Answer A. JSPT 6B, TEP2

Cold stream reversing describes a system that uses bypass air to produce reverse thrust. This is only possible with bypass turbofan engines.

6-24   AMP032

The purpose of cascade vanes in a thrust reversing system is to

A— form a solid blocking door in the jet exhaust path.

B— turn the exhaust gases forward just after exiting the exhaust nozzle.

C— turn to a forward direction the fan and/or hot exhaust gases that have been blocked from exiting through the exhaust nozzle.

6-24. Answer C. JSPT 6B, TEP2

The two types of thrust reversers in common use are the aerodynamic reversers and the mechanical blockage reversers. Aerodynamic, or cascade, reversers consist of a set of cascade vanes located ahead of the exhaust discharge that turn the escaping exhaust gases forward, which, in turn, produces reverse thrust. Mechanical blockage reversers typically consist of clamshell doors that extend into the exhaust stream and divert the flow of exhaust gases forward to create reverse thrust.

6-25   AMP032

Turbojet and turbofan thrust reverser systems are generally powered by

1. fuel pressure.

2. electricity.

3. hydraulic pressure.

4. pneumatic pressure.

A— 1, 3, and 4.

B— 1, 2, and 3.

C— 2, 3, and 4.

6-25. Answer C. JSPT 6B, TEP2

The most common type of actuators used on thrust reverser systems are pneumatic. However, electric and hydraulic actuators are also used in some applications.

6-26   AMP032

The rearward thrust capability of an engine with the thrust reverser system deployed is

A— less than its forward capability.

B— equal to or less than its forward capability, depending on ambient conditions and system design.

C— equal to its forward capability.

6-26. Answer A. JSPT 6B, FPH

Reversers are capable of producing between 35 and 50 percent of an engine's rated thrust in the reverse direction.

6-27   AMP008

Which statement is generally true regarding thrust reverser systems?

A— It is possible to move some aircraft backward on the ground using reverse thrust

B— Engine thrust reversers on the same aircraft usually will not operate independently of each other (must all be simultaneously)

C— Mechanical blockage system design permits a deployment position aft of the exhaust nozzle only

6-27. Answer A. JSPT 6B, TEP2

The thrust reverser systems on some aircraft do create enough reverse thrust to move the aircraft backwards. This is referred to as a power-back operation. However, creating that much reverse thrust burns a great deal of fuel and, therefore, is not very economical.

6-28   AMP032

What is the proper operating sequence when using thrust reversers to slow an aircraft after landing?

A— Advance thrust levers up to takeoff position as conditions require, select thrust reverse, de-select thrust reverser, retard thrust levers to ground idle

B— Retard thrust levers to ground idle, raise thrust reverser levers as required, and retard thrust levers to ground idle

C— Select thrust reverse, advance thrust reverser levers no higher than 75% N1, and retard thrust reverser levers to idle at approximately normal taxi speed

6-28. Answer B. JSPT 6B, TEP2

Thrust reverse can only be selected with the thrust levers in the ground-idle position. Therefore, to obtain reverse thrust, you must first retard the thrust levers to ground idle, then raise the thrust reverser levers attached to the power levers as required. Once the aircraft has decelerated sufficiently, the thrust reverser levers are returned to the ground idle position.

6-29   AMP068

The exhaust section of a turbine engine is designed to

A— impart a high exit velocity to the exhaust gases.

B— increase temperature, therefore increasing velocity.

C— decrease temperature, therefore decreasing pressure.

6-29. Answer A. JSPT 6B, FPH

The exhaust section of a turbine engine installed on a subsonic aircraft is comprised of several components performing multiple functions. However, all components must work together to direct the flow of hot gases rearward and impart a high exit velocity.

6-30   AMP032

Thrust reversers utilizing a pneumatic actuating system usually receive operating pressure from

A– the engine bleed air system.

B– an on board hydraulic or electrical powered compressor.

C– high pressure air reservoirs.

6-30. Answer A. JSPT 6B, TEP2

Turbine engine thrust reversers are typically operated hydraulically, using hydraulic system pressure, or pneumatically using compressor bleed air.

ENGINE FUEL AND FUEL METERING

CHAPTER 7

SECTION A — FUEL SYSTEMS
This section covers fuel system components common to reciprocating and turbine engine aircraft, including fuel pumps, filters, tanks, valves, primer systems and other similar components.

7-1   AMP054
A nine-cylinder radial engine, using a multiple-point priming system with a central spider, will prime which cylinders?

A– One, two, three, eight, and nine

B– All cylinders

C– One, three, five, and seven

7-1. Answer A. JSPT 7A, FPH
On radial engines, fluids tend to seep into the lower cylinders and cause liquid lock.To prevent adding to this problem, the priming system on a radial engine only primes the cylinders that are horizontal or pointing upward. Therefore, on a nine-cylinder radial engine, only cylinders one, two, three, eight, and nine are primed.

7-2   AMP037
During what period does the fuel pump bypass valve open and remain open?

A– When the fuel pump pressure is greater than the demand of the engine

B– When the boost pump pressure is greater than fuel pump pressure

C– When the fuel pump output is greater than the demand of the carburetor

7-2. Answer B. JSPT 7A, FGH
When an aircraft's boost pump pressure exceeds that of the primary fuel pressure pump, a bypass valve in the pressure pump opens and allows fuel to flow directly to the engine. This occurs during start, when the pressure pump is not operating, and any time the engine driven fuel pump becomes clogged or fails.

7-3   AMP041
Which of the following statements concerning a centrifugal-type fuel boost pump located in a fuel supply tank is NOT true?

A– Air and fuel vapors do not pass through a centrifugal-type pump.

B– Fuel can be drawn through the impeller section of the pump when it is not in operation.

C– The centrifugal-type pump is classified as a positive displacement pump.

7-3. Answer C. JSPT 7A, FGH
A positive displacement pump provides a fixed quantity of fuel per pump revolution. With a centrifugal-type fuel boost pump, once the pressure builds to a predetermined pressure, fuel bypasses the impeller and remains in the fuel tank. Therefore, the pump does not continually displace fuel and is not a positive displacement pump.

7-4   AMP041

Where is the engine fuel shutoff valve usually located?

A– Aft of the firewall

B– Adjacent to the fuel pump

C– Downstream of the engine-driven fuel pump

7-4. Answer A. JSPT 7A, 14 CFR 23.995

According to the 14 CFR 23.995, the engine fuel shutoff valve may not be located on the engine side of the firewall.

7-5   AMP041

Boost pumps in a fuel system

A– operate during takeoff only.

B– are primarily used for fuel transfer.

C– provide a positive flow of fuel to the engine pump.

7-5. Answer C. JSPT 7A, FGH

The primary purpose of a fuel boost pump is to provide a positive flow of fuel to the engine driven pump.

7-6   AMP041

What is the purpose of an engine-driven fuel pump bypass valve?

A– To divert the excess fuel back to the main tank

B– To prevent a damaged or inoperative pump from blocking the fuel flow of another pump in series with it

C– To divert the excess fuel from the pressure side of the pump to the inlet side of the pump

7-6. Answer B. JSPT 7A, FGH

When an aircraft's boost pump pressure is greater than that of the main pressure pump, a bypass valve in the pressure pump opens and allows fuel to flow directly to the engine. This prevents a damaged or inoperative pump from blocking fuel flow to the engine.

7-7   AMP041

Most large aircraft reciprocating engines are equipped with which of the following types of engine-driven fuel pumps?

A– Rotary-vane-type fuel pump

B– Centrifugal-type fuel pump

C– Gear-type fuel pump

7-7. Answer A. JSPT 7A, FGH

The purpose of the engine-driven fuel pump is to deliver a continuous supply of fuel at the proper pressure at all times during engine operation. Therefore, a positive displacement pump must be used. One type of positive displacement pump that is widely used is the rotary-vane-type fuel pump.

7-8   AMP041

The fuel pump relief valve directs excess fuel to the

A– fuel tank return line.

B– inlet side of the fuel pump.

C– inlet side of the fuel strainer.

7-8. Answer B. JSPT 7A, FGH

Engine-driven fuel pumps typically discharge more fuel than an engine requires. Therefore, fuel systems must incorporate a relief valve to prevent the build up of excessive fuel pressures at the carburetor. A typical fuel pump relief valve is spring-loaded and, when opened, allows excess fuel to flow back to the inlet side of the fuel pump.

7-9   AMP041

Which type of pump is commonly used as a fuel pump on reciprocating engines?

A– Gear

B– Impeller

C– Vane

7-9. Answer C. JSPT 7A, FGH

The purpose of the engine-driven fuel pump is to deliver a continuous supply of fuel at the proper pressure at all times during engine operation. Therefore, a positive displacement pump must be used. One type of positive displacement pump that is widely used is the rotary-vane-type fuel pump.

7-10   AMP041

The purpose of the diaphragm in most vane-type fuel pumps is to

A– maintain fuel pressure below atmospheric pressure.

B– equalize fuel pressure at all speeds.

C– compensate fuel pressures to altitude changes.

7-10. Answer C. JSPT 7A, FGH

In a compensated vane-type fuel pump, the fuel pressure delivered to the carburetor inlet varies with altitude and atmospheric pressure. This is done by allowing spring tension and either atmospheric or carburetor inlet air pressure to act on a diaphragm which controls the pump's relief valve. As the amount of pressure acting on the diaphragm varies, the pressure at which the relief valve bypasses fuel back to the pump's inlet varies.

7-11   AMP039

The primary condition(s) that allow(s) microorganisms to grow in the fuel in aircraft fuel tanks is (are)

A– warm temperatures and frequent fueling.

B– the presence of water.

C– the presence of dirt or other particulate contaminants.

7-11. Answer B. JSPT 7A, FGH

There are over 100 different varieties of microorganisms which can live in the free water which accumulates in the sumps of aircraft fuel tanks. Because they thrive in water, the best way to prevent their growth is to eliminate the water through proper fuel handling procedures.

7-12   AMP041

(Refer to figure 7.)

What is the purpose of the fuel transfer ejectors?

A– To supply fuel under pressure to the engine-driven pump

B– To assist in the transfer of fuel from the main tank to the boost pump sump

C– To transfer fuel from the boost pump sump to the wing tank

7-12. Answer B. JSPT 7A, FPH

A fuel transfer ejector helps transfer fuel from the main tank to the boost pump sump by creating a low pressure area at the fuel pick-up point. By pumping fuel past the venturi in the injector, a low pressure area is created that drains fuel into the line that feeds the boost pump sump.

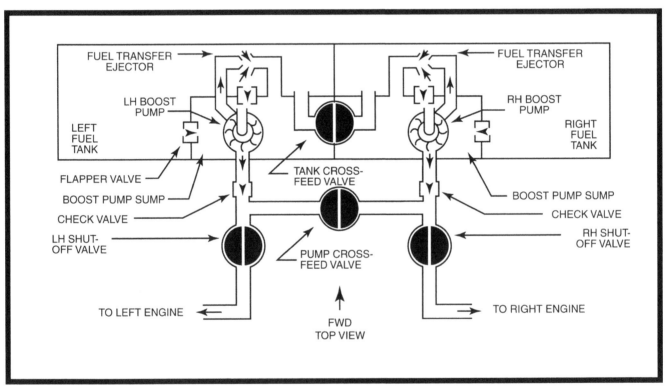

Figure 7. Fuel Systems.

7-13   AMP041

It is desirable that fuel lines have a gentle slope upward or downward and not have sharp curves or sharp rises and/or falls in order to

A– prevent vapor lock.

B– prevent stagnation or "pooling" of fuel in the fuel lines.

C– minimize the generation of static electricity by decreasing fluid friction in the lines.

7-13. Answer A. JSPT 7A

To reduce the possibility of vapor lock, fuel lines are kept away from heat sources, are sometimes wrapped with insulation, and are installed in a smooth, flowing manner with no sharp bends.

7-14   AMP041

The fuel systems of aircraft certificated in the standard classification must include which of the following?

A– An engine-driven fuel pump and at least one auxiliary pump per engine

B– A positive means of shutting off the fuel to all engines

C– A reserve supply of fuel, available to the engine only after selection by the flightcrew, sufficient to operate the engines at least 30 minutes at METO power

7-14. Answer B. JSPT 7A, 14 CFR 23.1189

According to 14 CFR 23.1189, aircraft that are certified in the normal category must have a positive means of shutting off the fuel to all engines.

7-15   AMP041

Where should the main fuel strainer be located in the aircraft fuel system?

A– Downstream from the wobble pump check valve

B– At the lowest point in the fuel system

C– At any point in the system lower than the carburetor strainer

7-15. Answer B. JSPT 7A, FGH

The main fuel strainer in an aircraft's fuel system is installed so that fuel flows through it before reaching the engine-driven pump. Furthermore, the strainer is typically located at the lowest point in the fuel system so that water and other debris can collect in the strainer, where they can be drained from the system.

7-16   AMP041
Where physical separation of the fuel lines from electrical wiring or conduit is impracticable, locate the fuel line

A— below the wiring and clamp the line securely to the airframe structure.

B— above the wiring and clamp the line securely to the airframe structure.

C— inboard of the wiring and clamp both securely to the airframe structure.

7-16. Answer A. JSPT 7A, AC 43.13-1B
Every effort should be made to physically separate electric wiring and lines carrying flammable fluids. However, when separation is impractical, electrical wire should be located above the flammable fluid line and both the electrical line and fluid line should be securely clamped to structure.

7-17   AMP041
What is a characteristic of a centrifugal-type fuel boost pump?

A— It separates air and vapor from the fuel.

B— It has positive displacement.

C— It requires a relief valve.

7-17. Answer A. JSPT 7A, FGH
The swirling action of a centrifugal boost pump impeller separates air and vapor from fuel before it enters the fuel line to the carburetor. By removing air and vapor, the possibility of vapor lock greatly decreases.

7-18   AMP041
The Federal Aviation Regulations require the fuel flow rate for gravity systems (main and reserve) to be

A— 125 percent of the takeoff fuel consumption of the engine.

B— 125 percent of the maximum, except takeoff, fuel consumption of the engine.

C— 150 percent of the takeoff fuel consumption of the engine.

7-18. Answer C. JSPT 7A, 14 CFR 23.955
According to 14 CFR 23.955, the fuel flow rate of a gravity-fed system must be at least 150 percent of the takeoff fuel consumption of the engine.

7-19   AMP041
Fuel boost pumps are operated

A— to provide a positive flow of fuel to the engine.

B— during takeoff only.

C— primarily for fuel transfer to another tank.

7-19. Answer A. JSPT 7A, FGH
The primary function of a fuel boost pump is to supply a positive flow of fuel to the engine-driven fuel pump. Secondary functions include supplying positive fuel flow to the engine, when the engine-driven pump fails, and transferring fuel.

7-20   AMP041
A fuel strainer or filter must be located between the

A– boost pump and tank outlet.

B– tank outlet and the fuel metering device.

C– boost pump and engine-driven fuel pump.

7-20. Answer B. JSPT 7A, FAR 23.997
According to FAR 23.997, there must be a fuel strainer or filter between the fuel tank outlet and the engine-driven pump or fuel metering device.

7-21   AMP041
Fuel pump relief valves designed to compensate for atmospheric pressure variations are known as

A– compensated-flow valves.

B– pressurized-relief valves.

C– balanced-type relief valves.

7-21. Answer C. JSPT 7A, FGH
Fuel pump relief valves designed to compensate for atmospheric pressure variations operate on the principle that, within the valve, a balance between fuel pressure and atmospheric or carburetor inlet air pressure is maintained. Thus, these valves are often referred to as balanced-type relief valves. "Compensated-flow valves" and "pressurized-relief valves" are terms that are not commonly applied to fuel pump relief valves.

7-22   AMP041
Fuel lines are kept away from sources of heat, and sharp bends and steep rises are avoided to reduce the possibility of

A– liquid lock.

B– vapor lock.

C– positive lock.

7-22. Answer B. JSPT 7A, FPH
To reduce the possibility of vapor lock, fuel lines are kept away from heat sources, are sometimes wrapped with insulation, and installed in a smooth, flowing manner with no sharp bends.

7-23   AMP041
Fuel crossfeed systems are used in aircraft to

A– purge the fuel tanks.

B– jettison fuel in an emergency.

C– maintain aircraft stability.

7-23. Answer C. JSPT 7A, FGH
The purpose of a fuel crossfeed system is to allow fuel from any tank to be fed to any engine. Unfortunately, this is not a choice.

7-24   AMP041

A fuel pressure relief valve is required on

A– engine-driven diaphragm-type fuel pumps.

B– engine-driven vane-type fuel pumps.

C– centrifugal fuel boost pumps.

7-24. Answer B. JSPT 7A, FGH

Since an engine-driven vane-type fuel pump discharges more fuel than an engine requires, there must be some way of routing excess fuel away from the carburetor inlet line to prevent excess pressure from building. This is accomplished by using a spring loaded relief valve that is adjusted to deliver fuel at the recommended pressure.

7-25   AMP041

A rotary-vane pump is best described as a

A– positive-displacement pump.

B– variable-displacement pump.

C– boost pump.

7-25. Answer A. JSPT 7A, FGH

Rotary-vane pumps used as main fuel supply pumps provide a fixed quantity of fuel per pump revolution. Therefore, rotary-vane pumps are positive displacement pumps.

7-26   AMP041

Fuel pressure produced by the engine-driven fuel pump is adjusted by the

A– bypass valve adjusting screw.

B– relief valve adjusting screw.

C– engine-driven fuel pump adjusting screw.

7-26. Answer B. JSPT 7A, FGH

Since engine-driven fuel pumps provide more fuel than an engine needs, they must employ some means of limiting the pressure they deliver to the carburetor. This is accomplished with a relief valve that directs fuel away from the carburetor inlet line when fuel pressure exceeds the carburetor's demand. This relief valve relies on spring tension that uses an adjusting screw to maintain the appropriate fuel pressure.

7-27   AMP039

Kerosene is used as turbine engine fuel because

A– kerosene has very high volatility which aids in ignition and lubrication.

B– kerosene has more heat energy per gallon and lubricates fuel system components.

C– kerosene does not contain any water.

7-27. Answer B. JSPT 7A, ASTM Spec. D-910, D-1655

Aviation gasoline (100LL) has a heat energy of 112,320 BTUs per gallon while kerosene (Jet A fuel) has a heat energy of 123,541 BTUs per gallon. In addition, kerosene's high viscosity allows it to act as a lubricant in pumps and fuel control units.

7-28   AMP041

Which of the following turbine fuel filters has the greatest filtering action?

A– Micron

B– Small wire mesh

C– Stacked charcoal

7-28. Answer A. JSPT 7A, FPH

Of the filters listed, the micron filter has the greatest filtering action. Micron filters can be made of cloth or paper and remove foreign matter measuring from 10 to 25 microns which equates to particles between .00001 and .000025 inch in size.

SECTION B — RECIPROCATING ENGINE FUEL METERING

Section B of Chapter 7 covers reciprocating engine fuel metering systems including float-type carburetors, pressure carburetors, and fuel injection systems.

7-29   AMP039

Which fuel/air mixture will result in the highest engine temperature (all other factors remaining constant)?

A– A mixture leaner than a rich best-power mixture of .085

B– A mixture richer than a full-rich mixture of .087

C– A mixture leaner than a manual lean mixture of .060

7-29. Answer C. JSPT 7B, FPH

The fuel/air mixture which will result in the highest engine temperature varies according to the engine's power setting. For example, at high power settings, lean mixtures produce the highest temperature. Therefore, a mixture leaner than a manual lean mixture of .060 will produce very high temperatures at high power settings. Although a mixture leaner than a rich best-power mixture of .085 will produce an elevated temperature, it will not produce the highest of the choices listed.

7-30   AMP056

Increased water vapor (higher relative humidity) in the incoming air to a reciprocating engine will normally result in which of the following?

A– Decreased engine power at a constant RPM and manifold pressure

B– Increased power output due to increased volumetric efficiency

C– A leaning effect on engines which use non-automatic carburetors

7-30. Answer A. JSPT 7B, FGH

When an engine takes in air with a high water vapor content, there is less oxygen available for combustion. Any time there is less oxygen available for combustion there is a corresponding decrease in engine power for any given RPM and manifold pressure.

7-31   AMP056

1. Preignition is caused by improper ignition timing.

2. Detonation occurs when an area of the combustion chamber becomes incandescent and ignites the fuel/air mixture in advance of normal timed ignition.

Regarding the above statements,

A– only No.1 is true.

B– both No.1 and No.2 are true.

C– neither No.1 nor No.2 is true.

7-31. Answer C. JSPT 7B, FPH

Both statements are false. Preignition occurs when the fuel/air mixture is ignited prior to the spark plugs firing and has nothing to do with how an ignition system is timed. Detonation, on the other hand, is the uncontrolled burning of the fuel/air mixture. Typical causes of detonation include use of the improper fuel grade and engine overheating.

7-32   AMP056

Which of the following conditions would most likely lead to detonation?

A– Late ignition timing

B– Use of fuel with too high an octane rating

C– Use of fuel with too low an octane rating

7-32. Answer C. JSPT 7B, FPH

Detonation is the uncontrolled burning of the fuel/air mixture. Typical causes of detonation include use of fuel with too low an octane rating, high manifold pressure, high intake air pressure, and engine overheating.

7-33   AMP039

Which statement pertaining to fuel/air ratios is true?

A– The mixture ratio which gives the best power is richer than the mixture ratio which gives maximum economy.

B– A rich mixture is faster burning than a normal mixture.

C– The mixture ratio which gives maximum economy may also be designated as best power mixture.

7-33. Answer A. JSPT 7B, FPH

For a given RPM, the fuel/air mixture that results in best power is always richer than the mixture used for best economy. One way to remember this is to associate best power with using more fuel and best economy with using less fuel. With this in mind there is no way the mixture used for maximum economy can also be used for best power.

7-34   AMP041

How are discharge nozzles in a fuel injected reciprocating engine identified to indicate the flow range?

A– By an identification letter stamped on one of the hexes of the nozzle body

B– By an identification metal tag attached to the nozzle body

C– By color codes on the nozzle body

7-34. Answer A. JSPT 7B, FPH

Fuel discharge nozzles are calibrated for several different flow ranges. In order to help identify the flow range of a specific nozzle a letter is stamped on the hex of the nozzle body.

7-35   AMP056

As a general rule, the mixture setting on a reciprocating engine operating at or near takeoff power that provides the best cooling is

A– FULL RICH.

B– LEAN.

C– FULL LEAN.

7-35. Answer A. JSPT 7B, FPH

Air-cooled aircraft engines rely to some degree on fuel to aid in cooling during high-power operations. Therefore, as a general rule the mixture should be set in the full rich position when operating at or near takeoff power. A rich mixture typically provides more fuel than is needed for combustion, leaving excess fuel to aid in engine cooling.

7-36   AMP056

A reciprocating engine automatic mixture control responds to changes in air density caused by changes in

A– altitude or humidity.

B– altitude only.

C– altitude or temperature.

7-36. Answer C. JSPT 7B, FPH

An automatic mixture control utilizes a sealed, helium-filled bellows that fluctuates with changes in air density. As air density decreases due to an increase in altitude or temperature, the helium pressure inside the bellows causes the bellows to expand and move a poppet valve that adjusts the fuel/air mixture.

7-37   AMP037

On a float-type carburetor, the purpose of the economizer valve is to

A– provide extra fuel for sudden acceleration of the engine.

B– maintain the leanest mixture possible during cruising best power.

C– provide a richer mixture and cooling at maximum power output.

7-37. Answer C. JSPT 7B, FPH

For an engine to develop maximum power at full throttle, the fuel mixture must be richer than that used at cruise power settings. The additional fuel is used to cool the engine and prevent detonation. One way to make sure the engine gets this additional fuel is with an economizer valve which automatically enriches the fuel/air mixture at throttle settings above 60 to 70 percent power.

7-38   AMP037

The fuel metering force of a conventional float-type carburetor in its normal operating range is the difference between the pressure acting on the discharge nozzle located within the venturi and the pressure

A– acting on the fuel in the float chamber.

B– of the fuel as it enters the carburetor.

C– of the air as it enters the venturi (impact pressure).

7-38. Answer A. JSPT 7B

The force that is responsible for discharging fuel into the throat of a float-type carburetor is a result of the differential pressure between the fuel discharge nozzle within the venturi and the pressure exerted on the fuel within the float chamber. As engine speed increases the amount of air flowing past the venturi increases causing a greater pressure differential and corresponding increase in fuel flow.

7-39   AMP038

If the main air bleed of a float-type carburetor becomes clogged, the engine will run

A– lean at rated power.

B– rich at rated power.

C– rich at idling.

7-39. Answer B. JSPT 7B, FPH

The main air bleed in a float-type carburetor allows air to be drawn into the carburetor venturi along with the fuel. The additional air helps decrease the fuel density and destroy surface tension, resulting in better vaporization and control of fuel discharge at lower engine speeds. If the main air bleed becomes clogged, it stands to reason that less air will be drawn into the engine and the fuel/air mixture will become excessively rich at high power settings.

7-40   AMP038

Which method is commonly used to adjust the level of a float in a float-type carburetor?

A– Lengthening or shortening the float shaft.

B– Add or remove shims under the needle-valve seat.

C– Change the angle of the float arm pivot.

7-40. Answer B. JSPT 7B

Most carburetor floats are adjusted by adding or removing shims between the needle seat and the throttle body. This method of adjustment is much more convenient and precise than adjusting the length of the float shaft or changing the angle of the float arm pivot.

7-41   AMP037

What is the possible cause of an engine running rich at full throttle if it is equipped with a float-type carburetor?

A– Float level too low

B– Clogged main air bleed

C– Clogged atmospheric vent

7-41. Answer B. JSPT 7B, FPH

The main air bleed in a float-type carburetor allows air to be drawn into the carburetor venturi along with the fuel. Therefore, if the air bleed becomes clogged, less air will be drawn into the engine and the fuel/air mixture will become excessively rich at high power settings.

7-42   AMP037

One of the things a metering orifice in a main air bleed helps to accomplish (at a given altitude) in a carburetor is

A– pressure in the float chamber to increase as airflow through the carburetor increases.

B– a progressively richer mixture as airflow through the carburetor increases.

C– better fuel vaporization and control of fuel discharge, especially at lower engine speeds.

7-42. Answer C. JSPT 7B, FPH

One way to help promote better fuel vaporization within the throat of a carburetor is to allow a calibrated amount of air from an air bleed to be mixed with the fuel as the fuel enters the carburetor throat. Mixing fuel and air also allows better control of the fuel discharge rate, especially at low engine speeds.

7-43   AMP037

A punctured float in a float-type carburetor will cause the fuel level to

A– lower, and enrich the mixture.

B– rise, and enrich the mixture.

C– rise, and lean the mixture.

7-43. Answer B. JSPT 7B, FPH

During engine operation, the carburetor float is responsible for maintaining the appropriate amount of fuel within the float bowl. When fuel is drawn from the bowl, the float lowers and fuel is allowed into the bowl. By the same token, if a float should become punctured, it would fill with fuel and sink. With the float resting on the bottom of the bowl, fuel would be allowed to continually enter the bowl and eventually enrich the fuel/air mixture.

7-44   AMP037

If an aircraft engine is equipped with a carburetor that is not compensated for altitude and temperature variations, the fuel/air mixture will become

A– leaner as either the altitude or temperature increases.

B– richer as the altitude increases and leaner as the temperature increases.

C– richer as either the altitude or temperature increases.

7-44. Answer C. JSPT 7B, FPH

As both altitude and temperature increase, the air becomes less dense. Therefore, as an airplane climbs or as the air temperature increases, the amount of oxygen drawn into an engine decreases. In either of these situations if an engine is not equipped with a carburetor that can be adjusted for increases in altitude and temperature, the fuel/air mixture will become excessively rich.

7-45   AMP037
Float-type carburetors which are equipped with economizers are normally set for

A– their richest mixture delivery and leaned by means of the economizer system.

B– the economizer system to supplement the main system supply at all engine speeds above idling.

C– their leanest practical mixture delivery at cruising speeds and enriched by means of the economizer system at higher power settings.

7-45. Answer C. JSPT 7B, FPH
For an engine to develop maximum power at full throttle, the fuel mixture must be richer than that used at cruise power. The additional fuel is used to cool the engine and prevent detonation. One way to make sure the engine gets this additional fuel is with an economizer valve which is set to the leanest practical mixture at cruise power settings, then automatically enriches the fuel/air mixture at throttle settings above 60 to 70 percent power.

7-46   AMP037
If a float-type carburetor becomes flooded, the condition is most likely caused by

A– a leaking needle valve and seat assembly.

B– the accelerating pump shaft being stuck.

C– a clogged back-suction line.

7-46. Answer A. JSPT 7B
A likely cause of float-type carburetor flooding is an improperly set float level or a leak at the needle valve and seat assembly. A stuck accelerating pump shaft is unlikely to flood an engine since it sprays a charge of fuel into the carburetor throat only when the shaft and pump are advanced rapidly.

7-47   AMP038
If an engine is equipped with a float-type carburetor and the engine runs excessively rich at full throttle, a possible cause of the trouble is a clogged

A– main air bleed.

B– back-suction line.

C– atmospheric vent line.

7-47. Answer A. JSPT 7B, FPH
The main air bleed in a float-type carburetor allows air to be drawn into a carburetor's venturi along with the fuel to improve vaporization. Therefore, if the air bleed becomes clogged, the engine will draw too much fuel and the fuel/air mixture will become excessively rich..

7-48   AMP056

Which of the following best describes the function of an altitude mixture control?

A– Regulates the richness of the fuel/air charge entering the engine.

B– Regulates the air pressure above the fuel in the float chamber.

C– Regulates the air pressure in the venturi.

7-48. Answer A. JSPT 7B, FPH

The function of a mixture control is to regulate the richness of the fuel/air mixture entering the engine.

7-49   AMP037

Select the correct statement concerning the idle system of a conventional float-type carburetor.

A– The low-pressure area created in the throat of the venturi pulls the fuel from the idle passage

B– Climactic conditions have very little effect on idle mixture requirements

C– The low pressure between the edges of the throttle valve and the throttle body pulls the fuel from the idle passage

7-49. Answer C. JSPT 7B, FPH

With the throttle valve closed at idling speed, air velocity through the venturi is so low that it cannot draw enough fuel from the main discharge nozzle to keep an engine running. Therefore, in order to allow the engine to idle, a fuel passageway called an idling jet is incorporated in the low pressure area between the throttle valve and throttle body that discharges fuel into the throttle body.

7-50   AMP022

On an engine equipped with a pressure-type carburetor, fuel supply in the idling range is ensured by the inclusion in the carburetor of

A– a spring in the unmetered fuel chamber to supplement the action of normal metering forces.

B– an idle metering jet that bypasses the carburetor in the idle range.

C– a separate boost venturi that is sensitive to the reduced airflow at start and idle speeds.

7-50. Answer A. JSPT 7B, FPH

In a pressure-type carburetor, fuel follows in the same path at idling as it does when the main metering system is in operation. However, because of the low air velocity through the venturi, insufficient differential pressure exists to displace the diaphragm that holds the poppet valve open and allows fuel to flow. Therefore, a spring is used to physically hold the poppet valve off its seat so fuel can flow while the engine is idling.

7-51   AMP037

The economizer system of a float-type carburetor performs which of the following functions?

A– It supplies and regulates the fuel required for all engine speeds.

B– It supplies and regulates the additional fuel required for all engine speeds above cruising.

C– It regulates the fuel required for all engine speeds and all altitudes.

7-51. Answer B. JSPT 7B, FPH

In order for an engine to effectively develop maximum power at full throttle, the fuel/air mixture must be richer than that used for cruise power settings. The additional fuel is used for cooling the engine to prevent detonation. One way to make sure the engine gets this additional fuel is with an economizer valve which automatically supplies and regulates the additional fuel needed at throttle settings above 60 to 70 percent power.

7-52   AMP037

The fuel level within the float chamber of a properly adjusted float-type carburetor will be

A– slightly higher than the discharge nozzle outlet.

B– slightly lower than the discharge nozzle outlet.

C– at the same level as the discharge nozzle outlet.

7-52. Answer B. JSPT 7B, FPH

In a float-type carburetor, a float chamber is provided between the fuel supply and the metering system to provide a nearly constant level of fuel to the main discharge nozzle. The fuel level in the float chamber is set slightly lower than the discharge nozzle outlet to allow differential pressure to draw the fuel into the carburetor throat. If the float chamber fuel level was higher or at the same level as the nozzle outlet, fuel would run out of the carburetor when the engine was shut down.

7-53   AMP037

Select the statement which is correct relating to a fuel level check of a float-type carburetor.

A– Use 5 pounds fuel pressure for the test if the carburetor is to be used in a gravity fuel feed system.

B– Block off the main and idle jets to prevent a continuous flow of fuel through the jets.

C– Do not measure the level at the edge of the float chamber.

7-53. Answer C. JSPT 7B

The fuel level in the float chamber of a carburetor should be one-eighth inch below the main discharge outlet. When measuring this level, your measurements should be taken away from the edge of the float chamber since the fuel tends to cling to the walls of the chamber. If a measurement were taken at the edge, an inaccurate measurement may result.

7-54   AMP022

What carburetor component measures the amount of air delivered to the engine?

A– Economizer valve

B– Automatic mixture control

C– Venturi

7-54. Answer C. JSPT 7B

A carburetor measures airflow through its induction system using a venturi. As air passes through the venturi, its velocity increases and its pressure drops. The pressure drop is proportional to the velocity and, therefore, is a measure of the airflow.

7-55   AMP037

Fuel is discharged for idling speeds on a float-type carburetor

A– from the idle discharge nozzle.

B– in the venturi.

C– through the idle discharge air bleed.

7-55. Answer A. JSPT 7B, FPH

The main discharge nozzle cannot be used at idle speeds because there is insufficient airflow through the venturi to create enough of a pressure differential to force fuel from the nozzle. Because of this, float-type carburetors employ an idle jet or idle discharge nozzle that takes advantage of the low pressure area between the throttle valve and throttle body. This idle jet provides sufficient fuel flow to allow an engine to run at low RPM.

7-56   AMP022

When air passes through the venturi of a carburetor, what three changes occur?

A– Velocity increases, temperature increases, and pressure decreases

B– Velocity decreases, temperature increases, and pressure increases

C– Velocity increases, temperature decreases, and pressure decreases

7-56. Answer C. JSPT 7B, FPH

To answer this question you must be familiar with Bernoulli's Principle and Charles' Gas Law. Bernoulli's Principle states that when air flows through a converging duct such as a carburetor venturi, its velocity rises and its pressure drops. Charles' Law, on the other hand, states that pressure and temperature are directly proportional. In other words, a decrease in pressure means a decrease in temperature. Therefore, when air passes through a carburetor venturi, air velocity decreases while air temperature and pressure decrease.

7-57   AMP037
Where is the throttle valve located on a float-type carburetor?

A– Between the venturi and the discharge nozzle

B– After the main discharge nozzle and venturi

C– After the venturi and just before the main discharge nozzle

7-57. Answer B. JSPT 7B, FPH
In a float-type carburetor, the throttle valve controls the mass airflow through the venturi and, therefore, must be located downstream of both the venturi and the main discharge nozzle. However, in pressure injection carburetors the throttle valve is located after the venturi and just before the main discharge nozzle.

7-58   AMP041
An aircraft carburetor is equipped with a mixture control in order to prevent the mixture from becoming too

A– lean at high altitudes.

B– rich at high altitudes.

C– rich at high speeds.

7-58. Answer B. JSPT 7B, FPH
Carburetors are calibrated at sea level, and the correct fuel/air mixture is established at that altitude with the mixture control set in the FULL RICH position. However, as altitude increases, the density of air entering the carburetor decreases while the density of the fuel remains the same. This means that at higher altitudes, the mixture becomes progressively richer. Therefore, the purpose of the mixture control is to allow the pilot to control the amount of fuel that is mixed with the incoming air.

7-59   AMP022
Which of the following is NOT a function of the carburetor venturi?

A– Proportions the air/fuel mixture

B– Regulates the idle system

C– Limits the airflow at full throttle

7-59. Answer B. JSPT 7B, FPH
The venturi in a carburetor performs three functions. It proportions the fuel/air mixture, it decreases pressure at the discharge nozzle, and it limits the airflow at full throttle.

7-60   AMP037
One purpose of an air bleed in a float-type carburetor is to

A– increase fuel flow at altitude.

B– meter air to adjust the mixture.

C– decrease fuel density and destroy surface tension.

7-60. Answer C. JSPT 7B, FPH
The main air bleed on a float-type carburetor allows air to be mixed with the fuel being drawn out of the main discharge nozzle to decrease fuel density and decrease surface tension. This results in better fuel vaporization and allows better control of fuel discharge rates, especially at low engine speeds.

7-61   AMP037

To determine the float level in a float-type carburetor, a measurement is usually made from the top of the fuel in the float chamber to the

A— parting surface of the carburetor.

B— top of the float.

C— centerline of the main discharge nozzle.

7-61. Answer A. JSPT 7B

The float level in a float-type carburetor is determined by measuring the distance from the top of the fuel to the parting surface of the carburetor body or the point where the float chamber separates.

7-62   AMP037

The throttle valve of float-type aircraft carburetors is located

A— ahead of the venturi and main discharge nozzle.

B— after the main discharge nozzle and ahead of the venturi.

C— between the venturi and the engine.

7-62. Answer C. JSPT 7B, FPH

In a float-type carburetor, the throttle valve controls the mass airflow through the venturi and, therefore, must be located downstream of the venturi and upstream of the engine. If the throttle valve were located ahead of the venturi the fuel/air charge delivered to the engine would not be uniform.

7-63   AMP056

Why must a float-type carburetor supply a rich mixture during idle?

A— Engine operation at idle results in higher than normal volumetric efficiency.

B— Because at idling speeds the engine may not have enough airflow around the cylinders to provide proper cooling.

C— Because of reduced mechanical efficiency during idle.

7-63. Answer B. JSPT 7B

When a reciprocating aircraft engine is idling, there is typically not enough air movement around the cylinders to provide sufficient cooling. Therefore, most float-type carburetors provide a rich mixture during idle to help cool the engine.

7-64   AMP022

What component is used to ensure fuel delivery during periods of rapid engine acceleration?

A— Acceleration pump

B— Water injection pump

C— Power enrichment unit

7-64. Answer A. JSPT 7B, FPH

When the throttle valve is opened quickly, a large volume of air rushes through the carburetor. To ensure that enough fuel is mixed with the onrush of air, carburetors are equipped with a small fuel pump called an accelerator pump that provides a short burst of fuel when the throttle is advanced rapidly.

7-65   AMP041

The device that controls the ratio of the fuel/air mixture to the cylinders is called a

A— throttle valve.

B— mixture control.

C— metering jet.

7-65. Answer B. JSPT 7B, FPH

A mixture control on a carburetor controls the ratio of the fuel/air mixture by allowing a pilot to regulate the amount of fuel introduced into the mixture. Depending on the type of carburetor, the mixture control can be a manual or an automatic device.

7-66   AMP041

The device that controls the volume of the fuel/air mixture to the cylinders is called a

A— mixture control.

B— metering jet.

C— throttle valve.

7-66. Answer C. JSPT 7B, FPH

The throttle valve controls the amount, or volume of fuel/air mixture that is allowed to pass through the carburetor to the cylinders.

7-67   AMP056

Which statement is correct regarding a continuous-flow fuel injection system used on many reciprocating engines?

A— Fuel is injected directly into each cylinder.

B— Fuel is injected at each cylinder intake port.

C— Two injector nozzles are used in the injector fuel system for various speeds.

7-67. Answer B. JSPT 7B

Some continuous-flow fuel injection systems used on aircraft engines have a fuel discharge nozzle located in each cylinder head. The nozzle outlet is directed into the intake port where fuel and air are mixed just prior to entering the cylinder.

7-68   AMP022

During the operation of an aircraft engine, the pressure drop in the carburetor venturi depends primarily upon the

A— air temperature.

B— barometric pressure.

C— air velocity.

7-68. Answer C. JSPT 7B, FPH

According to Bernoulli's Principle, when air flows at a continuous rate, its pressure is indirectly proportional to its velocity. Therefore, when air flow increases through the venturi of a carburetor, air pressure decreases. The faster the air flows through the venturi, the greater the pressure drop.

7-69   AMP022

Which of the following causes a single diaphragm accelerator pump to discharge fuel?

A– An increase in venturi suction when the throttle valve is open

B– An increase in manifold pressure that occurs when the throttle valve is opened

C– A decrease in manifold pressure that occurs when the throttle valve is opened

7-69. Answer B. JSPT 7B, FPH

The accelerator pump in a pressure injection carburetor responds to changes in manifold pressure. For example, when the throttle valve is opened rapidly manifold pressure increases and causes the accelerator pump to inject additional fuel into the carburetor throat to maintain the proper fuel/air mixture.

7-70   AMP037

At what engine speed does the main metering jet actually function as a metering jet in a float-type carburetor?

A– All RPMs

B– Cruising RPM only

C– All RPMs above idle range

7-70. Answer C. JSPT 7B, FPH

Fuel metering in a float-type carburetor is accomplished with either an idle jet or a main metering jet. At idle speeds, airflow through the venturi is not great enough to draw fuel from the main discharge nozzle, so an idle jet located between the throttle valve and throttle body supplies fuel at low speeds when the throttle valve is closed. However, at all speeds above idle, the main metering jet supplies the necessary fuel to keep the engine running.

7-71   AMP042

An aircraft engine continuous cylinder fuel injection system normally discharges fuel during which stroke(s)?

A– Intake

B– Intake and compression

C– All (continuously)

7-71. Answer C. JSPT 7B, FPH

This question is asking when the fuel injection system discharges fuel into the intake port, not when the fuel enters the cylinders. In a continuous cylinder fuel injection system, the injector pump is not timed to inject fuel into the intake port at a specific time. Instead, fuel is always available at all intake ports.

7-72   AMP022

What is the purpose of the carburetor accelerating system?

A– Supply and regulate the fuel required for engine speeds above idle

B– Temporarily enrich the mixture when the throttle is suddenly opened

C– Supply and regulate additional fuel required for engine speeds above cruising

7-72. Answer B. JSPT 7B, FPH
When the throttle valve is opened quickly, a large volume of air rushes through the carburetor. To ensure that enough fuel is mixed with the onrush of air, carburetors are equipped with a small fuel pump called an accelerator pump that provides a momentary burst of fuel that temporarily enriches the mixture when the throttle is opened rapidly.

7-73   AMP022

What is the relationship between the accelerating pump and the enrichment valve in a pressure injection carburetor?

A– No relationship since they operate independently.

B– Unmetered fuel pressure affects both units.

C– The accelerating pump actuates the enrichment valve.

7-73. Answer A. JSPT 7B

In a pressure injection carburetor, the accelerating pump and the enrichment valve operate independently of each other. The accelerating pump senses rapid changes in manifold pressure and injects fuel into the carburetor throat any time the throttle is opened rapidly. On the other hand, the enrichment valve responds to metered fuel pressure to increase fuel flow to the discharge nozzle when the engine runs at high power settings.

7-74   AMP022

What is the relationship between the pressure existing within the throat of a venturi and the velocity of the air passing through the venturi?

A– There is no direct relationship between the pressure and the velocity.

B– The pressure is directly proportional to the velocity.

C– The pressure is inversely proportional to the velocity.

7-74. Answer C. JSPT 7B, FPH
According to Bernoulli's Principle, as the velocity of a fluid increases, its internal pressure decreases. In other words, pressure is inversely proportional to velocity.

7-75   AMP042

Which of the following is least likely to occur during operation of an engine equipped with a direct cylinder fuel injection system?

A– After firing

B– Kickback during start

C– Backfiring

7-75. Answer C. JSPT 7B, FPH

Backfiring is a condition that occurs when the fuel/air mixture within the induction system ignites and explodes when the intake valve opens. In a direct cylinder fuel injection system, the intake valve only allows air to enter the cylinder, while the fuel is injected through a separate nozzle. This eliminates any mixing of fuel and air in the induction system which, in turn, prevents backfiring.

7-76

What carburetor component actually limits the desired maximum airflow to the engine at full throttle?

A– Throttle valve

B– Venturi

C– Manifold intake

7-76. Answer B. JSPT 7B, FPH

The throttle valve limits the airflow through the carburetor at all throttle settings except full throttle.

At full throttle, the throttle valve is opened all the way leaving only the venturi to limit the airflow. The manifold intake is comparatively large in relation to the venturi and, therefore, does not limit maximum airflow.

7-77   AMP022

On a carburetor without an automatic mixture control as you ascend to altitude, the mixture will

A– be enriched.

B– be leaned.

C– not be affected.

7-77. Answer A. JSPT 7B, FPH

As altitude increases, the air becomes less dense. Therefore, if the fuel/air mixture is not leaned as an aircraft ascends, the mixture will become excessively rich.

7-78   AMP023

The desired engine idle speed and mixture setting

A– is adjusted with engine warmed up and operating.

B– should give minimum RPM with maximum manifold pressure.

C– is usually adjusted in the following sequence; speed first, then mixture.

7-78. Answer A. JSPT 7B, FPH

When adjusting a carburetor's idle speed or mixture, the engine should be warmed up and operating in its normal temperature range, since fuel vaporization qualities are different in an engine when it is cold. Therefore, any adjustment made on a cold engine will not be accurate.

7-79   AMP037

What is a function of the idling air bleed in a float-type carburetor?

A– It provides a means for adjusting the mixture at idle speeds.

B– It vaporizes the fuel at idling speeds.

C– It aids in emulsifying/vaporizing the fuel at idle speeds.

7-79. Answer C. JSPT 7B, FPH

The idle jet in a float-type carburetor utilizes an idle air bleed that allows air to be mixed with the fuel before it enters the carburetor throat. This aids in vaporizing fuel before it is drawn into the cylinder. The idle air bleed does not adjust the mixture at idle speeds nor does it actually vaporize fuel at idle speeds.

7-80   AMP022

If the volume of air passing through a carburetor venturi is reduced, the pressure at the venturi throat will

A– decrease.

B– be equal to the pressure at the venturi outlet.

C– increase.

7-80. Answer C. JSPT 7B, FPH

According to Bernoulli's Principle, fluid pressure and velocity are inversely related. In other words, as the velocity of a fluid increases, its internal pressure decreases and when the velocity of a fluid decreases, its internal pressure increases. Therefore, if the volume of air flowing through a carburetor decreases, the pressure will increase.

7-81   AMP037

What will occur if the vapor vent float in a pressure carburetor loses its buoyancy?

A– The amount of fuel returning to the fuel tank from the carburetor will be increased

B– The engine will continue to run after the mixture control is placed in IDLE CUTOFF

C– A rich mixture will occur at all engine speeds

7-81. Answer A. FPH

Pressure carburetors employ vapor venting systems that take the excess fuel vapor created in the fuel system and direct it back to the fuel tank. With this type of system, air enters the vented chamber and displaces the fuel thereby lowering the fuel level. When the fuel level reaches a predetermined level, the float pulls down on the vapor vent valve and allows fuel vapor to flow back to the fuel tank. Based on this, if the vapor vent valve should stick open or the float become filled with fuel and sink, fuel and fuel vapor continuously flow back to the fuel tank.

7-82   AMP038

What method is ordinarily used to make idle speed adjustments on a float-type carburetor?

A– An adjustable throttle stop or linkage

B– An orifice and adjustable tapered needle

C– An adjustable needle in the drilled passageway which connects the airspace of the float chamber and the carburetor venturi

7-82. Answer A. JSPT 7B, FPH

Idle speed on engines using a float-type carburetor is adjusted by limiting how far the throttle valve will close. This is usually accomplished with an adjustable throttle stop or linkage.

7-83   AMP041

1. The mixture used at rated power in air cooled reciprocating engines is richer than the mixture used through the normal cruising range.

2. The mixture used at idle in air cooled reciprocating engines is richer than the mixture used at rated power.

Regarding the above statements,

A– only No. 1 is true.

B– only No. 2 is true.

C– both No. 1 and No. 2 are true.

7-83. Answer C. JSPT 7B, FPH

Both statements (1) and (2) are true. Rich mixtures are required at idle speeds and at full rated power to aid in engine cooling. However, since there is more airflow over the engine running at its rated power than when the engine is idling, the mixture used at idle is typically richer than the mixture used at rated power.

7-84   AMP023

During idle mixture adjustments, which of the following is normally observed to determine when the correct mixture has been achieved?

A– Changes in fuel/air pressure ratio

B– Fuel flowmeter

C– Changes in RPM or manifold pressure

7-84. Answer C. JSPT 7B, FPH

When adjusting the mixture on an idling engine, you should observe the engine RPM gauge on aircraft with a fixed-pitch propeller and the manifold pressure gauge on aircraft equipped with constant-speed propellers. In either case, the power output will increase to a maximum when the mixture is set properly.

7-85   AMP023
An indication that the optimum idle mixture has been obtained occurs when the mixture control is moved to IDLE CUTOFF and manifold pressure

A– decreases momentarily and RPM drops slightly before the engine ceases to fire.

B– increases momentarily and RPM drops slightly before the engine ceases to fire.

C– decreases and RPM increases momentarily before the engine ceases to fire.

7-85. Answer C. JSPT 7B, FPH
When the mixture is adjusted properly, engine power output will be at maximum as indicated by the manifold pressure gauge. Therefore, when the mixture is moved to the idle cutoff position, it will become excessively lean and engine power will decrease immediately, causing a decrease in manifold pressure. This drop in manifold pressure will allow the engine to momentarily rotate faster causing an increase in RPM before the engine ceases to fire.

7-86   AMP056
The use of less than normal throttle opening during starting will cause

A– a rich mixture.

B– a lean mixture.

C– backfire due to lean fuel/air ratio.

7-86. Answer A. JSPT 7B
The position of the throttle valve determines the amount of air that flows into the engine. When an engine is started, a high vacuum is created on the engine side of the throttle. Therefore, if the throttle valve opening is less than normal at this time, the high vacuum will draw excessive fuel from the idle jet and create a richer than normal mixture.

7-87   AMP023
When checking the idle mixture on a carburetor, the engine should be idling normally, then pull the mixture control toward the IDLE CUTOFF position. A correct idling mixture will be indicated by

A– an immediate decrease in RPM.

B– a decrease of 20 to 30 RPM before quitting.

C– an increase of 10 to 50 RPM before decreasing.

7-87. Answer C. JSPT 7B
On engines that do not use a manifold pressure gauge, you must observe the tachometer for an indication of correct idle mixture. In most cases, the idle mixture should be adjusted so that when the mixture control is pulled toward the idle cutoff position, a 10 to 50 RPM rise occurs prior to a rapid decrease as the engine ceases to fire.

7-88   AMP023

When a new carburetor is installed on an engine,

A– warm up the engine and adjust the float level.

B– do not adjust the idle mixture setting; this was accomplished on the flow bench.

C– and the engine is warmed up to normal temperatures, adjust the idle mixture, then the idle speed.

7-88. Answer C. JSPT 7B, FPH

When a new carburetor is installed on an engine, the idle speed and mixture must be set. These adjustments should be made after the engine has been operating long enough to achieve normal cylinder head temperatures.

7-89   AMP056

Reciprocating engine power will be decreased at all altitudes if the

A– air density is increased.

B– humidity is increased.

C– manifold pressure is increased.

7-89. Answer B. JSPT 7B, FGH

Water vapor is a non-combustible gas. Therefore, when humid air is drawn into an engine, the engine's volumetric efficiency decreases, causing a decrease in engine power.

7-90   AMP038

If the idling jet becomes clogged in a float-type carburetor, the

A– engine operation will not be affected at any RPM.

B– engine will not idle.

C– idle mixture becomes richer.

7-90. Answer B. JSPT 7B, FPH

At low engine speeds there is insufficient airflow through the carburetor to allow the main discharge nozzle to operate properly; therefore, a separate idle jet is installed in the low pressure area between the throttle valve and throttle body to supply fuel for idling. If an idle jet should become clogged, the engine will not idle.

7-91   AMP041

An aircraft engine equipped with a pressure-type carburetor is started with the

A– primer while the mixture control is positioned at IDLE CUTOFF.

B– mixture control in the FULL-RICH position.

C– primer while the mixture control is positioned at the FULL-LEAN position.

7-91. Answer A. JSPT 7B, FGH

Aircraft engines using pressure-type carburetors are generally started using the primer with the mixture control in the idle cutoff position. Then, as soon as the engine starts, the mixture control is moved to the full rich position while the primer is released as soon as the RPM indicates the engine is receiving fuel.

7-92   AMP056

One of the best ways to increase engine power and control detonation and preignition is to

A– enrich the fuel/air mixture.

B– use water injection.

C– lean the fuel/air mixture.

7-92. Answer B. JSPT 7B, FPH

A water injection system adds an alcohol-water compound to the fuel/air mixture to allow an engine to achieve higher manifold pressures and corresponding increase in power without promoting detonation.

7-93   AMP056

An excessively lean fuel/air mixture may cause

A– an increase in cylinder head temperature.

B– high oil pressure.

C– backfiring through the exhaust.

7-93. Answer A. JSPT 7B, FPH

When an engine is operated on a lean mixture, all the fuel in the mixture is used to support combustion and there is no excess fuel left to aid in engine cooling. Therefore, lean fuel/air mixtures typically cause an increase in cylinder head temperatures.

7-94   AMP041

The density of air is very important when mixing fuel and air to obtain a correct fuel-to-air ratio. Which of the following weighs the most?

A– 75 parts of dry air and 25 parts of water vapor

B– 100 parts of dry air

C– 50 parts of dry air and 50 parts of water vapor

7-94. Answer B. JSPT 7B, FGH

For a given volume, air containing water vapor weighs approximately five-eighths as much as dry air. Therefore, 100 percent dry air weighs more than a mixture of dry air and water vapor.

7-95   AMP041

An air/fuel mixture ratio of 11:1 normally refers to

A– a stoichiometric mixture.

B– 1 part air to 11 parts fuel.

C– 1 part fuel to 11 parts air.

7-95. Answer C. JSPT 7B, FPH

In any air/fuel mixture ratio, the larger number always refers to the amount of air in the mixture. Therefore, an air/fuel mixture ratio of 11:1 is 1 part fuel to 11 parts air.

7-96   AMP037

The economizer system in a float-type carburetor

A– keeps the fuel/air ratio constant.

B– functions only at cruise and idle speeds.

C– increases the fuel/air ratio at high power settings.

7-96. Answer C. JSPT 7B, FPH

In order for an engine to effectively operate at high power settings, the fuel/air mixture must be rich so there is additional fuel available to aid in cylinder cooling. On engines equipped with an economizer system, when the throttle is advanced beyond approximately 70 percent power the economizer valve opens and automatically enriches the fuel/air mixture.

7-97   AMP022

A carburetor is prevented from leaning out during quick acceleration by the

A– power enrichment system.

B– mixture control system.

C– accelerating system.

7-97. Answer C. JSPT 7B, FPH

When the throttle valve is opened quickly, a large volume of air rushes into the carburetor. To prevent the fuel/air mixture from becoming excessively lean when the additional air enters the engine, most carburetors are equipped with an accelerating system that provides a momentary burst of fuel to maintain the proper mixture.

7-98   AMP041

What could cause a lean mixture and high cylinder head temperature at sea level or low altitudes?

A– Mixture control valve fully closed

B– Automatic mixture control stuck in the extended position

C– Defective accelerating system

7-98. Answer B. JSPT 7B, FPH

To compensate for decreases in air density, an automatic mixture control decreases fuel flow from the carburetor as an aircraft climbs to higher altitudes. However, if the automatic mixture control were to malfunction and stick in the extended position, the fuel/air mixture would become progressively leaner as the aircraft descends to lower altitudes. With a lean mixture, there is little excess fuel available to aid in engine cooling, so engines that run on a lean mixture typically have high cylinder head temperatures.

7-99   AMP041

Detonation occurs when the air/fuel mixture

A– burns too fast.

B– ignites before the time of normal ignition.

C– is too rich.

7-99. Answer A. JSPT 7B, FPH

Detonation is the explosive, or rapid combustion of unburned fuel in a cylinder that results in an extremely rapid pressure rise. Detonation can happen any time an engine overheats or if the improper fuel grade is used.

7-100   AMP043

A major difference between the Teledyne-Continental and RSA (Precision Airmotive or Bendix) continuous flow fuel injection systems in fuel metering is that the

A– RSA system uses air pressure only as a metering force.

B– Continental system utilizes airflow as a metering force.

C– Continental system uses fuel pressure only as a metering force.

7-100. Answer C. JSPT 7B

The RSA fuel injection system relies on both air and fuel forces to provide the correct pressure differential across the primary metering jet. The Teledyne-Continental injection system, on the other hand, uses a special fuel pump to produce the fuel metering pressure.

7-101   AMP043

The function of the altitude compensating, or aneroid valve used with the Teledyne-Continental fuel injection system on many turbocharged engines is to

A– prevent an overly rich mixture during sudden acceleration.

B– prevent detonation at high altitudes.

C– provide a means of enriching the mixture during sudden acceleration.

7-101. Answer A. JSPT 7B

Some Teledyne Continental fuel injection systems employ an altitude compensating aneroid valve to prevent an overly rich mixture during sudden acceleration. To accomplish this, an evacuated bellows responds to upper deck pressure to control the size of a variable orifice. When the throttle is suddenly opened, the aneroid holds the orifice open until the volume of air flowing into the engine increases.

7-102   AMP041

The primary purpose of the air bleed openings used with continuous flow fuel injector nozzles is to

A– provide for automatic mixture control.

B– lean out the mixture.

C– aid in proper fuel vaporization.

7-102. Answer C. JSPT 7B, FPH

Some continuous flow fuel injector nozzles have air bleed holes that allow air to mix with fuel to help vaporize the fuel.

7-103   AMP056
(Refer to figure 6.)

Which curve most nearly represents an aircraft engine's fuel/air ratio throughout its operating range?

A– 1

B– 3

C– 2

7-103. Answer C. JSPT 7B, FPH
At idle speeds, an engine requires a rich fuel/air mixture so there is additional fuel available for cooling. However, as engine speed is increased to a cruise setting, the additional ram airflow created by the propeller and forward section of the aircraft cool the engine sufficiently and fuel requirements decrease. Then, as power output approaches maximum, additional fuel is again required to aid in cooling and help prevent detonation. Based on this, curve number two best represents an aircraft engine's fuel/air ratio throughout its operating range.

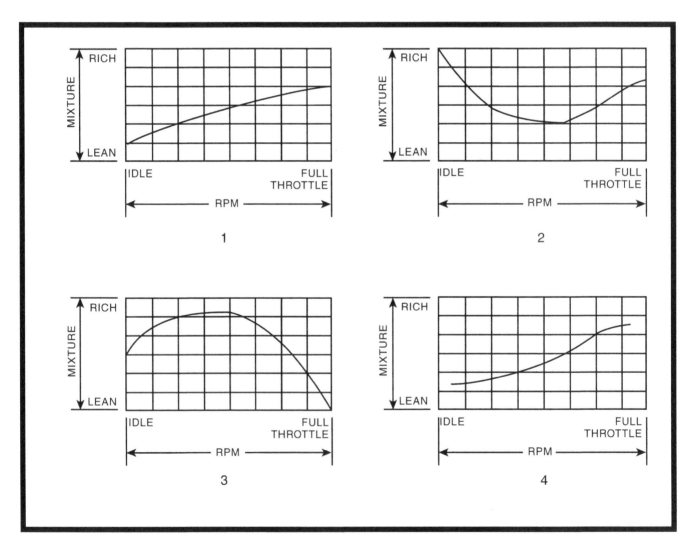

Figure 6. Fuel / Air Ratio Graphs.

7-104   AMP041

A pilot reports that the fuel pressure fluctuates and exceeds the upper limits whenever the throttle is advanced. The most likely cause of the trouble is

A– a ruptured fuel pump relief-valve diaphragm.

B– a sticking fuel pump relief valve.

C– an air leak at the fuel pump relief-valve body.

7-104. Answer B. JSPT 7B, FGH

During normal operation, the fuel pump delivers more fuel than the engine needs and, therefore, a fuel pump relief valve must be used to prevent excessive pressures from reaching the carburetor inlet. The relief valve is held closed by spring tension and, once opened by excessive fuel pressure, directs fuel back to the pump inlet. If a relief valve sticks closed when an engine accelerates, excessive fuel pressure will build until the relief valve opens. Therefore, a sticking fuel pump relief valve will cause fluctuating fuel pressure readings and, if the relief valve sticks enough, excessive pressure readings.

7-105   AMP038

If an engine equipped with a float-type carburetor backfires or misses when the throttle is advanced, a likely cause is that the

A– float level is too high.

B– main air bleed is clogged.

C– accelerating pump is not operating properly.

7-105. Answer C. JSPT 7B

When a carburetor's throttle valve is opened quickly, a large volume of air rushes into the carburetor. To prevent an excessively lean mixture from developing when this occurs, float-type carburetors employ an accelerator pump that injects a momentary burst of fuel into the engine to maintain the proper fuel/air mixture. If an accelerator pump does not operate properly, an excessively lean mixture that can lead to backfiring and missing will result when the throttle is advanced rapidly.

7-106   AMP038

How often should float carburetors be overhauled?

A– At engine overhaul

B– Annually

C– At engine change

7-106. Answer A. JSPT 7B

Although float carburetors typically have no required overhaul period, good operating practice dictates that a carburetor be completely overhauled when the engine is overhauled. Operating beyond this point can result in poor fuel metering, which could lead to detonation and subsequent damage to a freshly overhauled engine. Overhauling a carburetor on an annual basis would be a wasteful and unnecessary expense.

7-107   AMP038

What is the final authority for the details of carburetor overhaul?

A– The local FAA safety inspector

B– The Type Certificate Data Sheet for the engine

C– The manufacturer's recommendations

7-107. Answer C. JSPT 7B

A carburetor manufacturer's recommendations are FAA approved and represent the final authority for maintaining a carburetor. Only those alterations or repairs that are in the manufacturer's maintenance materials should be made.

7-108   AMP056

Excessively rich or lean idle mixtures result in

A– too rapid completion of combustion.

B– incomplete combustion.

C– incomplete cylinder scavenging.

7-108. Answer B. JSPT 7B

Excessively rich or lean idle mixtures typically result in incomplete combustion. For example, with an excessively rich mixture carbon deposits form on the spark plugs and cause subsequent plug fouling. Excessively lean mixtures, on the other hand, can burn so slowly that combustion can carry into the intake stroke and cause backfiring.

7-109   AMP042

Which statement is true regarding proper throttle rigging of an airplane?

A– The throttle stop on the carburetor must be contacted before the stop in the cockpit

B– The stop in the cockpit must be contacted before the stop on the carburetor

C– The throttle control is properly adjusted when neither stop makes contact

7-109. Answer A. JSPT 7B

Throttle and mixture controls must operate freely throughout their full range of travel, and the stops on the carburetor must be contacted before the cockpit control reaches its stop. Springback in the control system ensures that the carburetor control is fully actuated.

7-110   AMP023

What precaution should be taken when putting thread lubricant on a tapered pipe plug in a carburetor float bowl?

A– Put the thread lubricant only on the first thread.

B– Do not use thread lubricant on any carburetor fitting.

C– Engage the first thread of the plug, then put a small amount of lubricant on the second thread and screw the plug in.

7-110. Answer C. JSPT 7B

The use of thread lubricant on a float bowl plug helps prevent thread damage and provide a better seal. However, it is important that no thread lubricant be allowed to enter the carburetor bowl since the lubricant is insoluble and, therefore, can plug the fuel jets. When applying a thread lubricant, begin by screwing the plug one turn into the float bowl and applying lubricant to the second thread. This helps ensure that no lubricant enters the carburetor interior.

7-111   AMP056

Maximum power is normally considered to be developed in a reciprocating engine with an air/fuel mixture ratio of approximately

A– 8:1

B– 12:1

C– 15:1

7-111. Answer B. JSPT 7B, FPH

Valve timing and engine induction system design require a slightly rich mixture in order to produce maximum power. This mixture typically contains 12 parts air to every 1 part fuel, or 12:1.

7-112   AMP021

When operating an engine, the application of carburetor heat will have what effect on the fuel/air mixture?

A– Enriching the mixture because the AMC cannot make a correction for increased temperature

B– Enriching the mixture until the AMC can make a compensation

C– Leaning the mixture until the AMC can make a compensation

7-112. Answer B. JSPT 7B, FPH

When carburetor heat is turned on, warm, less dense air is drawn into the carburetor. However, if the mixture is not adjusted, the same amount of fuel continues to mix with the air. The combination of less dense air with no change in the amount of fuel supplied produces a mixture that is richer than it was before carburetor heat was applied. However, on carburetors equipped with an automatic mixture control (AMC) the mixture will only remain rich until the AMC can compensate.

SECTION C — TURBINE ENGINE FUEL METERING

Section C of Chapter 7 covers turbine engine fuel control units and fuel system components that are specific to turbine engine aircraft such as fuel heaters, dump valves, and other similar items.

7-113   AMP068
Which of the following influences the operation of an automatic fuel control unit on a turbojet engine?

A– Burner pressure

B– Mixture control position

C– Exhaust gas temperature

7-113. Answer A. JSPT 7C, FPH
Some of the variables that an automatic fuel control unit senses include the power lever position, engine RPM, either compressor inlet pressure or temperature, and burner pressure or compressor discharge pressure.

7-114   AMP068
What is the purpose of the dump valve used on aircraft gas turbine engines?

A– The fuel is quickly cut off to the nozzles and the manifolds are drained preventing fuel boiling as a result of residual engine heat.

B– The valve controls compressor stalls by dumping compressor bleed air from the compressor discharge port under certain conditions.

C– Maintains minimum fuel pressure to the engine fuel control unit inlet and dumps excessive fuel back to the inlet of the engine driven fuel pump.

7-114. Answer A. JSPT 7C, FPH
The dump valve is part of the fuel system in a turbine engine that automatically dumps fuel pressure at engine shut down. This prevents fuel boiling due to residual engine heat.

7-115   AMP068
A condition known as "hot streaking" in turbine engines is caused by

A– a partially clogged fuel nozzle.

B– a misaligned combustion liner.

C– excessive fuel flow.

7-115. Answer A. JSPT 7C, FPH
The term hot streaking describes a condition where a fuel nozzle shoots out an unatomized stream of fuel which can contact the combustion liner or other components creating hot spots.

7-116 AMP068

What factor is not used in the operation of an aircraft gas turbine engine fuel control unit?

A– Compressor inlet air temperature

B– Mixture control position

C– Power lever position

7-116. Answer B. JSPT 7C, FPH

Automatic fuel control units sense power lever position, engine RPM, compressor inlet air temperature and density, and burner pressure or discharge pressure. Since turbine engine aircraft do not utilize a mixture control, it is not a factor in the operation of the fuel control unit.

7-117 AMP069

In order to stabilize cams, springs, and linkages within the fuel control, manufacturers generally recommend that all final turbine engine trim adjustments be made in the

A– increase direction.

B– decrease direction.

C– decrease direction after over-adjustment.

7-117. Answer A. JSPT 7C

In order to stabilize internal components and ensure consistent results, most engine manufacturers specify that all trim adjustments be made in the increase direction. In other words, the engine will idle at a value just above the minimum idle speed and maximum thrust will be obtained slightly before the power levers reach the full forward position.

7-118 AMP069

When trimming a turbine engine, the fuel control is adjusted to

A– produce as much power as the engine is capable of producing.

B– set idle RPM and maximum speed or EPR.

C– allow the engine to produce maximum RPM without regard to power output.

7-118. Answer B. JSPT 7C, FPH

Field adjustments, or trimming adjustments made to turbine engine fuel controls are limited to idle RPM and maximum speed adjustments.

7-119 AMP068

A supervisory electronic engine control (EEC) is a system that receives engine operating information and

A– adjusts a standard hydromechanical fuel control unit to obtain the most effective engine operation.

B– develops the commands to various actuators to control engine parameters.

C– controls engine operation according to ambient temperature, pressure, and humidity.

7-119. Answer A. JSPT 7C

A supervisory electronic engine control (EEC) includes a computer that monitors several engine operating criteria and uses this information to adjust a standard hydromechanical fuel control unit (FCU) to obtain a constant thrust for a given power lever position.

7-120   AMP068

A full-authority electronic engine control (EEC) is a system that receives all the necessary data for engine operation and

A— adjusts a standard hydromechanical fuel control unit to obtain the most effective engine operation.

B— develops the commands to various actuators to control engine parameters.

C— controls engine operation according to ambient temperature, pressure, and humidity.

7-120. Answer B. JSPT 7C

A full-authority electronic engine control (EEC) performs all of the functions required to operate an engine. In other words, it receives data from the aircraft and engine systems and then issues commands to various actuators that control engine operating parameters.

7-121   AMP068

In a supervisory EEC system, any fault in the EEC that adversely affects engine operation

A— causes redundant or backup units to take over and continue normal operation.

B— usually degrades performance to the extent that continued operation can cause damage to the engine.

C— causes an immediate reversion to control by the hydromechanical fuel control unit.

7-121. Answer C. JSPT 7C

Any fault in a supervisory electronic engine control (EEC) automatically causes the EEC to relinquish engine control to the hydromechanical control unit. At the same time, the EEC sends a signal to the cockpit that illuminates an annunciator light to inform the flight crew of the change in operating mode.

7-122   AMP069

What should be checked/changed to ensure the validity of a turbine engine performance check if an alternate fuel is to be used?

A— Fuel specific gravity setting

B— Maximum RPM adjustment

C— EPR gauge calibration

7-122. Answer A. FGH

Turbine engines are designed to operate using a specific type of fuel with a given BTU value and specific gravity. Therefore, if a performance check is made on an engine using an alternate fuel, the specific gravity setting should be checked and changed as necessary on the fuel control unit to ensure proper performance.

7-123   AMP069

The generally acceptable way to obtain accurate on-site temperature prior to performing engine trimming is to

A— call the control tower to obtain field temperature.

B— observe the reading on the aircraft Outside Air Temperature (OAT) gauge.

C— hang a thermometer in the shade of the nose wheel-well until the temperature reading stabilizes.

7-123. Answer C. JSPT 7C, TEP2

Part of the procedure used for trimming an engine includes measuring engine inlet barometric pressure and ambient temperature. To ensure a temperature value that is accurate, it is common practice to hang a thermometer in the shade of the nose wheel-well.

7-124   AMP069

An aircraft should be facing into the wind when trimming an engine. However, if the velocity of the wind blowing into the intake is excessive, it is likely to cause a

A— false low exhaust gas temperature reading.

B— trim setting resulting in engine overspeed.

C— false high compression and turbine discharge pressure, and a subsequent low trim.

7-124. Answer C. JSPT 7C, TEP2

Facing an engine into a strong wind produces the same effect as improving the efficiency of the engine's compressor. Therefore, if an engine is trimmed while facing into an excessive wind, a false high compression and turbine discharge pressure, as well as a subsequent low trim are likely to occur.

7-125   AMP069

Generally, the practice when trimming an engine is to

A— turn all accessory bleed air off.

B— turn all accessory bleed air on.

C— make adjustments (as necessary) for all engines on the same aircraft with accessory bleed air settings the same—either on or off.

7-125. Answer A. JSPT 7C, FPH

When high-pressure air is bled from the compressor for various aircraft functions, it has the same effect as decreasing the compressor's efficiency. Therefore, if a trim adjustment is made with the bleeds on, an inaccurate or overtrimmed condition will result. Because of this, most engine manufacturers require that an engine be trimmed with the engine bleeds off.

7-126   AMP069

For what primary purpose is a turbine engine fuel control unit trimmed?

A— To obtain maximum thrust output when desired

B— To properly position the power levers

C— To adjust the idle RPM

7-126. Answer A. JSPT 7C, FPH

The primary reason for trimming a turbine engine is to ensure that the desired thrust is obtained when the power lever is in the full power position.

7-127   AMP041
Which type of fuel control is used on most of today's turbine engines?

A– Electromechanical

B– Mechanical

C– Hydromechanical or electronic

7-127. Answer C. JSPT 7C, FPH
Most fuel controls in use today are hydromechanical or electronic.

7-128   AMP069
Under which of the following conditions will the trimming of a turbine engine be most accurate?

A– High wind and high moisture

B– High moisture and low wind

C– No wind and low moisture

7-128. Answer C. JSPT 7C, FPH
The ideal conditions for trimming a turbine engine are no wind, low humidity, and standard temperature and pressure. Because standard day conditions seldom exist, engine manufacturers produce trim charts to compensate for nonstandard conditions.

7-129   AMP041
In turbine engines that utilize a pressurization and dump valve, the dump portion of the valve

A– cuts off fuel flow to the engine fuel manifold and dumps the manifold fuel into the combustor to burn just before the engine shuts down.

B– drains the engine manifold lines to prevent fuel boiling and subsequent deposits in the lines as a result of residual engine heat (at engine shutdown).

C– dumps extra fuel into the engine in order to provide for quick engine acceleration during rapid throttle advancement.

7-129. Answer B. JSPT 7C, FPH
With aircraft that utilize a pressurization and dump valve the "dump" feature refers to the dumping of fuel from the fuel manifold after engine shutdown. Manifold dumping sharply cuts off combustion and drains the manifold lines of fuel to prevent fuel boiling and eliminate solid deposits in the manifold.

7-130   AMP068
Which of the following is NOT an input parameter for a turbine engine fuel control unit?

A– Compressor inlet pressure

B– Compressor inlet temperature

C– Ambient humidity

7-130. Answer C. JSPT 7C, FPH
A typical fuel control senses a number of engine variables, depending upon the installation. For example, a standard fuel control unit can sense engine speed, inlet pressure, compressor discharge pressure, burner can pressure, and compressor inlet temperature. Based on this, the only choice listed that is not an input parameter for a fuel control unit is ambient humidity.

7-131   AMP041

What are the principal advantages of the duplex fuel nozzle used in many turbine engines?

A– Restricts the amount of fuel flow to a level where more efficient and complete burning of the fuel is achieved.

B– Provides better atomization and uniform flow pattern.

C– Allows a wider range of fuels and filters to be used.

7-131. Answer B. JSPT 7C, FPH

The principal advantages of duplex fuel nozzles over simplex fuel nozzles are that duplex nozzles provide better fuel atomization and a more uniform flow pattern at low engine speeds.

7-132   AMP068

It is necessary to control acceleration and deceleration rates in turbine engines in order to

A– prevent blowout or die-out.

B– prevent overtemperature.

C– prevent friction between turbine wheels and the case due to expansion and contraction.

7-132. Answer A. JSPT 7C, FPH

Because of the large changes in airflow associated with changes in power settings, turbine engines do not respond well to rapid power changes. For example, too rapid an acceleration or deceleration could cause a compressor stall, which could lead to a rich blowout or lean die out.

7-133   AMP041

What is the purpose of the flow divider in a turbine engine duplex fuel nozzle?

A– Allows an alternate flow of fuel if the primary flow clogs or is restricted.

B– Creates the primary and secondary fuel supplies.

C– Provides a flow path for bleed air which aids in the atomization of fuel.

7-133. Answer B. JSPT 7C, FPH

The flow divider in a duplex fuel nozzle divides the fuel supply into a primary and secondary flow that discharge through separate, concentric spray tips. Primary fuel flows at all power settings, while secondary fuel flows only when fuel pressure builds enough to unseat the flow divider.

7-134   AMP041

What causes the fuel divider valve to open in a turbine engine duplex fuel nozzle?

A– Fuel pressure

B– Bleed air after the engine reaches idle RPM

C– An electrically operated solenoid

7-134. Answer A. JSPT 7C, FPH

The flow divider in a turbine engine duplex fuel nozzle opens when the fuel pressure reaches approximately 90 PSIG. Once open, fuel is directed into the secondary chamber in the fuel nozzle and then discharges through the secondary tip into the combustion liner.

7-135   AMP041

What are the positions of the pressurization valve and the dump valve in a jet engine fuel system when the engine is shut down?

A— Pressurization valve closed, dump valve open

B— Pressurization valve open, dump valve open

C— Pressurization valve closed, dump valve closed

7-135. Answer A. JSPT 7C, FPH

The dump valve opens at shutdown to drain the fuel manifold. This prevents fuel from falling into the combustion cans and possibly causing an after-fire or carbonization of the fuel nozzles.

ELECTRICAL, STARTING, AND IGNITION SYSTEMS

CHAPTER 8

SECTION A — GENERATORS

Section A of Chapter 8 contains information related to D.C. generator theory, operation, maintenance, and troubleshooting.

8-1   AMP044

What device is used to convert alternating current, which has been induced into the loops of the rotating armature of a DC generator, to direct current?

A– A rectifier

B– A commutator

C– An inverter

8-1. Answer B. JSPT 8A, FGH

By replacing the slip rings of a basic AC generator with two half-cylinders, called a commutator, DC current is obtained. As the generator's armature rotates, the commutator elements act as a switch causing the current to flow in the same direction through the external circuit.

8-2   AMP044

The stationary field strength in a direct current generator is varied

A– by the reverse-current relay.

B– because of generator speed.

C– according to the load requirements.

8-2. Answer C. JSPT 8A, FGH

The stationary field strength in a direct-current generator is varied according to the load requirements. For example, as the load increases, the voltage regulator automatically increases the field current to allow the generator to provide the required current load.

8-3   AMP044

If a generator is malfunctioning, its voltage can be reduced to residual by actuating the

A– rheostat.

B– generator master switch.

C– master solenoid.

8-3. Answer B. JSPT 8A, FGH

A generator master switch is provided in most aircraft so that a malfunctioning generator may be disconnected from the aircraft electrical system to prevent damage to the generator or to the rest of the system. Operation of this switch deactivates the voltage coil in the voltage regulator, resulting in generator output being reduced to residual voltage.

8-4   AMP006

Aircraft that operate more than one generator connected to a common electrical system must be provided with

A– automatic generator switches that operate to isolate any generator whose output is less than 80 percent of its share of the load.

B– an automatic device that will isolate nonessential loads from the system if one of the generators fails.

C– individual generator switches that can be operated from the cockpit during flight.

8-4. Answer C. JSPT 8A, FAR 25.1351

According to FAR 25.1351, aircraft equipped with more than one generator connected to a common electrical system must have individual generator switches which can be operated from the cockpit during flight.

8-5   AMP044

The most effective method of regulating aircraft direct current generator output is to vary, according to the load requirements, the

A– strength of the stationary field.

B– generator speed.

C– number of rotating armature loops in use.

8-5. Answer A. JSPT 8A, FGH

Although all of the choices listed can be used to regulate generator output, varying the strength of the stationary field is the most effective and convenient means.

8-6   AMP044

As the generator load is increased (within its rated capacity), the voltage will

A– decrease and the amperage output will increase.

B– remain constant and the amperage output will increase.

C– remain constant and the amperage output will decrease.

8-6. Answer B. JSPT 8A, FGH

Generators are designed to operate at a specified voltage while generator ratings are usually given as the number of amperes a generator can supply at its rated voltage. Therefore, as the load on a generator increases, the amperage output increases up to the generator's limit, while the voltage remains constant.

8-7 AMP044
As the flux density in the field of a DC generator increases and the current flow to the system increases, the

A— generator voltage decreases.

B— generator amperage decreases.

C— force required to turn the generator increases.

8-7. Answer C. JSPT 8A, FAH
The greater the flux density in the field of a generator the greater the resistance to rotation. The greater the resistance to rotation the greater the force required to turn the generator.

8-8 AMP044
What is the purpose of a reverse-current cutout relay?

A— It eliminates the possibility of reversed polarity of the generator output current.

B— It prevents fluctuations of generator voltage.

C— It opens the main generator circuit whenever the generator voltage drops below the battery voltage.

8-8. Answer C. JSPT 8A, FGH
The purpose of the reverse-current cutout relay is to automatically disconnect the battery from the generator when generator output voltage is less than battery voltage. This prevents the battery from discharging through the generator and trying to drive it as a motor.

8-9 AMP026
Generator voltage will not build up when the field is flashed and solder is found on the brush cover plate.

These are most likely indications of

A— an open armature.

B— excessive brush arcing.

C— armature shaft bearings overheating.

8-9. Answer A. JSPT 8A, FGH
If voltage does not build when a generator's field is flashed, check for an open armature. To do this, remove the generator cover and inspect the commutator cover. If melted solder is found, then the armature is open.

8-10 AMP006
The reason for flashing the field in a generator is to

A— restore correct polarity and/or residual magnetism to the field poles.

B— increase generator capacity.

C— remove excessive deposits.

8-10. Answer A. JSPT 8A, FGH
Generators use field coils wrapped around soft iron cores to produce the magnetic field required to generate current. Soft iron retains little or no residual magnetism when the magnetizing field is removed. As a result, generator fields must be flashed to restore residual magnetism.

8-11   AMP026
The generating system of an aircraft charges the battery by using

A— constant current and varying voltage.

B— constant voltage and varying current.

C— constant voltage and constant current.

8-11. Answer B. JSGT 3C, FGH
A typical aircraft generating system produces a constant voltage that supplies power to the primary bus and charges the battery. This type of system utilizes a fixed voltage that is slightly higher than the battery voltage.

8-12   AMP006
It is necessary to determine that the electrical load limit of a 28-volt, 75-amp generator, installed in a particular aircraft, has not been exceeded. By making a ground check, it is determined that the battery furnished 57 amperes to the system when all equipment that can continuously draw electrical power in flight is turned on. This type of load determination

A— can be made, but the load will exceed the generator load limit.

B— can be made, and the load will be within the generator load limit.

C— cannot be made on direct current electrical systems.

8-12. Answer B. JSPT 8A, AC 43.13-1B
The electrical load check described in this question is an acceptable method for determining an aircraft's total electrical load. According to AC 43.13-1B, unless the aircraft is placarded or contains monitoring devices, the total continuous electrical load may be held to approximately 80% of the total rated generator output capacity. The total load on the system is only 76 percent of the generator's capacity. Therefore, the load is considered to be within the generator's load limit.

8-13   AMP044
Which of the following is regulated in a generator to control its voltage output?

A— Speed of the armature

B— Number of windings in the armature

C— The strength of the field

8-13. Answer C. JSPT 8A, FGH
Although all of the choices listed can be used to regulate generator output, varying the strength of the stationary field is the most effective and convenient means.

8-14   AMP006
Arcing at the brushes and burning of the commutator of a motor may be caused by

A— weak brush springs.

B— excessive brush spring tension.

C— low mica.

8-14. Answer A. JSPT 8A, FGH
Weak or worn brush springs allow the brushes to bounce, resulting in arcing and burned or pitted commutator surfaces.

8-15   AMP044

The maximum allowable voltage drop between the generator and the bus bar is

A– 1 percent of the regulated voltage.

B– 2 percent of the regulated voltage.

C– less than the voltage drop permitted between the battery and the bus bar.

8-15. Answer B. JSPT 8A, AC 43.13-1B

According to AC 43.13-1A, the voltage drop in the main power wires from the generator or the battery to the bus should not exceed 2 percent of the regulated voltage when the generator is carrying rated current or the battery is being discharged at the 5-minute rate.

8-16   AMP001

What speed must an eight-pole AC generator turn to produce 400-Hertz AC?

A– 400 RPM

B– 1,200 RPM

C– 6,000 RPM

8-16. Answer C. JSGT 3D, FGH

The frequency of AC produced by an AC generator is determined by the number of poles and the speed of the rotor and can be calculated using the formula:

$F = (P \div 2) \times (N \div 60)$

Where:

F = frequency of the AC in Hertz

P = number of poles in the rotating field

N = rotational speed of the generator in RPM

To solve for N, the formula becomes:

$N = (F \times 60) \div (P \div 2)$

Therefore:

$N = 400 \times 60 \div (8 \div 2)$

$N = 24,000 \div 4$

$N = 6,000$ RPM

8-17   AMP026

If the points in a vibrator-type voltage regulator stick in the closed position while the generator is operating, what will be the probable result?

A– Generator output voltage will decrease.

B– Generator output voltage will not be affected.

C– Generator output voltage will increase.

8-17. Answer C. JSPT 8A, AC65-9A

The opening and closing of the points in a vibrating-type voltage regulator controls the generator output. When the points are open, generator output decreases and when the points are closed, generator output increases. Therefore, if the points stick closed, the generator's output will increase to its maximum.

SECTION B — ALTERNATORS

Section B of Chapter 8 contains information related to AC generator (alternator) theory, operation, maintenance, and troubleshooting.

8-18   AMP001

Upon what does the output frequency of an AC generator (alternator) depend?

A– The speed of rotation and the strength of the field

B– The speed of rotation, the strength of the field, and the number of field poles

C– The speed of rotation and the number of field poles

8-18. Answer C. JSPT 8B, FGH

The output frequency of an alternator depends on the rotational speed of the rotor and the number of poles. The faster the rotor turns, the higher the frequency generated. By the same token, the more poles on a rotor, the higher the frequency for any given speed.

8-19   AMP001

Alternators (AC generators) that are driven by a constant-speed drive (CSD) mechanism are used to regulate the alternator to a constant

A– voltage output.

B– amperage output.

C– hertz output.

8-19. Answer C. JSPT 8B, FGH

Components that utilize alternators (AC generators) as a source for power, require a specific frequency or hertz output to function properly. One way to ensure that an alternator produces a specified frequency is to have the alternator driven by a constant speed drive (CSD) unit.

8-20   AMP001

Why is a constant-speed drive used to control the speed of some aircraft engine-driven generators?

A– So that the voltage output of the generator will remain within limits

B– To eliminate uncontrolled surges of current to the electrical system

C– So that the frequency of the alternating current output will remain constant

8-20. Answer C. JSPT 8B, FGH

Components that utilize alternators (AC generators) as a source of power require a specific frequency or number of cycles per second to function properly. One way to ensure that an alternator produces a specified frequency is to have the alternator driven by a constant speed drive (CSD) unit.

8-21　AMP026

According to the electron theory of the flow of electricity, when a properly functioning DC alternator and voltage regulating system is charging an aircraft's battery, the direction of current flow through the battery

A– is into the negative terminal and out the positive terminal.

B– is into the positive terminal and out the negative terminal.

C– cycles back and forth with the number of cycles per second being controlled by the rotational speed of the alternator.

8-21. Answer A. JSGT 3A, FGH

The electron theory of the flow of electricity states that the flow of electrons is from negative to positive. When this theory is applied to a charging battery, the current flow through the battery is from the negative terminal to the positive terminal. The theory of conventional flow states that electrons flow from the positive terminal to the negative terminal and is generally considered incorrect.

8-22　AMP001

Why is it unnecessary to flash the field of the exciter on a brushless alternator?

A– The exciter is constantly charged by battery voltage.

B– Brushless alternators do not have exciters.

C– Permanent magnets are installed in the main field poles.

8-22. Answer C. JSPT 8B, FGH

A brushless alternator utilizes permanent magnet interpoles in the exciter stator to provide enough magnetic flux to start producing electricity. Therefore, there is no need to flash the field to put residual magnetism into the field frame.

8-23　AMP001

How are the rotor windings of an aircraft alternator usually excited?

A– By a constant AC voltage from the battery

B– By a constant AC voltage

C– By a variable direct current

8-23. Answer C. JSPT 8B, FGH

In most brush-type alternators, the rotor winding is excited by direct current supplied by the battery and varied by a regulator. When the alternator load increases, the regulator supplies more current to the rotor windings and when the load decreases, less current is supplied.

8-24   AMP026

What is a basic advantage of using AC for electrical power for a large aircraft?

A– AC systems operate at higher voltage than DC systems and therefore use less current and can use smaller and lighter weight wiring.

B– AC systems operate at lower voltage than DC systems and therefore use less current and can use smaller and lighter weight wiring.

C– AC systems operate at higher voltage than DC systems and therefore use more current and can use smaller and lighter weight wiring.

8-24. Answer A. JSPT 8B, FGH

Electrical power is the product of voltage and current. Since direct current systems produce low voltage, the corresponding current must be large enough to produce sufficient power to sustain heavy electrical loads. As a result, conductors carrying direct current must be large and heavy to carry the high current. Alternating current, on the other hand, utilizes much higher voltages and, therefore, lower currents. Since low current can be carried in smaller wire, the use of AC power on large aircraft produces substantial weight savings.

8-25   AMP001

1. Alternators are rated in volt-amps, which is a measure of the apparent power being produced by the generator.

2. Alternating current has the advantage over direct current in that its voltage and current can easily be stepped up or down.

Regarding the above statements,

A– only No. 1 is true.

B– only No. 2 is true.

C– both No. 1 and No. 2 are true.

8-25. Answer C. JSPT 8B, FGH

Both statements (1) and (2) are correct. Alternating current is used on large aircraft to take advantage of the weight savings and the fact that AC can be easily stepped up or down. The alternators used in these systems are rated in volt-amps which are generally expressed in kilo-volt amps (KVA). A typical Boeing 727 AC alternator is rated at 45 KVA.

8-26   AMP026

What is the frequency of most aircraft alternating current?

A– 115-Hertz

B– 60-Hertz

C– 400-Hertz

8-26. Answer C. JSPT 8B, FGH

Most aircraft systems use 400-Hertz alternating current. At this high frequency, inductive reactance is high and current is low. As a result, motors can be wound with smaller wire, and transformers can be made much smaller and lighter.

8-27 AMP001

The part of a DC alternator power system that

prevents reverse flow of current from the battery to the alternator is the

A– reverse current relay.

B– voltage regulator.

C– rectifier.

8-27. Answer C. JSGT 4B, FGH

An alternator uses solid-state diodes in its rectifier circuit. These diodes act as electrical check valves and allow current to only flow in one direction. This isolates battery current from the alternator. Reverse current relays are used only with DC generators and voltage regulators supply current to the field to match the generator's output current to load demand.

SECTION C — MOTORS AND STARTING SYSTEMS

This section covers the theory of operation, maintenance, and troubleshooting of electric motors including starters, fuel pump motors, and turbine engine starter-generators.

8-28   AMP025
A certain direct current series motor mounted within an aircraft draws more amperes during start than when it is running under its rated load. The most logical conclusion that may be drawn is

A– the starting winding is shorted.

B– the brushes are floating at operating RPM because of weak brush springs.

C– the condition is normal for this type of motor.

8-28. Answer C. JSPT 8C, FGH
Because the windings in a series motor have such a low resistance, it is normal for these motors to draw a large amount when started. However, when this starting current passes through both the field and armature windings, a high starting torque is produced.

8-29   AMP025
What type of electric motor is generally used with a direct-cranking engine starter?

A– Direct current, shunt-wound motor

B– Direct current, series-wound motor

C– Synchronous motor

8-29. Answer B. JSPT 8C, FPH
A series-wound motor produces the highest torque of any of the motors listed. Furthermore, a typical starter motor is operated by a 12- or 24-volt direct current battery. Therefore, the most common starter found on reciprocating engines is a direct current series-wound motor.

8-30   AMP025
A high surge of current is required when a DC electric motor is first started. As the speed of the motor increases,

A– the counter EMF decreases proportionally.

B– the applied EMF increases proportionally.

C– the counter EMF builds up and opposes the applied EMF, thus reducing the current flow through the armature.

8-30. Answer C. JSPT 8C, FGH
When an armature in a motor rotates in a magnetic field, a voltage is induced into the windings that opposes the applied voltage. This back, or counter electromotive force (EMF) increases with motor speed and, therefore, reduces the current flowing through the armature.

8-31   AMP026

Electric motors are often classified according to the method of connecting the field coils and armature. Aircraft engine starter motors are generally of which type?

A– Compound

B– Series

C– Shunt (parallel)

8-31. Answer B. JSPT 8C, FPH

Of the types of motors listed, the series-wound motor develops the most torque. Therefore, series motors are generally used as starter motors.

8-32   AMP026

What are two types of AC motors that are used to produce a relatively high torque?

A– Shaded pole and shunt field

B– Shunt field and single phase

C– Three-phase induction and capacitor start

8-32. Answer C. JSPT 8C, FGH

The most common AC motors that produce a relatively high torque are the three-phase induction motor and the capacitor start motor.

8-33   AMP026

Which of the following aircraft circuits does NOT contain a fuse/circuit breaker?

A– Generator circuit

B– Air-conditioning circuit

C– Starter circuit

8-33. Answer C. JSPT 8C, FGH

An aircraft starter circuit does not have a fuse or circuit breaker because the current draw is so great that a fuse or circuit breaker would continually be blowing. Although generator circuits and air conditioning circuits draw high amperages, they use considerably less current than a starter and, therefore, use circuit breakers or fuses to protect the aircraft wiring.

8-34   AMP006

As a general rule, starter brushes are replaced when they are approximately

A– one-half their original length.

B– one-third their original length.

C– two-thirds their original length.

8-34. Answer A. JSGT 4C, FPH

Manufacturers specify the exact wear limits for their parts. However, as a general rule, starter brushes should be replaced when they are worn to approximately one-half of their original length. Allowing the wear to progress much farther will affect the spring tension and the ability of the brush to stay in contact with the commutator.

8-35   AMP068

When the starter switch to the aircraft gas turbine engine starter-generator is energized and the engine fails to rotate, one of the probable causes would be the

A– power lever switch is defective.

B– undercurrent solenoid contacts are defective.

C– starter solenoid is defective.

8-35. Answer C. JSPT 8C

Although the FAA does not list a figure to refer to for this question, it may be helpful to use figure 8-1 in this book. When the master switch is on and the start switch is placed in the start position, power is supplied to the starter generator. However, if the starter solenoid is defective, the starter will not rotate.

8-36   AMP026

(Refer to figure 5 on page 8-13.)

The type of system depicted is capable of operating with

A– external power only.

B– either battery or external power.

C– battery power and external power simultaneously.

8-36. Answer B. JSPT 8C

The system illustrated may be operated with either battery power or external power, but not both at the same time. To prevent both an external power source and the battery from operating simultaneously, an external power receptacle switch is placed just after the battery solenoid coil that removes power from the battery solenoid coil and, ultimately, battery power from the bus when external power is plugged in.

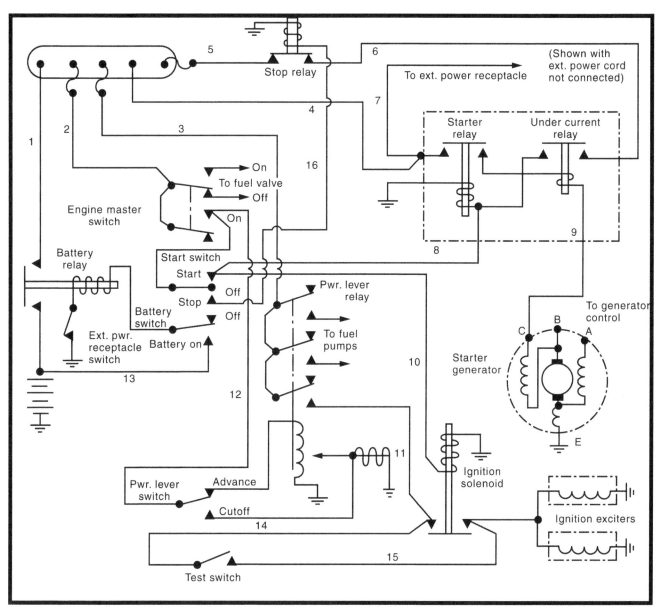

Figure 5. Starter-Generator Circuit

8-37　　AMP068

The purpose of an under current relay in a starter-generator system is to

A– provide a backup for the starter relay

B– disconnect power from the starter-generator and ignition when sufficient engine speed is reached.

C– keep current flow to the starter-generator under the circuit capacity maximum.

8-37. Answer B. JSPT 8C, FPH

In a system that uses an undercurrent relay, an engine start is initiated by placing the start switch in the start position for a few seconds to allow current to close both the starter and undercurrent solenoids. Once these solenoids are closed, the start sequence will support itself and the start switch can be turned off. Then, once the engine speed increases and starter current drops, the undercurrent relay opens to disconnect power from the starter-generator and ignition circuits and enable the generator circuit.

8-38　　AMP065

In a typical starter-generator system, under which of the following starting circumstances may it be necessary to use the start stop switch?

A– Hung start

B– Hot start

C– Contacts stick open

8-38. Answer A. JSPT 8C, FPH

When a hung start occurs, the engine fails to reach a self-sustaining speed and the starter continues to crank the engine. To abort a hung start, the start/stop switch must be pressed or toggled manually to de-energize the starter generator.

8-39　　AMP068

When using an electric starter motor, current usage

A– is highest at the start of motor rotation.

B– remains relatively constant throughout the starting cycle.

C– is highest just before starter cutoff (at highest RPM).

8-39. Answer A. JSPT 8C, FPH

Series-wound motors are typically used for starter motors because they are able to produce a high starting torque. However, this high starting torque requires a great deal of current. On the other hand, as engine and starter speed increase, counter electromotive forces build and limit the amount of current the starter can draw.

8-40　　AMP068

When using an electric starter motor, the current flow through it

A– is highest at the start of motor rotation.

B– remains relatively constant throughout the starting cycle.

C– is highest just before starter cutoff (at highest RPM).

8-40. Answer A. JSPT 8C, FGH

Current provided to a starter is high at the onset of engine rotation and decreases as engine speed builds. The voltage provided to a starter remains relatively constant throughout an engine start.

8-41   AMP026

(Refer to figure 5 on page 8-13.)

Placing the engine master switch and battery switch to the on position and advancing the power lever, allows current to flow from the bus to the

A– fuel valve, start switch, power lever switch, power lever relay coil, fuel pumps, and one side of the ignition relay contactor.

B– fuel valve, external power receptacles, undercurrent relay contacts, starter relay coil, and ignition relay contacts.

C– fuel valve, external power receptacles, power lever switch, power lever relay coil, and ignition relay coil.

8-41. Answer A. JSPT 8C

Closing the battery switch energizes the battery solenoid coil, which closes the battery solenoid and allows current to flow to the bus and one side of the start switch. Closing the engine master switch allows current to flow to the fuel valve and to the power lever switch. Once the power lever is advanced, the power lever switch moves to the Advance position and current flows to the power lever relay coil, causing the power lever relay to close and allow current to flow to the fuel pumps and one side of the ignition relay. Current is not made available to the starter relay or the ignition relay coil until the start switch is placed in the on position.

8-42   AMP026

(Refer to figure 5 on page 8-13.)

With power applied to the bus bar, what switch changes will allow the ignition exciters test switch to function?

A– Engine master switch and power lever switch

B– Engine master switch, start switch, and test switch

C– Engine master switch, battery switch, and power lever switch

8-42. Answer A. JSPT 8C

Only the engine master switch is necessary to be changed in order to allow the ignition exciters test switch to function. With start switch on, the test switch would be inoperative since exciters would already be activated. The test switch would be functional with the master switch and power lever switch on. The answer with master and power lever is chosen over the answer with master, battery and power lever since the battery switch would already be on to provide power to the bus, or if powered by external power, would be inoperative due to the external power receptacle switch.

8-43   AMP026
(Refer to figure 5 on page 8-13.)

If wire No.8 is broken or disconnected after rotation is initiated, and the power lever is advanced, the

A– starting sequence will continue normally.

B– starter will shut down, but the igniters will continue to fire.

C– starting sequence will discontinue.

8-43. Answer A. JSPT 8C
Wire 8 supplies current to the starter solenoid coil which makes the solenoid close. With the starter solenoid closed, power flows from the bus, through the undercurrent solenoid coil and on to the starter generator. Since current is flowing through the undercurrent solenoid coil, the solenoid will close and provide a secondary power source to keep the starter solenoid engaged and, as long as the start switch is closed, the start sequence progressing normally if wire 8 should break or become disconnected.

8-44   AMP026
(Refer to figure 5 on page 8-13.)

When an external power source is connected to the aircraft,

A– the battery cannot be connected to the bus.

B– both battery power and external power are available to the bus.

C– the start relay coil has a path to ground.

8-44. Answer A. JSPT 8C
The system illustrated may be operated with either battery power or external power, but not both at the same time. To prevent both an external power source and the battery from supplying power to the system simultaneously, an external power receptacle switch is placed just after the battery solenoid coil that removes power from the battery solenoid coil and, ultimately, battery power from the bus when external power is plugged in.

8-45   AMP063
The primary advantage of pneumatic (air turbine) starters over comparable electric starters for turbine engines is

A– a decreased fire hazard.

B– reduction gearing not required.

C– high power-to-weight ratio.

8-45. Answer C. JSPT 8C, FPH
The primary advantage of pneumatic starters over electric starters is that pneumatic starters have a much higher power-to-weight ratio. For example, a typical air turbine starter weighs from one-fourth to one-half as much as an electric starter capable of starting the same engine.

8-46   AMP064

A clicking sound heard at engine coast-down in a pneumatic starter incorporating a sprag clutch ratchet assembly is an indication of

A– gear tooth and/or pawl damage.

B– one or more broken pawl springs.

C– the pawls recontacting and riding on the ratchet gear.

8-46. Answer C. JSPT 8C, FPH

In a pneumatic starter that incorporates a sprag clutch ratchet assembly, the pawls are forced inward by small leaf springs to engage the sprag clutch ratchet when the engine is at rest. However, once the engine reaches a given RPM during a start, centrifugal force pulls the pawls outward, disengaging them from the sprag clutch ratchet. On coastdown the springs force the pawls to ride the ratchet gear until the engine comes to a stop.

8-47   AMP063

Pneumatic starters are usually designed with what types of airflow impingement systems?

A– Radial inward flow turbine and axial-flow turbine

B– Centrifugal compressor and axial-flow compressor

C– Double entry centrifugal outward flow and axial-flow turbines

8-47. Answer A. JSPT 8C

Pneumatic starters that utilize a low pressure, high volume air supply typically employ a radial inward flow turbine or an axial-flow turbine.

8-48   AMP064

Inspection of pneumatic starters by maintenance technicians usually includes checking the

A– oil level and magnetic drain plug condition.

B– stator and rotor blades for FOD.

C– rotor alignment.

8-48. Answer A. JSPT 8C

Because of their high rotational speed, pneumatic starters require frequent inspection of their oil level and the condition of their magnetic drain plugs.

8-49   AMP063

Air turbine starters are generally designed so that reduction gear distress or damage may be detected by

A– characteristic sounds from the starter assembly during engine start.

B– breakage of a shear section on the starter drive shaft.

C– inspection of a magnetic chip detector.

8-49. Answer C. JSPT 8C

Most air turbine starters utilize a self-contained lubrication system that incorporates a magnetic chip detector. When inspecting a chip detector, if metallic particles are found, it may indicate internal stress or damage to the starter's reduction gearing.

8-50   AMP063

Airflow to the pneumatic starter from a ground unit is normally prevented from causing starter overspeed during engine start by

A– stator nozzle design that chokes airflow and stabilizes turbine wheel speed.

B– activation of a flyweight cutout switch.

C– a preset timed cutoff of the airflow at the source.

8-50. Answer B. JSPT 8C

In the normal operation of a pneumatic starter, once the starter reaches a predetermined drive speed, the starter's air supply is cut off by a centrifugal cutout flyweight switch. If the cutout switch should fail, most pneumatic starters incorporate a stator nozzle that chokes the incoming airflow supply to stabilize the turbine wheel speed below the burst speed.

8-51   AMP063

A safety feature usually employed in pneumatic starters that is used if the clutch does not release from the engine drive at the proper time during start is the

A– flyweight cutout switch.

B– spring coupling release.

C– drive shaft shear point.

8-51. Answer C. JSPT 8C, FPH

To help protect pneumatic starters from being damaged if the clutch does not release from the engine drive at the proper speed, a drive shaft shear point is typically incorporated.

8-52   AMP063

A safety feature usually employed in direct-cranking starters that is used to prevent the starter from reaching burst speed is the

A– drive shaft shear point.

B– stator nozzle design that chokes airflow and stabilizes turbine wheel speed.

C– spring coupling release.

8-52. Answer C. JSPT 8C

The spring coupling release disengages the starter gear when the engine r.p.m. exceeds the starter limitations.

8-53   AMP065

In the event a pneumatic start valve will not operate and the manual override must be used, the starter T handle must be closed at scheduled starter drop out because

A– the starter will overheat.

B– the starter will overspeed at a given N_2.

C– the starter oil will be blown over board.

8-53. Answer B. JSPT 8C, TEP2

If the pneumatic starter on a turbine engine is inoperative, the engine can be started by manually actuating the start valve. This is typically done by pulling a T-handle on the start valve, turning the T-handle to the OPEN position, and holding it in this position until the start is self-sustaining. If the T-handle is not returned to the CLOSED position after a successful start, the starter will overspeed and fail.

8-54   AMP064

What is used to polish commutators or slip rings?

A– Very fine sandpaper

B– Crocus cloth or fine oilstone

C– Aluminum oxide or garnet paper

8-54. Answer A. JSPT 8C, FGH

A rough or pitted commutator should be smoothed using very fine sandpaper, such as 000, and then cleaned and polished with a clean, dry cloth.

SECTION D — ELECTRICAL SYSTEM COMPONENTS

Section D of Chapter 8 includes information on basic electrical system theory, maintenance practices, and troubleshooting procedures including nickel-cadmium and lead-acid batteries, electrical connectors, wiring, and other similar components

---

8-55   AMP002

What precaution is usually taken to prevent electrolyte from freezing in a lead acid battery?

A– Place the aircraft in a hangar.

B– Remove the battery and keep it under constant charge.

C– Keep the battery fully charged.

8-55. Answer C. AC 43.13-1B, 11-5, 65-9A

As the specific gravity of the electrolyte solution within a battery rises, its freezing point drops. Therefore, in cold climates, the state of charge in a storage battery should be kept at a maximum so it does not freeze.

8-56   AMP002

How many hours will a 140 ampere-hour battery deliver 15 amperes?

A– 1.40 hours

B– 9.33 hours

C– 14.0 hours

8-56. Answer B. JSGT 3C, FGH

The capacity of a storage battery is rated in ampere-hours which is the amount of electricity that can be taken out of a battery when a current of one ampere flows for one hour. This rating indicates the minimum amount of amperes that a battery can put out in one hour. Therefore, a battery that can supply 140 amperes in one hour can deliver 15 amps for 9.33 hours (140 amp-hour ÷ 15 amps = 9.33 hours).

8-57   AMP002

The constant current method of charging a ni-cad battery

A– will bring it up to fully charged in the shortest amount of time.

B– will lead to cell imbalance over a period of time.

C– is the method most effective in maintaining cell balance.

8-57. Answer C. JSGT 3C, FGH

A ni-cad battery can be charged using either the constant current or constant voltage method. With the constant current method the charge takes longer but is more effective in maintaining cell balance.

8-58   AMP006

The maximum number of terminals that may be connected to any one terminal stud in an aircraft electrical system is

A– two.

B– three.

C– four.

8-58. Answer C. JSPT 8D, AC 43.13-1B

According to AC 43.13-1B, no more than four terminals can be attached to a single terminal stud. If more than four terminals must be attached, use two adjacent studs connected by a small metal bus strap.

8-59   AMP006

What is the maximum number of bonding jumper wires that may be attached to one terminal grounded to a flat surface?

A– Two

B– Three

C– Four

8-59. Answer C. JSPT 8D, AC 43.13-1B

According to AC 43.13-1B, no more than four bonding jumper wires should be attached to one terminal that is grounded to a flat surface. If more than four jumper wires are used, a proper ground may not be obtained.

8-60   AMP006

When installing an electrical switch, under which of the following conditions should the switch be derated from its nominal current rating?

A– Conductive circuits

B– Capacitive circuits

C– Direct-current motor circuits

8-60. Answer C.

Electrical switches should be derated from their nominal current rating when they are used to control direct current motors. The reason for this is that DC motors will draw several times their rated current during starting. Therefore, if the switch is not derated, it will not have enough of a safety factor to prevent overloading.

8-61   AMP026

The resistance of the current return path through the aircraft is always considered negligible, provided the

A– voltage drop across the circuit is checked.

B– generator is properly grounded.

C– structure is adequately bonded.

8-61. Answer C. JSPT 8D, FPH

One of the purposes of bonding and grounding an aircraft structure is to provide current return paths. If the bonding and grounding is properly done, there should be virtually no resistance in the return path. Bonding is accomplished using bonding straps and braids.

8-62   AMP006

In order to reduce the possibility of ground shorting the circuits when the connectors are separated for maintenance, the AN and MS electrical connectors should be installed with the

A– socket section on the ground side of the electrical circuit.

B– pin section on the ground side of the electrical circuit.

C– pin section on the positive side of the electrical circuit.

8-62. Answer B. JSPT 8D, FPH

AN and MS electrical connectors consist of a female socket and a male connector with a set of pins. When installing an electrical connector, the socket should be installed on the voltage side while the pin section should be attached to the ground side. When assembled this way, the recessed sockets make it extremely difficult to short or ground a circuit.

8-63   AMP026

When does current flow through the coil of a solenoid-operated electrical switch?

A– Continually, as long as the aircraft's electrical system master switch is on

B– Continually, as long as the control circuit is complete

C– Only until the movable points contact the stationary points

8-63. Answer B. JSPT 8D, FGH

In a solenoid-operated electrical switch, part of the core is movable and is spring loaded open. When the control circuit to the solenoid is completed, a magnetic field pulls the solenoid closed. This completes the primary circuit. When power is removed from the control circuit the magnetic field dissipates causing the movable core to return to its original position and open the circuit. Therefore, as long as the control circuit is complete, current will flow through the coil and the switch will close. Although some solenoid-operated electrical switches are actuated by an aircraft's master switch, many switches have separate control circuits that must be complete before the solenoid closes.

8-64   AMP026

What type of lubricant may be used to aid in pulling electrical wires or cables through conduits?

A– Silicone grease

B– Soapstone talc

C– Rubber lubricant

8-64. Answer B. JSPT 8D

Prior to pulling electrical wires or cables through conduit, soapstone talc is dusted on the cables to act as a lubricant. The talc helps keep the wire from binding and chafing against the walls of the conduit.

8-65   AMP026

Bonding jumpers should be designed and installed in such a manner that they

A– are not subjected to flexing by relative motion of airframe or engine components.

B– provide a low electrical resistance in the ground circuit.

C– prevent buildup of a static electrical charge between the airframe and the surrounding atmosphere.

8-65. Answer B. JSPT 8D, FPH

One of the purposes of bonding jumpers is to provide a ground for electrical circuits. If the bonding and grounding is properly done, there should be virtually no resistance in the return path. Some guidelines to follow when attaching bonding jumpers is to make them as short as possible and install them in such a manner that the resistance of each connection does not exceed 0.003 ohm.

8-66   AMP006

ON-OFF two position engine electrical switches should be installed

A– so that the toggle will move in the same direction as the desired motion of the unit controlled.

B– under a guard.

C– so the ON position is reached by a forward or upward motion.

8-66. Answer C. JSPT 8D, AC 43.13-1B

Hazardous errors in switch operation can be avoided by logical and consistent installation. For example, when two-position on-off switches are installed, they should always be mounted so that the on position is reached by a forward or upward movement. Furthermore, when a switch controls movable aircraft elements such as landing gear or flaps, the switch should move in the same direction as the desired motion.

8-67   AMP026

When selecting an electrical switch for installation in an aircraft circuit utilizing a direct current motor,

A– a switch designed for DC should be chosen.

B– a derating factor should be applied.

C– only switches with screw-type terminal connections should be used.

8-67. Answer B.

Switches should be derated from their nominal current rating when they are used to control direct current motors, inductive circuits, and high in-rush circuits. The reason for this is that these types of circuits can draw several times their rated current when closed, so the switch must be capable of handling this without the contacts burning or welding together.

8-68   AMP026

When installing electrical wiring parallel to a fuel line, the wiring should be

A– in metal conduit.

B– in a non-conductive fire-resistant sleeve.

C– above the fuel line.

8-68. Answer C. JSPT 8D, AC 43.13-1B

An arcing fault between an electric wire and a metallic fluid line can puncture the line and result in a serious fire. Consequently, every effort should be made to physically separate electrical wire from lines or equipment containing oil, fuel, hydraulic fluid, or alcohol. When separation is impractical, locate the electric wire above the flammable fluid line and securely clamp it to the structure. When installed in this manner, a leaking fluid line is less likely to drip onto the electrical wire and ignite.

8-69   AMP026

How many basic types of circuit breakers are used in power plant installation electrical systems?

A– Two

B– Three

C– Four

8-69. Answer B. JSPT 8D

The three basic types of circuit breakers used in aircraft electrical systems are the push-to-reset type, the push/pull type, and the toggle type.

8-70   AMP006

Which Federal Aviation Regulation specifies that each resettable circuit protective device requires a manual operation to restore service after the device has interrupted the circuit?

A– 14 CFR Part 23

B– 14 CFR Part 43

C– 14 CFR Part 91

8-70. Answer A.

14 CFR Part 23, Airworthiness Standards: Normal, Utility, Acrobatic, and Commuter Category Airplanes, specifies the airworthiness standards for the issue of type certificates. Within this part, 14 CFR 23.1357 states that each resettable circuit protection device requires a manual operation to restore service after the device has interrupted the circuit.

8-71   AMP026

Which Federal Aviation Regulation requirement prevents the use of automatic reset circuit breakers?

A— 14 CFR Part 21

B— 14 CFR Part 23

C— 14 CFR Part 91

8-71. Answer B. JSPT 8D, 14 CFR 23.1357

14 CFR Part 23, Airworthiness Standards: Normal, Utility, Acrobatic, and Commuter Category Airplanes, specifies the airworthiness standards for the issue of type certificates. Within this part, 14 CFR 23.1357 states that each resettable circuit protection device (trip free device in which the tripping mechanism cannot be overridden by the operating control) must be designed so that:

1. A manual operation is required to restore service after tripping; and

2. If an overload or circuit fault exists, the device will open the circuit regardless of the position of the operating control.

8-72   AMP006

The time/current capacities of a circuit breaker or fuse must be

A— above those of the associated conductor.

B— equal to those of the associated conductor.

C— below those of the associated conductor.

8-72. Answer C. JSPT 8D, AC 43.13-1B

A circuit breaker or fuse should open a circuit before the associated conductor reaches its maximum capacity. To accomplish this, the time/current characteristics of the protective device must fall below that of the associated conductor.

8-73   AMP026

1. Most modern aircraft use circuit breakers rather than fuses to protect their electrical circuits.

2. Federal Aviation Regulations Part 23 requires that all electrical circuits incorporate some form of circuit protective device.

Regarding the above statements,

A— only No. 1 is true.

B— only No. 2 is true.

C— both No. 1 and No. 2 are true.

8-73. Answer A. JSPT 8D, 14 CFR 23.1357

Only statement (1) is correct. Most modern aircraft use circuit breakers rather than fuses to protect their electrical circuits because fuses are typically more cumbersome to replace. However, according to 14 CFR 23.1357, protective devices such as fuses or circuit breakers do not have to be installed in the main circuits of starter motors, or in nonhazardous circuits.

8-74   AMP026
Electrical switches are rated according to the

A– voltage and the current they can control.

B– resistance rating of the switch and the wiring.

C– resistance and the temperature rating.

8-74. Answer A. JSPT 8D, AC 43.13-1B, 11-16
Switches are rated according to both the voltage and current they can control. A typical aircraft switch may be rated for 5 amps at 125 volts, or 35 amps at 24 volts.

8-75   AMP026
Electrical circuit protection devices are installed primarily to protect the

A– switches.

B– units.

C– wiring.

8-75. Answer C. JSPT 8D, FGH
Circuit protection devices are installed primarily to protect the wiring. Therefore, circuit protection devices are rated based on the amount of current that can be safely carried in the wiring.

8-76   AMP006

1. Electrical circuit protection devices are rated based on the amount of current that can be carried without overheating the wiring insulation.

2. A "trip-free" circuit breaker makes it impossible to manually hold the circuit closed when excessive current is flowing.

Regarding the above statements,

A– only No. 1 is true.

B– only No. 2 is true.

C– both No. 1 and No. 2 are true.

8-76. Answer C. JSPT 8D, FGH
Both statements (1) and (2) are correct. Circuit protection devices are installed primarily to protect the wiring and, therefore, are rated based on the amount of current that can be carried without overheating the wire and insulation. A second requirement is that all aircraft circuit protection devices open the circuit regardless of the position of the operating control. This requirement is met by trip-free circuit breakers that cannot override an open circuit. In other words, this type of circuit breaker makes it impossible to manually hold the circuit closed when excessive current is flowing.

8-77   AMP026
Which of the following Federal Aviation Regulations require that all aircraft using fuses as the circuit protective devices carry "one spare set of fuses, or three spare fuses of each kind required"?

A– FAR Part 23

B– FAR Part 43

C– FAR Part 91

8-77. Answer C. JSPT 8D, 14 CFR 91.205
Within Part 91, 14 CFR 91.205 specifically requires that one spare set of fuses, or three spare fuses of each type be carried in the aircraft during flight.

8-78   AMP026
What is the smallest terminal stud allowed for aircraft electrical power systems?

A– No. 6

B– No. 8

C– No. 10

8-78. Answer C. JSPT 8D, FPH
The smallest terminal stud allowed for electrical power systems is a number 10. However, smaller studs are sometimes used with some smaller operational systems.

8-79   AMP026
A typical barrier type aircraft terminal strip is made of

A– paper-base phenolic compound.

B– polyester resin and graphite compound.

C– layered aluminum impregnated with compound.

8-79. Answer A. JSPT 8D
Most of the terminal strips in an aircraft electrical system are of the barrier type and are made of a strong paper-base phenolic compound.

8-80   AMP026
A term commonly used when two or more electrical terminals are installed on a single lug of a terminal strip is

A– strapping.

B– stepping.

C– stacking.

8-80. Answer C. JSPT 8D, FPH
When attaching the terminal end of wires to a terminal strip, fan the wires out from the bundles so they will align with the terminal studs. If two or more electrical terminals must be installed on a single lug you must "stack" the terminals as necessary.

8-81   AMP026

1. Electrical wires larger than 10 gauge use uninsulated terminals.

2. Electrical wires smaller than 10 gauge use uninsulated terminals.

Regarding the above statements,

A– only No. 1 is true.

B– only No. 2 is true.

C– neither No. 1 nor No. 2 is true.

8-81. Answer A. JSPT 8D, FPH
Only statement (1) is correct. Terminals on wires up to 10-gauge are pre-insulated and color coded to identify the size of wire they fit. Wires larger than 10 gauge, on the other hand, use uninsulated terminals.

8-82   AMP026
Aircraft electrical wire size is measured according to the

A– Military Specification system.

B– American Wire Gauge system.

C– Technical Standard Order system.

8-82. Answer B. JSPT 8D, FPH
Wire is measured according to the American Wire Gauge (AWG) system, with the smaller numbers used to identify the larger wire. The Military Specification system does not provide a means of measuring wire size and Technical Standard Orders certify that parts and appliances installed on aircraft meet certain quality standards.

8-83   AMP026
Aircraft copper electrical wire is coated with tin, silver, or nickel in order to

A– improve conductivity.

B– add strength.

C– prevent oxidization.

8-83. Answer C. JSPT 8D
Copper is a very corrosive metal. Therefore, aircraft electrical wire is coated with tin, silver, or nickel plating to help prevent oxidation.

8-84   AMP026

(Refer to figure 4.)

The following data concerning the installation of an electrical unit is known: current requirements for continuous operation – 11 amperes; measured cable length – 45 feet; system voltage – 28 volts (do not exceed 1 volt drop); cable in conduit and bundles.

What is the minimum size copper electrical cable that may be selected?

A– No. 10

B– No. 12

C– No. 14

8-84. Answer B. JSPT 8D, AC 43.13-1B

First, locate the column on the left side of the chart representing a 28V system with a 1 volt drop. Move down this column to a wire length of 45 feet, which is between the 40 and 50 foot callouts. From this point, project a line to the right just beyond the 10 amp diagonal line. Since this point is above curve 1, installation in a bundle carrying continuous current is permitted. Now, project a line down vertically to the bottom of the chart. The line falls on the #12 wire size. Therefore, a #12 wire is required.

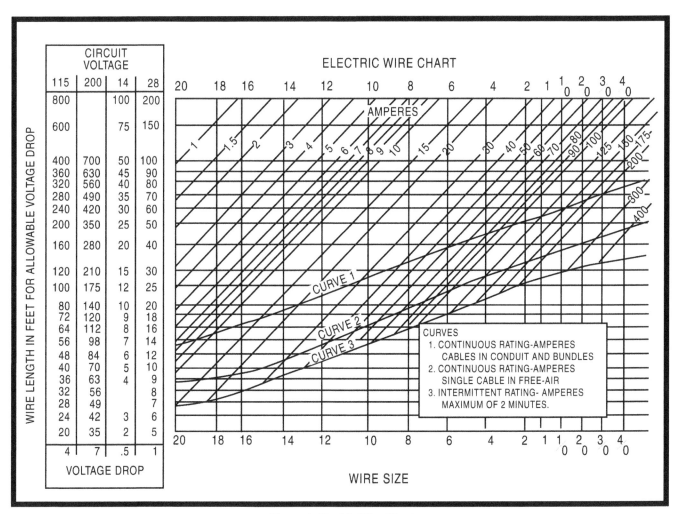

Figure 4. Electric Wire Chart.

8-85   AMP026
(Refer to figure 4 on page 8-29.)

In a 28-volt system, what is the maximum continuous current that can be carried by a single No.10 copper wire 25 feet long, routed in free air?

A– 20 amperes

B– 35 amperes

C– 28 amperes

8-86   AMP002
What is the ampere-hour rating of a storage battery that is designed to deliver 45 amperes for 2.5 hours?

A– 112.5 ampere-hour

B– 90.0 ampere-hour

C– 45.0 ampere-hour

8-85. Answer B. JSPT 8D, FAH
Begin by locating the 28-volt column on the left side of the chart. Move down this column until you hit the number 25 which represents the wire length. From here, move horizontally left until you intersect the vertical line representing No. 10 copper wire. Since this intersection is above curve 2, the wire can carry a continuous current in free air. To determine the maximum continuous current that can be carried, interpolate between the 30 amp and 40 amp diagonal lines. The answer is 35 amperes.

8-86. Answer A. JSGT 3C, FGH
The capacity of a storage battery is rated in ampere-hours which is the amount of electricity that can be taken out of a battery when a current of one ampere flows for one hour. This rating indicates the minimum amount of amperes that a battery can put out in one hour. Therefore, a battery which can deliver 45 amps for 2.5 hours has a 112.5 ampere-hour capacity (45 amps x 2.5 hours = 112.5 amp-hours).

SECTION E — RECIPROCATING ENGINE IGNITION SYSTEMS

Section E of Chapter 8 includes high- and low-tension ignition systems used on reciprocating engines, as well as information on spark plugs and ignition wiring.

8-87   AMP057

What tool is generally used to measure the crankshaft rotation in degrees?

A– Dial indicator

B– Timing disk

C– Prop protractor

8-87. Answer B. FPH

The timing disk is a more accurate crankshaft positioning device than timing reference marks. When setting up the ignition timing on an engine, a timing disk should be attached to the engine to measure the crankshaft rotation in degrees.

8-88   AMP063

If the ignition switch is moved from BOTH to either LEFT or RIGHT during an engine ground check, normal operation is usually indicated by a

A– large drop in RPM.

B– momentary interruption of both ignition systems.

C– slight drop in RPM.

8-88. Answer C. JSPT 8E, FPH

A magneto check is conducted with the propeller in the high RPM position at a speed between approximately 1,000 and 1,700 RPM. During this check, the ignition switch is moved from the BOTH to the RIGHT position, and then the BOTH to the LEFT position. While switching from BOTH to a single magneto position, a slight but noticeable drop in rpm should occur. If a large RPM drop occurs, or if there is a momentary interruption of both ignition systems, the ignition system is not operating properly.

8-89   AMP057

One of the best indicators of reciprocating engine combustion chamber problems is

A– excessive engine vibration.

B– starting difficulties.

C– spark plug condition.

8-89. Answer C.

One way of determining combustion chamber problems is by examining the condition of the spark plugs. For example, normal operation is indicated by a spark plug having a relatively small amount of light brown or tan deposit on the nose of the center electrode insulator. However, if heavy oily deposits are found on the spark plugs, it is a good indication that the rings or valve seals are worn and allowing oil to seep into the cylinder.

8-90   AMP047

When a magneto is disassembled, keepers are usually placed across the poles of the rotating magnet to reduce the loss of magnetism. These keepers are usually made of

A– chrome magnet steel.

B– soft iron.

C– cobalt steel.

8-90. Answer B. JSPT 8E, FGH

Almost all magnets, regardless of their retentivity, lose some of their magnetic strength when their lines of flux pass through the air. Therefore, during the overhaul of a magneto, when the rotating magnet is removed, it should be placed in a soft iron keeper to prevent loss of magnetism. A "keeper" is a piece of soft iron that is used to link the magnetic poles and provide a highly permeable path for the flux.

8-91   AMP047

How is the strength of a magneto magnet checked?

A– Hold the points open and check the output of the primary coil with an AC ammeter while operating the magneto at a specified speed.

B– Check the AC voltage reading at the breaker points.

C– Check the output of the secondary coil with an AC ammeter while operating the magneto at a specified speed.

8-91. Answer A. JSPT 8E

There are two common methods for checking the strength of a magneto magnet. If the magnet is removed from the magneto, it is checked with a magnetometer. However, if the magneto is assembled, the magnet's strength is checked by holding the points open and then checking the output of the primary with an AC ammeter as the magneto is rotated at a specified speed.

8-92   AMP047

The E-gap angle is usually defined as the number of degrees between the neutral position of the rotating magnet and the position

A– where the contact points close.

B– where the contact points open.

C– of greatest magnetic flux density.

8-92. Answer B. JSPT 8E, FPH

The number of degrees between the neutral position of the rotating magnet and the position where the contact points open is called the E-gap angle. When the rotor is at the E-gap angle the cam opens the breaker points and current stops flowing through the primary coil. This sudden stoppage of current flow causes the magnetic field in the coil core to collapse and induce a voltage into the secondary winding.

8-93   AMP046
The greatest density of flux lines in the magnetic circuit of a rotating magnet-type magneto occurs when the magnet is in what position?

A– Full alignment with the field shoe faces

B– A certain angular displacement beyond the neutral position, referred to as E-gap angle or position

C– The position where the contact points open

8-93. Answer A. JSPT 8E, FPH
The greatest flux density within a rotating magnet-type magneto occurs when the poles of the magnet are fully aligned with the field shoe faces. This position is known as the full register position.

8-94   AMP047
Magneto breaker point opening relative to the position of the rotating magnet and distributor rotor (internal timing) can be set most accurately

A– during the magneto-to-engine timing operation.

B– during assembly of the magneto before installation on the engine.

C– by setting the points roughly at the required clearance before installing the magneto and then making the fine breaker point adjustment after installation to compensate for wear in the magneto drive train.

8-94. Answer B. JSPT 8E, FPH
The internal timing of a magneto is most easily set when the magneto is being assembled prior to installation.

8-95   AMP046
Why are high-tension ignition cables frequently routed from the distributors to the spark plugs in flexible metallic conduits?

A– To eliminate high altitude flashover

B– To reduce the formation of corona and nitric oxide on the cable insulation

C– To reduce the effect of the high-frequency electromagnetic waves emanated during operation

8-95. Answer C. JSPT 8E, FPH
The ignition harness on reciprocating engines serve several purposes. It supports the wires going from the magneto to each spark plug and protects them from engine heat, vibration, and weather. Ignition harnesses also serve as a conductor for the stray magnetic fields that surround the wires as they momentarily carry high-voltage current. Therefore, by routing the ignition leads through metallic conduits, the stray magnetic fields are easily conducted to ground, thereby reducing electrical interference with aircraft radio equipment.

8-96   AMP047

What will be the results of increasing the gap of the breaker points in a magneto?

A– Retard the spark and increase its intensity.

B– Advance the spark and decrease its intensity.

C– Retard the spark and decrease its intensity.

8-96. Answer B. JSPT 8E, FPH

Any time the gap between the breaker points in a magneto is increased, the points will open early. When the points open early, the spark within the cylinder occurs in advance of when it is supposed to. Furthermore, early opening points also cause a decrease in spark intensity.

8-97   AMP047

What is the purpose of a safety gap in some magnetos?

A– To discharge the secondary coil's voltage if an open occurs in the secondary circuit

B– To ground the magneto when the ignition switch is off

C– To prevent flashover in the distributor

8-97. Answer A. JSPT 8E

Some magnetos contain a safety gap that protects the secondary coil. The safety gap is connected in series with the secondary circuit by two electrodes. One electrode is attached to the high tension brush holder and the other electrode is grounded to the ground plate. With this configuration, if excessive voltage builds in the secondary circuit due to an open that does not allow the spark to jump the spark plug electrodes, the excessive voltage jumps the safety gap to the ground connection. This helps ensure that the voltage cannot rise high enough to damage the insulation within the secondary coil.

8-98   AMP047

When timing a magneto internally, the alignment of the timing marks indicates that the

A– breaker points are just closing.

B– magnets are in the neutral position.

C– magnets are in the E-gap position.

8-98. Answer C. JSPT 8E, FPH

When the timing marks within a magneto are aligned, the magnets are in the E-gap position and the breaker points are just beginning to open.

8-99   AMP047
When internally timing a magneto, the breaker points begin to open when the rotating magnet is

A– fully aligned with the pole shoes.

B– a few degrees past full alignment with the pole shoes.

C– a few degrees past the neutral position.

8-99. Answer C. JSPT 8E, FPH
When internally timing a magneto, the breaker points should begin to open when the rotating magnet is a few degrees past the neutral position. The neutral position is defined as the point where the rotating magnet is 45 degrees past full alignment with the pole shoes.

8-100   AMP063
What is the electrical location of the primary capacitor in a high-tension magneto?

A– In parallel with the breaker points

B– In series with the breaker points

C– In a series with the primary and secondary winding

8-100. Answer A.
The primary electrical circuit in a magneto consists of a set of breaker contact points, a capacitor, and an insulated coil. The capacitor is wired in parallel with the breaker points to prevent arcing between the points when they open, and to hasten the collapse of the magnetic field around the primary coil. If a capacitor were connected in series with the breaker points the magneto would not operate.

8-101   AMP046
In a high-tension ignition system, the current in the magneto secondary winding is

A– conducted from the primary winding via the discharge of the capacitor.

B– induced when the primary circuit is interrupted.

C– induced when the primary circuit discharges via the breaker points.

8-101. Answer B. JSPT 8E, FPH
Current is induced into a magneto's secondary winding when the current within the primary winding is interrupted suddenly, causing a high rate of flux change. Current is interrupted by opening the primary breaker points when the rotating magnet is in the E-gap position.

8-102   AMP046

When a "Shower of Sparks" ignition system is activated at an engine start, a spark plug fires

A– as soon as the advance breaker points open.

B– only while both the retard and advance breaker points are closed.

C– only while both the retard and advance breaker points are open.

8-102. Answer C. JSPT 8E, FPH

With a "shower of sparks" ignition system, an electrically operated vibrator rapidly opens and closes. This action causes the current flowing through the primary coil to be interrupted several times per second which, in turn, causes the magnetic field surrounding the primary coil to build and collapse at the same rate. The rapid successions of separate voltages that are induced into the secondary coil by the pulsating magnetic field around the primary coil produce a "shower of sparks" across the selected spark plug when both of the breaker points are open.

8-103   AMP046

What is the radial location of the two north poles of a four-pole rotating magnet in a high-tension magneto?

A– 180° apart

B– 270° apart

C– 90° apart

8-103. Answer A. JSPT 8E, FPH

In a four-pole rotating magnet, the two north poles are located 180 degrees apart.

8-104   AMP047

Magneto timing drift is caused by erosion of the breaker points and

A– excessive spark plug gap.

B– wear of the cam followers.

C– loss of magnetism in the rotor.

8-104. Answer B. JSPT 8E, AC 65 -9A

If a set of points is worn, the internal timing of the magneto is advanced. The next most common cause of timing drift is wear of the breaker cam which causes the timing to be retarded.

8-105   AMP046

Capacitance after firing in most modern spark plugs is reduced by the use of

A– fine wire electrodes.

B– a built-in resistor in each plug.

C– aluminum oxide insulation.

8-105. Answer B. JSPT 8E

The shielding used on ignition leads to protect against radio interference can act as a capacitor and store electrical energy that is released when the spark jumps the spark plug gap. When this happens,the energy that is stored in the capacitance of the ignition harness is returned to the spark plug, and after firing occurs. To minimize this problem, spark plugs have a resistor installed inside the spark plug insulator that prevents the electrical energy stored in the harness from reaching the spark plug gap.

8-106   AMP063

What components make up the magnetic system of a magneto?

A– Pole shoes, the pole shoe extensions, and the primary coil

B– Primary and secondary coils

C– Rotating magnet, the pole shoes, the pole shoe extensions, and the coil core

8-106. Answer C. JSPT 8E, FPH

The magnetic circuit of a magneto consists of a permanent rotating magnet, a pair of soft iron pole shoes and pole shoe extensions, and a coil core.

8-107   AMP046

In an aircraft ignition system, one of the functions of the capacitor is to

A– regulate the flow of current between the primary and secondary coil.

B– facilitate a more rapid collapse of the magnetic field in the primary coil.

C– stop the flow of magnetic lines of force when the points open.

8-107. Answer B. JSPT 8E, FPH

The purpose of the capacitor in the primary electrical circuit is to prevent arcing between the points when they are opened, and to hasten the collapse of the magnetic field surrounding the primary coil.

8-108   AMP063

When will the voltage in the secondary winding of a magneto, installed on a normally operating engine, be at its highest value?

A– Just prior to spark plug firing

B– Toward the latter part of the spark duration when the flame front reaches its maximum velocity

C– Immediately after the breaker points close

8-108. Answer A.

A high voltage is induced into the secondary winding when there is a rapid change in the magnetic field surrounding the primary coil. The amount of voltage within the secondary winding builds from its lowest value immediately before the breaker points close to a maximum value just prior to the spark plug firing.

8-109   AMP046

When the switch is off in a battery ignition system, the primary circuit is

A– grounded.

B– opened.

C– shorted.

8-109. Answer B. JSPT 8E, FPH

In a battery ignition system, when the ignition switch is on, current is supplied to the primary coil. However, when the switch is off, the primary circuit opens and current cannot flow to the primary coil.

8-110   AMP046

As an aircraft engine's speed is increased, the voltage induced in the primary coil of the magneto

A– remains constant.

B– increases.

C– varies with the setting of the voltage regulator.

8-110. Answer B. JSPT 8E, FPH

The amount of voltage induced in the primary coil of a magneto varies with the rate at which the magnet'slines of flux are cut. Therefore, the faster an engine runs, the faster the flux lines are cut and the greater the induced voltage.

8-111   AMP047

When internally timing a magneto, the breaker points begin to open when

A– the piston has just passed TDC at the end of the compression stroke.

B– the magnet poles are a few degrees beyond the neutral position.

C– the magnet poles are fully aligned with the pole shoes.

8-111. Answer B. JSPT 8E, FPH

When internally timing a magneto, the breaker points should begin to open when the rotating magnet is a few degrees past the neutral position. The neutral position is defined as the point where the rotating magnet is 45 degrees past full alignment with the pole shoes.

8-112   AMP063

The purpose of a safety gap in a magneto is to

A– prevent burning out the primary winding.

B– protect the high-voltage winding from damage.

C– prevent burning of contact points.

8-112. Answer B. JSPT 8E

Some magnetos contain a safety gap that protects the secondary coil. The safety gap is connected in series with the secondary circuit by two electrodes. One electrode is attached to the high tension brush holder while the other electrode is grounded to the ground plate. With this configuration, if excessive voltage builds in the secondary circuit due to an open that does not allow the spark to jump the spark plug electrodes, the excessive voltage jumps the safety gap to the ground connection. This helps ensure that the voltage cannot rise high enough to damage insulation within the secondary coil.

8-113   AMP064

A defective primary capacitor in a magneto is indicated by

A– a fine-grained frosted appearance of the breaker points.

B– burned and pitted breaker points.

C– a weak spark.

8-113. Answer B. JSPT 8E, FPH

One of the purposes of a capacitor in a magneto is to prevent arcing across the breaker points once the points open. Therefore, a good indication of a defective capacitor is breaker points that are burned or pitted from arcing.

8-114   AMP046

A magneto ignition switch is connected

A– in series with the breaker points.

B– parallel to the breaker points.

C– in series with the primary capacitor and parallel to the breaker points.

8-114. Answer B. JSPT 8E, FPH

The ignition switch in a magneto circuit is wired in parallel with the breaker points and the primary capacitor. With the ignition switch closed, no current flows through the coil and the breaker points. With the ignition switch open, current flows through the coil, and when the breaker points open, the current stops and the field collapses sending high voltage to the spark plug.

8-115   AMP046

The spark is produced in a magneto ignition system when the breaker points are

A– fully open.

B– beginning to open.

C– fully closed.

8-115. Answer B. JSPT 8E, FPH

Current is induced into the secondary winding to produce a spark when the breaker points begin to open, causing the magnetic field surrounding the primary coil to collapse. The spark has subsided by the time the points are fully open, and when the points are fully closed no spark is produced because there is no collapsing field to induce current in the secondary coil.

8-116   AMP063

Shielding is used on spark plug and ignition wires to

A– protect the wires from short circuits as a result of chafing and rubbing.

B– prevent outside electromagnetic emissions from disrupting the operation of the ignition system.

C– prevent interference with radio reception.

8-116. Answer C. JSPT 8E, FPH

The shielding used on spark plug and ignition wires serves to prevent or reduce interference with radio reception. Without this shielding, the stray magnetic fields that surround the wires when they momentarily carry the high-voltage current could make radio communication virtually impossible. Protecting the wires from physical wear such as chafing and abrasionis the job of the ignition wire's insulation and other protective sleeves.

8-117   AMP046

What is the purpose of using an impulse coupling with a magneto?

A– To absorb impulse vibrations between the magneto and the engine

B– To compensate for backlash in the magneto and the engine gears

C– To produce a momentary high rotational speed of the magneto

8-117. Answer C. JSPT 8E, FPH

An impulse coupling is designed to induce a momentary high rotational speed which increases the rate at which the lines of flux in the primary coil are cut. This produces a more intense spark that aids in starting.

8-118   AMP063

The purpose of staggered ignition is to compensate for

A– short ignition harness.

B– rich fuel/air mixture around exhaust valve.

C– diluted fuel/air mixture around exhaust valve.

8-118. Answer C. JSPT 8E

In a dual-ignition system, the spark plugs may be set to fire at the same instant (synchronized) or at slightly different intervals (staggered). When a staggered ignition is used, the spark plug in the exhaust side of the cylinder is always fired first to compensate for the slower burn rate of the diluted fuel/air mixture in this portion of the cylinder.

8-119   AMP046

Aircraft magneto housings are usually ventilated in order to

A– prevent the entrance of outside air which may contain moisture.

B– allow heated air from the accessory compartment to keep the internal parts of the magneto dry.

C– provide cooling and remove corrosive gases produced by normal arcing.

8-119. Answer C. JSPT 8E, FPH

Magnetos require adequate drains and proper ventilation to provide cooling and prevent moisture from building inside a magneto and shorting across the internal components. In addition, good magneto ventilation helps ensure that the corrosive gases produced by normal arcing across the distributor air gap are carried away.

8-120   AMP063

Failure of an engine to cease firing after turning the magneto switch off is an indication of

A– an open high tension lead.

B– an open P-lead to ground.

C– a grounded magneto switch.

8-120. Answer B. JSPT 8E, FPH

In a magneto ignition system, if the engine does not stop firing when the ignition switch is turned off, there is an open P-lead to ground.

8-121   AMP047

Alignment of the marks provided for internal timing of a magneto indicates that the

A– breaker points are just beginning to close for No.1 cylinder.

B– magneto is in E-gap position.

C– No.1 cylinder is on TDC of compression stroke.

8-121. Answer B. JSPT 8E, FPH

When the timing marks within a magneto are aligned, the magnets are in the E-gap position and the breaker points are just beginning to open.

8-122   AMP047

When using a timing light to time a magneto to an aircraft engine, the magneto switch should be placed in the

A– BOTH position.

B– OFF position.

C– LEFT or RIGHT position (either one).

8-122. Answer A. JSPT 8E, FPH

When using a timing light to time a magneto to an engine, the ignition switch is placed in the BOTH position. If the magneto switch is in the OFF position, the timing light will not indicate when the breaker points open, and if the magneto switch is in either the LEFT or RIGHT position, you could only time one of the magnetos.

8-123   AMP064

What test instrument could be used to test an ignition harness for suspected leakage?

A– A high-tension lead tester

B– A high voltage DC voltmeter

C– A high amperage DC ammeter

8-123. Answer A. JSPT 8E, FPH

Several different types of test devices are used for determining the serviceability of a high-tension ignition harness. One common type of tester is capable of applying a direct current voltage up to 15,000 volts. Once voltage is applied to an ignition harness, a high-tension lead tester is used to measure any current that leaks through the insulation. Neither a high voltage DC voltmeter nor a high amperage DC ammeter is sensitive enough to detect leakage current from a high-tension harness.

8-124   AMP046

The amount of voltage generated in any magneto secondary coil is determined by the number of windings and by the

A– rate of buildup of the magnetic field around the primary coil.

B– rate of collapse of the magnetic field around the primary coil.

C– amount of charge released by the capacitor.

8-124. Answer B. JSPT 8E

The amount of voltage induced into the secondary coil of a magneto is determined by the ratio of the number of turns of wire in the two coils and the speed at which the magnetic field around the primary coil collapses. The faster the magnetic coil collapses the greater the induced voltage.

8-125   AMP063

Magneto breaker points must be timed to open when the

A– rotating magnet is positioned a few degrees before neutral.

B– greatest magnetic field stress exists in the magnetic circuit.

C– rotating magnet is in the full register position.

8-125. Answer B. JSPT 8E, AC 65-21A

With the primary breaker points closed, the rotating magnet's flux generates an opposing magnetic field in the magneto coil. This opposing force is the source of magnetic field stress, and the point where this stress is highest is a few degrees beyond the neutral position or the E-gap position. It is here that the points open to induce the highest possible voltage into the secondary coil.

8-126   AMP063

In reference to a "Shower of Sparks" ignition system:

1. the retard breaker points are designed to keep the affected ignition system operating if the advance breaker points should fail during normal engine operation (after start).

2. the timed opening of the retard breaker points is designed to prevent engine "kickback" during start.

Regarding the above statements,

A– only No. 1 is true.

B– only No. 2 is true.

C– both No. 1 and No. 2 are true.

8-126. Answer B. JSPT 8E, FPH

Only statement number (2) is correct. The retard points are timed so that they open later than the normal points. This retarded timing ensures that the engine will not kick-back when it fires. Both sets of points must be open for the Shower of Sparks system to operate. After the starter switch is released, the retard points have no function.

8-127   AMP063

A certain nine-cylinder radial engine used a noncompensated single-unit, dual-type magneto with a four-pole rotating magnet and separately mounted distributors. Which of the following will have the lowest RPM at any given engine speed?

A– Breaker cam

B– Engine crankshaft

C– Distributors

8-127. Answer C. JSPT 8E, FPH

A distributor used with any four-cycle engine must rotate at one-half the engine's speed to fire each spark plug in every two crankshaft revolutions. However, the speed of a magneto with an uncompensated cam is calculated by dividing the number of cylinders by twice the number of poles on the magnet. In this case, magneto speed is 1.125 times the crankshaft speed (9 ÷ (4 x 2) = 1.125). Based on this, the distributor rotates at the slowest speed.

8-128   AMP064

What will be the effect if the spark plugs are gapped too wide?

A– Insulation failure

B– Hard starting

C– Lead damage

8-128. Answer B. JSPT 8E, FPH

Spark plugs that are gapped too wide generally lead to hard starting. The reason for this is that the wider gap requires a higher voltage to produce a spark that will jump the gap. Since the production of a higher voltage requires the magneto to rotate faster, starting becomes more difficult. Excessive spark plug gaps can cause insulation damage and ignition lead damage over time, but hard starting is much more immediate.

8-129   AMP064

When removing a shielded spark plug, which of the following is most likely to be damaged?

A– Center electrode

B– Shell section

C– Core insulator

8-129. Answer C. JSPT 8E, FPH

Before a spark plug is removed, its ignition harness lead must be disconnected. If the lead is not pulled straight out of the plug barrel, damage to the core insulator and the ceramic lead terminal may result. The center electrode and shell section are unlikely to be damaged unless the spark plug is dropped.

8-130   AMP064

What likely effect would a cracked distributor rotor have on a magneto?

A– Ground the secondary circuit through the crack

B– Fire two cylinders simultaneously

C– Ground the primary circuit through the crack

8-130. Answer A. JSPT 8E, FPH

One end of a magneto secondary coil is grounded to the primary coil or the coil core while the other end is connected to the distributor rotor. Therefore, if the distributor rotor in a magneto is cracked, the current in the secondary coil has a less resistive path to ground through the crack to the metal shaft of the magneto.

8-131   AMP064

Which of the following breaker point characteristics is associated with a faulty capacitor?

A– Crowned

B– Fine grained

C– Coarse grained

8-131. Answer C. JSPT 8E, FPH

One purpose of the capacitor in a magneto ignition system is to prevent arcing between the breaker points. Therefore, a faulty capacitor can be suspected if the breaker points take on a coarseg-rained or sooty appearance. Crowned points have a concave center and a convex rim and are the result of improper dressing, not a faulty capacitor, and points having a fine-grained appearance indicates normal capacitor operation.

8-132   AMP063

How are most radial engine spark plug wires connected to the distributor block?

A– By use of cable-piercing screws

B– By use of self-locking cable ferrules

C– By use of terminal sleeves and retaining nuts

8-132. Answer A. JSPT 8E, FPH

Spark plug wires on most radial engines are normally connected to the distributor block with cable-piercing screws. Neither self-locking cable ferrules nor terminal sleeves and retaining nuts are used to attach spark plug wires to a distributor block.

8-133   AMP063

Capacitance after firing of a spark plug is caused by

A– the stored energy in the ignition shielded lead unloading after normal timed ignition.

B– excessive center electrode erosion.

C– constant polarity firing.

8-133. Answer A. JSPT 8E

The shielding used on ignition leads to protect against radio interference can sometimes act as a capacitor and store residual electrical energy as the high voltage charge flows through the lead to the spark plug. When this happens, the energy stored in the ignition harness is returned to the spark plug after the primary spark has occurred. Although center electrode erosion is not the cause of capacitance after firing, it is a typical consequence.

8-134   AMP063

If it is found that a shielded ignition system does not adequately reduce ignition noise, it may be necessary to install

A– a second layer of shielding.

B– a filter between the magneto and magneto switch.

C– bonding wires from the shielding to ground.

8-134. Answer A. JSPT 8E, FPH

If a typical shielded ignition system does not adequately reduce ignition noise, a second layer of shielding is typically installed.

8-135   AMP047

When a magneto is operating, what is the probable cause for a shift in internal timing?

A– The rotating magnet looses its magnetism.

B– The distributor gear teeth are wearing on the rotor gear teeth.

C– The cam follower wears and/or the breaker points wear.

8-135. Answer C. JSPT 8E, FPH

A magneto is internally timed to ensure that the breaker points open at the E-gap position to produce the greatest flux change around the primary coil. Since the breaker points are opened by a cam, wear to either the cam or the breaker points themselves could cause a magneto's internal timing to shift.

8-136   AMP047

What should be used to clean grease or carbon tracks from capacitors or coils that are used in magnetos?

A– Solvent

B– Acetone

C– Naphtha

8-136. Answer B. JSPT 8E, FPH

When inspecting a magneto, all accessible condensers should be cleaned with a lint-free cloth moistened with acetone. However, you should always observe the magneto manufacturer's recommendations since some cleaners can damage the protective coating on some components.

8-137   AMP063

The electrical circuit from the spark plug back to the magneto is completed by grounding through the

A– engine structure.

B– P-lead.

C– cockpit switch.

8-137. Answer A. JSPT 8E

In a typical magneto-type ignition system, the magneto produces a high voltage charge that flows through the distributor to the ignition leads and spark plugs. To complete the circuit, the electrical charge jumps the gap in the spark plug which is grounded through the engine structure.

8-138   AMP064

Spark plugs are considered worn out when the

A– electrodes have worn away to about one-half of their original dimensions.

B– center electrode edges have become rounded.

C– electrodes have worn away to about two-thirds of their original dimensions.

8-138. Answer A. JSPT 8E

Any spark plug whose electrodes have worn to approximately one-half their original dimension should be replaced. Spark plug electrodes become rounded fairly quickly, and replacing them at this point would be wasteful and expensive. However, waiting until the electrodes are two-thirds worn brings a greater risk of plug malfunction.

8-139   AMP064

Which of the following could cause damage to the nose ceramic or to the electrode of an aircraft sparkplug?

A– Plug installed without a copper gasket

B– Improper gapping procedures

C– Excessive magneto voltage

8-139. Answer B. JSPT 8E, FPH

When gapping spark plugs, you typically decrease the clearance between the center electrode and the ground electrode. However, it is not recommended that a gap be widened after it has been inadvertently decreased too much since damage to the center electrode insulator typically results. Neither the lack of a copper gasket nor excessive magneto voltage will damage the nose ceramic or electrode.

8-140   AMP057
After spark plugs from an opposed engine have been serviced, in what position should they be reinstalled?

A— Next in firing order to the one from which they are removed

B— Swapped bottom to top

C— Next in firing order to the one from which they were removed and swapped bottom to top

8-140. Answer C. JSPT 13B
When a spark occurs between the electrodes of a spark plug, metal is taken from one electrode and deposited onto another. Therefore, when a spark plug fires positively, the ground electrode wears more than the center electrode and when a spark plug fires negatively, the center electrode wears more than the ground electrode. Futhermore, lead and other impurities produced during the combustion process tend to precipitate to the lower spark plugs, causing them to wear. To help equalize spark plug wear, each time spark plugs are removed they should be replaced in the cylinder next in the firing order to the one from which they were removed and switched from the top to bottom.

8-141   AMP063
Sharp bends should be avoided in ignition leads primarily because

A— weak points may develop in the insulation through which high tension current can leak.

B— ignition lead wire conductor material is brittle and may break.

C— ignition lead shielding effectiveness will be reduced.

8-141. Answer A. JSPT 8E
Although newer ignition harnesses are flexible and can be installed with smaller bend radii, older ignition cables have a low tolerance for sharp bends. Over time, the stress imposed by sharp bends on an ignition lead's insulation can cause the insulation to break down and allow current to leak.

8-142   AMP063
In a high-tension ignition system, a primary capacitor of too low a capacity will cause

A— excessive primary voltage.

B— excessively high secondary voltage.

C— the breaker contacts to burn.

8-142. Answer C. JSPT 8E, FPH
One of the purposes of the capacitor in a magneto is to prevent arcing and burning of the breaker points. Therefore, if the capacitor lacks sufficient capacity, arcing will occur and the points will burn.

8-143   AMP064
Which of the following, obtained during magneto check at 1,700 RPM, indicates a short (grounded) circuit between the right magneto primary and the ignition switch?

A– BOTH-1,700 RPM, R-1,625 RPM, L-1,700 RPM, OFF-1,625 RPM

B– BOTH-1,700 RPM, R-0 RPM, L-1,700 RPM, OFF-0 RPM

C– BOTH-1,700 RPM, R-0 RPM, L-1,675 RPM, OFF-0 RPM

8-143. Answer B. JSPT 8E, FPH
The ignition switch for a magneto ignition system eliminates current flow from the primary circuit by grounding the magneto primary leads. Therefore, if the primary lead to the right magneto is grounded, no current flows from the magneto to the spark plug. A grounded right magneto is identified during a magneto check by the engine quitting when the ignition switch is moved to the RIGHT position. However, in the BOTH position and in the LEFT position, the engine will run at the established rpm setting (1,700 RPM).

8-144   AMP063
If an aircraft ignition switch is turned off and the engine continues to run normally, the trouble is probably caused by

A– an open ground lead in the magneto.

B– arcing magneto breaker points.

C– primary lead grounding.

8-144. Answer A. JSPT 8E, FPH
The ignition switch for a magneto ignition system shuts an engine down by supplying a path to ground through the ignition switch. If the engine does not shut down when the ignition switch is turned to the OFF position, there is either an open ground lead in the magneto or a faulty ignition switch.

8-145   AMP063
When the ignition switch of a single (reciprocating) engine aircraft is turned to the OFF position,

A– the primary circuits of both magnetos are grounded.

B– the secondary circuits of both magnetos are opened.

C– all circuits are automatically opened.

8-145. Answer A. JSPT 8E, FPH
The ignition switch for a magneto ignition system shuts an engine down by supplying a path to ground for both magnetos through the ignition switch. The ignition switch neither opens the secondary circuits nor automatically opens all circuits when it is placed in the OFF position.

8-146   AMP064
A spark plug's heat range is the result of

A– the area of the plug exposed to the cooling airstream.

B– its ability to transfer heat from the firing end of the spark plug to the cylinder head.

C– the heat intensity of the spark.

8-146. Answer B. JSPT 8E, FPH
The heat range of a spark plug refers to the ability of the insulator and center electrode to conduct heat away from the plug tip and transfer it to the cylinder head. "Hot" plugs have a long insulator that creates a long heat transfer path while "cold" plugs have a short insulator that rapidly transfers heat to the cylinder head

8-147   AMP063

If staggered ignition timing is used, the

A— spark plug nearest the exhaust valve will fire first.

B— spark will be automatically advanced as engine speed increases.

C— spark plug nearest the intake valve will fire first.

8-147. Answer A. JSPT 8E

When staggered ignition timing is used, the spark plug nearest the exhaust valve fires first. This is done because the fuel/air mixture nearest the exhaust valve is diluted and burns more slowly.

8-148   AMP064

The term "reach," as applied to spark plug design and/or type, indicates the

A— linear distance from the shell gasket seat to the end of the threads on the shell skirt.

B— length of center electrode exposed to the flame of combustion.

C— length of the shielded barrel.

8-148. Answer A. JSPT 8E, FPH

The reach of a spark plug is the linear distance from the shell gasket to the end of the threads on the plug skirt. This does not include any space taken up by the gasket. In simple terms, it is how far a plug extends into the cylinder head. Reach does not refer to either the length of the center electrode exposed to the combustion flame or the length of the shielded barrel.

8-149   AMP063

The numbers appearing on the ignition distributor block indicate the

A— sparking order of the distributor.

B— relation between distributor terminal numbers and cylinder numbers.

C— firing order of the engine.

8-149. Answer A. JSPT 8E, FPH

The numbers on a distributor block always indicate the sparking order of the distributor. These numbers do not indicate the relationship between the distributor terminals and the cylinder numbers nor do they indicate the engine's firing order.

8-150   AMP064

When testing a magneto distributor block for electrical leakage, which of the following pieces of test equipment should be used?

A— A high-tension harness tester

B— A continuity tester

C— A high-range ammeter

8-150. Answer A. JSPT 8E, FPH

In addition to being able to check ignition leads, a high-tension harness tester can also be used to indicate the condition of the distributor block. If the majority of ignition leads being tested show excessive leakage, there is a good possibility that the distributor block is at fault.

8-151   AMP064

1. The platinum and iridium ground electrodes used on fine wire spark plugs are extremely brittle and can be broken if they are improperly handled or adjusted.

2. When gapping massive-electrode spark plugs, a wire gauge should be inserted between the center and ground electrodes while moving the ground electrode in order to avoid setting the gap too close.

Regarding the above statements,

A– only No. 1 is true.

B– only No. 2 is true.

C– both No. 1 and No. 2 are true.

8-151. Answer A. JSPT 8E
Only statement (1) is true. Although fine wire electrodes are easier to gap than massive electrode plugs, extreme care must be taken because both platinum and iridium are extremely brittle and can break if improperly handled. For massive electrode spark plugs, the wire gauge must not be between the electrodes when you move the ground electrode over since this will place a side load on the center electrode which could crack the ceramic.

8-152   AMP056
Hot spark plugs are generally used in aircraft power plants

A– with comparatively high compression or high operating temperatures.

B– with comparatively low operating temperatures.

C– which produce high power per cubic inch displacement.

8-152. Answer B. JSPT 8E, FPH
The heat range of a spark plug refers to the ability of the insulator and the center electrode to conduct heat away from the plug tip. Hot spark plugs, or plugs that have a long insulator, slowly transfer heat and are typically used in engines whose cylinder temperatures are relatively low. Cold spark plugs, on the other hand, have a short insulator that rapidly transfers heat which makes them appropriate for hot running, high-compression engines.

8-153   AMP063
If a spark plug lead becomes grounded, the

A– magneto will not be affected.

B– distributor rotor finger will discharge to the next closest electrode within the distributor.

C– capacitor will break down.

8-153. Answer A.
In a normally operating ignition system, when a spark plug fires, current from the magneto passes to ground by jumping the spark plug's air gap. Therefore, if a spark plug lead becomes grounded, current would simply flow through the lead to ground with no effect on the magneto.

8-154   AMP064

Which of the following statements most accurately describes spark plug heat range?

A– The length of the threaded portion of the shell usually denotes the spark plug heat range.

B– A hot plug is designed so that the insulator tip is reasonably short to hasten the rate of heat transfer from the tip through the spark plug shell to the cylinder head.

C– A cold plug is designed so that the insulator tip is reasonably short to hasten the rate of heat transfer from the tip through the spark plug shell to the cylinder head.

8-154. Answer C. JSPT 8E, FPH

The heat range of a spark plug is a measure of a spark plug's ability to transfer heat to the cylinder head. The primary factor in determining the heat range of a plug is the length of the nose core. For example, cold plugs have a relatively short insulator to provide a rapid transfer of heat to the cylinder head while hot plugs have a long insulator nose that creates a long heat transfer path.

8-155   AMP063

When does battery current flow through the primary circuit of a battery ignition coil?

A– Only when the breaker points are open

B– At all times when the ignition switch is on

C– When the breaker points are closed and the ignition switch is on

8-155. Answer C. JSPT 8E, FPH

In a battery ignition system, current is supplied by the battery through the ignition switch with a return to ground through the breaker points. Therefore, in order for current to flow, the ignition switch must be on and the breaker points closed.

8-156   AMP063

In order to turn a magneto off, the primary circuit must be

A– grounded.

B– opened.

C– shorted.

8-156. Answer A. JSPT 8E, FPH

In a magneto ignition system, the purpose of the ignition switch is to ground out the primary of the magneto when the switch is OFF. Once grounded, the breaker points are effectively shorted making the magneto inoperative.

8-157   AMP063

When performing a magneto ground check on an engine, correct operation is indicated by

A— a slight increase in RPM.

B— no drop in RPM.

C— a slight drop in RPM.

8-157. Answer C. JSPT 8E, FPH

When performing a magneto ground check, the engine is operated at a specified RPM and the ignition switch is moved from BOTH to LEFT and back to BOTH; then from BOTH to RIGHT and back to BOTH. When this check is performed there should be a small drop in rpm at the LEFT and the RIGHT positions. This occurs because with only one magneto selected, only one spark plug fires in each cylinder thereby causing a slight decrease in power output.

8-158   AMP064

Defective spark plugs will cause the engine to run rough at

A— high speeds only.

B— low speeds only.

C— all speeds.

8-158. Answer C. JSPT 2A

A defective spark plug, meaning a plug which is not firing or is firing intermittently, will cause the engine to miss at all engine speeds.

8-159   AMP064

Which of the following would be cause for rejection of a spark plug?

A— Carbon fouling of the electrode and insulator

B— Insulator tip cracked

C— Lead fouling of the electrode and insulator

8-159. Answer B. JSPT 8E, FPH

A spark plug whose insulator tip is cracked should be replaced. This condition can affect the firing of the plug as well as its ability to transfer heat. Carbon fouling and lead fouling happens during the combustion process and can be removed from a spark plug in the shop. Therefore, neither of these conditions would be cause for rejection.

8-160   AMP064

What will be the result of using too hot a spark plug?

A– Fouling of plug

B– Preignition

C– Burned capacitor

8-160. Answer B. JSPT 8E, FPH

The heat range of a spark plug refers to the ability of the insulator and the center electrode to conduct heat away from the plug tip. Hot spark plugs, or plugs that have a long insulator, slowly transfer heat and are typically used in an engine whose cylinder temperatures are relatively low. Cold spark plugs, on the other hand, have a short insulator that rapidly transfers heat which makes them appropriate for hot running, high-compression engines. An engine which runs hot requires a relatively cold spark plug, whereas an engine which runs cool requires a relatively hot spark plug. If a hot spark plug is installed in an engine which runs hot, the tip of the plug could overheat and cause pre-ignition. Plug fouling is caused by an excessively rich mixture or by an intermittently firing spark plug, but not by a hot spark plug. Using a hot spark plug will not cause a burned capacitor.

8-161   AMP007

Upon inspection of the spark plugs in an aircraft engine, the plugs were found caked with a heavy black soot. This indicates

A– worn oil seal rings.

B– a rich mixture.

C– a lean mixture.

8-161. Answer B. JSPT 8E, FPH

Carbon fouling of spark plugs appears as a heavy black soot on the plug tip. The most common cause of carbon fouling is running an engine with an excessively rich fuel/air mixture.

8-162   AMP064

Spark plug heat range is determined by

A– the reach of the spark plug.

B– its ability to transfer heat to the cylinder head.

C– the number of ground electrodes.

8-162. Answer B. JSPT 8E, FPH

The heat range of a spark plug is a measure of a plug's ability to transfer heat to the cylinder head. The primary factor in determining the heat range of a plug is the length of the nose core. For example, cold plugs have a relatively short insulator to provide a rapid transfer of heat to the cylinder head while hot plugs have a long insulator nose that creates a long heat transfer path. A spark plug's reach is the threaded portion of the spark plug and does not affect the plug's ability to transfer heat. The number of ground electrodes also has no affect on heat range.

8-163   AMP064
Ignition check during engine run-up indicates excessive RPM drop during operation on the right magneto. The major portion of the RPM loss occurs rapidly after switching to the right magneto position (fast drop). The most likely cause is

A— faulty or fouled spark plugs.

B— incorrect ignition timing on both magnetos.

C— one or more dead cylinders.

8-163. Answer A. JSPT 8E, FPH
When performing a magneto check on an engine, an excessive and rapid RPM drop is usually the result of faulty or failed spark plugs or a faulty ignition harness.

8-164   AMP064
If new breaker points are installed in a magneto on an engine, it will be necessary to time the

A— magneto internally and the magneto to the engine.

B— breaker points to the No.1 cylinder.

C— magneto drive to the engine.

8-164. Answer A. JSPT 8E, FPH
When installing new breaker points in a magneto, the internal timing of the magneto must be checked to ensure that the point opening coincides with the E-gap position of the rotor. The timing of the magneto to the engine must also be checked to ensure that the firing of the spark plugs occurs at the proper time in relation to piston position.

8-165   AMP063
Using a cold spark plug in a high-compression aircraft engine would probably result in

A— normal operation.

B— a fouled plug.

C— detonation.

8-165. Answer A. JSPT 8E, FPH
The heat range of a spark plug refers to the ability of the plug's insulator and center electrode to conduct heat away from the tip. Hot spark plugs, or plugs that have a long insulator, slowly transfer heat and are typically used in an engine whose cylinder temperatures are relatively low. Cold spark plugs, on the other hand, have a short insulator that rapidly transfers heat which makes them appropriate for hot running, high-compression engines. Therefore, when a cold spark plug is used in a high-compression engine the engine will run normally.

8-166   AMP063

Spark plug fouling caused by lead deposits occurs most often

A– during cruise with rich mixture.

B– when cylinder head temperatures are relatively low.

C– when cylinder head temperatures are high.

8-166. Answer B. JSPT 8E, FPH

Lead fouling can occur at any power setting, however, it is most frequently associated with cruising power settings with lean mixtures. At these power settings, the cylinder head temperature is relatively low and there is an excess of oxygen above that needed to consume all the fuel in the fuel/air mixture. The excess oxygen ends up combining with lead and builds up in layers on the cool cylinder walls and the spark plugs.

8-167   AMP063

In a four-stroke cycle aircraft engine, when does the ignition event take place?

A– Before the piston reaches TDC on compression stroke

B– After the piston reaches TDC on power stroke

C– After the piston reaches TDC on compression stroke

8-167. Answer A. JSPT 8E, FPH

The ignition event in a four-stroke engine occurs before the piston reaches top dead center on the compression stroke. This ensures complete combustion of the fuel/air charge by the time the piston is slightly past top dead center. If the fuel/air charge were ignited after TDC, power output would decrease substantially.

8-168   AMP064

When installing a magneto on an engine, the

A– piston in the No.1 cylinder must be a prescribed number of degrees before top center on the compression stroke.

B– magneto breaker points must be just closing.

C– piston in the No.1 cylinder must be a prescribed number of degrees after top center on the intake stroke.

8-168. Answer A. JSPT 8E, FPH

Magneto to engine timing is based on having the magneto in the E-gap, or firing position and the number one cylinder a prescribed number of degrees before top dead center on the compression stroke. This position represents the point in which the fuel/air mixture ignites.

8-169   AMP064

The spark occurs at the spark plug when the ignition's

A– secondary circuit is completed.

B– primary circuit is completed.

C– primary circuit is broken.

8-169. Answer C. JSPT 8E, FPH

In both a battery and magneto ignition system, the spark occurs at the spark plug when voltage is induced into the secondary winding. Voltage is induced when the primary circuit is opened at the breaker points.

8-170   AMP064

Ignition check during engine run-up indicates a slow drop in RPM. This is usually caused by

A– defective spark plugs.

B– a defective high-tension lead.

C– incorrect ignition timing or valve adjustment.

8-170. Answer C. JSPT 8E, FPH

When performing a magneto check, a slow drop in RPM is usually caused by incorrect ignition timing or faulty valve adjustment. With late ignition timing, the fuel/air charge is ignited late in relation to piston travel and maximum combustion pressures are not obtained. The result is a gradual power loss when checking a single magneto.

8-171   AMP063

If the ground wire of a magneto is disconnected at the ignition switch, the result will be the

A– affected magneto will be isolated and the engine will run on the opposite magneto.

B– engine will stop running.

C– engine will not stop running when the ignition switch is turned off.

8-171. Answer C. JSPT 8E, FPH

In a magneto ignition system, the purpose of the ignition switch is to ground out the primary circuit when the switch is OFF. By grounding out the primary circuit continuously, insufficient voltage is induced into the secondary coil to produce a spark. Therefore, if the ground wire to the ignition switch is disconnected, the engine will continue running when the ignition is turned to the OFF position.

8-172   AMP063

Which of the following are advantages of dual ignition in aircraft engines?

1. Gives a more complete and quick combustion of the fuel.

2. Provides a backup magneto system.

3. Increases the output power of the engine.

4. Permits the use of lower grade fuels.

5. Increases the intensity of the spark at the spark plugs.

A– 2, 3, and 4

B– 2, 3, and 5

C– 1, 2, and 3

8-172. Answer C. JSPT 8E, DSA-25

The principal advantages of a dual magneto-ignition system are that if any part of one magneto should fail to operate, the other magneto will continue to furnish ignition. Furthermore, a dual ignition system firing two spark plugs ignites the fuel/air mixture in each cylinder simultaneously at two different places, resulting in more complete and quick combustion and increased engine power. Based on this, choices 1, 2, and 3 are correct.

8-173   AMP064

How does high-tension ignition shielding tend to reduce radio interference?

A— Prevents ignition flashover at high altitudes.

B— Reduces voltage drop in the transmission of high-tension current.

C— Receives and grounds high-frequency waves coming from the magneto and high-tension ignition leads.

8-173. Answer C. JSPT 8E, FPH

The shielding used on an ignition harness serves as a conductor to receive and ground stray magnetic fields that are produced when high-voltage current passes through the leads. By conducting these magnetic lines of force to ground, the ignition harness cuts down electrical interference with the aircraft radio and other electrically sensitive equipment.

8-174   AMP063

Which of the following are distinct circuits of a high-tension magneto?

1. Magnetic

2. Primary

3. E-gap

4. P-lead

5. Secondary

A— 1, 2, and 5

B— 1, 3, and 4

C— 2, 4, and 5

8-174. Answer A. JSPT 8E, FPH

A high-tension magneto system is divided into three distinct circuits: the magnetic, the primary, and the secondary. The E-gap represents a specific position of a magneto's rotating magnet just before the breaker points open. The P-lead, on the other hand, identifies the wire that is used to ground a magneto.

8-175   AMP064

What are two parts of a distributor in an aircraft engine ignition system?

1. Coil

2. Block

3. Stator

4. Rotor

5. Transformer

A– 2 and 4

B– 3 and 4

C– 2 and 5

8-175. Answer A. JSPT 8E, FPH

The distributor in a magneto ignition system consists of two parts. The revolving part is called a distributor rotor and the stationary part is called a distributor block.

8-176   AMP064

What is a result of "flashover" in a distributor?

A– Intense voltage at the spark plug

B– Reversal of current flow

C– Conductive carbon trail

8-176. Answer C. JSPT 8E, FPH

Flashover in a distributor can lead to carbon tracking, which appears as a fine pencil-like carbon trail where the flashover occurred. This carbon trail typically collects on the distributor and forms a conductive path to ground which increases the potential for additional flashover to occur.

8-177   AMP063

What is the relationship between distributor and crankshaft speed of aircraft reciprocating engines?

A– The distributor turns at one-half crankshaft speed.

B– The distributor turns at one and one-half crankshaft speed.

C– The crankshaft turns at one-half distributor speed.

8-177. Answer A. JSPT 8E, FPH

In order for a magneto to provide a spark at the appropriate time in the four-stroke process, the distributor must turn at one-half the crankshaft speed. Another way to look at this is that it takes two revolutions of the crankshaft to fire all the cylinders and, therefore, the distributor only needs to rotate at half the crankshaft speed.

8-178   AMP063
At what RPM is a reciprocating engine ignition switch check made?

A– 1,500 RPM

B– The slowest possible RPM

C– Full throttle RPM

8-178. Answer B. JSPT 8E, FPH
An ignition switch check requires that the ignition be momentarily turned to the OFF position and then back to BOTH while the engine is running to see if all magneto ground leads are electrically grounded. To prevent backfiring when the ignition switch is returned to the BOTH position, an ignition switch check is usually made at the slowest possible RPM setting, typically between 500 and 700 RPM.

8-179   AMP064
What is the approximate position of the rotating magnet in a high-tension magneto when the points first close?

A– Full register

B– Neutral

C– A few degrees after neutral

8-179. Answer A. JSPT 8E, FPH
The primary breaker points in a magneto close at approximately the full register position. In this position, the poles of the magnet are perfectly aligned with the pole shoes and the maximum number of flux lines flow through the magnetic circuit.

8-180   AMP064
What component of a dual magneto is shared by both ignition systems?

A– High-tension coil

B– Rotating magnet

C– Capacitor

8-180. Answer B. JSPT 8E, FPH
A dual magneto incorporates two magnetos in one housing. This configuration allows somewhat of a weight savings because one rotating magnet and one cam can be used for both magnetos.

8-181   AMP063
What would be the result if a magneto breaker point mainspring did not have sufficient tension?

A– The points will stick.

B– The points will not open to the specified gap.

C– The points will float or bounce.

8-181. Answer C. JSPT 8E, FPH
If a breaker point mainspring does not apply sufficient tension to the breaker points, the points could bounce or float at higher speeds. A bouncing or floating point would prevent the normal induction buildup within the magneto thereby reducing the magneto output.

8-182   AMP063
The secondary coil of a magneto is grounded through the

A– ignition switch.

B– primary coil.

C– grounded side of the breaker points.

8-182. Answer B. JSPT 8E, FPH
The secondary coil of a magneto is made up of a winding containing approximately 13,000 turns of fine, insulated wire. One end of the wire is electrically grounded to the primary coil or coil core, while the other end is connected to the distributor rotor.

8-183   AMP063
In the aircraft magneto system, if the P-lead is disconnected, the magneto will be

A– on regardless of ignition switch position.

B– grounded regardless of ignition switch position.

C– open regardless of ignition switch position.

8-183. Answer A. JSPT 8E, FPH
The magneto ground lead, or P-lead, grounds the primary side of the magneto coil when the magneto switch is in the OFF position. This effectively shorts the breaker points, rendering the magneto inoperable. Therefore, if the P-lead should become disconnected or broken, the magneto will be on all the time regardless of the ignition switch position.

8-184   AMP064
A spark plug is fouled when

A– its spark grounds by jumping electrodes.

B– it causes preignition.

C– its spark grounds without jumping electrodes.

8-184. Answer C. FPH
A spark plug is fouled when it becomes contaminated with foreign matter to the point that the spark flows through the foreign matter to ground rather than jumping the air gap at the electrode.

8-185   AMP046
Which of the following statements regarding magneto switch circuits is NOT true?

A– In the BOTH position, the right and left magneto circuits are grounded.

B– In the OFF position, neither the right nor left magneto circuits are open.

C– In the RIGHT position, the right magneto circuit is open and the left magneto circuit is grounded.

8-185. Answer A. JSPT 8E, FPH
When a magneto switch is in the BOTH position, neither magneto is grounded.

SECTION F — TURBINE ENGINE IGNITION SYSTEMS
This section covers turbine engine ignition system maintenance and troubleshooting, including igniter plugs..

8-186   AMP068
One way that the automatic ignition relight systems are activated on gas turbine engines is by a

A— drop in compressor discharge pressure.

B— sensing switch located in the tailpipe.

C— drop in fuel flow.

8-186. Answer A. JSPT 8F
The automatic ignition relight system is activated differently on different aircraft. One popular method of activating the system is to use pressure sensors installed at the compressor discharge. When used this way, a drop in discharge pressure automatically activates the ignition system.

8-187   AMP068
The capacitor-type ignition system is used almost universally on turbine engines primarily because of its high voltage and

A— low amperage.

B— long life.

C— high-heat intensity.

8-187. Answer C. JSPT 8F, FPH
Turbine engine ignition systems must deliver a high-heat intense spark to ignite fuel at low temperatures or high altitudes. To accomplish this, turbine engines employ a capacitor-ignition system that delivers a high amperage spark.

8-188   AMP063
How does the ignition system of a gas turbine engine differ from that of a reciprocating engine?

A— One igniter plug is used in each combustion chamber.

B— Magneto-to-engine timing is not critical.

C— A high-energy spark is required for ignition.

8-188. Answer C. JSPT 8F, FPH
Unlike the ignition system for a reciprocating engine that produces a high voltage, low amperage spark, turbine engine ignition systems deliver a high-energy spark with a substantially higher amperage. This high-energy spark is needed to ignite the fuel/air mixture in low temperatures and at high altitudes.

8-189   AMP068

In a turbine engine DC capacitor discharge ignition system, where are the high-voltage pulses formed?

A– At the breaker

B– At the triggering transformer

C– At the rectifier

8-189. Answer B. JSPT 8F, FPH

A high-voltage capacitor discharge ignition system in a turbine engine produces high voltage pulses at what is called a trigger transformer. Current is supplied to the trigger transformer through a gas discharge tube. When the voltage is high enough to jump the gas discharge tube, the energy in the storage capacitor and trigger capacitor are allowed to flow to the trigger transformer where a high-voltage pulse is formed and sent to the igniter.

8-190   AMP063

Why are turbine engine igniters less susceptible to fouling than reciprocating engine spark plugs?

A– The high-intensity spark cleans the igniter.

B– The frequency of the spark is less for igniters.

C– Turbine igniters operate at cooler temperatures.

8-190. Answer A. JSPT 8F, FPH

Turbine engine igniters are far less susceptible to electrode fouling than reciprocating engine spark plugs because the heat of the high-intensity spark produced tends to clean the igniter electrodes. Although the frequency of the spark is lower for igniters, this has little bearing on plug fouling characteristics.

8-191   AMP069

Generally, when removing a turbine engine igniter plug, in order to eliminate the possibility of the technician receiving a lethal shock, the ignition switch is turned off and

A– disconnected from the power supply circuit.

B– the igniter lead is disconnected from the plug and the center electrode grounded to the engine after disconnecting the transformer-exciter input lead and waiting the prescribed time.

C– the transformer-exciter input lead is disconnected and the center electrode grounded to the engine after disconnecting the igniter lead from the plug and waiting the prescribed time.

8-191. Answer B. JSPT 8F, FPH

To minimize the risk of shock when removing an igniter plug, it is important that you take all necessary precautions. As a general rule, you should begin removing an igniter plug by disconnecting the transformer exciter input lead and waiting the time prescribed by the manufacturer. Once this is complete, disconnect the igniter lead and ground the center electrode to the engine. When these steps are followed, the chances of receiving a shock are nearly eliminated.

8-192   AMP063
Great caution should be exercised in handling damaged hermetically sealed turbine engine igniter transformer units because

A– compounds in the unit may become a fire or explosion hazard when exposed to the air.

B– some contain radioactive material.

C– some contain toxic chemicals.

8-192. Answer B.
Great caution should be exercised in handling damaged transformer units from turbine engine ignition systems since some units may have radioactive material on the air gap points. This material is used to calibrate the discharge points to a preset voltage. No igniter transformer units contain compounds that present fire or explosion hazards. Although the radioactive compounds present in these units do present a toxicity hazard, their radioactivity is the primary concern.

8-193   AMP068
Igniter plugs used in turbine engines are subjected to high intensity spark discharges and yet they have a long service life because they

A– operate at much lower temperatures.

B– are not placed directly into the combustion chamber.

C– do not require continuous operation.

8-193. Answer C. JSPT 8F
The high-energy current used to fire turbine engine igniters, if used continuously, would quickly cause electrode erosion. However, since combustion in a turbine engine is self-supporting, igniter plugs are only used for short periods and, therefore, they maintain a relatively long service life. The ignition system is used primarily to start an engine and ensure ignition during takeoff, icing conditions, landing, and moderate to severe turbulence.

8-194   AMP063
Which statement is correct regarding the ignition system of a turbine engine?

A– The system is normally de-energized as soon as the engine starts.

B– It is energized during the starting and warm-up periods only.

C– The system generally includes a polar inductor-type magneto.

8-194. Answer A. JSPT 8F, FPH
The high-energy current used to fire the turbine engine igniter, if used continuously, would quickly cause electrode erosion. However, since combustion is continuous once a turbine engine is started, the ignition system is typically de-energized soon after the engine starts.

8-195   AMP068
The type of ignition system used on most turbine aircraft engines is

A– high resistance.

B– low tension.

C– capacitor discharge.

8-195. Answer C. JSPT 8F, FPH
Because of the high-energy spark required to ignite a turbine engine, the capacitor discharge type ignition system is most often used on turbine engines.

8-196   AMP063

Why do turbine engine ignition systems require high energy?

A– To ignite the fuel under conditions of high altitude and high temperatures

B– Because the applied voltage is much greater

C– To ignite the fuel under conditions of high altitude and low temperatures

8-196. Answer C. JSPT 8F, FPH

The fuel/air mixture in turbine engines can be ignited readily in standard atmospheric conditions. However, since turbine engines often operate in the low temperatures of high altitudes, it is imperative that their ignition systems be capable of supplying the high-intensity spark needed to ignite the mixture under these conditions.

8-197   AMP063

Which of the following are included in a typical turbine engine ignition system?

1. Two igniter plugs

2. Two transformers

3. One exciter unit

4. Two intermediate ignition leads

5. Two low-tension igniter leads

6. Two high-tension igniter leads

A– 2, 3, and 4

B– 1, 4, and 5

C– 1, 3, and 6

8-197. Answer C. JSPT 8F, TEP2

A typical turbine engine ignition system includes 2 plugs, 2 exciter units, and 2 high-tension leads. However, in some aircraft the exciter units may be contained in a single housing.

LUBRICATION SYSTEMS

SECTION A — ENGINE LUBRICATING OILS

This section contains questions regarding the requirements and characteristics of engine oils and other lubricants used in reciprocating- or turbine-powered aircraft..

9-1   AMP057

Which condition would be the least likely to be caused by failed or failing engine bearings?

A– Excessive oil consumption

B– High oil temperatures

C– Low oil temperatures

9-1. Answer C. FPH

If a bearing fails or is in the process of failing, metal to metal contact is occurring. The friction which accompanies this metal to metal contact generates a great deal of heat and can cause high oil temperatures. The higher the oil temperature, the more oil is consumed. Since the question asks for the condition that is least likely to be caused by a failed bearing, low oil temperatures is the best choice.

9-2   AMP029

What will be the result of operating an engine in extremely high temperatures using a lubricant recommended by the manufacturer for a much lower temperature?

A– The oil pressure will be higher than normal

B– The oil temperature and oil pressure will be higher than normal

C– The oil pressure will be lower than normal

9-2. Answer C. FPH

The viscosity, or the resistance of oil to flow, changes with temperature. For example, as the temperature drops, highly viscous oils become extremely thick and do not circulate. Therefore, low viscosity oils are typically recommended for use in reciprocating engines operating in cold climates. However, if a low viscosity oil is used when an engine is operated in extremely high temperatures, the oil can become so thin that a lower than normal oil pressure can result.

9-3   AMP029

1. Gas turbine and reciprocating engine oils can be mixed or used interchangeably.

2. Most gas turbine engine oils are synthetic.

Regarding the above statements,

A— only No. 2 is true.

B— both No. 1 and No. 2 are true.

C— neither No.1 nor No. 2 is true.

9-3. Answer A. JSPT 9A, FPH
Only statement (2) is correct. Because of the unique operating requirements, synthetic oils are typically used in gas turbine engines. Furthermore, because of the differences between turbine and reciprocating engine oils, they should not be mixed or used interchangeably.

9-4   AMP029
The time in seconds required for exactly 60 cubic centimeters of oil to flow through an accurately calibrated orifice at a specific temperature is recorded as a measurement of the oil's

A— flash point.

B— specific gravity.

C— viscosity.

9-4. Answer C. JSPT 9A, FPH
The viscosity of commercial aviation oils is measured by a testing instrument called a Saybolt Universal Viscosimeter. This instrument consists of a tube that holds a specific oil quantity at an exact temperature and a calibrated orifice. The time in seconds required for exactly 60 cubic centimeters of oil to flow through the orifice is recorded as the oil's viscosity.

9-5   AMP029
Upon what quality or characteristic of a lubricating oil is its viscosity index based?

A— Its resistance to flow at a standard temperature as compared to high grade paraffin-base oil at the same temperature

B— Its rate of change in viscosity with temperature change

C— Its rate of flow through an orifice at a standard temperature

9-5. Answer B. JSPT 9A
Viscosity index is a measure of the change in an oil's viscosity for a given change in temperature. The smaller the change in viscosity for a given temperature change, the higher the viscosity index.

9-6   AMP029

Lubricating oils with high viscosity index ratings are oils

A— in which the viscosity does not vary much with temperature change.

B— in which the viscosity varies considerably with temperature change.

C— which have high SAE numbers.

9-6. Answer A. JSPT 9A

Viscosity index is a measure of the change in an oil's viscosity for a given change in temperature. The smaller the change in viscosity for a given temperature change, the higher the viscosity index. In other words, a high viscosity index indicates that an oil's viscosity does not change very much with changes in temperature.

9-7   AMP029

The oil used in reciprocating engines has a relatively high viscosity due to

A— the reduced ability of thin oils to maintain adequate film strength at altitude. (reduced atmospheric pressure).

B— the relatively high rotational speeds.

C— large clearances and high operating temperatures.

9-7. Answer C. JSPT 9A, FPH

Reciprocating engines require large engine operating clearances because of the relatively large size of the moving parts and high operating temperatures. Therefore, the oil used in reciprocating engines must have relatively high viscosity in order to maintain an adequate film between moving parts.

9-8   AMP029

If all other requirements can be met, what type of oil should be used to achieve theoretically perfect engine lubrication?

A— The thinnest oil that will stay in place and maintain a reasonable film strength

B— An oil that combines high viscosity and low demulsibility

C— An oil that combines a low viscosity index and a high neutralization number

9-8. Answer A. JSPT 9A, FPH

The oil selected for aircraft engine lubrication must be thin enough to circulate freely, yet heavy enough to provide the proper film strength at operating temperatures.

9-9   AMP029

In addition to lubricating (reducing friction between moving parts), engine oil performs what functions?

1. Cools

2. Seals

3. Cleans

4. Prevents corrosion

5. Cushions impact (shock) loads

A– 1, 2, 3, and 4

B– 1, 2, 3, 4, and 5

C– 1, 3, and 4

9-9. Answer B. JSPT 9A, FPH

In addition to reducing friction, one of the primary functions of oil is to circulate through the engine and absorb heat to aid in engine cooling. In addition, engine oil also helps to form a seal between the piston rings and cylinder walls, clean the engine interior by carrying foreign particles to the filter, coat engine parts to prevent corrosion, and act as a cushion between the metal parts during the combustion process. This cushioning effect is particularly important for such parts as crankshafts and connecting rods.

9-10   AMP029

The viscosity of a liquid is a measure of its

A– resistance to flow.

B– rate of change of internal friction with change in temperature.

C– weight or density.

9-10. Answer A. JSPT 9A, FPH

The resistance of an oil to flow is known as its viscosity.

9-11   AMP029

Which of the following factors helps determine the proper grade of oil to use in a particular engine?

A– Adequate lubrication in various attitudes of flight

B– Positive introduction of oil to the bearings

C– Operating speeds of bearings

9-11. Answer C. JSPT 9A, FPH

Some of the factors considered when determining the proper grade of oil to use in a particular engine include the engine's operating loads, rotational speeds, and operating temperatures.

9-12   AMP029
Specific gravity is a comparison of the weight of a substance to the weight of an equal volume of

A– oil at a specific temperature.

B– distilled water at a specific temperature.

C– mercury at a specific temperature.

9-12. Answer B. JSPT 9A, FPH
All liquids have a specific gravity. Specific gravity is a comparison of the weight of a substance to the weight of an equal volume of distilled water at a specific temperature.

9-13   AMP029
What advantage do mineral base lubricants have over vegetable oil base lubricants when used in aircraft engines?

A– Cooling ability

B– Chemical stability

C– Friction resistance

9-13. Answer B. JSPT 9A
In general, vegetable based oils are chemically unstable at high temperatures, perform poorly at low temperatures, and are unsuited for aircraft engine lubrication. Mineral based oils, on the other hand, tend to be much more chemically stable and suited for aircraft use.

9-14   AMP029
The recommended aircraft engine lubricants are

A– mineral or synthetic based.

B– vegetable, mineral, or synthetic based.

C– animal, mineral, or synthetic based.

9-14. Answer A. JSPT 9A
In general, animal and vegetable based lubricants are chemically unstable at high temperatures, often perform poorly at low temperatures, and are unsuited for aircraft engine lubrication. However, neither mineral based nor synthetic based oils have these limitations and, therefore, perform well as aircraft engine lubricant.

9-15   AMP029
High tooth pressures and high rubbing velocities, such as occur with spur-type gears, require the use of

A– an EP lubricant.

B– straight mineral oil.

C– metallic ash detergent oil.

9-15. Answer A. JSPT 9A
EP (extreme pressure) lubricants are intended for use with spur-type gears operating at high speeds and under high pressure loads. Under these conditions, straight mineral oil would allow metal to metal contact resulting in excessive wear.

9-16   AMP029

What type of oil do most engine manufacturers recommend for new reciprocating engine break-in?

A– Ashless-dispersant oil

B– Straight mineral oil

C– Semi-synthetic oil

9-16. Answer B. JSPT 9A

Most engine manufacturers recommend the use of straight mineral oil for at least the first 50 hours of the break-in period in new or newly overhauled reciprocating engines.

9-17   AMP029

What type of oil do most engine manufacturers recommend after new reciprocating engine break-in?

A– Metallic-ash detergent oil

B– Ashless-dispersant oil

C– Straight mineral oil

9-17. Answer B. JSPT 9A

Ashless dispersant or AD oil is the most commonly used lubricant for reciprocating engines after breakin.

9-18   AMP056

From the following, identify the factor that has the least effect on the oil consumption of a specific engine.

A– Mechanical efficiency

B– Engine RPM

C– Lubricant characteristics

9-18. Answer A. JSPT 9A, FPH

The factors that affect oil consumption are engine speed, engine temperature, operating clearances, oil condition, and characteristics of the lubricant being used. An engine's mechanical efficiency has little effect on oil consumption.

9-19   AMP030

What is the source of most of the heat that is absorbed by the lubricating oil in a reciprocating engine?

A– Crankshaft main bearings

B– Exhaust valves

C– Pistons and cylinder walls

9-19. Answer C. JSPT 9A, FPH

As oil circulates through a reciprocating engine, it absorbs heat from the engine. Since the pistons and cylinder walls are exposed to the highest temperatures during the combustion process, they are the source of the greatest amount of heat that is absorbed by the oil.

SECTION B — RECIPROCATING ENGINES

Section B of Chapter 9 contains information regarding lubrication system requirements, maintenance, and troubleshooting for reciprocating engines.

9-20   AMP030

The floating control thermostat, used on some reciprocating engine installations, helps regulate oil temperature by

A— controlling oil flow through the oil cooler.

B— recirculating hot oil back through the sump.

C— controlling air flow through the oil cooler.

9-20. Answer C. JSPT 9B, FPH

One of the most widely used automatic oil temperature control devices is the floating control thermostat. This unit provides both manual and automatic control of the amount of air that passes through the oil cooler by controlling the oil cooler air-exit door.

9-21   AMP056

If the oil pressure of a cold engine is higher than at normal operating temperatures, the

A— oil system relief valve should be readjusted.

B— engine's lubrication system is probably operating normally.

C— oil dilution system should be turned on immediately.

9-21. Answer B. JSPT 9B, FPH

On engines that are equipped with a compensated oil pressure relief valve, a higher oil pressure is maintained when the oil is cold. This helps ensure adequate lubrication when the oil is partially congealed. However, as the oil heats up, the relief valve automatically lowers the system pressure to the normal operating range.

9-22   AMP057

If an engine operates with a low oil pressure and a high oil temperature, the problem may be caused by a

A— leaking oil dilution valve.

B— sheared oil pump shaft.

C— clogged oil cooler annular jacket.

9-22. Answer A. JSPT 9B, FPH

Some lubrication systems provide a means of diluting oil with fuel. When oil is diluted, less power is needed for starting and starting is accomplished more rapidly. However, if an oil dilution valve leaks, the oil will become excessively thin and cause a reduction in oil pressure. Furthermore, because fuel thinned-oil cannot transfer heat as readily as normal oil, an engine operated with diluted oil will have higher oil temperatures.

9-23   AMP030

An oil separator is generally associated with which of the following?

A– Engine-driven oil pressure pump

B– Engine-driven vacuum pump

C– Cuno oil filter

9-23. Answer B. JSPT 9B, FAH

A wet-type engine-driven vacuum pump uses an air-oil separator to separate the oil that mixes with the air that passes through the pump. The separator is installed in the pump's discharge line where it removes oil from the air and returns it to the engine sump.

9-24   AMP056

The engine oil temperature regulator is usually located between which of the following on a dry sump reciprocating engine?

A– The engine oil supply pump and the internal lubrication system

B– The scavenger pump outlet and the oil storage tank

C– The oil storage tank and the engine oil supply pump

9-24. Answer B. JSPT 9B, FPH

The oil temperature regulator controls oil temperature by directing oil through the core of the cooler or to the oil tank without cooling. Therefore, the engine oil temperature regulator must sense the oil's temperature as it leaves the scavenger pump but before it proceeds to the storage tank.

9-25   AMP031

What will happen to the return oil if the oil line between the scavenger pump and the oil cooler separates?

A– Oil will accumulate in the engine

B– The return oil will be pumped overboard

C– The scavenger return line check valve will close and force the oil to bypass directly to the intake side of the pressure pump

9-25. Answer B. JSPT 9B, FPH

If the return line between the scavenge pump and oil cooler should separate, the return oil would be pumped overboard.

9-26   AMP068

At cruise RPM, some oil will flow through the relief valve of a gear-type engine oil pump. This is normal as the relief valve is set at a pressure which is

A– lower than the pump inlet pressure.

B– lower than the pressure pump capabilities.

C– higher than pressure pump capabilities.

9-26. Answer B. JSPT 9B, FPH

The purpose of an oil pressure relief valve is to maintain the correct system pressure. On most engines, the desired maximum oil pressure is reached before the engine reaches cruise RPM. Therefore, the relief valve is typically set at a pressure that is lower than the oil pump's maximum capabilities. This means that when an engine reaches cruise rpm, the relief valve must open slightly to maintain the correct oil pressure.

9-27   AMP030

What prevents pressure within the lubricating oil tank from rising above or falling below ambient pressure (reciprocating engine)?

A– Oil tank check valve

B– Oil pressure relief valve

C– Oil tank vent

9-27. Answer C. JSPT 9B, FPH

To ensure proper tank ventilation at all flight attitudes reciprocating engine oil tanks are fitted with vent lines. These lines are usually connected to the engine crankcase and indirectly vent the oil tank to the atmosphere. This indirect venting prevents the tank pressure from rising above or falling below the outside ambient pressure.

9-28   AMP031

What unit in an aircraft engine lubrication system is adjusted to maintain the desired system pressure?

A– Oil pressure relief valve

B– Oil viscosity valve

C– Oil pump

9-28. Answer A. JSPT 9B, FPH

In most aircraft engine lubrication systems the oil pump typically supplies more pressure than the system can handle. Therefore, the appropriate system pressure must be maintained by the oil pressure relief valve.

9-29   AMP031

Low oil pressure can be detrimental to the internal engine components. However, high oil pressure

A– should be limited to the engine manufacturer's recommendations.

B– has a negligible effect.

C– will not occur because of pressure losses around the bearings.

9-29. Answer A. JSPT 9B, FPH

An oil pressure relief valve limits oil pressure to a value specified by the engine manufacturer. If the relief valve should stick closed and allow the oil pressure to become excessive, leakage and damage to the oil system could result. Therefore, high oil pressure should always be limited to the engine manufacturer's recommendations.

9-30   AMP030

Some larger reciprocating engines use a compensating oil pressure relief valve to

A– provide a high engine oil pressure when the oil is cold and automatically lower the oil pressure when the oil warms up.

B– compensate for changes in atmospheric pressure that accompany altitude changes.

C– automatically keep oil pressure nearly the same whether the oil is warm or cold.

9-30. Answer A. JSPT 9B, DSA-25

Some larger reciprocating engines require high oil pressure to force cold oil through the bearings during starting and warm-up. However, after the oil has warmed up, lower oil system pressure is preferred to minimize oil consumption. One way of providing varying oil pressures is with a compensating oil pressure relief valve.

9-31   AMP030

In order to relieve excessive pump pressure in an engine's internal oil system, most engines are equipped with a

A– vent.

B– bypass valve.

C– relief valve.

9-31. Answer C. JSPT 9B, FPH

Almost all engine driven oil pumps provide excessive oil pressure at higher power settings. Therefore, most oil systems are equipped with a pressure relief valve that maintains the correct system pressure.

9-32   AMP030

How are the teeth of the gears in the accessory section of an engine normally lubricated?

A– By splashed or sprayed oil

B– By submerging the load-bearing portions in oil

C– By surrounding the load-bearing portions with baffles or housings within which oil pressure can be maintained

9-32. Answer A. JSPT 9B, FPH

The gear teeth within an accessory section of a reciprocating engine are typically lubricated by oil that is sprayed by the accessory bearings and by oil that is splashed in the accessory case.

9-33   AMP031

What is the purpose of the check valve generally used in a dry sump lubrication system?

A— To prevent the scavenger pump from losing its prime

B— To prevent the oil from the supply tank from seeping into the crankcase during inoperative periods

C— To prevent the oil from the pressure pump from entering the scavenger system

9-33. Answer B. JSPT 9B, FPH

Reciprocating engines using dry-sump oil systems often have a check valve installed in the oil filter. This check valve is held closed by a light spring load of one to three pounds when the engine is not operating and prevents oil from draining out of the supply tank and into the engine crankcase.

9-34   AMP030

Which of the following lubrication system components is never located between the pressure pump and the engine pressure system?

A— Oil temperature bulb

B— Fuel line for oil dilution system

C— Check valve

9-34. Answer B. JSPT 9B, FPH

The fuel line for an oil dilution system is never located between the pressure pump and the engine pressure system. The reason for this is that with an oil dilution system, the fuel must be introduced into unpressurized oil so there is almost no chance for oil to flow back through the dilution system and enter the fuel supply.

9-35   AMP030

As an aid to cold-weather starting, the oil dilution system thins the oil with

A— kerosene.

B— alcohol.

C— gasoline.

9-35. Answer C. JSPT 9B, FPH

Oil dilution systems thin engine oil for cold-weather starting by allowing the pilot to add fuel (gasoline) to the engine oil just prior to engine shut down. Although kerosene and alcohol can also be used to dilute engine oil, neither is typically carried on reciprocating engine aircraft.

9-36   AMP056

Where is the oil temperature bulb located on a dry sump reciprocating engine?

A— Oil inlet line

B— Oil cooler

C— Oil outlet line

9-36. Answer A. JSPT 9B, FPH

It is important for pilots to know the temperature of the oil just before it enters the engine. Therefore, indry-sump lubricating systems, the oil temperature bulb may be located anywhere in the oil inlet line between the supply tank and the engine.

9-37   AMP030
Cylinder walls are usually lubricated by

A– splashed or sprayed oil.

B– a direct pressure system fed through the crankshaft, connecting rods, and the piston pins to the oil control ring groove in the piston.

C– oil that is picked up by the oil control ring when the piston is at bottom center.

9-37. Answer A. JSPT 9B, FPH
In most reciprocating engines, the cylinder walls receive oil spray from the crankshaft and crankpin bearings. Some of the oil coming from the crankshaft is also splashed onto the cylinder walls.

9-38   AMP030
If a full-flow oil filter is used on an aircraft engine, and the filter becomes completely clogged, the

A– oil supply to the engine will be blocked.

B– oil will be bypassed back to the oil tank hopper where larger sediments and foreign matter will settle out prior to passage through the engine.

C– bypass valve will open and the oil pump will supply unfiltered oil to the engine.

9-38. Answer C. JSPT 9B, FPH
Full-flow oil filters used on aircraft engines are always equipped with a bypass valve which allows unfiltered oil to bypass the filter and enter the engine should the oil filter become clogged.

9-39   AMP031
What is the primary purpose of changing aircraft engine lubricating oils at predetermined periods?

A– The oil becomes diluted with gasoline washing past the pistons into the crankcase.

B– The oil becomes contaminated with moisture, acids, and finely divided suspended solid particles.

C– Exposure to heat and oxygen causes a decreased ability to maintain a film under load.

9-39. Answer B. JSPT 9B, FPH
Oil in an engine is constantly exposed to many harmful substances that reduce its ability to protect moving parts. These contaminants include moisture, acids, dirt, carbon, and metallic particles. Therefore, it is important that the oil be changed at regular intervals.

9-40   AMP030
What is the primary purpose of the hopper located in the oil supply tank of some dry sump engine installations?

A– To reduce the time required to warm the oil to operating temperatures

B– To reduce surface aeration of the hot oil and thus reduce oxidation and the formation of sludge and varnish

C– To impart a centrifugal motion to the oil entering the tank so that the foreign particles in the oil will separate more readily

9-40. Answer A. JSPT 9B, FPH
Some oil tanks have a built-in hopper, or temperature accelerating well, that extends from the oil return fitting on top of the oil tank to the outlet fitting in the sump in the bottom of the oil tank. The primary purpose of the hopper is to separate the circulating oil from the surrounding oil in the tank so the circulating oil warms quickly after the engine is started.

9-41   AMP056
The purpose of the flow control valve in a reciprocating engine oil system is to

A– direct oil through or around the oil cooler.

B– deliver cold oil to the hopper tank.

C– compensate for volumetric increases due to foaming of the oil.

9-41. Answer A. JSPT 9B, FPH
A flow control valve determines whether the oil passes through or around the oil cooler. When oil is cold, the flow control valve directs the oil around the cooler and back to the tank for circulation. However, when the oil is hot, the flow control valve directs the oil through the oil cooler.

9-42   AMP030
Why is an aircraft reciprocating engine oil tank on a dry sump lubrication system equipped with a vent line?

A– To prevent pressure buildup in the reciprocating engine crankcase

B– To eliminate foaming in the oil tank

C– To prevent pressure buildup in the oil tank

9-42. Answer C. JSPT 9B, FPH
Reciprocating engine oil tanks are equipped with vent lines to ensure proper tank ventilation in all flight attitudes and prevent pressure buildup in the oil tank. The vent line is usually connected to the engine crankcase which is vented to the atmosphere through the crankcase breather.

9-43   AMP030

The pumping capacity of the scavenger pump in a dry sump aircraft engine's lubrication system

A— is greater than the capacity of the oil supply pump.

B— is less than the capacity of the oil supply pump.

C— is usually equal to the capacity of the oil supply pump in order to maintain constant oiling conditions.

9-43. Answer A. JSPT 9B, FPH

The scavenger pump in a dry sump lubrication system is responsible for pumping circulated oil from the sump back to the oil tank. However, because the oil thermally expands once it gets to the sump, scavenger pumps must have a greater capacity than the pressure pump to prevent oil from collecting in the sump.

9-44   AMP030

In which of the following situations will the oil cooler automatic bypass valve be open the greatest amount?

A— Engine oil above normal operating temperature

B— Engine oil below normal operating temperature

C— Engine stopped with no oil flowing after run-up

9-44. Answer B. JSPT 9B, FPH

The bypass valve on an oil cooler regulates the amount of oil that flows through the oil cooler. When the engine oil is below normal operating temperature the bypass valve is fully open so the oil can bypass the oil cooler. However, once the oil reaches its operating temperature, the bypass valve closes and allows the oil to pass through the oil cooler.

9-45   AMP056

In order to maintain a constant oil pressure as the clearances between the moving parts of an engine increase through normal wear, the supply pump output

A— increases as the resistance offered to the flow of oil increases.

B— remains relatively constant (at a given RPM) with less oil being returned to the pump inlet by the relief valve.

C— remains relatively constant (at a given RPM) with more oil being returned to the pump inlet by the relief valve.

9-45. Answer B. JSPT 9B, FPH

Most oil pumps used in aircraft engines provide excessive oil pressure when run at a high RPM and, therefore, a relief valve must be used to maintain a constant pressure. When the relief valve opens, oil is directed back to the oil pump inlet for recirculation. With this type of system, as the clearances between moving parts increase, the pump output remains constant but less oil is returned to the pump inlet by the relief valve.

9-46   AMP030

What will result if an oil filter becomes completely blocked?

A– Oil will flow at a reduced rate through the system

B– Oil flow to the engine will stop

C– Oil will flow at the normal rate through the system

9-46. Answer C. JSPT 9B, FPH

Aircraft engine oil systems are equipped with a bypass valve that allows oil to flow at a normal rate around the filter in the event the filter should become clogged or the oil becomes too congealed to flow through it.

9-47   AMP030

An engine lubrication system pressure relief valve is usually located between the

A– oil cooler and the scavenger pump.

B– scavenger pump and the external oil system.

C– pump and the internal oil system.

9-47. Answer C. JSPT 9B, FPH

To prevent internal engine damage caused by excessive oil pressure, an oil pressure relief valve is typically installed between the pressure pump and the internal oil system. This way, if the pump output pressure exceeds the recommended system pressure, the relief valve can relieve the excess pressure before the oil enters the engine.

9-48   AMP030

Where is the oil of a dry sump reciprocating engine exposed to the temperature control valve sensing unit?

A– Oil cooler inlet

B– Engine outlet

C– Engine inlet

9-48. Answer A. JSPT 9B, FPH

The temperature control valve, sometimes called the flow control valve, is located at the oil cooler inlet and determines whether or not the oil passes through the oil cooler. When the oil is cold, the flow control valve directs oil around the jacket surrounding the cooler to allow the oil to warm quickly. However, when the oil reaches its operating temperature, the flow control valve closes and directs oil through the oil cooler core.

9-49   AMP030

Under which of the following conditions is the oil cooler flow control valve open on a reciprocating engine?

A– When the temperature of the oil returning from the engine is too high

B– When the temperature of the oil returning from the engine is too low

C– When the scavenger pump output volume exceeds the engine pump input volume

9-49. Answer B. JSPT 9B, FPH

The temperature control valve, or flow control valve, is located at the oil cooler inlet and determines whether or not the oil passes through the oil cooler. When the oil is cold, the flow control valve is open and directs oil around the jacket surrounding the cooler to allow the oil to warm quickly. However, when the oil reaches its operating temperature, the flow control valve closes and directs oil through the oil cooler core.

9-50   AMP030

In a reciprocating engine, oil is directed from the pressure relief valve to the inlet side of the

A– scavenger pump.

B– oil temperature regulator.

C– pressure pump.

9-50. Answer C. JSPT 9B, FPH

To avoid damage to an engine's internal lubrication system, an oil pressure relief valve is installed after the oil pressure pump outlet that relieves excess pressure by directing some of the excess oil back to the inlet side of the pressure pump.

9-51   AMP030

If the oil in the oil cooler core and annular jacket becomes congealed, what unit prevents damage to the cooler?

A– Oil pressure relief valve

B– Airflow control valve

C– Surge protection valve

9-51. Answer C. JSPT 9B, FPH

If the oil in an oil cooler becomes congealed, the scavenge pump could build up enough pressure in the system to cause damage. To prevent this high pressure from damaging the oil cooler, some engines are equipped with a surge protection valve in either the oil cooler or the oil return line.

9-52   AMP030

The primary source of oil contamination in a normally operating reciprocating engine is

A– metallic deposits as a result of engine wear.

B– atmospheric dust and pollution.

C– combustion deposits due to combustion chamber blow-by and oil migration on the cylinder walls.

9-52. Answer C. JSPT 9B, FPH

The primary source of oil contamination in a reciprocating engine is combustion by-products that escape past the piston rings (blow-by), and oil carbonizing that occurs when oil becomes trapped in the pores of the cylinder walls and is burned.

9-53   AMP030

A drop in oil pressure may be caused by

A– the temperature regulator sticking open.

B– the bypass valve sticking open.

C– foreign material under the relief valve.

9-53. Answer C. JSPT 9B, FPH

When oil pressure in an engine becomes excessive, the pressure relief valve unseats and excess oil is directed back to the inlet of the pressure pump. If foreign matter causes the relief valve to stick open, oil would continue to be bypassed even when the pressure was not excessive. This would cause a reduced amount of oil to flow to the engine which, in turn, would cause a low oil pressure.

9-54   AMP030

The main oil filters strain the oil at which point in the system?

A– Immediately after it leaves the scavenger pump

B– Immediately before it enters the pressure pump

C– Just as it leaves the pressure pump

9-54. Answer C. JSPT 9B, FPH

In most aircraft oil systems, the main oil filter is located immediately downstream of the pressure pump to ensure clean oil enters the engine.

9-55   AMP030

An oil tank having a capacity of 5 gallons must have an expansion space of

A– 2 quarts.

B– 4 quarts.

C– 5 quarts.

9-55. Answer A. JSPT 9B, FAR 23.1013

According to FAR 23.1013, an oil tank must have an expansion space of 10 percent or 0.5 gallon, whichever is greater. In this example, 10 percent of 5 gallons is 2 quarts which is equivalent to 0.5 gallon.

9-56   AMP030

Why is expansion space required in an engine oil supply tank?

A– To eliminate oil foaming

B– For oil enlargement and collection of foam

C– For proper oil tank ventilation

9-56. Answer B. JSPT 9B, FPH

All oil tanks are provided with expansion space that allows for thermal expansion and foaming. The complete elimination of oil foaming is impossible and proper tank ventilation is provided by a vent line to the engine crankcase which, in turn, is vented to the atmosphere.

9-57   AMP031

The basic oil pressure relief valve setting for a newly overhauled engine is made

A– within the first 30 seconds of engine operation.

B– when the oil is at a higher than normal temperature to assure high oil pressure at normal oil temperature.

C– in the overhaul shop.

9-57. Answer C. JSPT 9B, FPH

Initial adjustment on the oil pressure relief valve for a newly overhauled engine is made in the overhaul shop. The adjustment is fine tuned after the engine is installed in a test stand and run. To help eliminate the risk of oil starvation, the initial adjustment should not wait until the engine is run.

9-58   AMP030

The vent line connecting the oil supply tank and the engine in some dry sump engine installations permits

A– pressurization of the oil supply to prevent cavitation of the oil supply pump.

B– oil vapors from the engine to be condensed and drained into the oil supply tank.

C– the oil tank to be vented through the normal engine vent.

9-58. Answer C. JSPT 9B, FPH

Oil tanks are equipped with vent lines to ensure proper tank ventilation in all flight attitudes. These lines are usually connected to the engine crankcase which is vented to the atmosphere through the crankcase breather. Therefore, the oil tank is indirectly vented through the engine vent.

9-59   AMP030

Oil tank fillers on reciprocating engines are marked with the word

A– "oil," and tank capacity, in accordance with 14 CFR Part 45.

B– "oil," type, and grade, in accordance with 14 CFR Part 33.

C– "oil," in accordance with 14 CFR Part 23.

9-59. Answer C. JSPT 9B, FAR 23.1557

FAR 23.1557 specifies that oil filler openings be marked with "Oil" and the permissible oil designations or reference to the Airplane Flight Manual for permissible oil designations.

SECTION C — TURBINE ENGINES

Section C of Chapter 9 contains information regarding lubrication system requirements, maintenance, and troubleshooting for turbine engines

9-60   AMP068

What is the possible cause when a turbine engine indicates no change in power setting parameters, but oil temperature is high?

A– High scavenge pump oil flow

B– Engine main bearing distress

C– Turbine damage and/or loss of turbine efficiency

9-60. Answer B. JSPT 9C, FPH

In the early stages of engine main bearing distress, increased friction can cause oil temperatures to rise while power parameters remain within normal limits. However, as a main bearing gets closer to failing, the engine's power parameters will change.

9-61   AMP029

Compared to reciprocating engine oils, the types of oils used in turbine engines

A– are required to carry and disperse a higher level of combustion by-products.

B– may permit a somewhat higher level of carbon formation in the engine.

C– have less tendency to produce lacquer or coke.

9-61. Answer C. JSPT 9C, FPH

Synthetic turbine engine oil has two principle advantages over petroleum oil. It has less tendency to deposit lacquer and coke, and is less likely to evaporate at high temperatures.

9-62   AMP029

Which of these characteristics is desirable in turbine engine oil?

A– Low flash point

B– High flash point

C– High volatility

9-62. Answer B. JSPT 9C, FPH

The flash point of oil is an important characteristic when selecting a lubricant. Flash point is determined by laboratory tests and represents the temperature at which a liquid will begin to give off ignitable vapors. The safest liquids are those that expel ignitable vapors at very high temperatures (high flash point). Therefore, it is desirable for aircraft engine oils to have a high flash point.

9-63   AMP030

What type of oil system is usually found on turbine engines?

A– Dry sump, pressure, and spray

B– Dry sump, dip, and splash

C– Wet sump, spray, and splash

9-63. Answer A. JSPT 9C, FPH

Both wet- and dry-sump lubrication systems are used in gas turbine engines. However, most turbo-jet engines are of the axial flow configuration and use a dry-sump lubrication system. With this type of system, the engine's bearings are pressure lubricated and the gearboxes are pressure and spray lubricated.

9-64   AMP031

Manufacturers normally require turbine engine oil servicing within a short time after engine shutdown primarily to

A– prevent over servicing.

B– help dilute and neutralize any contaminants that may already be present in the engine's oil system.

C– provide a better indication of any oil leaks in the system.

9-64. Answer A. JSPT 9C, TEP2

In an operating turbine engine the oil scavenge pump returns oil from the main bearing galleries to the oil reservoir. However, after an engine is shut down, the oil in the tank tends to seep down to the engine's lower components. This causes the oil level in the reservoir to decrease and give a faulty oil level indication. Therefore, the best way to prevent overfilling the reservoir is to service the oil system within 30 minutes after engine shutdown.

9-65   AMP068

The type of oil pumps most commonly used on turbine engines are classified as

A– positive displacement.

B– variable displacement.

C– constant speed.

9-65. Answer A. JSPT 9C, TEP2

The three most common types of oil pumps used on turbine engines are the vane, gerotor, and geartypes. All are classified as positive displacement pumps since they pump a fixed quantity of oil for each revolution.

9-66   AMP027

1. Fuel may be used to cool oil in gas turbine engines.

2. Ram air may be used to cool oil in gas turbine engines.

Regarding the above statements,

A– only No.1 is true.

B– only No. 2 is true.

C– both No. 1 and No. 2 are true.

9-66. Answer C. JSPT 9C, FPH

Both statements (1) and (2) are correct. In gas turbine engines, fuel and ram air are both used to cool the oil. The fuel-cooled oil cooler acts as a fuel/oil heat exchanger in that the fuel cools the oil and the oil heats the fuel. The air-cooled oil cooler normally is installed at the front of the engine and is similar to those used on reciprocating engines.

9-67   AMP068

What is the purpose of the last chance oil filters?

A– To prevent damage to the oil spray nozzle

B– To filter the oil immediately before it enters the main bearings

C– To ensure a clean supply of oil to the lubrication system

9-67. Answer B. JSPT 9C, FPH

In addition to the main oil filters, turbine engine oil systems utilize multiple secondary filters located throughout the system. For example, fine mesh screens called last chance filters are often used to strain the oil just before it enters the main bearing compartment.

9-68   AMP027

In a jet engine which uses a fuel-oil heat exchanger, the oil temperature is controlled by a thermostatic valve that regulates the flow of

A– fuel through the heat exchanger.

B– both fuel and oil through the heat exchanger.

C– oil through the heat exchanger.

9-68. Answer C. JSPT 9C, FPH

In oil systems using a fuel-oil heat exchanger, fuel flowing to the engine must pass through the heat exchanger. However, a thermostatic bypass valve controls the flow of oil through the heat exchanger to regulate the oil temperature.

9-69   AMP068

Oil picks up the most heat from which of the following turbine engine components?

A– Rotor coupling.

B– Compressor bearing.

C– Turbine bearing.

9-69. Answer C. JSPT 9C, FPH

The hottest section within a turbine engine where oil flows is the turbine section. Therefore, of the choices given, the oil will pick up the most amount of heat from the turbine bearing. In fact, the amount of heat absorbed by the turbine bearing is so great that the quantity of oil supplied to the bearing or bearings is often greater than to any of the other engine bearings.

9-70   AMP027

Which of the following is a function of the fuel-oil heat exchanger on a turbojet engine?

A– Aerates the fuel

B– Emulsifies the oil

C– Increases fuel temperature

9-70. Answer C. JSPT 9C, FPH

The fuel-oil heat exchanger is designed to exchange, or transfer heat from the engine oil to the fuel. This process warms the fuel sufficiently enough to prevent fuel icing.

9-71   AMP031

According to Federal Aviation Regulations (FAR's), oil tank fillers on turbine engines must be marked with the word

A– "oil" and the type and grade of oil specified by the manufacturer.

B– "oil" and tank capacity.

C– "oil".

9-71. Answer C. JSPT 9C, FAR 33.71

According to FAR 33.71, oil filler openings for turbine engines must be marked with the word "oil".

9-72   AMP031

After making a welded repair to a pressurized-type turbine engine oil tank, the tank should be pressure checked to

A– not less than 5 PSI plus the maximum operating pressure of the tank.

B– not less than 5 PSI plus the average operating pressure of the tank.

C– 5 PSI.

9-72. Answer A. JSPT 9C, FAR 33.71

FAR 33.71 states that pressurized oil tanks may not leak when subjected to their maximum operating temperature and an internal pressure that is not less than 5 PSI plus the maximum operating pressure of the tank.

9-73   AMP069

Possible failure related ferrous-metal particles in turbine engine oil cause an (electrical) indicating-type magnetic chip detector to indicate their presence by

A– disturbing the magnetic lines of flux around the detector tip.

B– bridging the gap between the detector center (positive) electrode and the ground electrode.

C– generating a small electric current that is caused by the particles being in contact with the dissimilar metal of the detector tip.

9-73. Answer B. JSPT 9C, TEP2

Chip detector systems warn of the presence of a substantial number of ferrous-metal particles in the engine oil. The warning feature on this type of system consists of an electrical circuit that is completed once debris bridges the gap between the magnetic positive electrode and the ground electrode (shell) of the chip detector probe.

9-74   AMP027

What is the primary purpose of the oil-to-fuel heat exchanger?

A– Cool the fuel

B– Cool the oil

C– De-aerate the oil

9-74. Answer B. JSPT 9C, FPH

The primary purpose of an oil-to-fuel heat exchanger in a turbine engine is to cool the engine oil. The heat exchanger does this by allowing the warm engine oil to transfer excess heat energy to the fuel.

9-75   AMP030

What is the primary purpose of the oil breather pressurization system that is used on turbine engines?

A– Prevents foaming of the oil

B– Allows aeration of the oil for better lubrication because of the air/oil mist

C– Provides a proper oil spray pattern from the main bearing oil jets

9-75. Answer C. JSPT 9C, FPH

The breather pressurizing system of a turbine engine ensures a proper spray pattern from the main bearing oil jets and furnishes a pressure head to the scavenge system. If the pressure within the bearing housings were allowed to drop as atmospheric pressure dropped with changes in altitude, the flow of oil from the oil jets would change. Therefore, to maintain a relatively constant flow rate the breather pressurizing system maintains a relatively constant pressure within the bearing compartments and oil tank as the aircraft climbs.

9-76   AMP030

1. Wet sump oil systems are most commonly used in gas turbine engines.

2. In most turbine engine oil tanks, a slight pressurization of the tank is desired to ensure a positive flow of oil.

Regarding the above statements,

A– both No. 1 and No. 2 are true.

B– only No. 2 is true.

C– neither No. 1 nor No. 2 is true.

9-76. Answer B. JSPT 9C, FPH

Only statement number (2) is correct. Although wet sump oil systems were used on some early turbine engines, they are not commonly used today. However, most turbine engine oil tanks are pressurized slightly to ensure a positive flow of oil.

9-77   AMP030

A turbine engine dry sump lubrication system of the self-contained, high-pressure design

A– has no heat exchanger.

B– consists of pressure, breather, and scavenge subsystems.

C– stores oil in the engine crankcase.

9-77. Answer B. JSPT 9C, FPH

The dry-sump lubrication system of a typical turbine engine consists of pressure, scavenge, and breather subsystems. The pressure system supplies oil to the main engine bearings and to the accessory drives, while the scavenge system returns the oil to the engine oil tank for recirculation. The breather system vents the individual bearing compartments and the oil tank to atmosphere through a breather pressurizing valve.

9-78   AMP030

Lube system last chance filters in turbine engines are usually cleaned

A– during annual inspection.

B– during 100-hour inspections.

C– during overhaul.

9-78. Answer C. JSPT 9C, FPH

Last chance filters in turbine engines are typically located at the oil jets within the bearing housing. Since bearing housings are not readily available for disassembly and inspection, last chance filters are typically cleaned when an engine is overhauled.

9-79   AMP068

The purpose of a relief valve installed in the tank venting system of a turbine engine oil tank is to

A– prevent oil pump cavitation by maintaining a constant pressure on the oil pump inlet.

B– maintain internal tank air pressure at the ambient atmospheric level regardless of altitude or rate of change in altitude.

C– maintain a positive internal pressure in the oil tank after shutdown to prevent oil pump cavitation on engine start.

9-79. Answer A. JSPT 9C

In most turbine engine oil tanks, a slight pressure buildup is desired to ensure a positive flow of oil to the oil pump inlet. This pressure buildup is accomplished by installing an adjustable check relief valve in the tank overboard vent line. This check valve is set between three to six psig to maintain positive pressure within the oil tank.

9-80   AMP030

Which type valve prevents oil from entering the main accessory case when the engine is not running?

A– Bypass

B– Relief

C– Check

9-80. Answer C. JSPT 9C, FPH

In both reciprocating and turbine dry-sump lubrication systems, check valves are installed between the oil tank and the engine. These valves are set at two to five PSI, and their purpose is to prevent oil from draining into the engine when the engine is not operating.

9-81   AMP069

As a general rule, a small amount of small fuzzy particles or gray metallic paste on a turbine engine magnetic chip detector

A– is considered to be the result of normal wear.

B– indicates an imminent component failure.

C– indicates accelerated generalized wear.

9-81. Answer A. JSPT 9C

Normal turbine engine operation results in small fuzzy particles or a gray metallic paste accumulating on the chip detector. Imminent component failure and accelerated generalized wear are typically identified by larger particles of different metals.

9-82   AMP068

The purpose of a dwell chamber in a turbine engine oil tank is to provide

A– a collection point for sediments.

B– for a pressurized oil supply to the oil pump inlet.

C– separation of entrained air from scavenged oil.

9-82. Answer C. JSPT 9C, FPH

A dwell chamber, sometimes referred to as a de-aerator, provides a means of separating entrained air from scavenge oil. Turbine engine oil tanks do not have separate collection points for sediments.

9-83   AMP030

Why are fixed orifice nozzles used in the lubrication system of gas turbine engines?

A– To provide a relatively constant oil flow to the main bearings at all engine speeds

B– To keep back pressure on the oil pump, thus preventing an air lock

C– To protect the oil seals by preventing excessive pressure from entering the bearing cavities

9-83. Answer A. JSPT 9C, FPH

To lubricate a turbine engine's main bearings, pressurized oil is sprayed on the bearings through fixed orifice nozzles. These nozzles provide a relatively constant flow of oil at all engine operating speeds thereby ensuring adequate lubrication.

9-84   AMP031

What would be the probable result if the oil system pressure relief valve should stick in the open position on a turbine engine?

A– Increased oil pressure

B– Decreased oil temperature

C– Insufficient lubrication

9-84. Answer C. FPH

If the oil system pressure should become excessive in a turbine engine, the pressure relief valve would open and direct oil back to the supply pump inlet before the oil reached any moving parts. Therefore, if the pressure relief valve should stick in the open position, system pressure would decrease below acceptable levels and insufficient lubrication be provided to moving parts.

9-85   AMP029

In regard to using a turbine engine oil analysis program, which of the following is NOT true?

A– Generally, an accurate trend forecast can be made after an engines first oil sample analysis.

B– It is best to start an oil analysis program on an engine when it is new.

C– A successful oil analysis program should be run over an engine's total operating life so that normal trends can be established.

9-85. Answer A. JSPT 9C, FPH

Oil analysis programs, when run over an engine's total operating life, can identify trends in engine wear. You cannot get any trend information by examining only at the first oil sample analysis.

CHAPTER 10

COOLING SYSTEMS

SECTION A — RECIPROCATING ENGINES

This section covers reciprocating engine cooling, including engine cylinder baffles, augmentor tubes, and cowl flaps.

10-1   AMP056

The primary purpose of baffles and deflectors installed around cylinders of air-cooled aircraft engines is to

A– create a low pressure area aft of the cylinders.

B– force cooling air into close contact with all parts of the cylinders.

C– increase the volume of air used to cool the engine.

10-1. Answer B. JSPT 10A, FPH

Many reciprocating engines utilize cylinder baffles to help direct cooling air into close contact with all cylinder parts.

10-2   AMP056

What is the purpose of an augmenter used in some reciprocating engine exhaust systems?

A– To reduce exhaust back pressure

B– To aid in cooling the engine

C– To assist in displacing the exhaust gases

10-2. Answer B. JSPT 10A, FPH

In an augmenter system, engine exhaust gases are discharged into a stainless steel augmenter tube. The flow of high velocity exhaust gases within the tube creates an area of low pressure at the augmenter inlet that draws additional air from within the cowl into the augmenter tube where is it discharged overboard with the exhaust. This process increases the airflow over the engine and aids in cooling.

10-3   AMP028

Cracks in cooling fins that do not extend into the cylinder head, may be repaired by

A– filling the extremities of the crack with liquid metal.

B– removing the affected area and contour filing within limits.

C– welding and then grinding or filing to original thickness.

10-3. Answer B. JSPT 10A, FPH

Cracks in the cooling fins of a cylinder are allowed, provided they are within the manufacturer's allowable limits. To repair a cracked cooling fin, you should remove the damaged fin then contour file the affected area. In general, neither filling the extremities of a crack with liquid metal nor welding and grinding cylinder cooling fins is considered an acceptable repair.

10-4   AMP024

Which of the following should a mechanic consult to determine the maximum amount of cylinder cooling fin that could be removed when cracks are found?

A– AC 43.13-1

B– Engine manufacturer's service or overhaul manual

C– Engine Structure repair manual

10-4. Answer B. JSPT 10A, FPH

When performing repairs to a cylinder's cooling fins, the engine manufacturer's service or overhaul manual should be consulted to ensure the repair is within limits.

10-5   AMP028

A bent cooling fin on an aluminum cylinder head

A– should be sawed off and filed smooth.

B– should be left alone if no crack has formed.

C– should be stop drilled or a small radius filed at the point of the bend.

10-5. Answer B. JSPT 10A, FPH

If a cooling fin is inadvertently bent on an aluminum cylinder head and no crack forms, the fin should be left alone. Aluminum cooling fins are very brittle, and any attempt to straighten them could cause them to crack or break.

10-6   AMP027

Where are cooling fins usually located on air-cooled engines?

A– Exhaust side of the cylinder head, inside the pistons, and connecting rods

B– Cylinder head, cylinder walls, and inside the piston skirt

C– Cylinder head, cylinder barrel, and inside the piston head

10-6. Answer C. JSPT 10A, FPH

On an air-cooled reciprocating engine, cooling fins are located on the cylinder head, cylinder barrel, and on the underside of the piston head. Neither connecting rods nor piston skirts require cooling fins to dissipate excess heat.

10-7   AMP056

How do cowl flaps aid in cooling a horizontally opposed aircraft engine?

A– Recirculates air through the engine cylinders

B– Directs air through the engine cylinders

C– Controls the amount of air flowing around the cylinders

10-7. Answer C. JSPT 10A, FPH

Cowl flaps are typically located on the bottom of an engine cowl and provide a means of controlling the amount of air that exits the cowl which, in turn, controls the amount of air flowing around the cylinders. For example, opening the cowl flaps increases the air exit area which effectively increases the amount of air that can circulate over the cylinder fins. Furthermore, the outside airstream flowing over an opened cowl flap creates a low pressure area which further assists in removing heat from the engine compartment.

10-8   AMP027

The position of the cowl flaps during normal cruise flight conditions is

A– closed.

B– open.

C– one half open.

10-8. Answer A. JSPT 10A, FPH

Cowl flaps are small doors at the rear of an engine cowling that are opened to vary the amount of cooling air that flows through the engine compartment. In normal cruise flight, the forward motion of the aircraft typically produces enough airflow over the engine that the cowl flaps can remain closed.

10-9   AMP028

Generally, a small crack just started in a cylinder baffle

A– requires repair by reinforcing, such as installation of a doubler over the area.

B– requires no action unless it grows or is branched into two cracks.

C– may be stop drilled.

10-9. Answer C. JSPT 10A, FPH

Cylinder baffles are sheet metal shields located in an engine compartment that channel air around the cylinders for cooling. If a small crack develops in a cylinder baffle it is acceptable to stop drill the crack.

10-10   AMP027

Which of the following assists in removing heat from the metal walls and fins of an air-cooled cylinder assembly?

A– An intercooler system

B– A baffle and cowl arrangement

C– An engine induction system

10-10. Answer B. JSPT 10A, FPH

An engine's cowling and baffles are designed to channel air over the engine cylinders to aid in removing heat from the engine. The cowling is responsible for receiving impact air and making it flow around the engine while the baffles direct the air close to the cylinder fins to prevent hot spots from forming.

10-11   AMP056

During ground operation of an engine, the cowl flaps should be in what position?

A– Fully closed

B– Fully open

C– Opened according to ambient conditions

10-11. Answer B. JSPT 10A, FPH

Cowl flaps are small doors at the rear of an engine cowling that are used to vary the amount of cooling air that flows through the engine compartment. When an engine is operated on the ground, the airflow through the cowl is limited due to the lack of forward motion. Therefore, to keep the engine from overheating, the cowl flaps should be placed in the full open position to allow the maximum amount of cooling air to flow through the engine compartment.

10-12   AMP028

During an operational check of an electrically powered radial engine cowl flap system, the motor fails to operate. Which of the following is the first to be checked?

A– Flap actuator motor circuit breaker

B– Cockpit control switch

C– Flap actuator motor

10-12. Answer A. FGH

Any time an electrical component fails to operate, the first action should be to check the component's fuse or circuit breaker.

10-13   AMP027

1. Some aircraft exhaust systems include an augmenter system to draw additional air over the engine for cooling.

2. Augmenter systems are used to create a low pressure area at the lower rear of the aircraft engine cowling.

Regarding the above statements,

A– only No.1 is true.

B– both No.1 and No.2 are true.

C– only No.2 is true.

10-13. Answer B. JSPT 10A, FPH

An augmenter system consists of tubes running from the engine compartment to the rear of the nacelle. The exhaust collectors feed exhaust gas into the inner augmenter tubes where the highvelocity flow creates an area of low pressure at the augmenter inlet. This low pressure draws additional air through the cowling to aid in cooling.

10-14   AMP056
Which of the following defects would likely cause a hot spot on a reciprocating engine cylinder?

A– Too much cooling fin area broken off

B– A cracked cylinder baffle

C– Cowling air seal leakage

10-14. Answer A. JSPT 10A, FPH
The cooling fins on reciprocating aircraft engines are designed with a precise surface area to dissipate a certain amount of heat. Therefore, if a large piece of cooling fin breaks off from a cylinder, a hot spot can develop. Although a cracked cylinder baffle or a leaking cowling air seal would reduce the efficiency of the engine's cooling system, neither would cause a localized hot spot on a cylinder.

10-15   AMP027
What part of an air-cooled cylinder assembly has the greatest fin area per square inch?

A– Cylinder barrel

B– Rear of the cylinder head

C– Exhaust valve port

10-15. Answer C. JSPT 10A, FPH
The hottest area on a cylinder head is around the exhaust valve and, therefore, requires the greatest fin area per square inch.

10-16   AMP027
Reciprocating engines used in helicopters are cooled by

A– the downdraft from the main rotor.

B– a fan mounted on the engine.

C– blast tubes on either side of the engine mount.

10-16. Answer B. JSPT 10A
When operating a reciprocating engine-powered helicopter, ram air pressure from the rotor system is usually not sufficient to cool the engine, particularly when the helicopter is hovering. Therefore, many helicopters utilize large engine-driven fans to maintain a strong flow of air around the engine.

10-17   AMP027
The greatest portion of heat generated by combustion in a typical aircraft reciprocating engine is

A– converted into useful power.

B– carried out with the exhaust gases.

C– dissipated through the cylinder walls and heads.

10-17. Answer B. JSPT 10A, FPH
In a typical aircraft reciprocating engine, about 40 percent of the heat generated in the engine is carried out with the exhaust gas while approximately 30 percent is removed by the oil and the engine's cooling system. The remaining 30 percent is converted into useful power. Therefore, the majority of heat generated by combustion is carried out with the exhaust gases.

10-18   AMP028

A broken cooling fin on a cylinder head

A– is cause for rejection of the head.

B– may be filed to smooth contours if damage and/or repair limits are not exceeded.

C– should be left alone.

10-18. Answer B. JSPT 10A, FPH

Although a broken cooling fin reduces cooling efficiency, it is not necessarily cause for rejection. For example, if the manufacturer's service limits have not been exceeded, the cooling fin may be filed to produce smooth contours and remain in service.

10-19   AMP009

Cylinder head temperatures are measured by means of an indicator and a

A– resistance bulb sensing device.

B– Wheatstone bridge sensing device.

C– thermocouple sensing device.

10-19. Answer C. JSPT 10A, FAH

Cylinder head temperature is usually measured with a thermocouple sensing device. A thermocouple consists of a circuit with two dissimilar metal wires that are joined at both ends to form two junctions. When one junction is heated, the thermocouple generates an electric current that can be measured by a galvanometer. The hotter the high temperature junction, the greater the current produced. By calibrating the galvanometer in degrees, it becomes a thermometer.

10-20   AMP056

Prolonged idling of an engine will usually result in

A– excessive cylinder head temperatures.

B– increased oil consumption.

C– foreign material buildup on spark plugs.

10-20. Answer C. FPH

When an engine is operated for a long period at idle RPM, a rich fuel/air mixture must be used to keep cylinder head temperatures within acceptable limits. However, after prolonged operation, the excess fuel has a tendency to build up and foul out the spark plugs.

10-21   AMP027

The most common method and generally the best conduction of heat from the inside of a cylinder barrel to the cooling air is accomplished by

A– machining fins directly on the outside of the barrel.

B– shrinking on a jacket or muff of aluminum cooling fins around a steel cylinder sleeve.

C– machining fins directly on the outside of the barrel and shrinking on a jacket or muff of aluminum cooling fins around a steel cylinder sleeve (on different areas of the barrel).

10-21. Answer A. JSPT 10A, FPH

Almost all reciprocating engine cylinder barrels have cooling fins machined directly onto their outside surfaces to help dissipate heat. These fins allow heat to be conducted away from the inside of the cylinder, allowing the use of stronger, lighter alloys.

10-22   AMP027

What is the function of a blast tube as found on aircraft engines?

A– A means of cooling the engine by utilizing the propeller backwash

B– A tube used to load a cartridge starter

C– A device to cool an engine accessory

10-22. Answer C. JSPT 10A, FPH

Many reciprocating engines use blast tubes to direct cooling air to inaccessible areas of an engine compartment. A blast tube is simply a small pipe or duct that channels air from the main cooling air stream onto heat-sensitive components such as spark plugs and alternators.

10-23   AMP056

What is the position of the cowl flaps during engine starting and warm-up operations under normal conditions?

A– Full open at all times

B– Full closed at all times

C– Open for starting, closed for warm-up

10-23. Answer A. JSPT 10A, FPH

Cowl flaps are used to control the amount of air that flows over an engine. During ground operations, many aircraft engines have a tendency to overheat due to the decreased airflow into the cowling. Therefore, during most ground operations the cowl flaps are typically left fully open to provide maximum cooling.

10-24   AMP028

Aircraft reciprocating engine cylinder baffles and deflectors should be repaired as required to prevent loss of

A– power.

B– fin area.

C– cooling.

10-24. Answer C. JSPT 10A, FPH

Cylinder deflectors and baffles are designed to force air over the cylinder cooling fins to ensure proper cooling. Therefore, if a cylinder baffle or deflector is damaged, it should be repaired as soon as possible to prevent a loss of cooling efficiency. Even a small amount of damage could cause a localized hot spot and an eventual engine malfunction.

SECTION B — TURBINE ENGINES

Section B of Chapter 10 covers the cooling features and requirements for turbine engines..

10-25   AMP068

The active clearance control (ACC) portion of an EEC system aids turbine engine efficiency by

A– adjusting stator vane position according to operating conditions and power requirements.

B– ensuring turbine blade to engine case clearances are kept to a minimum by controlling case temperatures.

C– automatically adjusting engine speed to maintain a desired EPR.

10-25. Answer B. JSPT 10B

The active clearance control (ACC) portion of an electronic engine control (EEC) system controls turbine blade-to-engine case clearances by controlling the amount of air that is directed through the engine case. By keeping clearances to a minimum, pressure losses caused by air leakage at the blade tips is minimized.

10-26   AMP068

Which statement is true regarding the air passing through the combustion section of a jet engine?

A– Most is used for engine cooling

B– Most is used to support combustion

C– A small percentage is frequently bled off at this point to be used for air-conditioning and/or other pneumatic powered systems

10-26. Answer A. JSPT 10B, FPH

Approximately 25 percent of the air passing through a turbine engine's combustion chamber is used to support combustion while the other 75 percent is used to propel the turbine and cool the engine.

10-27   AMP027

How are combustion liner walls cooled in a gas turbine engine?

A– By secondary air flowing through the combustion chamber

B– By the pattern of holes and louvers cut in the diffuser section

C– By bleed air vented from the engine air inlet

10-27. Answer A. JSPT 10B, FPH

The airflow coming off the compressor is typically divided into primary and secondary flows. The primary flow is used to support combustion and drive the turbine while the secondary flow is used to cool the combustion and turbine sections.

ENGINE FIRE PROTECTION

SECTION A — FIRE DETECTION SYSTEMS

Section A of Chapter 11 addresses fire detection systems used on reciprocating and turbine engine aircraft including smoke and flame detection systems, and warning systems.

11-1   AMP034
Which of the following fire detectors are commonly used in the power section of an engine nacelle?

A– CO detectors

B– Smoke detectors

C– Rate-of-temperature-rise detectors

11-1. Answer C. JSPT 11A, FPH
A typical fire detection system used in reciprocating engine aircraft incorporates a thermocouple system that uses a series of rate-of-temperature-rise detectors. With this type of system a warning will not sound when an engine warms up slowly or when a short circuit develops. However, if temperatures in the engine compartment should rise rapidly, such as when a fire exists, the detectors will sound a warning horn in the cockpit.

11-2   AMP034
What is the function of a fire detection system?

A– To discharge the power plant fire-extinguishing system at the origin of the fire

B– To activate a warning device in the event of a power plant fire

C– To identify the location of a power plant fire

11-2. Answer B. JSPT 11A, FPH
The function of a fire detection system is to activate a warning device in the event of a power plant fire. It is important to remember that a fire detection system only warns the pilot of a fire, it does not pinpoint a fire's location or try to extinguish it.

11-3   AMP034
A continuous-loop fire detector is what type of detector?

A– Spot detector

B– Overheat detector

C– Rate-of-temperature-rise detector

11-3. Answer B. JSPT 11A, FPH
A continuous-loop fire detection system consists of a loop of one or two conductors installed around an engine compartment that, when overheated, sends electrical current to a warning indicator in the cockpit.

11-4   AMP034

What is the operating principle of the spot detector sensor in a fire detection system?

A– Resistant core material that prevents current flow at normal temperatures

B– A conventional thermocouple that produces a current flow

C– A bimetallic thermoswitch that closes when heated to a high temperature

11-4. Answer C. JSPT 11A, FPH

Spot detector fire detection systems consist of a bimetallic thermal switch installed between two loops of wire. When the thermal switch is heated to a predetermined temperature, the switch closes and completes the circuit between the two wire loops. With the circuit completed, electrical current flows to the fire warning horn in the cockpit.

11-5   AMP034

Which of the following is NOT used to detect fires in reciprocating engine nacelles?

A– Smoke detectors

B– Rate-of-temperature-rise detectors

C– Flame detectors

11-5. Answer A. JSPT 11A, FPH

Some of the common devices used to detect fires on reciprocating engine aircraft include: overheat detectors, rate-of-temperature-rise detectors, flame detectors, and observation by crewmembers. Smoke detectors, on the other hand, are only effective in relatively still air where materials burn slowly or smolder and, therefore, are not used in reciprocating engine nacelles.

11-6   AMP034

What is the principle of operation of the continuous-loop fire detector system sensor?

A– Fuse material which melts at high temperatures

B– Core resistance material which prevents current flow at normal temperatures

C– A bimetallic thermoswitch which closes when heated to a high temperature

11-6. Answer B. JSPT 11A, FPH

In a continuous-loop fire detection system, an electrical wire or wires are surrounded by a material with a resistance value that prevents the flow of current at normal temperatures. However, when the material is heated, the resistance decreases and allows current within the wires to find a path to ground. This completes the circuit and allows current to flow to the warning horn in the cockpit.

11-7   AMP034

Why does one type of Fenwal fire detection system use spot detectors wired in parallel between two separate circuits?

A– To provide an installation that is equal to two separate systems: a primary system and a secondary, or back-up system

B– So that a double fault may exist in the system without sounding a false alarm

C– So that a single fault may exist in the system without sounding a false alarm

11-7. Answer C. JSPT 11A, FPH

The Fenwal fire-detection system utilizes spot detectors that are wired in parallel between two separate circuits so that a short or fault in either leg of the system will not cause a false fire warning. The system is wired so that one leg of the circuit supplies current to the detectors while the other leg serves as a path to ground. If the ground leg should develop a short, a false fire warning will not occur because this portion of the circuit is already grounded. If the powered leg shorts, the rapid increase in current flow will trip a relay which causes the powered leg to become the ground and the grounded leg to become powered.

11-8   AMP034

Which of the following fire detection systems measures temperature rise compared to a reference temperature?

A– Thermocouple

B– Thermal switch

C– Lindberg continuous element

11-8. Answer A. JSPT 11A, FPH

The thermocouple fire warning system senses the rate of temperature rise and, therefore, only provides a warning when the temperature increases rapidly. In each thermocouple, there is a cold, or reference junction that is enclosed in an insulated air space and a hot junction which is installed in an uninsulated space. If both of these junctions heat up at the same rate, no fire warning is given regardless of the temperature. However, if the hot junction should be exposed to an extreme amount of heat, a temperature imbalance between the two junctions will exist causing current to flow to the warning horn.

11-9   AMP034

A fire detection system operates on the principle of a buildup of gas pressure within a tube proportional to temperature. Which of the following systems does this statement define?

A– Kidde continuous-loop system

B– Lindberg continuous-element system

C– Thermal switch system

11-9. Answer B. JSPT 11A, FAH

The Lindberg continuous-element fire detection system is a continuous-element type detector consisting of a stainless steel tube filled with an inert gas, typically helium. The principle of operation is based on the fact that if the volume of the gas is held constant, its pressure will increase as temperature increases. Thus the helium within the enclosed tube will exert a pressure proportional to the temperature along the entire length of the tube. If the pressure within the tube becomes excessive, it mechanically actuates a diaphragm in a responder unit which sets off the fire alarm.

11-10   AMP034

The fire detection system that uses a single wire surrounded by a continuous string of ceramic beads in a tube is the

A– Fenwal system.

B– Kidde system.

C– thermocouple system.

11-10. Answer A. JSPT 11A, FPH

The Fenwal fire detection system consists of an Inconel® tube with one wire running through it. The wire carries an electrical potential and the tube is the source to ground. The potential and ground are separated by a core material which, when cold, acts as a resistor. However, when the core material is heated to a specified temperature, it acts as a conductor and allows the potential to find a path to ground. When this circuit is completed, it causes a fire alarm to sound.

11-11   AMP034

The fire detection system that uses two wires imbedded in a ceramic core within a tube is the

A– Fenwal system.

B– Lindberg system.

C– Kidde system.

11-11. Answer C. JSPT 11A, FPH

The Kidde fire detection system consists of an inconel tube with two wires running through it. One of the wires has a positive electrical potential while the other is a source to ground. The two wires are separated by a core material which, when cold, acts as a resistor. However, when the core material is heated to a specific temperature it acts as a conductor and allows the potential to find a path to ground.

11-12   AMP034

A fire detection system that operates on the rate-of-temperature rise is a

A– continuous-loop system.

B– thermocouple system.

C– thermal switch system.

11-12. Answer B. JSPT 11A, FPH

The thermocouple fire warning system senses the rate of temperature rise and, therefore, only provides a warning when the temperature increases rapidly. In each thermocouple, there is a cold, or reference junction that is enclosed in an insulated air space and a hot junction which is installed in an uninsulated space. If both of these junctions heat up at the same rate, no fire warning is given regardlessof the temperature. However, if the hot junction should be exposed to an extreme amount of heat, a temperature imbalance between the two junctions will exist causing current to flow to the warning horn.

11-13   AMP034

Two continuous-loop fire detection systems that will not test due to a broken detector element are the

A— Kidde system and the Lindberg system.

B— Kidde system and the Fenwal system.

C— thermocouple system and the Lindberg system.

11-13. Answer B. JSAT 16A, FAH

Both the Kidde and Fenwal systems are continuous-loop fire detection systems that rely on a complete, unbroken circuit to allow the press-to-test operation to function. However, both systems can experience a break and still give a fire warning.

11-14   AMP034

Which of the following fire detection systems will detect a fire when an element is inoperative but will not test when the test circuit is energized?

A— The Kidde system and the thermocouple system

B— The Kidde system and the Fenwal system

C— The thermocouple system and the Lindberg system

11-14. Answer B. JSPT 11A, FAH

Both the Kidde and Fenwal systems are continuous-loop fire detection systems that rely on a complete, unbroken circuit to allow the press-to-test operation to function. However, both systems can experience a break and still give a fire warning.

11-15   AMP034

Which of the following fire detection systems uses heat in the normal testing of the system?

A— The thermocouple system and the Lindberg system

B— The Kidde system and the Fenwal system

C— The thermocouple system and the Fenwal system

11-15. Answer A. JSPT 11A, FAH

When testing either the thermocouple or the Lindbergh fire detection systems, heat must be applied to the detectors to simulate a fire condition and sound the warning horn in the cockpit.

11-16   AMP034

After a fire is extinguished, or overheat condition removed in aircraft equipped with a Systron-Donner fire detector, the detection system

A— must be manually reset.

B— automatically resets.

C— sensing component must be replaced.

11-16. Answer B. JSPT 11A, ITP-A2

The Systron-Donner fire detector system continuously monitors temperatures and automatically resets after an overheat condition is removed or the fire extinguished.

SECTION B — FIRE EXTINGUISHING SYSTEMS

Section B of Chapter 11 addresses fire extinguishing systems that are used on reciprocating and turbine engine aircraft, including fire extinguisher agents.

11-17   AMP034

How are most aircraft turbine engine fire-extinguishing systems activated?

A– Electrically discharged cartridges

B– Manual remote control valve

C– Pushrod assembly

11-17. Answer A. JSPT 11B, FPH

In a turbine engine powered aircraft, the fire extinguishing portion of a fire protection system typically includes a cylinder of extinguishing agent for each engine and nacelle area. The container of agent is normally equipped with two discharge valves that are operated by electrically discharged cartridges. The electrical current needed to discharge the cartridges is released by the fire handles in the cockpit.

11-18   AMP036

How does carbon dioxide (CO_2) extinguish an aircraft engine fire?

A– Contact with the air converts the liquid into snow and gas which smothers the flame

B– By lowering the temperature to a point where combustion will not take place

C– The high pressure spray lowers the temperature and blows out the fire

11-18. Answer A. JSPT 11B, FPH

When liquid CO2 leaves the fire extinguisher nozzle u der pressure, it converts into a gas that extinguishes flame by displacing the oxygen around the flame and smothering it.

11-19   AMP036

What retains the nitrogen charge and fire-extinguishing agent in a high rate of discharge (HRD) container?

A– Breakable disk and fusible disk

B– Pressure switch and check tee valve

C– Pressure gauge and cartridge

11-19. Answer A. JSPT 11B, FPH

The nitrogen charge within a typical high rate of discharge container is retained, or held in by a discharge plug and a safety discharge connection. The discharge plug is sealed with a breakable disk combined with an explosive charge that is electrically detonated to discharge the contents of the bottle. The safety discharge connection, or fusible disk, is capped at the inboard side of the engine strut with a red indication disk. If the temperature rises beyond a predetermined safe value, the disk will rupture, dumping the agent overboard.

11-20   AMP036
How is the fire-extinguishing agent distributed in the engine section?

A– Spray nozzles and fluid pumps

B– Nitrogen pressure and slinger rings

C– Spray nozzles and perforated tubing

11-20. Answer C. JSPT 11B, FPH
In a typical engine fire extinguishing system, the extinguishing agent is distributed through spray nozzles and perforated tubing. The perforated tubing distribution system is more common with reciprocating engines, while spray nozzles are typically used with turbine engines.

11-21   AMP036
Which of the following is the safest fire-extinguishing agent to use from a standpoint of toxicity and corrosion hazards?

A– Dibromodifluoromethane (Halon 1202)

B– Bromochlorodifluoromethane (Halon 1211)

C– Bromotrifluoromethane (Halon 1301)

11-21. Answer C. JSPT 11B, FAH
Bromotrifluoromethane (Halon 1301) is one of the most effective fire extinguishing agents. In addition, it is non-toxic and non-corrosive.

11-22   AMP036
The most satisfactory extinguishing agent for a carburetor or intake fire is

A– carbon dioxide.

B– dry chemical.

C– methyl bromide.

11-22. Answer A. JSAT 16B, FGH
Carbon dioxide is the most satisfactory agent to use for a carburetor or intake fire and, when used properly, will not damage the engine. Dry chemical and methyl bromide, on the other hand, can cause damage when used to extinguish intake fires.

11-23   AMP036
The explosive cartridge in the discharge valve of a fire-extinguisher container is

A– a life-dated unit.

B– not a life-dated unit.

C– mechanically fired.

11-23. Answer A. JSAT 16B, FAH
The service life of fire extinguisher discharge cartridges is specified by the manufacturer and stated in hours. The service life of a typical discharge cartridge is 5,000 hours.

11-24   AMP036

The pulling out (or down) of an illuminated fire handle in a typical large jet aircraft fire protection system commonly accomplishes what events?

A– Closes all firewall shutoff valves, disconnects the generator, and discharges a fire bottle

B– Closes fuel shutoff, closes hydraulic shutoff, disconnects the generator field, and arms the fire-extinguishing system

C– Closes fuel shutoff, closes hydraulic shutoff, closes the oxygen shutoff, disconnects the generator field, and arms the fire-extinguishing system

11-24. Answer B. JSAT 16B, FPH

When the pilot pulls the fire handle it arms the fire extinguisher system, disconnects the generator field relay, and shuts off the fuel and hydraulics to the engine.

11-25   AMP010

A fuel or oil fire is defined as a

A– class B fire.

B– class A fire.

C– class C fire.

11-25. Answer A. JSPT 11B, FAH

Class B fires involve combustible liquids such as gasoline, engine oil, turbine fuel, hydraulic oil, and many solvents and paint thinners used in aviation maintenance.

11-26   AMP010

A fire involving energized electrical equipment is defined as a

A– class B fire.

B– class D fire.

C– class C fire.

11-26. Answer C. JSPT 11B, FAH

Class C fires are those which involve electrical equipment. When attempting to extinguish a class C fire, special care must be exercised because of the dangers of electricity, as well as those from the fire itself.

11-27   AMP036

In a fixed fire-extinguishing system, there are two small lines running from the system and exiting overboard. These line exit ports are covered with a blowout type indicator disc. Which of the following statements is true?

A— When the red indicator disc is missing, it indicates the fire-extinguishing system has been normally discharged.

B— When the yellow indicator disc is missing, it indicates the fire-extinguishing system has been normally discharged.

C— When the green indicator disc is missing, it indicates the fire-extinguishing system has had a thermal discharge.

11-27. Answer B. JSPT 11B, FAH

In a typical fixed fire extinguishing system, a yellow and a red colored disk are used to indicate the status of the extinguishing agent. The yellow disk blows when the agent has been emptied by a normal discharge and the red disk blows when the agent is blown overboard due to an over-temperature condition.

11-28   AMP010

The most satisfactory extinguishing agent for an electrical fire is

A— carbon tetrachloride.

B— carbon dioxide.

C— methyl bromide.

11-28. Answer B. JSPT 11B, FAH

Of the choices given, carbon dioxide is the most satisfactory extinguishing agent for fires involving electrical equipment. However, halogenated hydrocarbon and dry powder extinguishers may also be used.

11-29   AMP010

The use of water on class D fires

A— is most effective if sprayed in a fine mist.

B— will cause the fire to burn more violently and can cause explosions.

C— has no effect.

11-29. Answer B. JSPT 11B, FGH

A class D fire is one in which some metal, such as magnesium, is burning. Class D fires are put out using dry powder or halogenated extinguishers and under no circumstances should water be used. The application of water to a class D fire will cause the fire to burn more violently and can cause explosions.

11-30   AMP036

For fire detection and extinguishing purposes, aircraft power plant areas are divided into fire zones based on

A– hot and cold sections of the engine.

B– the volume and smoothness of the airflow through engine compartments.

C– engine type and size.

11-30. Answer B. JSPT 11B, FAH

For fire detection and extinguishing purposes, aircraft power plant areas are divided into fire zones based on the volume and smoothness of airflow passing through the area.

11-31   AMP036
(Refer to figure 2.)

Determine the fire-extinguisher container pressure limits when the temperature is 75°F.

A– 326 minimum and 415 maximum

B– 330 minimum and 419 maximum

C– 338 minimum and 424 maximum

11-31. Answer C. JSAT 16B, FPH

Since the question specifies a temperature of 75°C you must interpolate between the minimum and maximum limits for both 70°F and 80°F. To interpolate find the difference between the two readings, divide the difference by two and add the quotient to the lower pressure. The minimum container pressure at 70°F is 319 PSIG and 356 PSIG at 80°F. Therefore, the minimum pressure at 75°F is 338 PSIG (356 − 319 = 37 ÷ 2 = 18.5 + 319 = 337.5). The maximum pressure at 70°F is 405 PSIG and 443 PSIG at 80°F. Therefore, the maximum pressure at 75°F is 424 PSIG (443 − 405 = 38 ÷ 2 = 19 + 405 = 424).

CONTAINER PRESSURE VERSUS TEMPERATURE		
TEMPERATURE °F	CONTAINER PRESSURE (PSIG)	
	MINIMUM	MAXIMUM
−40	60	145
−30	83	165
−20	105	188
−10	125	210
0	145	230
10	167	252
20	188	275
30	209	295
40	230	317
50	255	342
60	284	370
70	319	405
80	356	443
90	395	483
100	438	523

Figure 2. Fire Extinguisher Pressure Chart

11-32   AMP036
(Refer to figure 3.)

What are the fire-extinguisher container pressure limits when the temperature is 50°F?

A– 425 - 575 PSIG

B– 435 - 605 PSIG

C– 475 - 625 PSIG

11-32. Answer C. JSAT 16B, FPH
To answer this question, begin by locating 50°F at the bottom of the chart. From here, follow the line up to intersect the minimum gauge reading curve. From this intersection, draw a horizontal line to the left that intersects the pressure axis at 475 PSIG. Next, go back to the 50°F line and follow it up to intersect the maximum gauge reading curve. From this intersection, draw a horizontal line to the left that intersects the pressure axis at 625 PSIG. Based on this chart, the minimum and maximum container pressure at 50°F is 475 PSIG and 625 PSIG respectively.

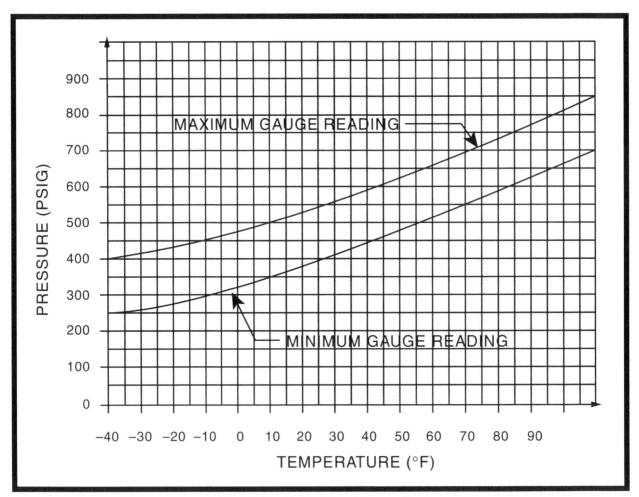

Figure 3. Fire Extinguisher Pressure Chart

CHAPTER 12

PROPELLERS

SECTION A — PROPELLER PRINCIPLES

This section contains information regarding the construction and aerodynamic principles of propellers.

12-1 AMP053
What operational force causes the greatest stress on a propeller?

A– Aerodynamic twisting force

B– Centrifugal force

C– Thrust bending force

12-1. Answer B. JSPT 12A, FPH
The greatest stress on a propeller is the centrifugal force created by the propeller's rotation. Depending on a blade's weight and RPM, centrifugal force can be greater than 25 tons.

12-2 AMP053
What operational force tends to increase propeller blade angle?

A– Centrifugal twisting force

B– Aerodynamic twisting force

C– Thrust bending force

12-2. Answer B. JSPT 12A, FPH
A propeller blade is an airfoil and is subject to the same aerodynamic forces as any other airfoil. On all propeller blades, the center of lift, or center of pressure, is forward of the blade's center of rotation. Therefore, when a propeller blade is producing lift (thrust), the blade tends to rotate to a higher angle. This is called aerodynamic twisting force.

12-3 AMP053
How does the aerodynamic twisting force affect operating propeller blades?

A– It tends to turn the blades to a high blade angle.

B– It tends to bend the blades forward.

C– It tends to turn the blades to a low blade angle.

12-3. Answer A. JSPT 12A, FPH
A propeller blade is an airfoil and is subject to the same aerodynamic forces as any other airfoil. On all propeller blades, the center of lift, or center of pressure, is forward of the blade's center of rotation. Therefore, when a propeller blade is producing lift (thrust), the blade tends to rotate to a higher angle. This is called aerodynamic twisting force.

12-4   AMP053

The propeller blade angle is defined as the acute angle between the airfoil section chord line (at the blade reference station) and which of the following?

A– The plane of rotation

B– The relative wind

C– The axis of blade rotation during pitch change

12-4. Answer A. JSPT 12A, FPH

The propeller blade angle is the acute angle between the airfoil section chord line at the proper reference station and the propeller's rotational plane. The reference station is typically at a point approximately 75 percent of the distance from the hub to the tip.

12-5   AMP053

The actual distance a propeller moves forward through the air during one revolution is known as the

A– effective pitch.

B– geometric pitch.

C– relative pitch.

12-5. Answer A. JSPT 12A, FPH

Effective pitch is the actual distance a propeller moves through the air in one revolution.

12-6   AMP053

Propeller blade stations are measured from the

A– index mark on the blade shank.

B– hub centerline.

C– blade base.

12-6. Answer B. JSPT 12A, FPH

Propeller blade stations are measured from the hub centerline. Each blade has its own set of stations starting from station zero at the hub centerline and increasing out to the blade tip.

12-7   AMP053

The thrust produced by a rotating propeller is a result of

A– an area of low pressure behind the propeller blades.

B– an area of decreased pressure immediately in front of the propeller blades.

C– the angle of relative wind and rotational velocity of the propeller.

12-7. Answer B. JSPT 12A, FPH

A propeller is a rotating airfoil and creates thrust the same way an airplane's wing creates lift. When the propeller rotates, an area of decreased pressure forms in front of the propeller blade, while an area of constant or higher pressure forms in back of the propeller. The pressure differential between the front and back of the propeller is the source of thrust.

12-8   AMP053
The angle-of-attack of a rotating propeller blade is measured between the blade chord or face and which of the following?

A– Plane of blade rotation

B– Full low-pitch blade angle

C– Relative airstream

12-8. Answer C. JSPT 12A, FPH
Propeller angle of attack is the acute angle between the blade chord and the relative wind.

12-9   AMP053
The centrifugal twisting moment of an operating propeller tends to

A– increase the pitch angle.

B– reduce the pitch angle.

C– bend the blades in the direction of rotation.

12-9. Answer B. JSPT 12A, FPH
When an object rotates, its center of mass tends to align with its center of rotation. A propeller's center of mass is typically ahead of its center of rotation. Therefore, when a propeller rotates, centrifugal force tries to pull the propeller's center of mass in line with its center of rotation thereby decreasing the propeller's pitch angle.

12-10   AMP053
Which of the following is identified as the cambered or curved side of a propeller blade, corresponding to the upper surface of a wing airfoil section?

A– Blade back

B– Blade chord

C– Blade face

12-10. Answer A. JSPT 12A, FPH
The curved, or cambered side of a propeller blade is called the blade back and the flat side is called the blade face.

12-11   AMP053
Blade angle is an angle formed by a line perpendicular to the crankshaft and a line formed by the

A– relative wind.

B– chord of the blade.

C– blade face.

12-11. Answer B. JSPT 12A, FPH
Blade angle is the acute angle formed by a line perpendicular to the crankshaft centerline and the chord of the blade at a specified reference station.

12-12   AMP053
Propeller blade station numbers increase from

A– hub to tip.

B– tip to hub.

C– leading edge to trailing edge.

12-12. Answer A. JSPT 12A, FPH
Propeller blade stations are measured from the hub centerline. Each blade has its own set of stations starting from station zero at the hub centerline and increasing out to the blade tip.

12-13   AMP053
The aerodynamic force acting on a rotating propeller blade operating at a normal pitch angle tends to

A– reduce the pitch angle.

B– increase the pitch angle.

C– bend the blades rearward in the line of flight.

12-13. Answer B. JSPT 12A, FPH
A propeller blade is an airfoil and is subject to the same aerodynamic forces as any other airfoil. On all propeller blades, the center of lift, or center of pressure, is forward of the blade's center of rotation. Therefore, when a propeller blade is producing lift (thrust), the blade tends to rotate to a higher angle. This is called aerodynamic twisting force.

12-14   AMP053
The blade angle of a fixed-pitch propeller

A– is greatest at the tip.

B– is smallest at the tip.

C– increases in proportion to the distance each section is from the hub.

12-14. Answer B. JSPT 12A, FPH
A propeller's blade angle decreases from the hub to the tip. This is necessary because the further a blade station is from the hub, the faster the airfoil moves through the air. Therefore, in order to maintain a relatively equal amount of thrust along the entire blade length, the blade angle must decrease from the hub to the tip.

12-15   AMP053
Most engine-propeller combinations have one or more critical ranges within which continuous operation is not permitted. Critical ranges are established to avoid

A– severe propeller vibration.

B– low or negative thrust conditions.

C– inefficient propeller pitch angles.

12-15. Answer A. JSPT 12A
Propellers are subject to aerodynamic vibrations when the blade tips travel at near sonic speeds. In addition, mechanical vibrations are transmitted from the engine to the propeller. At certain combinations of airspeed and engine rpm these vibrations can create harmonic stresses that could lead to metal fatigue and eventual propeller blade failure. Therefore, the Type Certificate Data Sheets for engine/propeller combinations identify any critical RPM ranges that are to be avoided to prevent severe vibration. Regulations require that these ranges be marked on the tachometer with a red arc.

12-16   AMP053

The primary purpose of a cuff on a propeller is to

A– distribute anti-icing fluid.

B– strengthen the propeller.

C– increase the flow of cooling air to the engine nacelle.

12-16. Answer C. JSPT 12A, FPH

A blade cuff is a metal, wood, or plastic structure that is attaches to the shank of a propeller blade. The cuff surface transforms the round shank into an airfoil section and is designed primarily to increase the flow of cooling air to the engine nacelle.

12-17   AMP053

The primary purpose of a propeller is to

A– create lift on the fixed airfoils of an aircraft.

B– change engine horsepower to thrust.

C– provide static and dynamic stability of an aircraft in flight.

12-17. Answer B. FPH

The primary purpose of a propeller is to convert engine horsepower to useful thrust. Modern propellers can convert up to 85 percent of an engine's brake horsepower to thrust horsepower.

12-18   AMP053

The centrifugal twisting force acting on a propeller blade is

A– greater than the aerodynamic twisting force and tends to move the blade to a higher angle.

B– less than the aerodynamic twisting force and tends to move the blade to a lower angle.

C– greater than the aerodynamic twisting force and tends to move the blade to a lower angle.

12-18. Answer C. JSPT 12A, FPH

The centrifugal twisting force, sometimes called centrifugal twisting moment, acting on a propeller is greater than the aerodynamic twisting force and tries to decrease a propeller's blade angle.

12-19   AMP053

Geometric pitch of a propeller is defined as the

A– effective pitch minus slippage.

B– effective pitch plus slippage.

C– angle between the blade chord and the plane of rotation.

12-19. Answer B. JSPT 12A, FPH

A propeller's geometric pitch is the theoretical distance that the propeller will move forward in one revolution. Effective pitch, on the other hand, is the actual distance that the propeller moves forward in one revolution. The difference between geometric pitch and effective pitch is called slippage. Therefore, effective pitch plus slippage is equal to geometric pitch.

12-20   AMP053
Propeller blade angle is the angle between the

A— chord of the blade and the relative wind.

B— relative wind and the rotational plane of the propeller.

C— chord of the blade and the rotational plane of the propeller.

12-20. Answer C. JSPT 12A, FPH
Propeller blade angle is the acute angle formed by the propeller blade chord line and the rotational plane of the propeller.

12-21   AMP053
What operational force causes propeller blade tips to lag in the opposite direction of rotation?

A— Thrust-bending force

B— Aerodynamic-twisting force

C— Torque-bending force

12-21. Answer C. JSPT 12A, FPH
Torque bending force, in the form of air resistance, tends to bend cause a propeller's tips to lag in the direction of rotation.

12-22   AMP053
What operational force tends to bend the propeller blades forward at the tip?

A— Torque-bending force

B— Centrifugal-twisting force

C— Thrust-bending force

12-22. Answer C. JSPT 12A, FPH
Thrust bending force tends to bend the propeller tips forward as the propeller pulls an aircraft through the air. This force is comparable to the coning action of a helicopter rotor blade, except that the thrust bending force acts forward instead of upward.

SECTION B — FIXED-PITCH PROPELLERS

Section B of Chapter 12 contains information related to fixed-pitch propeller designs, including information on fixed-pitch propeller maintenance and identification.

12-23   AMP053

What is the primary purpose of the metal tipping which covers the blade tips and extends along the leading edge of each wood propeller blade?

A– To increase the lateral strength of the blade

B– To prevent impact damage to the tip and leading edge of the blade

C– To increase the longitudinal strength of the blade

12-23. Answer B. JSPT 12B, FPH

Metal tipping is applied to the leading edge and tip of wood propeller blades to prevent damage from small stones or debris which might strike the prop during ground operations. This tipping is attached to the blade with countersunk screws in the thick blade sections and with copper rivets in the thin sections.

12-24   AMP053

What is the basic purpose of the three small holes (No. 60 drill) in the tipping of wood propeller blades?

A– To provide a means for inserting balancing shot when necessary

B– To provide a means for periodically impregnating the blade with preservation materials

C– To allow the moisture which may collect between the tipping and the wood to escape (vent the tipping)

12-24. Answer C. JSPT 12B, FPH

The three small holes (No. 60 drill) in the metal tipping of a wooden propeller serve to ventilate and release moisture formed by condensation between the tipping and the wooden blade.

SECTION C — ADJUSTABLE-PITCH PROPELLERS

Section C of Chapter 12 contains information related to adjustable-pitch propeller designs, including information on adjustable-pitch propeller maintenance and identification. Constant-speed propeller governor theory and operation is also covered in this section.

12-25   AMP053

What is the basic operational sequence for reducing the power output of an engine equipped with a constant-speed propeller?

A– Reduce the RPM, then the manifold pressure.

B– Reduce the manifold pressure, then retard the throttle to obtain the correct RPM.

C– Reduce the manifold pressure, then the RPM.

12-25. Answer C. JSPT 12C, FPH
When reducing power on an engine equipped with a constant speed propeller, care should be taken to never let the manifold pressure get too high for a given RPM. To do this, the throttle should be pulled back to reduce the manifold pressure first followed by a slow reduction in RPM.

12-26   AMP053

To reduce the power output of an engine equipped with a constant-speed propeller and operating near maximum BMEP, the

A– manifold pressure is reduced with the throttle control before the RPM is reduced with the propeller control.

B– manifold pressure is reduced with the propeller control before the RPM is reduced with the throttle control.

C– RPM is reduced with the propeller control before the manifold pressure is reduced with the throttle control.

12-26. Answer A. JSPT 12C, FPH
When reducing power on an engine equipped with a constant speed propeller, care should be taken to never let the manifold pressure get too high for a given RPM. To do this, the throttle should be pulled back to reduce the manifold pressure first followed by a slow reduction in RPM.

12-27   AMP053

A power plant using a hydraulically controlled constant-speed propeller is operating within the propeller's constant-speed range at a fixed throttle setting. If the tension of the propeller governor control spring (speeder spring) is reduced by movement of the cockpit propeller control, the propeller blade angle will

A– increase, engine manifold pressure will increase, and engine RPM will decrease.

B– decrease, engine manifold pressure will increase, and engine RPM will decrease.

C– decrease, engine manifold pressure will decrease, and engine RPM will increase.

12-27. Answer A. JSPT 12C, FPH

On aircraft that utilize a constant-speed propeller, the pitch of the propeller blades is controlled by a governor consisting of an oil pump, pilot valve, speeder spring, and flyweights. When the propeller is in an on-speed condition, the centrifugal force exerted on the rotating flyweights is exactly balanced by the force exerted by the speeder spring and the propeller blade angle remains constant. If the speeder spring force is reduced through the use of the propeller control, the flyweights tilt outward into an over-speed position and the pilot valve allows oil to drain out of the propeller hub. This results in an increased blade angle, a reduction in RPM, and an increase in manifold pressure.

12-28   AMP052

Why is the pulley stop screw on a propeller governor adjustable?

A– To limit the maximum engine speed during takeoff

B– To maintain the proper blade angle for cruising

C– To limit the maximum propeller pitch for takeoff

12-28. Answer A. JSPT 12C, FPH

The pulley stop screw limits the amount of tension put on the governor speeder spring which, in turn, limits the maximum engine speed with full power applied.

12-29   AMP053

During engine operation at speeds lower than those for which the constant-speed propeller control can govern in the IN-CREASE RPM position, the propeller will

A– remain in the full HIGH PITCH position.

B– maintain engine RPM in the normal manner until the HIGH PITCH stop is reached.

C– remain in the full LOW PITCH position.

12-29. Answer C. JSPT 12C, FPH

When an engine operates at speeds lower than those the governor can govern in the INCREASE RPM position, the propeller will remain in the full LOW PITCH position. This occurs because, at low engine speeds the governor senses an underspeed condition and directs oil to position the propeller blades in the low pitch position in an effort to reduce engine load and increase rpm.

12-30 AMP053

When engine power is increased, the constant-speed propeller tries to function so that it will

A– maintain the RPM, decrease the blade angle, and maintain a low angle of attack.

B– increase the RPM, decrease the blade angle, and maintain a low angle of attack.

C– maintain the RPM, increase the blade angle, and maintain a low angle of attack.

12-30. Answer C. JSPT 12C, FPH

When engine power is increased, the propeller governor senses an over-speed condition. In an overspeed condition, centrifugal force causes the governor flyweights to tip outward causing the pilot valve to allow oil to drain from the propeller hub. As the oil drains, the propeller blade angle increases so the selected RPM can be maintained.

12-31 AMP053

The propeller governor controls the

A– oil to and from the pitch changing mechanism.

B– spring tension on the boost pump speeder spring.

C– linkage and counterweights from moving in and out.

12-31. Answer A. JSPT 12C, FPH

The propeller governor controls the flow of oil into and out of the pitch change mechanism in the propeller hub assembly.

12-32 AMP053

During the on-speed condition of a propeller, the

A– centrifugal force acting on the governor flyweights is greater than the tension of the speeder spring.

B– tension on the speeder spring is less than the centrifugal force acting on the governor flyweights.

C– centrifugal force of the governor flyweights is equal to the speeder spring force.

12-32. Answer C. JSPT 12C, FPH

On aircraft that utilize a constant-speed propeller, the pitch of the propeller blades is controlled by a governor consisting of an oil pump, pilot valve, speeder spring, and flyweights. When the propeller is in an on-speed condition, the centrifugal force exerted on the rotating flyweights is exactly balanced by the force exerted by the speeder spring and the propeller blade angle remains constant.

12-33   AMP053

What actuates the pilot valve in the governor of a constant-speed propeller?

A– Engine oil pressure

B– Governor flyweights

C– Governor pump oil pressure

12-33. Answer B. JSPT 12C, FPH

When a propeller over-speeds, centrifugal force causes the governor flyweights to overcome the speeder spring force and raise the pilot valve. During an under-speed, the speeder spring force overcomes the centrifugal force of the flyweights and lowers the pilot valve. Since speeder spring is not an answer, the governor flyweights is the only correct answer.

12-34   AMP053

What will happen to the propeller blade angle and the engine RPM if the tension on the propeller governor control spring (speeder spring) is increased?

A– Blade angle will decrease and RPM will decrease.

B– Blade angle will increase and RPM will decrease.

C– Blade angle will decrease and RPM will increase.

12-34. Answer C. JSPT 12C, FPH

When the propeller control in the cockpit is moved forward, governor speeder spring tension increases and causes the governor flyweights to tilt inward. This causes the pilot valve to lower and port oil in the direction necessary to decrease the propeller blade angle and increase RPM.

12-35   AMP053

How is the speed of a constant-speed propeller changed in flight?

A– By varying the output of the governor booster pump

B– By advancing or retarding the throttle

C– By changing the load tension against the flyweights in the governor

12-35. Answer C. JSPT 12C, FPH

To change the rotational speed of a constant-speed propeller in flight, the pilot adjusts the prop lever which varies the spring tension on the governor speeder spring. Moving the prop control forward increases spring tension which tilts the governor flyweights inward and lowers the pilot valve. On the other hand, moving the prop control aft decreases spring tension which allows the flyweights to tilt outward and raise the pilot valve.

12-36   AMP053
When the centrifugal force acting on the propeller governor flyweights overcomes the tension on the speeder spring, a propeller is in what speed condition?

A– On-speed

B– Under-speed

C– Over-speed

12-37   AMP053
During which of the following conditions of flight will the blade pitch angle of a constant-speed propeller be the greatest?

A– Approach to landing

B– Climb following takeoff

C– High-speed, high-altitude cruising flight

12-38   AMP053
What is the result of moving the throttle on a reciprocating engine when the propeller is in the constant-speed range with the engine developing cruise power?

A– Opening the throttle will cause an increase in blade angle.

B– The RPM will vary directly with any movement of the throttle.

C– Movement of the throttle will not affect the blade angle.

12-36. Answer C. JSPT 12C, FPH
When a propeller over-speeds, centrifugal force causes the governor flyweights to overcome the speeder spring force and raise the pilot valve. Oil pressure is decreased in counterweighted propellers or increased in non-counterweighted propellers, forcing the blades to a higher pitch and slowing the propeller to the selected RPM.

12-37. Answer C. JSPT 12C, FPH
To obtain the maximum amount of engine power during takeoff and climb a low propeller blade angle is used. However, during high-speed, high-altitude cruising flight, less engine power is needed and, therefore, the propeller blade angle is typically greater.

12-38. Answer A. JSPT 12C, FPH
When the throttle is opened on an engine which has a constant-speed propeller operating in the constant-speed range, the propeller governor increases the blade angle to absorb the additional engine power and maintain the desired RPM.

12-39   AMP053
Why is a constant-speed counterweight propeller normally placed in full HIGH PITCH position before the engine is stopped?

A– To prevent exposure and corrosion of the pitch changing mechanism

B– To prevent hydraulic lock of the piston when the oil cools

C– To prevent overheating of the engine during the next start

12-39. Answer A. JSPT 12C, FPH
Some constant-speed counterweight propellers use an exposed actuating piston to change the pitch of the propeller blade. Therefore, when shutting down an engine equipped with this type of propeller, the propeller should be placed in the full HIGH PITCH position so that the actuating piston is covered and somewhat protected from corrosion causing moisture by the propeller hub.

12-40   AMP052
The low pitch stop on a constant-speed propeller is usually set so that

A– the engine will turn at its rated takeoff RPM at sea level when the throttle is opened to allowable takeoff manifold pressure.

B– maximum allowable engine RPM cannot be exceeded with any combination of manifold pressure, altitude, or forward speed.

C– the limiting engine manifold pressure cannot be exceeded with any combination of throttle opening, altitude, or forward speed.

12-40. Answer A. JSPT 12C, 14 CFR 23.33
The low pitch stop on a constant-speed propeller is set so that the engine can develop its rated power at sea level at the RPM specified by the propeller manufacturer. If the low pitch stop is improperly set, the engine could fail to attain rated power.

12-41   AMP053
Which of the following best describes the blade movement of a full-feathering, constant-speed propeller that is in the LOW RPM position when the feathering action is begun?

A– High pitch through low pitch to feather position

B– High pitch directly to feather position

C– Low pitch through high pitch to feather position

12-41. Answer B. JSPT 12C, FPH
When a propeller is set in the LOW RPM position, the blade pitch is high. Therefore, when feathering is begun, the propeller blades move directly from high pitch into the feather position.

12-42   AMP053

Which of the following forces or combination of forces operates to move the blades of a constant-speed counterweight-type propeller to the HIGH PITCH position?

A— Engine oil pressure acting on the propeller piston-cylinder arrangement and centrifugal force acting on the counterweights

B— Centrifugal force acting on the counterweights

C— Prop governor oil pressure acting on the propeller piston-cylinder arrangement

12-42. Answer B. JSPT 12C, FPH

With counterweight-type propellers, centrifugal force acting on a set of counterweights tends to rotate the blades to a high pitch angle.

12-43   AMP052

The purpose of permanently sealing and partially filling some models of McCauley propeller hubs with dyed oil is to

A— provide an always clean separate lubrication of the internal parts.

B— dampen pressure surges and prevent too rapid changes in propeller blade angle.

C— make the location of cracks readily apparent.

12-43. Answer C. JSPT 12C

Some models of McCauley propellers use dyed oil to aid in the detection of cracks. The propeller hub is permanently sealed and partially filled with red-dyed oil. If red dye appears on the hub or blades, some component in the hub has failed and the propeller should be removed and serviced.

12-44   AMP053

Which of the following best describes the blade movement of a feathering propeller that is in the HIGH RPM position when the feathering action is begun?

A— High pitch through low pitch to feather position

B— Low pitch through reverse pitch to feather position

C— Low pitch through high pitch to feather position

12-44. Answer C. JSPT 12C, FPH

When a propeller is set in the HIGH RPM position, the blade pitch is low. Therefore, when the feathering action begins, the blades must rotate from low pitch through high pitch and then to the feather position.

12-45   AMP053

What controls the constant-speed range of a constant-speed propeller?

A– Engine RPM

B– Angle of climb and descent with accompanying changes in airspeed

C– The mechanical limits in the propeller pitch range

12-45. Answer C. JSPT 12C, FPH

Mechanical stops in the propeller hub limit the constant-speed range of a constant-speed propeller.

12-46   AMP053

For takeoff, a constant-speed propeller is normally set in the

A– HIGH PITCH, high RPM position.

B– HIGH PITCH, low RPM position.

C– LOW PITCH, high RPM position.

12-46. Answer C. JSPT 12C, FPH

To allow an engine to develop its rated takeoff power, a constant-speed propeller is normally set in the low pitch, high RPM position. This places the lightest load on the engine, allowing it to develop maximum power.

12-47   AMP052

Where are the high and low pitch stops of a Hamilton Standard constant-speed or two-position counterweight propeller located?

A– In the hub and blade assembly

B– In the counterweight assembly

C– In the dome assembly

12-47. Answer B. JSPT 12C

The high and low pitch stops of Hamilton Standard propellers are located in the counterweight assembly. However, in some of the more modern constantspeed propeller assemblies, the pitch stops are located in the dome assembly.

12-48   AMP053

Which of the following statements about constant-speed counterweight propellers is also true when referring to two-position counterweight propellers?

A— Blade angle changes are accomplished by the use of two forces, one hydraulic and the other centrifugal.

B— Since an infinite number of blade angle positions are possible during flight, propeller efficiency is greatly improved.

C— The pilot selects the RPM and the propeller changes pitch to maintain the selected RPM.

12-48. Answer A. JSPT 12C, FPH

The two-position and the constant-speed counterweight propellers both use hydraulic force to decrease blade angle and centrifugal force acting on counterweights to increase blade angle. The major difference between the two is that the constant-speed propeller utilizes a governor to boost the oil pressure to a higher level and automatically control the oil flow to and from the propeller, while the two-position propeller operates at engine lubrication system pressure with the oil flow controlled by a manual selector valve.

12-49   AMP053

The purpose of a three-way propeller valve is to

A— direct oil from the engine oil system to the propeller cylinder.

B— direct oil from the engine through the governor to the propeller.

C— permit constant-speed operation of the propeller.

12-49. Answer A. JSPT 12C, DSA-25

A three-way propeller valve is a selector valve used in a two-position propeller control system. The three-way valve directs oil from the engine lubrication system to the propeller to control a propeller blade's pitch angle.

12-50   AMP053

A constant-speed propeller provides maximum efficiency by

A— increasing blade pitch as the aircraft speed decreases.

B— adjusting blade angle for most conditions encountered in flight.

C— increasing the lift coefficient of the blade.

12-50. Answer B. JSPT 12C, FPH

A constant-speed propeller achieves maximum efficiency by allowing the pilot to adjust the propeller blade angle as necessary to produce the most efficient blade angle for most conditions encountered in flight.

12-51   AMP053

What are the rotational speed and blade pitch angle requirements of a constant-speed propeller during takeoff?

A– Low-speed and high-pitch angle

B– High-speed and low-pitch angle

C– High-speed and high-pitch angle

12-51. Answer B. JSPT 12C, FPH

During takeoff, a constant-speed propeller is set for high speed and a low pitch angle so the engine can develop its maximum rated power. Cruising flight, on the other hand, does not require maximum power so the propeller can be set for low speed and a high pitch angle.

12-52   AMP053

1. During takeoff, propeller thrust (pull) is greatest if the blade angle of attack is low and the engine power setting is high.

2. With the aircraft stationary, propeller thrust is greatest if the blade angle of attack is high and the engine power setting is high. Regarding the above statements,

A– only No.1 is true.

B– only No.2 is true.

C– both No.1 and No.2 are true.

12-52. Answer A. JSPT 12C, FPH

Only statement (1) is correct. During takeoff, when maximum power and thrust are required, the propeller blades are set to a low blade angle that allows the engine to turn at a high RPM.

12-53   AMP053

Constant-speed non-feathering McCauley, Hartzell, and other propellers of similar design without counterweights increase pitch angle using

A– oil pressure.

B– spring pressure.

C– centrifugal twisting moment.

12-53. Answer A. JSPT 12C, FPH

Most non-counterweight propellers use oil pressure to increase the propeller's blade angle.

12-54   AMP053

Counterweights on constant-speed propellers are generally used to aid in

A– increasing blade angle.

B– decreasing blade angle.

C– unfeathering the propellers.

12-54. Answer A. FPH

On constant-speed propellers equipped with counterweights, centrifugal force acting on the counterweights is used to increase a propeller's blade angle.

12-55   AMP053

The primary purpose of a feathering propeller is to

A– prevent further engine damage when an engine fails in flight.

B– prevent propeller damage when an engine fails in flight.

C– eliminate the drag created by a windmilling propeller when an engine fails in flight.

12-55. Answer C. JSPT 12C, FPH

When an engine is shut down in flight, the propeller blades create a substantial amount of drag which decreases aircraft performance. Feathering propellers eliminate this drag by driving the propeller blades to a 90 degree angle. Although feathering a propeller prevents it from windmilling and causing further engine damage, the primary purpose of feathering is to eliminate drag.

12-56   AMP053

What normally prevents a Hartzell Compact propeller from going to feather when the engine is shut down on the ground?

A– Propeller cylinder air pressure

B– A latch mechanism composed of springs and lock pins

C– Accumulator provided oil pressure

12-56. Answer B. JSPT 12C, FPH

Hartzell® Compact propellers utilize a latch stop called the automatic high pitch stop to hold the blades in a low angle when the engine is shut down on the ground. The latch mechanism is comprised of springs and lock pins that prevent the propellers from feathering once engine RPM falls below a predetermined value.

SECTION D — TURBOPROP PROPELLERS

This section contains information related to turboprop propeller designs, including turboprop propeller operations and maintenance.

12-57 AMP053

How is a propeller controlled in a large aircraft with a turboprop installation?

A– Independently of the engine

B– By varying the engine RPM except for feathering and reversing

C– By the engine power lever

12-57. Answer C. JSPT 12D, FPH

On turboprop engines, the fuel control unit and propeller governor are interconnected. Therefore, in flight, when a pilot moves the power lever, the fuel control and governor establish the correct combination of RPM, fuel flow, and propeller blade angle to provide the desired power output.

12-58 AMP053

Which of the following best describes the blade movement of a feathering propeller that is in the HIGH RPM position when reversing action is begun?

A– Low pitch directly to reverse pitch

B– Low pitch through high pitch to reverse pitch

C– Low pitch through feather position to reverse pitch

12-58. Answer A. JSPT 12D, FPH

When a propeller control is in a HIGH RPM position, there is a relatively low pitch on the propeller blades. When a propeller moves to reverse pitch, the blades rotate through the low blade angle and into a negative blade angle. Therefore, if a propeller blade is in a low pitch position when reverse pitch is selected, the blades will move directly to the reverse pitch position.

12-59 AMP053

An aircraft's propeller system beta range

A– is used to produce zero or negative thrust.

B– is used to achieve maximum thrust during takeoff.

C– refers to the most fuel efficient pitch range to use at a given engine RPM.

12-59. Answer A. JSPT 12D, FPH

Beta range refers to a reversing-type propeller that can operate in a zero or negative thrust range. During operation in beta range, propeller governor operation is locked out and all propeller control is accomplished with the power lever.

SECTION E — AUXILIARY PROPELLER SYSTEMS

Section E of Chapter 12 includes information related to auxiliary propeller systems including propeller synchronization, and anti-ice systems.

12-60   AMP053
How is aircraft electrical power for propeller deicer systems transferred from the engine to the propeller hub assembly?

A– By slip rings and segment plates

B– By slip rings and brushes

C– By flexible electrical connectors

12-60. Answer B. JSPT 12E, FPH
A typical electric propeller deice system utilizes a set of brush blocks and slip rings to transfer electrical power from the engine to the rotating propeller assembly. The brush blocks are mounted on the engine case just behind the propeller while the slip rings are mounted on the back of the propeller hub assembly.

12-61   AMP016
How is anti-icing fluid ejected from the slinger ring on a propeller?

A– By pump pressure

B– By centripetal force

C– By centrifugal force

12-61. Answer C. JSPT 12E, FPH
A slinger ring is a U-shaped circular channel mounted on the rear of a propeller hub assembly that incorporates a discharge for each propeller blade. When an anti-icing system is on, a pump forces anti-icing fluid into the slinger ring where centrifugal force discharges the fluid from the slinger ring through the discharge tubes and onto the propeller blades.

12-62   AMP053
On most reciprocating multiengine aircraft, automatic propeller synchronization is accomplished through the actuation of the

A– throttle levers.

B– propeller governors.

C– propeller control levers.

12-62. Answer B. JSPT 12E, FPH
A propeller synchronization system provides a means of synchronizing engine RPM by varying the pitch of the propeller blades through a set of propeller governors.

12-63   AMP016
Propeller fluid anti-icing systems generally use which of the following?

A– Ethylene glycol

B– Isopropyl alcohol

C– Ethyl alcohol

12-63. Answer B. JSPT 12E, FPH
Propeller fluid anti-icing systems typically use isopropyl alcohol because of its availability and low cost.

12-64   AMP053

What is a function of the automatic propeller synchronizing system on multiengine aircraft?

A– To control the tip speed of all propellers

B– To control engine RPM and reduce vibration

C– To control the power output of all engines

12-64. Answer B. JSPT 12E, FPH

A propeller synchronization system provides a means of synchronizing engine RPM by varying the pitch of the propeller blades through the propeller governors. Synchronization reduces vibration and eliminates the annoying pulsating produced by unsynchronized propellers.

12-65   AMP016

Ice formation on propellers, when an aircraft is in flight, will

A– decrease thrust and cause excessive vibration.

B– increase aircraft stall speed and increase noise.

C– decrease available engine power.

12-65. Answer A. JSPT 12E, FPH

Ice formations destroy a propeller's aerodynamic profile which, in turn, reduces thrust. Furthermore, the formation of ice can also cause an unbalanced condition that can induce excessive vibration.

12-66   AMP016   What unit in the propeller anti-icing system controls the output of the pump?

A– Pressure relief valve

B– Rheostat

C– Cycling timer

12-66. Answer B. JSPT 12E, FPH

A typical fluid anti-icing system consists of a tank to hold a supply of anti-icing fluid, a pump, and a control inside the cockpit. The control system typically consists of a rheostat that allows the pilot to control the pump output.

12-67   AMP053

Proper operation of electric deicing boots on individual propeller blades may best be determined by

A– feeling the sequence of boot heating and have an assistant observe the loadmeter indications.

B– observing the ammeter or loadmeter for current flow.

C– feeling the boots to see if they are heating.

12-67. Answer A. JSPT 12E

About the only way to tell if an individual electric deicing boot is operating properly is to turn on the system and feel each boot in sequence while someone else watches the ammeter for proper sequencing.

12-68   AMP053

1A propeller synchrophasing system allows a pilot to reduce noise and vibration by

A– adjusting the phase angle between the propellers on an aircraft's engines.

B– adjusting the plane of rotation of all propellers.

C– setting the pitch angle of all propellers exactly the same.

2-68. Answer A. JSPT 12E

Synchrophasing is a form of synchronization that allows the pilot to adjust the phase angle between the propellers to reduce propeller noise and vibration. With this type of system, a pulse generator is keyed to the same blade of each propeller. Each generator produces a signal that is compared to the signal emanating from the opposite generator. If the signals don't match, a signal is sent to the slave governor which establishes the phase angle selected by the pilot.

SECTION F — PROPELLER INSPECTION, MAINTENANCE, INSTALLATION

Section F of Chapter 12 includes information regarding propeller inspection, maintenance, and installation procedures including blade tracking, propeller balancing, blade dressing, and other similar operations.

12-69   AMP029
Which of the following determines oil and grease specifications for lubrication of propellers?

A– Airframe manufacturers

B– Engine manufacturers

C– Propeller manufacturers

12-69. Answer C. JSPT 12F, FPH
Propeller manufacturers are responsible for determining and publishing the oil and grease specifications as well as the proper lubrication procedures for the propellers they produce.

12-70   AMP053
Grease used in aircraft propellers reduces the frictional resistance of moving parts and is easily molded into any form under pressure. This statement defines

A– antifriction and plasticity characteristics of grease.

B– antifriction and chemical stability of grease.

C– viscosity and melting point of grease.

12-70. Answer A. JSPT 12F
The reduction of frictional resistance refers to a lubricant's anti-friction characteristics, while the ease at which a lubricant is molded under pressure refers to a lubricant's plasticity characteristics.

12-71   AMP052
What type of imbalance will cause a two-blade propeller to have a persistent tendency to come to rest in a horizontal position (with the blades parallel to the ground) while being checked on a propeller balancing beam?

A– Vertical

B– Horizontal

C– Harmonic

12-71. Answer A. JSPT 12F, FPH
When a propeller is placed in a vertical position on a balancing stand and it rotates to a horizontal position, it is said to be vertically imbalanced.

12-72   AMP052

What is the purpose of an arbor used in balancing a propeller?

A– To support the propeller on the balance knives

B– To level the balance stand

C– To mark the propeller blades where weights are to be attached

12-72. Answer A. JSPT 12F, FPH

The basic components of a typical propeller static balance stand include the bushing, arbor, knife edges, and balancing stand. The bushings are placed in a propeller's engine shaft hole while the arbor is inserted through the bushings. The arbor is designed to support and permit free rotation of the propeller on the knife edges which rest on the balancing stand.

12-73   AMP052

If a blade of a particular metal propeller is shortened because of damage to the tip, the remaining blade(s) must be

A– reset (blade angle) to compensate for the shortened blade.

B– returned to the manufacturer for alteration.

C– reduced to conform with the shortened blade.

12-73. Answer C. JSPT 12F, AC 43.13-1B

All of the blades on a conventional propeller assembly must be precisely the same length, profile, and weight to prevent severe vibration. Therefore, if the shape or length of one blade is changed, the opposite blade must also be changed.

12-74   AMP052

The application of more protective coating on one blade than the other when refinishing a wood propeller

A– has little or no effect on operating characteristics.

B– should never be done.

C– may be necessary to achieve final balancing.

12-74. Answer C. JSPT 12F, AC 43.13-1B

Minor horizontal propeller imbalances on a wood propeller may be corrected by applying an additional protective coating to the light blade.

12-75   AMP052

Apparent engine roughness is often a result of propeller unbalance. The effect of an unbalanced propeller will usually be

A– approximately the same at all speeds.

B– greater at low RPM.

C– greater at high RPM.

12-75. Answer C. JSPT 12F, FPH

Centrifugal force increases as an object's rotational speed increases. As a result, vibration emanating from an unbalanced propeller increases with an increase in propeller RPM.

12-76   AMP052
Which of the following is used to correct horizontal unbalance of a wood propeller?

A– Brass screws

B– Shellac

C– Solder

12-76. Answer C. JSPT 12F, AC 43.13-1B
To correct a horizontal imbalance on a wooden propeller, a small amount of solder is melted onto the face side of the metal tip cap of the light blade and filed smooth.

12-77   AMP052
Propeller aerodynamic (thrust) imbalance can be largely eliminated by

A– correct blade contouring and angle setting.

B– static balancing.

C– keeping the propeller blades within the same plane of rotation.

12-77. Answer A. JSPT 12F, FPH
Aerodynamic thrust imbalance results when one propeller blade produces more thrust then the other blade. This type of unbalance can largely be eliminated by making sure all propeller blades are contoured properly and that they all have the same blade angle setting.

12-78   AMP052
Propellers exposed to salt spray should be flushed with

A– stoddard solvent.

B– fresh water.

C– soapy water.

12-78. Answer B. JSPT 12F, FPH
If a propeller has been exposed to salt water, it should be flushed with fresh water until all traces of salt have been removed. This should be accomplished as soon as possible after the salt water has been splashed on a propeller. After flushing, all parts should be dried thoroughly.

12-79   AMP052
How can a steel propeller hub be tested for cracks?

A– By anodizing

B– By magnetic particle inspection

C– By etching

12-79. Answer B. JSPT 12F, FPH
Of the choices given, magnetic particle inspection is the preferred method for inspecting a steel propeller hub for cracks.

12-80   AMP052

Which of the following functions requires the use of a propeller blade station?

A– Measuring blade angle

B– Indexing blades

C– Propeller balancing

12-80. Answer A. JSPT 12F, FPH

When measuring a propeller's blade angle, a reference blade angle measuring station is always specified by the propeller manufacturer. Therefore, you must be familiar with and use a propeller blade station to measure a propeller's blade angle.

12-81   AMP052

Inspection of propeller blades by dye-penetrant inspection is accomplished to detect

A– cracks or other defects.

B– corrosion at the blade tip.

C– torsional stress.

12-81. Answer A. JSPT 12F, AC 43.13-1B

Dye-penetrant inspection is normally used to detect cracks or other defects that are open to the surface.

12-82   AMP052

Which of the following defects is cause for rejection of wood propellers?

A– Solder missing from screw heads securing metal tipping

B– An oversize hub or bolt hole, or elongated bolt holes

C– No protective coating on propeller

12-82. Answer B. JSPT 12F, AC 43.13-1B

Oversize or elongated bolt holes on a wooden propeller are typically cause for rejection. However, some oversize or worn bolt holes may be repaired by the use of metal inserts to restore the original diameter. This is a major repair and must be performed by a certificated repair station.

12-83   AMP059

1. A mechanic certificate with a power plant rating authorizes the holder to repair deep scars, nicks, and dents on aluminum propeller blades.

2. A mechanic certificate with a power plant rating authorizes the holder to perform minor straightening of steel propeller blades

Regarding the above statements,

A– only No.1 is true.

B– both No.1 and No.2 are true.

C– neither No.1 nor No.2 is true.

12-83. Answer C. JSGT 15A, 14 CFR 43 Appendix A,14 CFR 65.81

Neither statement (1) nor (2) is correct. A certificated mechanic may perform minor repairs or alterations to propeller blades. Deep scars, nicks, and dents on aluminum propeller blades and the straightening of propeller blades are major repairs. These repairs may be performed by a properly certificated repair station or the propeller manufacturer.

12-84   AMP052
Longitudinal (fore and aft) clearance of constant-speed propeller blades or cuffs must be at least 1/2 inch (12.7 mm) between propeller parts and stationary parts of the aircraft. This clearance is with the propeller blades

A– at takeoff pitch (maximum thrust) angle.

B– feathered or in the most critical pitch configuration.

C– at the lowest pitch angle.

12-84. Answer B. JSPT 12F, 14 CFR 23.925
Federal Aviation Regulations require that the longitudinal clearance between the propeller blades or cuffs and stationary parts of the airplane be at least one-half inch measured with the propeller in the most adverse pitch position.

12-85   AMP052
When lubricating a Hartzell propeller blade with grease, to prevent damage to the blade seals, the service manual may recommend on some models to

A– pump grease into both zerk fittings for the blade simultaneously.

B– remove the seals prior to greasing and reinstall them afterwards.

C– remove one of the two zerk fittings for the blade and grease the blade through the remaining fitting.

12-85. Answer C. JSPT 12F
Hartzell propellers have two grease fittings (zerks) on their hubs. When lubricating these propellers, one zerk should be removed while grease is pumped into the other zerk. This prevents pressure buildup in the grease chamber and helps avoid damaging the blade seals.

12-86   AMP052

Which of the following occurs to cause front cone bottoming during propeller installation?

A– The front cone becomes bottomed in the front propeller hub cone seat before the rear propeller hub cone seat has engaged the rear cone.

B– The front cone enters the front propeller hub cone seat at an angle causing the propeller retaining nut to appear tight when it is only partially tightened.

C– The front cone contacts the ends of the shaft splines, preventing the front and rear cones from being tightened against the cone seats in the propeller hub.

12-86. Answer C. JSPT 12F, FPH

Front cone bottoming occurs during the installation of a spline shaft propeller when the apex of the front cone contacts the ends of the shaft splines. This happens when the rear cone is too far back on the propeller shaft. When this occurs, neither front nor rear cone can be tightened into the propeller hub's cone seats. The only way to correct this is to move the rear cone forward.

12-87   AMP052

What is indicated when the front cone bottoms while installing a propeller?

A– Propeller-dome combination is incorrect

B– Blade angles are incorrect

C– Rear cone should be moved forward

12-87. Answer C. JSPT 12F, FPH

Front cone bottoming occurs during the installation of a spline shaft propeller when the apex of the front cone contacts the ends of the shaft splines. This happens when the rear cone is too far back on the propeller shaft. When this occurs, neither front nor rear cone can be tightened into the propeller hub's cone seats. The only way to correct this is to move the rear cone forward.

12-88   AMP052

The primary purpose of the front and rear cones for propellers that are installed on splined shafts is to

A– position the propeller hub on the splined shaft.

B– prevent metal-to-metal contact between the propeller and the splined shaft.

C– reduce stresses between the splines of the propeller and the splines of the shaft.

12-88. Answer A. JSPT 12F, FPH

The purpose of the cones for a spine shaft propeller installation is to support and align the propeller hub on the shaft. This is similar to the action of tapered bearings which position and support a wheel on an axle.

12-89   AMP052

Which of the following statements concerning the installation of a new fixed-pitch wood propeller is true?

A– If a separate metal hub is used, final track should be accomplished prior to installing the hub in the propeller.

B– NAS close-tolerance bolts should be used to install the propeller.

C– Inspect the bolts for tightness after the first flight and again after the first 25 hours of flying.

12-89. Answer C. JSPT 12F, AC 43.13-1B

AC 43.13-1B specifies that when a fixed pitch wooden propeller has been installed, the bolts should be checked for tightness after the first flight, after the first 25 hours of flying, and at least every 50 flying hours thereafter. This is because the moisture content of the wood fibers can cause shrinkage after exposure to heat, causing the bolts to become loose. The fibers can also swell from humidity, which will cause the bolts to be too tight.

12-90   AMP052

If propeller cones or hub cone seats show evidence of galling and wear, the most likely cause is

A– the pitch change stops were located incorrectly, causing the cone seats to act as the high pitch stop.

B– the propeller retaining nut was not tight enough during previous operation.

C– the front cone was not fully bottomed against the crankshaft splines during installation.

12-90. Answer B. JSPT 12F, FPH

A loose retaining nut on a spine shaft propeller installation allows movement between the propeller cones and the hub cone seats. If not corrected, this movement can lead to galling or wear on both the front and rear cones and the cone seats.

12-91   AMP053

On aircraft equipped with hydraulically operated constant-speed propellers, all ignition and magneto checking is done with the propeller in which position?

A– High RPM

B– Low RPM

C– High pitch range

12-91. Answer A. JSPT 12F, FPH

Hydraulically operated constant-speed propellers should be placed in the high rpm, low pitch position for all ignition and magneto checking. This causes the propeller to operate as a fixed-pitch propeller and provides a standard RPM for determining the operating condition of the engine.

12-92   AMP052

Maximum taper contact between crank-shaft and propeller hub is determined by using

A— bearing blue color transfer.

B— a micrometer.

C— a surface gauge.

12-92. Answer A. JSPT 12F

Bearing blue color transfer, sometimes called Prussian blue, is used to determine the amount of surface contact between a tapered propeller shaft and the propeller hub. At least 70 percent surface contact is required.

12-93   AMP052

Propeller blade tracking is the process of determining

A— the plane of rotation of the propeller with respect to the aircraft longitudinal axis.

B— that the blade angles are within the specified tolerance of each other.

C— the positions of the tips of the propeller blades relative to each other.

12-93. Answer C. JSPT 12F, FPH

Propeller blade tracking is the process of determining the blade tip positions relative to each other. A propeller out-of-track condition may indicate a bent propeller shaft or a blade that is bent.

12-94   AMP052

A fixed-pitch wooden propeller that has been properly installed and the attachment bolts properly torqued exceeds the out-of-track allowance by 1/16 inch. The excessive out-of-track condition may be corrected by

A— slightly overtightening the attachment bolts adjacent to the most forward blade.

B— discarding the propeller since out-of-track conditions cannot be corrected.

C— placing shims between the inner flange and the propeller.

12-94. Answer C. JSPT 12F, APC

Correction of an out-of-track condition on a fixed pitch wooden propeller is made by inserting paper or brass shims between the inner flange of the metal hub and the propeller boss. On flange type shaft propeller installations, the shim should be placed between the propeller boss and the propeller shaft flange.

12-95   AMP053

In what position is the constant-speed propeller control placed to check the magnetos?

A– Full decrease, low propeller blade pitch angle

B– Full increase, high propeller blade pitch angle

C– Full increase, low propeller blade pitch angle

12-95. Answer C. JSPT 12F, FPH

Hydraulically operated constant-speed propellers should be placed in the high RPM, low pitch position when conducting any ignition or magneto checking. This results in a set blade angle that provides a standard RPM for determining the operating condition of the magneto.

12-96   AMP053

If a flanged propeller shaft has dowel pins

A– install the propeller so that the blades are positioned for hand propping.

B– the propeller can be installed in only one position.

C– check carefully for front cone bottoming against the pins.

12-96. Answer B. JSPT 12F, FPH

A flanged propeller shaft with dowel pins allows propeller installation in only one position on the crankshaft.

12-94   AMP052

A fixed-pitch wooden propeller that has been properly installed and the attachment bolts properly torqued exceeds the out-of-track allowance by 1/16 inch. The excessive out-of-track condition may be corrected by

A– slightly overtightening the attachment bolts adjacent to the most forward blade.

B– discarding the propeller since out-of-track conditions cannot be corrected.

C– placing shims between the inner flange and the propeller.

12-94. Answer C. JSPT 12F, APC

Correction of an out-of-track condition on a fixed pitch wooden propeller is made by inserting paper or brass shims between the inner flange of the metal hub and the propeller boss. On flange type shaft propeller installations, the shim should be placed between the propeller boss and the propeller shaft flange.

12-95   AMP053

In what position is the constant-speed propeller control placed to check the magnetos?

A– Full decrease, low propeller blade pitch angle

B– Full increase, high propeller blade pitch angle

C– Full increase, low propeller blade pitch angle

12-95. Answer C. JSPT 12F, FPH

Hydraulically operated constant-speed propellers should be placed in the high RPM, low pitch position when conducting any ignition or magneto checking. This results in a set blade angle that provides a standard RPM for determining the operating condition of the magneto.

12-96   AMP053

If a flanged propeller shaft has dowel pins

A– install the propeller so that the blades are positioned for hand propping.

B– the propeller can be installed in only one position.

C– check carefully for front cone bottoming against the pins.

12-96. Answer B. JSPT 12F, FPH

A flanged propeller shaft with dowel pins allows propeller installation in only one position on the crankshaft.

12-97   AMP052

Repairs of aluminum alloy adjustable pitch propellers are not permitted to be made on which of the following propeller blade areas?

A– Shank

B– Face

C– Back

12-97. Answer A. JSPT 12F, AC 43.13-1B

The shank, or base of an adjustable pitch propeller is subject to more stress than any other portion of the propeller blade. Therefore, no repairs are permitted to the shanks of aluminum alloy adjustable pitch propeller blades.

12-98   AMP052
Which of the following methods is used to straighten bent aluminum propeller blade that is within repairable limits?

A– Careful heating to accomplish straightening, followed by heat treatment to restore original strength

B– Either hot or cold straightening, depending on the location and severity of damage

C– Cold straightening only

12-98. Answer C. JSPT 12F, AC 43.13-1B

An aluminum alloy propeller blade should only be straightened in accordance with the propeller manufacturer's approved procedures. When blade straightening is allowed, it's cold worked only.

12-99   AMP052
It is important that nicks in aluminum alloy propeller blades be repaired as soon as possible in order to

A– maintain equal aerodynamic characteristics between the blades.

B– eliminate stress concentration points.

C– equalize the centrifugal loads between the blades.

12-99. Answer B. JSPT 12F, AC 43.13-1B

Rotating propellers are constantly subjected to high centrifugal loads and severe vibration. Therefore, any scratch, nick, or gouge can create a stress concentration that could develop into a crack and lead to fatigue failure.

12-100   AMP052
Generally, unless otherwise specified by the manufacturer, repairs of nicks, scratches, gouges, etc. on aluminum propeller blades must be made

A– parallel to the length of the blade.

B– perpendicular to the blade axis.

C– so as to return the damaged area to the original dimensions.

12-100. Answer A. JSPT 12F, AC 43.13-1B0 Repairs of minor defects on aluminum propeller blades should be made parallel to the length of the propeller blade.

12-101   AMP052

Minor surface damage located in a repairable area, but not on the leading or trailing edges of aluminum blades, may be repaired by first

A– filing with a riffle file.

B– filing with a half round or flat file.

C– rough sanding and applying a proper filler.

12-101. Answer A. JSPT 12F

Repairs on the face or back of a propeller blade are made with a spoon-like riffle file, which is used to dish out the damaged area.

12-102   AMP052

After proper removal of aluminum blade damage, the affected surface should be polished with

A– fine steel wool.

B– very fine sandpaper.

C– powdered soapstone.

12-102. Answer B. JSPT 12F, AC 43.13-1B

To make sure that all minor scratches or file marks are removed after a repair is made to an aluminum propeller blade you should polish the affected surface with very fine sandpaper. The sandpaper should be moved parallel to the length of the blade and, once the sanding is complete, the repaired area should be treated with an appropriate protective coating.

12-103   AMP052

When preparing a propeller blade for inspection it should be cleaned with

A– mild soap and water.

B– steel wool.

C– methyl ethyl ketone.

12-103. Answer A. JSPT 12F, FPH

When preparing a propeller blade for inspection it should be cleaned with mild soap and water.

12-104   AMP052

What method would be used to inspect an aluminum propeller blade when a crack is suspected

A– use a bright light.

B– magnetic particle.

C– dye-penetrant.

12-104. Answer C. JSPT 12F, AC 43.13-1B

Of the choices given, dye-penetrant inspection is the most effective method of detecting cracks on an aluminum propeller blade.

12-105   AMP052
Removal of propeller blade tips within Type Certificate Data Sheet limits when correcting a defect is

A– a major alteration.

B– a major repair.

C– permitted under the privileges and limitations of a power plant rating.

12-105. Answer B. JSGT 14A, FAR 43, Appendix A
According to FAR Part 43, Appendix A, shortening propeller blades, or retipping wooden blades, is a major repair. All propeller major repairs must be performed by an appropriately certificated repair station or the propeller manufacturer.

12-106   AMP052
Surface treatment to counter the effects of dye-penetrant inspection on a propeller is accomplished by

A– washing off with solvent.

B– wiping with alcohol.

C– rinse the blade in alodine solution.

12-106. Answer A. JSPT 12F, AC 43.13-1B
After performing a dye-penetrant inspection on a propeller, all penetrant residue should be removed using a solvent approved by both the penetrant and propeller manufacturer.

12-107   AMP052
One of the advantages of inspecting an aluminum propeller utilizing dye-penetrant inspection procedure is that

A– defects just below the surface are indicated.

B– it shows whether visible lines and other marks are actually cracks rather than scratches.

C– it indicates overspeed condition.

12-107. Answer B. JSPT 12F, AC 43.13-1B
Dye penetrant inspections allow a properly trained technician to differentiate between cracks and scratches on aluminum propeller blades.

12-108   AMP052
The primary reason for careful inspection and prompt repairing of minor surface defects such as scratches, nicks, gouges, etc. on aluminum alloy propellers is to prevent

A– corrosion.

B– unbalanced aerodynamics.

C– fatigue failure.

12-108. Answer C. JSPT 12F, AC 43.13-1B
Rotating propellers are constantly subjected to high centrifugal loads and severe vibration. Therefore, any scratch, nick, or gouge can create stress concentrations that could develop into a crack and lead to fatigue failure.

12-109   AMP052
Which of the following generally renders an aluminum alloy propeller unrepairable?

A– Any repairs that would require shortening and re-contouring of blades

B– Any slag inclusions or cold shuts

C– Transverse cracks of any size

12-109. Answer C. JSPT 12F, AC 43.13-1B
A transverse crack is a crack that is parallel to a propeller blade's chord. Transverse cracks of any size are not repairable and render a propeller un-airworthy.

12-110   AMP052
Cold straightening a bent aluminum propeller blade may be accomplished by

A– the holder of a mechanic certificate with a power plant rating.

B– an appropriately rated repair station or the manufacturer.

C– a person working under the supervision of the holder of a mechanic certificate with both airframe and power plant ratings.

12-110. Answer B. JSPT 12F, AC 43.13-1B
Cold straightening a bent aluminum propeller blade is considered a major repair and, therefore, can only be performed by an appropriately rated repair station or the propeller manufacturer.

POWERPLANT AND PROPELLER AIRWORTHINESS INSPECTIONS

CHAPTER 13

SECTION A — AIRWORTHINESS INSPECTION CRITERIA

Section A of Chapter 13 includes information on the conduct of required airworthiness inspections. The information includes the types of airworthiness inspections, who may conduct them, and the required maintenance record entries for each type of inspection.

13-1   AMP072

A Cessna 180 aircraft has a McCauley propeller Model No.2A34C50/90A. The propeller is severely damaged in a ground accident, and this model propeller is not available for replacement. Which of the following should be used to find an approved alternate replacement?

A– Summary of Supplemental Type Certificates

B– Aircraft Specifications/Type Certificate Data Sheets

C– Aircraft Engine and Propeller Specifications/ Type Certificate Data Sheets

13-1. Answer B. JSGT 14A, FGH

The Aircraft Specifications or Type Certificate Data Sheet for an aircraft lists the engines and propellers approved for use on the aircraft. If there is more than one approved propeller for the Cessna 180, it will be listed in one of these documents.

13-2   AMP058

1. Airworthiness Directives are Federal Aviation Regulations and must be complied with unless specific exemption is granted.

2. Airworthiness Directives of an emergency nature require immediate compliance upon receipt.

Regarding the above statements,

A– only No. 1 is true.

B– only No. 2 is true.

C– both No. 1 and No. 2 are true.

13-2. Answer C. JSGT 14A, FGH

Both statements (1) and (2) are correct. Airworthiness Directives (ADs) are part of 14 CFR Part 39 and must be complied with unless a specific exemption is granted. Statement (2) is also true on most occasions, because emergency ADs generally do require immediate compliance. Furthermore, if an AD is issued that identifies an emergency condition, compliance is typically required upon receipt.

13-3   AMP048
Which of the following contains a minimum checklist for 100-hour inspections of engines?

A– 14 CFR Part 33, Appendix A

B– 14 CFR Part 43, Appendix D

C– Engine Specifications or Type Certificate Data Sheets

13-3. Answer B. JSPT 13B, 14 CFR Part 43, Appendix D
14 CFR Part 43 contains the minimum checklist for a 100-hour inspection of an engine and airframe.

13-4   AMP072
Which of the following contains a table that lists the engines to which a given propeller is adaptable?

A– Aircraft Type Certificate Data Sheets

B– Propeller Type Certificate Data Sheets

C– Engine Type Certificate Data Sheets

13-4. Answer B. JSPT 13A, FPH
To find out what engines a particular propeller is adaptable to, you must look at the propeller's Type Certificate Data Sheet.

13-5   AMP045
Select the Airworthiness Directive applicability statement which applies to an IVO-355 engine, serial number T8164, with 2,100 hours total time and 300 hours since rebuilding.

A– Applies to all IVO-355 engines, serial numbers T8000 through T8300, having less than 2,400 hours total time

B– Applies to all IVO-355 engines, serial numbers T8000 through T8900 with 2,400 hours or more total time

C– Applies to all I.O. and TV10-355 engines, all serial numbers regardless of total time or since overhaul

13-5. Answer A. FGH
Applies to the engine identified because it gives the model number as IVO-355; the serial numbers include the number of the listed engine; and the hours of time in service apply to the listed engine. The number of hours the engine has accumulated since rebuilding does not matter in relation to this question.

13-6   AMP058
Each power plant installed on an airplane with a Standard Airworthiness Certificate must have been

A— type certificated.

B— manufactured under the TSO system.

C— originally certificated for that aircraft.

13-6. Answer A. JSGT 14A, 14 CFR 23.903
Each airplane having a standard airworthiness certificate must be equipped with an engine which is type certificated and, if it is prop driven, a type certificated propeller.

13-7   AMP048
When inspecting an aircraft reciprocating engine what document is used to determine if the proper magnetos are installed?

A— Instructions for continued airworthiness issued by the engine manufacturer

B— Engine Manufacturer's Maintenance Manual

C— Aircraft Engine Specifications or Type Certificate Data Sheets

13-7. Answer C. JSPT 13A, FGH
When inspecting an engine, it is important to make sure that it conforms to its original type design. The original type design for an engine manufactured before 1959 is contained in the Aircraft Engine Specifications. However, for engines that were manufactured after 1959 the type design information is in the Type Certificate Data Sheet.

13-8   AMP048
What publication is used for guidance to determine whether a power plant repair is major or minor?

A— Airworthiness Directives

B— Federal Aviation Regulations, Part 43, appendix A

C— Technical Standard Orders

13-8. Answer B. JSGT 14A, 14 CFR Part 43, Appendix A
A list of what constitutes a power plant major repair or alteration is provided in FAR Part 43, Appendix A. However, this list is only a guide and does not identify all possible repairs and alterations.

13-9   AMP058
The airworthiness standards for the issue of type certificates for small airplanes with nine or less passenger seats in the normal, utility, and acrobatic categories may be found in the

A— Supplemental Type Certificate.

B— Federal Aviation Regulations, Part 23.

C— Federal Aviation Regulations, Part 21.

13-9. Answer B. JSPT 13A, FAR 23.1
FAR Part 23 entitled, Airworthiness Standards: Normal, Utility, Acrobatic and Commuter Category Airplanes, prescribes the airworthiness standards for the issue of type certificates for small airplanes in the normal, utility, and acrobatic categories that have a passenger seating configuration, excluding pilot seats, of 9 seats or less.

13-10   AMP048

Which of the following contains approved data for performing a major repair to an aircraft engine?

A– Engine Type Certificate Data Sheets

B– Supplemental Type Certificates

C– Manufacturer's maintenance instructions when FAA approved

13-10. Answer C. JSGT 14A, AC 65-19E

Manufacturer's maintenance instructions are acceptable to use when performing a major repair to an engine, providing they are FAA approved. FAA approval must be stamped on the manual before it can be used as approved data.

13-11   AMP058

What maintenance record(s) is/are required following a major repair of an aircraft engine?

A– Entries in engine maintenance records and a list of discrepancies for the FAA

B– Entries in the engine maintenance record and FAA Form 337

C– Entry in logbook

13-11. Answer B. JSGT 14A, FAR 43.9

When a major repair is performed on an engine, an entry must be made in the engine's maintenance records and an FAA Form 337 must be filled out. One copy of the Form 337 stays with the maintenance records and a second copy is sent to the FAA. An exception to this would be if the repair was done by a certified repair station. If approved data was used, the repair station would not be required to fill out a Form 337.

13-12   AMP048

Where would one find type design information for an R1830-92 engine certificated under the Civil Air Regulations (CAR) and installed on a DC-3?

A– The Aircraft Specifications and Type Certificate Data Sheet

B– The Aircraft Engine Specifications

C– The Aircraft Engine Type Certificate Handbook

13-12. Answer B. JSPT 13A

Both the R1830-92 and DC-3 were certified under the older Civil Aeronautics Regulations and, therefore, Type Certificate Data Sheets were not published for either the engine or the aircraft. Therefore, the only place to find type design information for an R1830-92 engine that is installed on a DC-3 is in the aircraft engine specifications.

13-13   AMP045
(Refer to figure 1.)

Determine which portion of the AD is applicable for Model 0-690 series engine, serial No.5863-40 with 283 hours time in service.

A– (B)(1)

B– (A)

C– (B)(2)

13-13. Answer A. JSPT 13A, AC 39-7B
Paragraph B in the AD applies to all model 0-690 engines with serial numbers 5265-40 to 6129-40. The engine and serial number listed in the question fall within this listing. Paragraph 1 also applies to the listed engine because it identifies engines with more than 275 hours time in service.

This is the compliance portion of an FAA Airworthiness Directive.

Compliance required as indicated:

(A)   For model O-690 series engines, serial Nos. 101-40 through 5264-40 and IO-690 series engines, serial Nos. 101-48 through 423-48, compliance with (C) required within 25 hours' time in service after the effective date of this AD and every 100 hours' time in service thereafter.

(B)   For model O-690 series engines, serial Nos. 5265-40 through 6129-40 and IO-690 series engines, serial Nos. 424-48 through 551-48, compliance with (C) required as follows:

   (1)   Within 25 hours' time in service after the effective date of this AD and every 100 hours' time in service thereafter for engines with more than 275 hours' time in service on the effective date of this AD.

   (2)   Prior to the accumulation of 300 hours total time in service and every 100 hours' time in service thereafter for engines with 275 hours or less time in service on the effective date of this AD.

(C)   Inspect the oil pump drive shaft (P/N 67512) on applicable engines in accordance with instructions contained in Connin Service Bulletin No. 295. Any shafts which are found to be damaged shall be replaced before further flight. These inspections shall be continued until Connin P/N 67512 (redesigned) or P/N 74641 oil pump drive shaft is installed at which time the inspections may be discontinued.

Figure 1. Airworthiness Directive Excerpt

13-14   AMP007
Which of the following may inspect and approve an engine major repair for return to service?

A– Certificated mechanic with airframe and power plant ratings

B– Certificated mechanic with a power plant rating

C– Certificated mechanic with inspection authorization

13-14. Answer C. JSGT 14A, 14 CFR 65.95
Although a certificated airframe and power plant technician is authorized to perform a major repair, it takes a person with the inspection authorization to return the repair to service.

13-15   AMP012

1. Power plant instrument range markings show whether the current state of power plant operation is normal, acceptable for a limited time, or unauthorized.

2. Power plant instrument range markings are based on installed engine operating limits which may not exceed (but are not necessarily equal to) those limits shown on the engine Type Certificate Data Sheet.

Regarding the above statements,

A– both No.1 and No.2 are true.

B– neither No.1 nor No.2 is true.

C– only No.1 is true.

13-15. Answer A. JSGT 14A, FPH
Both statements (1) and (2) are correct. Power plant range markings show minimum, continuous, limited, and maximum ranges. These ranges may not exceed the engine's Type Certificate Data Sheet specifications and, in some cases, may be less than those specified.

13-16   AMP057
What is required by 14 CFR Part 43 appendix D when performing an annual/100-hour inspection on a reciprocating engine aircraft?

A– Magneto timing check

B– Cylinder compression check

C– Valve clearance check

13-16. Answer B. JSPT 13B, Part 43, Appendix D
According to 14 CFR 43, Appendix D, a cylinder compression check is required when performing an annual/100-hour inspection on a reciprocating engine aircraft. Although a magneto timing check and a valve clearance check on nonhydraulic lifters are valuable checks that should be done periodically, they are not required on a 100-hour inspection.

13-17   AMP057

Which of the following component inspections is to be accomplished on a 100-hour inspection?

A– Check internal timing of magneto.

B– Check cylinder compression.

C– Check valve timing.

13-17. Answer B. JSPT 13B, 14 CFR Part 43, Appendix D

According to Appendix D of 14 CFR Part 43 a 100-hour inspection on an engine requires that a cylinder compression check be performed.

13-18   AMP068

The basic gas turbine engine is divided into two main sections: the cold section and the hot section. (1) The cold section includes the engine inlet, compressor, and turbine sections. (2) The hot section includes the combustor, diffuser, and exhaust sections. Regarding the above statements,

A– only No.1 is true.

B– only No.2 is true.

C– neither No.1 nor No.2 is true.

13-18. Answer C. JSPT 13C, FPH

Neither statement (1) nor (2) is correct. The cold section includes the engine inlet, compressor, and diffuser sections. The hot section, on the other hand, includes the combustor, turbine, and exhaust sections.

13-19   AMP007

Hot section inspections for many modern turbine engines are required

A– only at engine overhaul.

B– only when an overtemperature or overspeed has occurred.

C– on a time or cycle basis.

13-19. Answer C. JSPT 13C, FPH

Almost all of the components on a turbine engine, including the hot section, are required to be inspected on a time or cycle basis. Additional times when a hot section must be inspected include during an overhaul or when an overtemperature or overspeed incident occurs.

13-20   AMP069
Which of the following may be used to accomplish internal inspection of an assembled turbine engine?

1. Infrared photography

2. Ultrasound

3. A borescope

4. Fluorescent penetrant and ultraviolet light

A– 1, 2, and 3

B– 1 and 3

C– 3

13-20. Answer C. JSPT 13C, TEP2
In recent years the borescope has become one of the most effective ways of inspecting the inner parts of the engine.

13-21   AMP069
A turbine engine hot section is particularly susceptible to which kind of damage?

A– Scoring

B– Cracking

C– Galling

13-21. Answer B. JSPT 13C, FPH
Due to the extremely high temperatures and vibration that exist in a hot section, cracking is the most common problem encountered.

13-22   AMP008
Hot spots in the combustion section of a turbojet engine are possible indicators of

A– faulty igniter plugs.

B– dirty compressor blades.

C– malfunctioning fuel nozzles.

13-22. Answer C. JSPT 13C, FPH
Hot spots within the combustion section are possible indicators of a serious condition, such as malfunctioning fuel nozzles or other fuel system malfunctions. Therefore, whenever hotspots are present they must be interpreted carefully.

13-23   AMP069

Which of the following can cause fan blade shingling in a turbofan engine?

1. Engine overspeed

2. Engine overtemperature

3. Large, rapid throttle movements

4. FOD

A– 1 and 2

B– 1, 2, 3, and 4

C– 1 and 4

13-23. Answer C. JSPT 13C

Fan blade shingling is the term used to describe the overlapping of midspan shrouds on fan blades. Any time rotating fan blades encounter a resistance that forces a blade sideways shingling occurs. Shingling is typically caused by an overspeed, FOD, a bird strike, or a compressor stall.

13-24   AMP069

The hot section of a turbine engine is particularly susceptible to which of the following kind of damage?

A– Galling

B– Pitting

C– Cracking

13-24. Answer C. JSPT 13C, FPH

Because of the high heat encountered in the hot section of a turbine engine, cracks frequently develop on turbine blades, stator vanes, and exhaust system components.

13-25   AMP069

Which of the following indicates that a combustion chamber of a jet engine is not operating properly?

A– Clam shells stick in thrust reverse position.

B– Hot spots on the tail cone.

C– Warping of the exhaust duct liner.

13-25. Answer B. JSPT 13C, FPH

A malfunctioning fuel nozzle or combustion chamber disrupts the normal flow of gases through the turbine and exhaust sections of a turbine engine. These defects can typically be detected by the presence of hot spots on the exhaust duct or tail cone.

POWERPLANT TROUBLESHOOTING

SECTION A — TROUBLESHOOTING PRINCIPLES

Section A of Chapter 14 contains information related to basic troubleshooting techniques, procedures, and tools that are used in identifying and isolating engine and propeller malfunctions.

14-1   AMP057

An engine misses in both the right and left positions of the magneto switch. The quickest method for locating the trouble is to

A– check for one or more cold cylinders.

B– perform a compression check.

C– check each spark plug.

14-1. Answer A. JSPT 14A, FPH

The cold cylinder check determines the operating characteristics of each cylinder of an air-cooled engine. The tendency for any cylinder or cylinders to be cold or to be only slightly warm after the engine was running indicates either a lack of combustion or incomplete combustion. If an engine misses in both the right and left positions of the magneto switch, combustion is not taking place in one or more cylinders. Any time there is a lack of combustion or incomplete combustion, the cylinder(s) affected will feel cooler than the cylinder(s) where complete combustion is occurring.

SECTION B - RECIPROCATING ENGINE TROUBLESHOOTING

Section B of Chapter 14 contains guidance information for typical reciprocating engine faults and methods for identifying and isolating various types of faults.

14-2   AMP057

During ground check an engine is found to be rough-running, the magneto drop is normal, and the manifold pressure is higher than normal for any given RPM. The trouble may be caused by

A— several spark plugs fouled on different cylinders.

B— a leak in the intake manifold.

C— a dead cylinder.

14-2. Answer C. JSPT 14B, FPH

The most likely cause of a rough running engine which has normal magneto drop and high manifold pressure is a dead cylinder.

14-3   AMP056

What is the best indication of worn valve guides?

A— High oil consumption

B— Low compression

C— Low oil pressure

14-3. Answer A. JSPT 14B, FPH

If the valve guides of an engine are worn, there will be excessive clearance between the valve guide and the valve stem. The excessive clearance allows oil to seep by the valve stems and enter the intake and exhaust ports, causing high oil consumption.

14-4   AMP056

Backfiring through the carburetor generally results from the use of

A— an excessively lean mixture.

B— excessively atomized fuel.

C— an excessively rich mixture.

14-4. Answer A. JSPT 14B, FPH

An extremely lean mixture will either not burn at all or burn so slowly that combustion continues until the intake valve opens near the end of the exhaust stroke. When this happens, the flame in the cylinder ignites the contents in the intake manifold causing an explosion known as a backfire.

14-5   AMP056

One cause of after firing in an aircraft engine is

A– sticking intake valves.

B– an excessively lean mixture.

C– an excessively rich mixture.

14-5. Answer C. JSPT 14B, FPH

After firing refers to a condition when unburned fuel from an excessively rich fuel/air mixture combines with air in the exhaust stacks and ignites, or fires, in the exhaust system.

14-6   AMP056

Which of the following would most likely cause a reciprocating engine to backfire through the induction system at low RPM operation?

A– Idle mixture too rich

B– Clogged derichment valve

C– Lean mixture

14-6. Answer C. JSPT 14B, FPH

An extremely lean mixture will either not burn at all or burn so slowly that combustion continues until the intake valve opens near the end of the exhaust stroke. When this happens, the flame in the cylinder ignites the contents in the intake manifold causing an explosion, or backfire within the induction manifold.

14-7   AMP038

If a float-type carburetor leaks fuel when the engine is stopped, a likely cause is that the

A– float needle valve is worn or otherwise not seated properly.

B– float level is adjusted too low.

C– main air bleed is clogged.

14-7. Answer A. JSPT 14B

If a float type carburetor leaks when an engine is shut down, either the needle valve is not firmly seated or the float level is adjusted too high.

14-8   AMP057

When troubleshooting an engine for too rich a mixture

to allow the engine to idle, what would be a possible cause?

A– A primer line open.

B– Mixture setting too rich.

C– Air leak in the intake manifold.

14-8. Answer B. JSPT 14B, FPH

A carburetor mixture set too rich is likely to cause the mixture to be too rich to allow the engine to idle properly.

14-9   AMP023

What corrective action should be taken when a carburetor is found to be leaking fuel from the discharge nozzle?

A– Replace the needle valve and seat.

B– Raise the float level.

C– Turn the fuel off each time the aircraft is parked.

14-9. Answer A. JSPT 14B, FPH

If a carburetor leaks fuel from the discharge nozzle, it is an indication that the fuel level is too high in the float chamber. A high fuel level can be caused by a float that is adjusted too high, a leaking or saturated float, dirt trapped between the needle and seat, or a worn needle and seat. Based on this and the choices given, the only logical choice would be to replace the needle valve and seat.

14-10   AMP057

Under which of the following conditions would an engine run lean even though there is a normal amount of fuel present?

A– The use of too high an octane rating fuel

B– Incomplete fuel vaporization

C– The carburetor air heater valve in the HOT position

14-10. Answer B. JSPT 14B, FPH

To ensure efficient combustion, fuel must be properly mixed with air, or atomized, before it enters the cylinders. The more fully a mixture is vaporized, the greater the efficiency of the combustion process.

On the other hand, if the fuel is not fully vaporized, less fuel mixes with the intake air and the mixture becomes lean even though there is an abundance of fuel present.

SECTION C - TURBINE ENGINE TROUBLESHOOTING

Section C of Chapter 14 contains guidance information for typical turbine engine faults and methods for identifying and isolating various types of malfunctions. FAA questions for this topic are covered in Chapter 4 of this test guide.

14-11   AMP068

What would be the possible cause if a gas turbine engine has high exhaust gas temperature, high fuel flow, and low RPM at all engine power settings?

A– Fuel control out of adjustment

B– Loose or corroded thermocouple probes for the EGT indicator

C– Turbine damage or loss of turbine efficiency

14-11. Answer C. JSPT 14C, FPH

A possible cause of high EGT, high fuel flow, and low RPM in a gas turbine engine is turbine section damage or loss of turbine efficiency. The purpose of the turbine blades is to convert the energy from the gases coming off the combustor into rotary motion to drive the compressor. If the turbine is damaged, it won't convert as much energy and the RPM will remain low, the exhaust gas temperature will increase, and the engine will burn more fuel at given RPM settings.

LEARNING STATEMENT CODES AND LEARNING STATEMENTS

Learning Statement Codes and Learning Statements for Inspection Authorization

Code	Learning Statement
IAR001	Calculate alteration specification
IAR002	Calculate center of gravity
IAR003	Calculate electrical load
IAR004	Calculate proof loading
IAR005	Calculate repair specific
IAR006	Calculate sheet metal repair
IAR007	Calculate temperature conversion
IAR008	Calculate weight and balance - adjust weight / fuel
IAR009	Determine alteration parameters
IAR010	Determine alteration requirements
IAR011	Determine Correct data
IAR012	Determine data application
IAR013	Determine design specific
IAR014	Determine fabrication specification
IAR015	Determine process specific
IAR016	Determine regulatory requirement
IAR017	Determine regulatory requirements
IAR018	Determine repair parameters
IAR019	Determine repair requirements
IAR020	Interpret data
IAR021	Interpret regulations
IAR022	Recall alteration / design fundamentals
IAR023	Recall engine repair fundamentals
IAR024	Recall fundamental inspection principles - airframe / engine
IAR025	Recall MEL requirements
IAR026	Recall principles of corrosion control
IAR027	Recall principles of sheet metal forming
IAR028	Recall principles of system fundamentals
IAR029	Recall principles of weight and balance
IAR030	Recall regulatory requirements
IAR031	Recall regulatory specific
IAR032	Recall repair fundamentals

Learning Statement Codes and Learning Statements for Aviation Mechanic - General Exams

Code	Learning Statement
AMG001	Ability to draw / sketch repairs / alterations
AMG002	Calculate center of gravity
AMG003	Calculate weight and balance
AMG004	Determine correct data
AMG005	Determine regulatory requirement.
AMG006	Interpret drag ratio from charts
AMG007	Recall aerodynamic fundamentals
AMG008	Recall air density
AMG009	Recall aircraft cleaning - materials / techniques
AMG010	Recall aircraft component markings
AMG011	Recall aircraft control cables - install / inspect / repair / service
AMG012	Recall aircraft corrosion - principles / control / prevention
AMG013	Recall aircraft drawings - detail / assembly
AMG014	Recall aircraft drawings / blueprints - lines / symbols / sketching
AMG015	Recall aircraft electrical system - install / inspect / repair / service
AMG016	Recall aircraft engines - performance charts
AMG017	Recall aircraft hardware - bolts / nuts / fasteners / fittings / valves
AMG018	Recall aircraft instruments - tachometer indications / dual tachometers
AMG019	Recall aircraft metals - inspect / test / repair / identify / heat treat
AMG020	Recall aircraft metals - types / tools / fasteners
AMG021	Recall aircraft publications - aircraft listings
AMG022	Recall aircraft records - required / destroyed
AMG023	Recall aircraft repair - major
AMG024	Recall airframe - inspections
AMG025	Recall airworthiness certificates - validity / requirements
AMG026	Recall ATA codes
AMG027	Recall basic physics - matter / energy / gas
AMG028	Recall data - approved
AMG029	Recall dissymmetry
AMG030	Recall effects of frost / snow on airfoils
AMG031	Recall electrical system - components / operating principles / characteristics/ symbols
AMG032	Recall environmental factors affecting maintenance performance
AMG033	Recall external loading
AMG034	Recall flight characteristics - autorotation / compressibility
AMG035	Recall flight operations - air taxi
AMG036	Recall fluid lines - install / inspect / repair / service
AMG037	Recall fluid lines - material / coding
AMG038	Recall forces acting on aircraft - angle of incidence

AMG039	Recall forces acting on aircraft - yaw / adverse yaw
AMG040	Recall fuel - types / characteristics / contamination / fueling / defueling / dumping
AMG041	Recall fundamental inspection principles - airframe / engine
AMG042	Recall fundamental material properties
AMG043	Recall generator system - components / operating principles / characteristics
AMG044	Recall geometry
AMG045	Recall ground operations - start / move / service / secure aircraft
AMG046	Recall helicopter engine control system
AMG047	Recall helicopter flight controls
AMG048	Recall information on an Airworthiness Directive
AMG049	Recall instrument panel mounting
AMG050	Recall maintenance error management
AMG051	Recall maintenance publications - service / parts / repair
AMG052	Recall maintenance resource management
AMG053	Recall mathematics - percentages / decimals / fractions / ratio / general
AMG054	Recall penalties - falsification / cheating
AMG055	Recall physics - work forces
AMG056	Recall pitch control - collective / cyclic
AMG057	Recall precision measuring tools - meters / gauges / scales / calipers
AMG058	Recall reciprocating engine - components / operating principles / characteristics
AMG059	Recall regulations - aircraft inspection / records / expiration
AMG060	Recall regulations - aircraft operator certificate
AMG061	Recall regulations - aircraft registration / marks
AMG062	Recall regulations - Airworthiness Directives
AMG063	Recall regulations - airworthiness requirements / responsibilities
AMG064	Recall regulations - certificate of maintenance review requirements
AMG065	Recall regulations - Certificate of Release
AMG066	Recall regulations - certification of aircraft and components
AMG067	Recall regulations - change of address
AMG068	Recall regulations - check periods
AMG069	Recall regulations - determine mass and balance
AMG070	Recall regulations - display / inspection of licences and certificates
AMG071	Recall regulations - emergency equipment
AMG072	Recall regulations - flight / operating manual marking / placard
AMG073	Recall regulations - housing and facility requirements
AMG074	Recall regulations - instrument / equipment requirements
AMG075	Recall regulations - maintenance control / procedure manual
AMG076	Recall regulations - maintenance reports / records / entries
AMG077	Recall regulations - maintenance requirements
AMG078	Recall regulations - minimum equipment list
AMG079	Recall regulations - minor / major repairs
AMG080	Recall regulations - persons authorized for return to service
AMG081	Recall regulations - persons authorized to perform maintenance

AMG082   Recall regulations - privileges / limitations of maintenance certificates / licences
AMG083   Recall regulations - privileges of approved maintenance organizations
AMG084   Recall regulations - reapplication after revocation / suspension
AMG085   Recall regulations - reporting failures / malfunctions / defects
AMG086   Recall regulations - return to service
AMG087   Recall regulations - special airworthiness certificates / requirements
AMG088   Recall regulations - special flight permit
AMG089   Recall regulations - weighing an aircraft
AMG090   Recall repair fundamentals - turnbuckles
AMG091   Recall rotor system - components / operating principles / characteristics
AMG092   Recall rotorcraft vibration - characteristics / sources
AMG093   Recall starter / ignition system - components / operating principles / characteristics
AMG094   Recall starter system - starting procedures
AMG095   Recall turbine engines - components / operational characteristics / associated instruments
AMG096   Recall turbine engines - install / inspect / repair / service / hazards
AMG097   Recall type certificate data sheet (TCDS) / supplemental type certificate (STC)
AMG098   Recall welding types / techniques / equipment
AMG099   Recall work / power / force / motion

AMG100   Recall mathematics - extract roots / radicals / scientific notation
AMG101   Recall positive / negative algebraic operations - addition / subtraction / multiplication / division
AMG102   Recall aircraft electrical circuit diagrams - read / interpret / troubleshoot
AMG103   Define maintenance resource management
AMG104   Recall human reliability in maintenance errors
AMG105   Recall environmental factors leading to maintenance errors
AMG106   Recall fatigue in maintenance errors causes / interventions
AMG107   Recall error management
AMG108   Recall maintenance resource management
AMG109   Recall error management in shift turnover
AMG110   Recall error capture / duplicate inspection
AMG111   Recall ergonomic interventions to maintenance errors
AMG112   Recall interventions to prevent cross-connection maintenance errors
AMG113   Recall interventions to prevent shift / task turnover errors
AMG115   Recall environmental factors affecting maintenance performance - lighting / temperature / noise / air quality
AMG116   Recall error intervention - interruptions / access

Learning Statement Codes and Learning Statements for Aviation Mechanic - Airframe Exam

Code	Learning Statement
AMA001	Recall aerodynamic fundamentals
AMA002	Recall air conditioning system - components / operating principles / characteristics
AMA003	Recall aircraft component markings
AMA004	Recall aircraft components material - flame resistant
AMA005	Recall aircraft cooling system - charging / leaking / oil / pressure / water
AMA006	Recall aircraft cooling system - components / operating principles / characteristics
AMA007	Recall aircraft corrosion - principles / control / prevention
AMA008	Recall aircraft engines - indicating system
AMA009	Recall aircraft exterior lighting - systems / components
AMA010	Recall aircraft flight indicator system
AMA011	Recall aircraft hardware - bolts / nuts / fasteners / fittings / valves
AMA012	Recall aircraft heating system - exhaust jacket inspection
AMA013	Recall aircraft instruments - install / inspect / adjust / repair / markings
AMA014	Recall aircraft instruments - types / components / operating principles / characteristics
AMA015	Recall aircraft lighting - install / inspect / repair / service
AMA016	Recall aircraft metals - inspect / test / repair / identify
AMA017	Recall aircraft metals - types / tools / fasteners
AMA018	Recall aircraft warning systems - navigation / stall / takeoff
AMA019	Recall airframe - inspections
AMA020	Recall airframe - repair / component installation
AMA021	Recall airframe design - structures / components
AMA022	Recall alternators - components / operating principles / characteristics
AMA023	Recall antenna system - install / inspect / repair / service
AMA024	Recall anti-icing / deicing - methods / systems
AMA025	Recall autopilot - components / operating principles / characteristics
AMA026	Recall autopilot - install / inspect / repair / service
AMA027	Recall avionics - components / operating principles / characteristics
AMA028	Recall avionics - install / inspect / repair / service
AMA029	Recall basic hand tools / torque values
AMA030	Recall batteries - capacity / charging / types / storage / rating / precautions
AMA031	Recall brake system - components / operating principles / characteristics
AMA032	Recall brake system - install / inspect / repair / service
AMA033	Recall carburetor - icing / anti-icing
AMA034	Recall chemical rain repellant
AMA035	Recall combustion heaters - components / operating principles / characteristics
AMA036	Recall compass - components / operating principles / characteristics
AMA037	Recall composite materials - types / repairs / techniques / processes
AMA038	Recall control cables - install / inspect / repair / service
AMA039	Recall DC electric motors - components / operating principles / characteristics

AMA040	Recall dope and fabric - materials / techniques / hazards
AMA041	Recall electrical system - components / operating principles / characteristics / symbols
AMA042	Recall electrical system - install / inspect / repair / service
AMA043	Recall electronic test equipment
AMA044	Recall Emergency Locator Transmitter (ELT) - operation / battery / testing
AMA045	Recall fiberglass - install / troubleshoot / service / repair
AMA046	Recall fire detection system - types / components / operating principles / characteristics
AMA047	Recall fire detection systems - install / inspect / repair / service
AMA048	Recall fire extinguishing systems - components / operating principles / characteristics
AMA049	Recall flap overload valve
AMA050	Recall flight characteristics - longitudinal stability / instability
AMA051	Recall fluid lines - material / coding
AMA052	Recall fuel - types / characteristics / contamination / fueling / defueling / dumping
AMA053	Recall fuel / oil - anti-icing / deicing
AMA054	Recall fuel system - components / operating principles / characteristics
AMA055	Recall fuel system - install / troubleshoot / service / repair
AMA056	Recall fuel system - types
AMA057	Recall fuel/air mixture - idle rich mixture - RPM rise
AMA058	Recall fundamental material properties
AMA059	Recall fuselage stations
AMA060	Recall helicopter control system
AMA061	Recall helicopter control system - collective
AMA062	Recall helicopter drive system - free wheeling unit
AMA063	Recall hydraulic systems - components / operating principles / characteristics
AMA064	Recall hydraulic systems - fluids
AMA065	Recall hydraulic systems - install / inspect / repair / service
AMA066	Recall instrument panel installation - shock mounts
AMA067	Recall instruments - manifold pressure indicating system
AMA068	Recall landing gear system - components / operating principles / characteristics
AMA069	Recall landing gear system - install / inspect / repair / service
AMA070	Recall maintenance publications - service / parts / repair
AMA071	Recall navigation / communication systems - types / operational characteristics
AMA072	Recall oxygen system - components / operating principles / characteristics
AMA073	Recall oxygen system - install / inspect / repair / service / precautions
AMA074	Recall oxygen system - quality / types / contamination / cylinders / pressure
AMA075	Recall physics - work forces
AMA076	Recall pitot-static system - components / operating principles / characteristics
AMA077	Recall pitot-static system - install / inspect / repair / service
AMA078	Recall plastic fundamentals - installation / cleaning / repair / characteristics
AMA079	Recall pneumatic system - components / operating principles / characteristics
AMA080	Recall pressurization system - components / operating principles / characteristics
AMA081	Recall primary flight controls - inspect / adjust / repair
AMA082	Recall primary flight controls - types / purpose / functionality

AMA083	Recall radar altimeter - indications
AMA084	Recall radar altimeter - signals
AMA085	Recall radio system - components / operating principles / characteristics
AMA086	Recall radio system - install / inspect / repair / service
AMA087	Recall radio system - licence requirements / frequencies
AMA088	Recall regulations - airworthiness requirements / responsibilities
AAM089	Recall regulations - maintenance reports / records / entries
AMA090	Recall regulations - privileges / limitations of maintenance certificates / licences
AAM091	Recall rotor system - components / operating principles / characteristics
AMA092	Recall secondary flight control system - inspect / adjust / repair
AMA093	Recall secondary flight control system - types / purpose / functionality
AMA094	Recall sheet metal fabrication - blueprints / shaping / construction
AMA095	Recall smoke detection systems - types / components / operating principles / characteristics
AMA096	Recall static pressure system - install / inspect / repair / service
AMA097	Recall tires - install / inspect / repair / service / storage
AMA098	Recall turbine engines - components / operational characteristics / associated instruments
AMA099	Recall type certificate data sheet (TCDS) / supplemental type certificate (STC)
AMA100	Recall weight and balance - equipment installation / CG / general principles
AMA101	Recall welding / soldering - types / techniques / equipment
AMA102	Recall wooden components - failures / decay / patching / gluing / substitutions

Learning Statement Codes and Learning Statements for Aviation Mechanic - Powerplant Exam

Code	Learning Statement
AMP001	Recall aircraft alternators - components / operating principles / characteristics
AMP002	Recall aircraft batteries - capacity / charging / types / storage / rating / precautions
AMP003	Recall aircraft carburetor - icing / anti-icing
AMP004	Recall aircraft component markings
AMP005	Recall aircraft cooling system - components / operating principles / characteristics
AMP006	Recall aircraft electrical system - install / inspect / repair / service
AMP007	Recall aircraft engine - inspections / cleaning
AMP008	Recall aircraft engines - components / operating principles / characteristics
AMP009	Recall aircraft engines - indicating system
AMP010	Recall aircraft fire classifications
AMP011	Recall aircraft hydraulic systems - components / operating principles / characteristics
AMP012	Recall aircraft instruments - types / components / operating principles / characteristics / markings
AMP013	Recall airflow systems - Bellmouth compressor inlet
AMP014	Recall airframe - inspections
AMP015	Recall altitude compensator / aneroid valve
AMP016	Recall anti-icing / deicing - methods / systems
AMP017	Recall Auxiliary Power Units - components / operating principles / characteristics
AMP018	Recall Auxiliary Power Units - install / inspect / repair / service
AMP019	Recall axial flow compressor - components / operating principles / characteristics
AMP020	Recall basic physics - matter / energy / gas
AMP021	Recall carburetor - effects of carburetor heat / heat control
AMP022	Recall carburetors - components / operating principles / characteristics
AMP023	Recall carburetors - install / inspect / repair / service
AMP024	Recall data - approved
AMP025	Recall DC electric motors - components / operating principles / characteristics
AMP026	Recall electrical system - components / operating principles / characteristics
AMP027	Recall engine cooling system - components / operating principles / characteristics
AMP028	Recall engine cooling system - install / inspect / repair / service
AMP029	Recall engine lubricating oils - function / grades / viscosity / types
AMP030	Recall engine lubricating system - components / operating principles / characteristics
AMP031	Recall engine lubricating system - install / inspect / repair / service
AMP032	Recall engine operations - thrust / thrust reverser
AMP033	Recall engine pressure ratio - EPR
AMP034	Recall fire detection system - types / components / operating principles / characteristics
AMP035	Recall fire detection systems - install / inspect / repair / service
AMP036	Recall fire extinguishing systems - components / operating principles / characteristics
AMP037	Recall float type carburetor - components / operating principles / characteristics

AMP038	Recall float type carburetor - install / inspect / repair / service
AMP039	Recall fuel - types / characteristics / contamination / fueling / defueling / dumping
AMP040	Recall fuel / oil - anti-icing / deicing
AMP041	Recall fuel system - components / operating principles / characteristics
AMP042	Recall fuel system - install / troubleshoot / service / repair
AMP043	Recall fuel system - types
AMP044	Recall generator system - components / operating principles / characteristics
AMP045	Recall information on an Airworthiness Directive
AMP046	Recall magneto - components / operating principles / characteristics
AMP047	Recall magneto - install / inspect / repair / service
AMP048	Recall maintenance publications - service / parts / repair
AMP049	Recall piston assembly - components / operating principles / characteristics
AMP050	Recall powerplant design - structures / components
AMP051	Recall pressure type carburetor - components / operating principles / characteristics
AMP052	Recall propeller system - install / inspect / repair / service
AMP053	Recall propeller system - types/ components / operating principles / characteristics
AMP054	Recall radial engine - components / operating principles / characteristics
AMP055	Recall radial engine - install / inspect / repair / service
AMP056	Recall reciprocating engine - components / operating principles / characteristics
AMP057	Recall reciprocating engine - install / inspect / repair / service
AMP058	Recall regulations - maintenance reports / records / entries
AMP059	Recall regulations - privileges / limitations of maintenance certificates / licences
AMP060	Recall regulations - privileges of approved maintenance organizations
AMP061	Recall rotor system - components / operating principles / characteristics
AMP062	Recall sea level - standard temperature / pressure
AMP063	Recall starter / ignition system - components / operating principles / characteristics
AMP064	Recall starter / ignition system - install / inspect / repair / service
AMP065	Recall starter system - starting procedures
AMP066	Recall thermocouples - components / operating principles / characteristics
AMP067	Recall thermocouples - install / inspect / repair / service
AMP068	Recall turbine engines - components / operational characteristics / associated instruments
AMP069	Recall turbine engines - install / inspect / repair / service / hazards
AMP070	Recall turbocharger system - components / operating principles / characteristics
AMP071	Recall turbojet - components / operating principles / characteristics
AMP072	Recall type certificate data sheet (TCDS) / supplemental type certificate (STC)
AMP073	Recall welding types / techniques / equipment

POWERPLANT ORAL AND PRACTICAL EXAM STUDY GUIDE

This appendix of the Powerplant Study Guide has been developed to aid you in preparing for the FAA Powerplant Mechanic on how applicants from Aviation Maintenance Technician Schools (AMTS), the military, or persons applying for certification through occupational experience can best prepare, apply for, and take the exam.

The second area of the appendix includes sample oral exam questions and **answers**, divided by subject area. These are typical questions that an examiner is likely to ask during testing. It should be noted that, since the FAA allows DMEs the flexibility to create their own Oral questions and **answers**, it is impossible for this or any study guide to provide the exact questions that the examiner will use. However, if you understand these questions, you should be adequately prepared to pass the test. The **answers** to the questions are provided along with references that can be used as an additional source of study material concerning each question.

The final part of this appendix includes sample practical projects that an examiner may assign during your test. Since the testing facilities and equipment vary between examiners, it is impossible to cover all the projects that you may be tested on. However, if you are able to perform the sample projects presented in this test guide, you should be adequately prepared to pass the FAA Practical Exam. The projects are divided into subject areas and follow the corresponding Oral questions.

The practical projects also include a skill level that must be reached in order to satisfactorily complete the projects. The completion standards are:

- Projects that require Level 1 skills are accomplished by your showing or explaining basic principles without using any manipulative skills.

- Level 2 projects require you to have knowledge of general principles, and you must demonstrate limited practical application. For these projects, you will likely be required to demonstrate sufficient manipulative skills to perform basic operations.

- Level 3 projects require you to have a high degree of knowledge of general principles and to demonstrate a high degree of practical application. To complete Level 3 projects satisfactorily, you are required to demonstrate the ability to complete the project to simulate a return-to-service condition.

Finally, each project includes a list of materials that the examiner will make available for you to use to complete the project. The examiner must provide you with access to current publications, and also will provide you with special tools and equipment. However, you should verify what tools you will be required to provide when you schedule the test. In most cases, you will at least need basic hand tools, including an inspection mirror(s), flashlight, sockets with ratchets, screwdrivers, wrenches, and safety equipment.

REQUIREMENTS FOR CERTIFICATION
The requirements for the certification of aircraft mechanics are outlined in Title 14 of the Code of Federal Regulations (14 CFR, Part 65)

ELIGIBILITY REQUIREMENTS
To be eligible for a mechanic certificate, a person must:

1. Be at least 18 years of age.

2. Be able to read, write, speak, and understand the English language (unless the applicant is to be employed outside the United States by a U.S. air carrier, in which case the certificate will have a limitation to be effective only outside the United States).

3. Have passed all of the prescribed Airman Knowledge Exams within a period of 24 calendar months. If the application is for an original issuance for a mechanic certificate, depending on the rating sought, you must have passed the General and Airframe Knowledge Exams, or General and Powerplant Knowledge Exams, within 24 calendar months of taking the Oral and Practical Exams.

4. Comply with other applicable regulations of Part 65 as detailed below.

EXPERIENCE AND APPLICATION REQUIREMENTS
There are two ways in which an applicant may meet the FAA requirements to be eligible to obtain a Mechanic Certificate. The first way is to present a certificate of completion from an Aviation Maintenance Technician School (AMTS) to an

examiner that is affiliated with the school. If you take the Airman Knowledge, Oral, or Practical Exams with an examiner that is affiliated with your AMTS, the school will provide two copies of FAA Form 8610-2 (Airman Certificate and/or Rating Application), and authorize you to take the required tests. If you are a graduate of an AMTS and wish to complete the Airman Knowledge or Oral and Practical Exams at a facility other than the AMTS that you attended, you must go to an FAA FSDO to have an Airworthiness Inspector authorize you to take the tests. At that time, the inspector will have you fill out two copies of the FAA Form 8610-2 and will ask you for a photo identification. Before you can begin any FAA required tests, you must present both forms with original signatures and photo identification. DO NOT LOSE THE FORMS and do not allow the Airman Knowledge Testing Center personnel to keep either of the originals (although they may make a photocopy for their records).

The second way to qualify for an Airman Mechanic Certificate is to present the FAA with documentary evidence showing work or military experience applicable to the rating(s) sought. This documentation should include descriptions of the work showing that the procedures, practices, materials, and equipment generally used in constructing, maintaining, or altering airframes or powerplants has been obtained. It is helpful if the documentation includes a contact phone number for a person that served in a supervisory position in case the FAA inspector needs further verification. For applicants with military experience, military discharge Form DD-214 may be used along with any training certificates received during military service. Part 65 requires a minimum of 18 months experience maintaining airframes to qualify for the Airframe Rating, or 30 months combined experience maintaining airframes and powerplants to qualify for both an Airframe and Powerplant rating. The work experience should essentially reflect the equivalent of a forty-hour workweek, although the work does not need to be consecutive.

THE ORAL AND PRACTICAL EXAM

The FAA Oral and Practical Exam for an Aircraft Mechanic Certificate is probably one of the most difficult FAA exams to prepare for because of the large amount of material that must be learned. For this reason, test preparation plays an important role in your ability to successfully pass the exams. However, in no way do we encourage you to memorize our test preparation materials. Instead, use your test guide as an aid to gain an in-depth understanding of concepts and procedures. Ultimately, you will find that the knowledge gained will benefit you throughout your career as an Aviation Maintenance Technician.

The purpose of this section of the appendix is to help **answer** some of the questions you may have about the oral and practical exams. With an understanding of the testing procedures, you will likely have less apprehension during the exam, allowing you to focus on the tasks that the examiner assigns you.

WHO CONDUCTS THE ORAL AND PRACTICAL EXAMS?

The Oral and Practical Exam may be given either by a Designated Mechanic Examiner (DME) or an FAA inspector. In most areas of the country, the FAA does not have the manpower to conduct the exam, in which case you will need to schedule your exams with a DME.

HOW DO I LOCATE A DME?

If you are a graduate of an AMTS, it is likely that the oral and practical exams will be conducted by a DME that is on staff with the school. If you're applying for a Mechanic's Certificate by showing occupational or military experience, you will need to locate a DME on your own to make arrangements for testing. The names and phone numbers of DMEs in your area are available by calling your local FAA Flight Standards District Office (FSDO). The phone numbers for these offices are generally found in your local phone directory under United States Government, Federal Aviation Administration, or Department of Transportation.

HOW MUCH DO THE EXAMS COST?

If you take your exam from a DME, they will have their own fee for each section of the exam that you take. The fees are set by the DME and vary between examiners. It is advisable for you to shop around and talk to different DMEs about their fees. Also, ask what method of payment is required. Some DMEs will only accept cash, while others will accept checks or even credit cards.

HOW LONG DO THE EXAMS TAKE?

There is no established maximum time limit for the exams. However, there is a minimum time requirement. The minimum time allocated for the General Oral and Practical Exams is 2 hours, while the Airframe or Powerplant Exams require 4 hours each to complete. If you do not already hold a Mechanic Certificate, you will be required to take both the General and Airframe or Powerplant Exams for a total minimum time of 6 hours. However, if you already hold an Aircraft Mechanic Certificate with one rating, you will not be required to retake the General Mechanic Exam to obtain the other rating. Although these minimum times have been established, the actual times vary. It is not uncommon for the exams to take two or three times longer than the minimum requirements. Ask the examiner about typical time requirements when making arrangements to take the exams, and plan your schedule to allow adequate time to complete them.

WHAT ITEMS SHOULD I BRING FOR THE EXAMS?

Since you and the examiner must schedule a large block of time for the exams, it is critical that you come with all the required materials. The following items should be organized and readily available to you no later than one day before your scheduled exam. If you fail to bring any of the following items with you for the exam, the examiner may not begin administering any portion of the exam, and you will have to reschedule another time with the examiner. To verify that you have the required items, use the following list to check off items before departing to take the exam. The required items include:

✓ Two copies of FAA Form 8610-2 with original signatures — if you obtained these documents from an FAA Airworthiness Inspector, the inspector's original signature must be included.

✓ Original Airman Knowledge Exam results — copies are not accepted and if the originals are lost, you must request a replacement from the FAA. The address and information that must be included with the request are given in the introduction section of this test guide. Keep in mind that the replacements may take over a week to obtain

✓ Photo Identification — acceptable photo identifications include a state issued driver's license or photo identification, government identification card, passport, alien residency (green) card, or military identification card.

✓ Examiner's Fee — correct cash or other form of payment as arranged with the examiner.

✓ Basic Hand Tools — assorted ratchets and sockets, screwdrivers, wrenches, mirror, flashlight, and other hand tools as required by the examiner.

✓ Reference Materials — consider bringing the General, Powerplant, and/or Airframe Textbooks, AC 43.13-1B and 2A, and other reference materials that you may find useful. You can use the reference materials while taking the practical portion of the test but cannot use any references during the oral portion of the exam, except those given to you by the examiner.

✓ Calculator, pencil, black ink pen, and paper.

WHAT AREAS WILL I BE TESTED ON?

The Oral and Practical Exam is designed so that the examiner can evaluate your performance to determine that you will be a competent and safe aircraft mechanic and that you at least meet the minimum requirements for certification. To verify that you are knowledgeable in all areas required by FAR Part 65, you will be tested in each subject area for the General Mechanic Certificate. These subjects include the following:

1. Aircraft Assembly and Rigging

2. Sheet Metal Structures

3. Wood Structures

4. Aircraft Welding

5. Aircraft Covering

5. Aircraft Finishes

6. Aircraft Electrical Systems

7. Hydraulic and Pneumatic Power Systems

8. Aircraft Landing Gear Systems

9. Position and Warning Systems

10. Aircraft Instrument Systems

11. Communication and Navigation Systems

12. Ice and Rain Control Systems

13. Cabin Atmosphere Control Systems

14. Aircraft Fuel Systems

15. Fire Protection Systems

16. Airframe Inspection

HOW IS THE ORAL EXAM CONDUCTED?

The oral exam may be conducted in different ways depending on the examiner. Some examiners conduct the oral exam first before having you do any of the practical portions of the test, while others may ask you oral questions while you perform the practical portion of the exam. In either case, the examiner will ask you a minimum of four questions that relate to each subject area. Of these four questions, you must correctly **answer** 3 out of 4 to pass. If you miss more than one question, at the discretion of the examiner, additional questions may be asked to further evaluate your knowledge of the subject area. If additional questions are asked, you must correctly **answer** 70% of all the questions to pass the subject area.

If you do not already hold an Aircraft or Powerplant Mechanic Certificate, you will also be required to take the General Mechanic oral exam. These may be administered before the General exams, or in some cases, the examiner may elect to vary the order. Regardless of the order that the exams are taken, you must pass all the oral questions in both the General and Airframe or Powerplant subject areas. This means that you B-4 General Oral and Practical Exam Study Guide Appendix B.qxd 10/19/07 1:54 PM Page B-4 will be required to **answer** a minimum of 48 General questions (12 subject areas) and 68 Airframe or Powerplant questions (17 subject areas).

When taking the oral exam, it is best to listen carefully to the question and formulate your **answer** before responding. Try to keep your **answer**s as direct to the question as possible. This will save time and keep the examiner from feeling the need to delve further into the subject area if your explanation is confusing.

If you do not understand the question, you can ask the examiner to elaborate further. In some cases, the examiner can rephrase the question, but in others the examiner will only repeat the question if they feel you should understand what is being asked. Regardless of the examiner's response, there is no harm in asking for clarification. Also, keep in mind that in no case is the examiner allowed to teach during the exam. If they feel that further elaboration may cause them to give you more information than they should divulge, they may elect to keep the questions very specific. In most cases, the examiner will try to remain personable, but they will keep focused on the task of administering the exam.

The examiner will also use a worksheet to keep track of your results and will likely take additional notes throughout the exam. It is required for the examiner to keep these records, so don't be concerned to see them writing after each question.

HOW IS THE PRACTICAL EXAM CONDUCTED?

The examiner will assign you projects from each of the subject areas required for the rating(s) you apply for. Depending on the examiner, you may be assigned a separate project for each subject, or you may be given a project that entails an evaluation of many subjects. For example, you may be given a project to install an up-limit switch on a landing gear. This project could allow the examiner to evaluate multiple subject areas including electrical systems, landing gear, position and warning systems, maintenance publications, and others. Regardless of the actual number of assignments that you are given, you must perform at least one practical project for each subject area. In addition, you will be required to complete an FAA Form 337 (Major Alteration and Repair Form), and to calculate a sample weight-and-balance change problem.

As mentioned earlier, the examiner will have technical manuals and special tools that you will need to complete the assigned projects. However, the examiner may not make these readily available to you. Part of the exam process includes evaluating whether you know what tools, materials and technical information you will need to work on an actual aircraft. Do not hesitate to ask the examiner where you can locate these items.

WHAT AM I REQUIRED TO DO IF I FAIL PART OF THE EXAM?

The examiner will normally advise you of your progress throughout the test and give you the option to discontinue the test at any time. However, you should try to complete the exam to identify all the areas that you may be deficient in. If you complete the exam and only have a few failed subject areas, you will only be tested on the failed subjects if you retest with the same examiner. However, if you go to another examiner, you will be required to repeat the entire test.

In the event you fail any subject area, Part 65 requires that you wait 30 days before reapplying for the exam, unless you receive additional instruction from an airman holding the rating that you are seeking. The person that provides you with the additional instruction should give you a written statement detailing the number of hours of instruction they provided along with a brief description of what subject areas were covered. In addition, the statement should contain the person's signature, certificate type, and airman certificate number.

WHEN DO I RECEIVE MY AIRMAN'S CERTIFICATE?

If you pass all areas of the oral and practical exam, you will be issued a Temporary Airman's Certificate that is immediately effective. The examiner may issue the temporary certificate on the day of the exam, or depending on the arrangements between the local FSDO and the examiner, it may be issued later by mail by the FSDO. In either case, the temporary certificate is effective for 120 days from the date of issuance. If you do not receive a permanent Airman's Certificate in the mail before your temporary certificate expires, you should contact your local FSDO to track your records and make an arrangement to issue you another temporary certificate. An FSDO inspector is the only person authorized to reissue a temporary certificate.

SUGGESTIONS FOR MILITARY APPLICANTS

Applicants coming from the military typically show a lack of experience with the civil aircraft manufacturer's technical manuals and Federal Aviation Administration documents. If you are applying for certification based on military experience, it is strongly recommended that you receive supplementary instruction in the use of civil aircraft manufacturer's illustrated parts catalogs, service manuals, and service information literature. You should also review federal publications such as Type Certificate Data Sheets, Airworthiness Directives, Advisory Circulars, and Supplemental Type Certificate Data Sheets before applying for the test.

In most cases, additional practical instruction in these areas can be received at a local AMTS or a Fixed Base Operation maintenance shop where you can contract with someone to instruct you. In some cases, you might even work with the DME that will be giving you your exam. This is not objectionable since the DME will likely not teach you the exam, but instead will teach you the material needed to be a safe and competent mechanic. Once the exam commences, the examiner will not provide any instruction, and they will evaluate you solely on your ability to do the work on your own.

Aside from these areas of study, most military applicants have adequate exposure to the tools, equipment, and maintenance practices to complete the FAA exams with the same amount of preparation as applicants coming from an AMTS. Regardless of whether you are coming from a military or civil background, the best way to guarantee success is with preparation. Our General Test Guide assures that you have the most thorough and complete test preparation materials available.

NOTES

CHAPTER 1 — RECIPROCATING ENGINES

ORAL QUESTIONS

1. What is the purpose of dynamic dampers on crankshafts?

    Answer – They reduce engine vibration. (Page Reference: JSPT 1-8)

2. What types of bearings are generally found in reciprocating engines?

    Answer – Plain, ball and roller bearings. (Page Reference: JSPT 1-10)

3. Are the connecting rods used in each cylinder of a radial engine the same? Explain.

    Answer – No. Radial engines use master and articulating rod assemblies. (Page Reference: JSPT 1-12)

4. Name the different types of piston rings.

    Answer – Oil control, compression and oil scraper. (Page Reference: JSPT 1-15)

5. Where should piston ring gaps be installed relative to each other, and why?

    Answer – Compression ring gaps should be staggered so that they do not align. This prevents excessive blow-by. (Page Reference: JSPT 1-15)

6. What could result from incorrectly installed piston rings?

    Answer – Excessive oil consumption. (Page Reference: JSPT 1-16)

7. What purpose do oil control rings serve?

    Answer – They regulate the thickness of the oil film on the cylinder walls. (Page Reference: JSPT 1-16)

8. What is used to help prevent valve surge or floating in an aircraft engine?

    Answer – Two or more springs are used on each valve. (Page Reference: JSPT 1-22)

9. On engines equipped with hydraulic valve lifters, what should the running valve clearance be?

    Answer – Zero. (Page Reference: JSPT 1-25)

10. What is the purpose of valve overlap?

    Answer – It allows better volumetric efficiency and lowers cylinder operating temperatures. (Page Reference: JSPT 1-39)

PRACTICAL TEST

1. Project: Identify crankshaft parts. (Level 3)

    Given: A crankshaft, associated parts, and reference material.

    Performance Standard: The applicant will identify each part of the crankshaft.

2. Project: Identify reciprocating engine cylinder parts. (Level 2)

    Given: An air-cooled cylinder and reference material.

    Performance Standard: The applicant will point out the major parts of the cylinder.

3. Project: Identify and inspect various types of engine bearings. (Level 3)

    Given: Plain, needle, roller, and ball bearings, tools, and reference materials.

    Performance Standard: The applicant will identify the type of bearing and inspect it for defects.

4. Project: Identify an engine by type without reference material. (Level 2)

    Given: An aircraft engine with data plate.

    Performance Standard: The applicant will visually inspect and list the information from the engine data plate.

CHAPTER 2 — RECIPROCATING ENGINE OPERATION, INSTRUMENTS, MAINTENANCE, AND OVERHAUL

ORAL QUESTIONS

1. What indications are given in the event of a leaking or open primer while the engine is running?

   Answer – The engine will not idle properly. (Page Reference: JSPT 14-11)

2. A cold cylinder is found when troubleshooting a running engine. What does this indicate?

   Answer – No combustion in that cylinder. (Page Reference: JSPT 14-5)

3. When pulling a propeller through, a hissing sound is heard, indicating valve blow-by. What procedure should be performed next?

   Answer – A compression check should be performed to identify the faulty cylinder. (Page Reference: JSPT 2-18)

4. What is the purpose of performing a compression test?

   Answer – To determine if the valves, pistons and rings are sealing properly. (Page Reference: JSPT 2-18)

5. When an engine is overhauled, how is its total time affected? When an engine is rebuilt, how is its operating history affected?

   Answer – The total time on the engine must be continued and the time since major overhaul is entered into the engine log. If the manufacturer rebuilds the engine, it is granted a zero-time status and is considered to have no previous operating history. (Page Reference: JSPT 2-25)

6. What inspections should be performed after a propeller strike without sudden stoppage?

   Answer – 1. Inspect engine mounts, the crankcase, and the nose section for damage. 2. Inspect the oil and oil filters/screens for metal particles. 3. Inspect the crankshaft or driveshaft for cracks and misalignment. (Page Reference: JSPT 2-25)

7. Name some of the precautions that should be performed prior to engine removal.

   Answer – Disconnect the battery, turn off the fuel valves, chock the wheels, and if necessary, install a tail stand. (Page Reference: JSPT 2-27)

8. When inspecting a piston, where are cracks most likely to be found?

   Answer – In those areas that are highly stressed; usually the base of the piston bosses, inside at the junction of the bore and the walls, and the ring lands. (Page Reference: JSPT 2-36)

9. What does it mean if an engine part is within "serviceable limits"?

   Answer – It means that the part is within the manufacturer's limits and can be used in an engine (does not require replacement). (Page Reference: JSPT 2-32)

10. What tools or instruments are used to inspect a cylinder barrel for out-of-roundness?

    Answer – A dial indicator or an inside micrometer is usually used to measure the top of the cylinder and at the skirt. A telescopic gauge and micrometer can also be used. Two readings should be taken 90# to each other. (Page Reference: JSPT 2-42)

11. How can a loose stud in an engine crankcase be repaired?

    Answer – Remove the loose stud and inspect the hole for size and thread condition. It may be necessary to use an oversize stud or Heli-Coil® insert. (Page Reference: JSPT 2-47)

12. What publication is used to check an engine for normal operation?

    Answer – Manufacturer's maintenance manual. (Page Reference: JSPT 2-13)

13. A weak cylinder is found during a compression check. What must be inspected?

     Answer - Pressure is transmitted equally in all directions. (Page Reference: JSPT 2-17)14.

14. What purpose does an oil analysis serve?

     Answer – Metal particles in the oil show normal and abnormal wear of the engine. This helps in evaluating the engine's internal condition. (Page Reference: JSPT 2-25)

15. What inspection should be performed on an engine that has been in storage?

     Answer – Perform an inspection to determine if there is any corrosion damage. (Page Reference: JSPT 2-54)

16. Where would a carburetor air temperature bulb be located?

     Answer – In the ram air intake duct. (Page Reference: JSPT 2-3)

17. What is the fuel pressure range on float-type carburetors?

     Answer – 3 to 5 psi. (Page Reference: JSPT 2-4)

18. Name the basic components of a fuel indicator system.

     Answer – The transmitter and the indicator. (Page Reference: JSPT 2-5)

19. What unit of measure is generally used to indicate fuel flow?

     Answer – Pounds or gallons per hour. (Page Reference: JSPT 2-6)

20. Why is fuel flow monitored?

     Answer – To determine fuel consumption and engine performance. (Page Reference: JSPT 2-6)

21. What does the manifold gauge indicate and how is it calibrated?

     Answer – It measures the absolute pressure in the engine manifold and is calibrated in inches of mercury. (Page Reference: JSPT 2-6)

22. What directly controls manifold pressure?

     Answer – Throttle opening and engine r.p.m. (Page Reference: JSPT 2-6)

23. During engine operation, where should the propeller control be set when checking the manifold pressure?

     Answer – Low pitch, high r.p.m. (Page Reference: JSPT 2-6)

24. Is the aircraft electrical system required to power a cylinder head temperature gauge?

     Answer – No. A thermocouple is used as the electrical source. (Page Reference: JSPT 2-8)

25. What are the possible indications of an oil pressure transmitter or indicator malfunction?

     Answer – A severe or sudden drop in oil pressure while the oil temperature remains normal and the oil supply remains full. (Page Reference: JSPT 2-8)

26. What does a tachometer indicate on a reciprocating engine?

     Answer – Engine r.p.m. (Page Reference: JSPT 2-10)

27. Where should the thermocouple be installed on a reciprocating engine using a single probe cylinder head temperature system?

     Answer – On the hottest cylinder. (Page Reference: JSPT 2-9)

PRACTICAL TEST

1. Project: Perform an engine cylinder runout inspection. (Level 3)

   Given: An engine cylinder, tools, and reference materials.

   Performance Standard: The applicant will locate the procedures to inspect an engine cylinder to determine if its dimensions and taper are within serviceable limits.

2. Project: Repair or replace a cylinder mounting stud. (Level 3)

   Given: A reciprocating-engine crankcase with a cylinder mounting stud, tools, and reference material.

   Performance Standard: The applicant will remove and replace a cylinder mounting stud in accordance with the engine manufacturer's procedures.

3. Project: Perform a runout inspection of a crankshaft. (Level 3)

   Given: A crankshaft, inspection equipment, and reference material.

   Performance Standard: The applicant will inspect a crankshaft, record the dimensions, and determine if it is within serviceable tolerances.

4. Project: Perform a crankshaft propeller flange runout inspection. (Level 3)

   Given: A crankshaft, inspection equipment, and reference material.

   Performance Standard: The applicant will inspect the crankshaft flange runout and determine if the crankshaft is within the manufacturer's tolerances for return-to-service.

5. Project: Replace a crankshaft front oil seal. (Level 3)

   Given: An engine, tools, oil seal, and reference material.

   Performance Standard: The applicant will replace the crankshaft front oil seal.

6. Project: Install a cylinder on an engine. (Level 3)

   Given: A cylinder assembly, an engine, seals, gaskets, tools, and reference materials.

   Performance Standard: Using the manufacturer's instructions, the applicant will install the cylinder on the engine.

7. Project: Install a piston and rings in a cylinder. (Level 3)

   Given: A cylinder, piston, rings, tools, and reference materials.

   Performance Standard: The applicant will install the piston and rings in the cylinder in accordance with the manufacturer's instructions.

8. Project: Perform a differential compression test on a cylinder. (Level 3)

   Given: An aircraft engine, differential compression tester, tools, and reference materials.

   Performance Standard: The applicant will test the compression on the cylinder while taking appropriate safety measures and determine the condition of the cylinder.

9. Project: Adjust exhaust and intake valve clearances on an engine with solid lifters. (Level 3)

   Given: An engine with adjustable intake and exhaust rocker arms, tools, and reference material.
   Performance Standard: The applicant will adjust the rocker arms according to the manufacturer's instructions.

10. Project: Adjust valve clearances on an engine with hydraulic valve lifters. (Level 3)

    Given: An aircraft engine, tools, equipment, and reference materials.

    Performance Standard: The applicant will use the proper tools, reference materials, and procedures to adjust the "dry tappet" clearance on the exhaust and intake valves.

11. Project: Replace and/or adjust engine shock mounts. (Level 3)

     Given: An aircraft with engine, an engine mount, hoist, tools, and reference materials.

     Performance Standard: The applicant will install and torque the engine mount in accordance with the reference material.

12. Project: Inspect the integrity of structural engine mounts. (Level 3)

     Given: An aircraft with engine installed, tools, and reference materials.

     Performance Standard: The applicant will visually inspect the engine mounts and determine serviceability.

13. Project: Adjust oil pressure. (Level 3)

     Given: An operable engine, tools, and reference material.

     Performance Standard: The applicant will adjust the engine oil pressure to specifications.

14. Project: The applicant will adjust the engine oil pressure to specifications. (Level 3)

     Given: An aircraft engine, timing disk, piston locator, tools, and reference materials.

     Performance Standard: The applicant will locate top-dead-center of a piston and verify the timing mark position on the engine.

15. Project: Inspect the rigging of engine controls. (Level 3)

     Given: An aircraft engine, tools, and reference material.

     Performance Standard: The applicant will inspect cable and push-pull engine control rigging, and rig the system as necessary to meet the manufacturer's requirements.

16. Project: Replace packing seals on a pushrod housing. (Level 3)

     Given: An engine, tools, seals, and reference materials.

     Performance Standard: The applicant will remove a pushrod housing, replace the seals, and install the housing.

17. Project: Repair or replace a sparkplug threaded boss. (Level 3)

     Given: An engine, tools, replacement insert, and reference tools.

     Performance Standard: The applicant will remove a sparkplug threaded insert and replace it in accordance with the manufacturer's instructions.

18. Project: Check engine controls for defects, improper travel, and freedom of operation. (Level 3)

     Given: An aircraft engine and reference materials.

     Performance Standard: The applicant will conduct an operational check of the engine controls in accordance with reference materials.

19. Project: Inspect an engine for fluid leaks. (Level 3)

     Given: An aircraft engine and reference materials.

     Performance Standard: The applicant will inspect an engine for fluid leaks.

20. Project: Inspect r.p.m. gauge markings. (Level 3)

     Given: An r.p.m. gauge and reference material.

     Performance Standard: The applicant will review the reference material and inspect an r.p.m. gauge for proper markings.

21. Project: Remove and install a tachometer generator. (Level 3)

     Given: An aircraft engine or mockup with a tachometer generator, tools, and reference materials.

     Performance Standard: The applicant will remove and reinstall a tachometer generator in accordance with the reference materials.

22. Project: Measure the resistance of a thermocouple. (Level 3)

   Given: A thermocouple, tools, and reference material.

   Performance Standard: The applicant will measure resistance in a thermocouple to determine its serviceability.

23. Project: Troubleshoot a cylinder head temperature (CHT) indicating system. (Level 3)

   Given: Pilot reports, schematics of a CHT system, and reference materials.

   Performance Standard: The applicant will analyze the pilot reports and determine the possible cause or causes of the system malfunction(s).

24. Project: Install a cylinder head temperature thermocouple. (Level 3)

   Given: A thermocouple assembly, tools, and reference materials.

   Performance Standard: The applicant will install a cylinder head thermocouple assembly, and check the operation.

CHAPTER 3 — TURBINE ENGINES

ORAL QUESTIONS

1. Explain the main difference and advantage of turbofan over turbojet engines.

    Answer – A turbofan engine uses a fan to bypass some air around the engine core and to provide thrust. The advantage is that this provides additional thrust without increasing fuel flow. (Page Reference: JSPT 3-4)

2. Name the major components in a gas turbine engine.

    Answer – Air inlet, compressor section, combustion section, turbine section, exhaust section, gearbox and accessory section. (Page Reference: JSPT 3-8)

3. What determines the amount of airflow through a turbine engine?

    Answer – The forward speed of the aircraft, compressor speed, and air density. (Page Reference: JSPT 3-8)

4. Name the two types of compressors commonly used in turbine engines.

    Answer – Axial and centrifugal flow compressors. (Page Reference: JSPT 3-12)

5. Name two different methods for attaching turbine engine rotor blades to the rotor disks.

    Answer –Dovetail-type root -or- Bulb-type root -or- Fir tree-type root (Page Reference: JSPT 3-15)

6. What is a split compressor system?

    Answer – Also called dual or twin spool compressors, these are connected to the turbine section with two rotor shafts, one inside the other. (Page Reference: JSPT 3-17)

7. What are the different types of combustion chambers used in turbine engines?

    Answer – Can, annular, can-annular, and reverse flow annular. (Page Reference: JSPT 3-20)

8. What prevents the combustion chambers from burning?

    Answer – Cooling air along the inside of the liner. (Page Reference: JSPT 3-21)

9. What is the purpose of the interconnecting tubes attached between can-type combustion chambers?

    Answer – For flame propagation during start. (Page Reference: JSPT 3-22)

10. What functions do axial flow turbine nozzles perform?

    Answer – They direct the mass airflow to drive the turbine rotor at a specific angle. (Page Reference: JSPT 3-20)

11. How is thermal stress relieved on a turbine disc?

    Answer – By directing bleed air onto the face of the disk, or by grooves being cut in the disk. (Page Reference: JSPT 3-27)

12. What are carbon seals used for in turbine engines?

    Answer – They are used as oil seals for the rotor shaft bearings. (Page Reference: JSPT 3-33)

13. What is shaft horsepower?

    Answer – It is an indication of the torque developed by a turboprop or turboshaft engine. (Page Reference: JSPT 3-35)

14. Name the main components of a typical APU.

    Answer – A small power turbine for power and bleed air, and an electrical generator. (Page Reference: JSPT 3-34)

15. When is the greatest demand placed on an APU?

    Answer – When supplying bleed air. (Page Reference: JSPT 3-35)

16. How is an APU generally started?

    Answer – With its own electrical starter and battery power. (Page Reference: JSPT 3-35)

17. Where does the APU get its fuel supply?

    Answer – From one of the aircraft's main fuel tanks. (Page Reference: JSPT 3-35)

18. At what speed does a gas turbine APU operate and how is this speed maintained?

    Answer – At or near its rated speed regardless of electrical or pneumatic loads imposed. The APU fuel control automatically adjusts the fuel flow to maintain the rated speed. (Page Refer**ence: JSPT** 3-35)

19. What is used to prevent a heavily loaded APU from exceeding its maximum EGT?

    Answer – A load control valve modulates the pneumatic load to maintain EGTs within limits. (Page Reference: JSPT 3-35)

20. How is an APU shut down and why is this procedure used?

    Answer – After the APU is unloaded by closing the bleed air valve, it is run for a specified amount of time to allow the EGT to cool and stabilize. This cool down period is typically three minutes. If a heavily loaded APU is abruptly shut down without any cooling down period, damage could occur as a result of thermal shock. (Page Reference: JSPT 3-35)

21. What powers the variable inlet guide vanes used on some APUs to regulate compressor intake airflow?

    Answer – Fuel pressure. (Page Reference: JSPT 3-35)

22. What is fan blade shingling?

    Answer – It is the overlapping of the midspan shrouds of the fan blade. (Page Reference: JSPT 3-15)

23. When a turbofan or turbojet engine is shut down, what should a mechanic listen for during coastdown?

    Answer – Any rubbing sound or other unusual noises from the engine. (Page Reference: JSPT 3-15)

PRACTICAL TEST

1. Project: Identify major components of turbine engines. (Level 2)

    Given: Unlabeled drawings of turbojet or turbofan engines and a list of component nomenclatures.

    Performance Standard: The applicant will label major components of turbine engines.

2. Project: Identify characteristics of different turbine compressors. (Level 2)

    Given: Unlabeled drawings of various types of compressors and a list of characteristics.

    Performance Standard: The applicant will label the drawings of compressors with characteristics.

3. Project: Identify airflow direction and pressure changes in turbojet or turbofan engines. (Level 2)

    Given: Unlabeled drawings of turbojet or turbofan engines.

    Performance Standard: The applicant will label, with arrows, the direction of airflow through a turbojet or turbofan engine, and note any change of air pressure between sections.

CHAPTER 4 — TURBINE ENGINE OPERATION, INSTRUMENTS, MAINTENANCE, AND OVERHAUL

ORAL QUESTIONS

1. Why are compressor washes performed and what methods are commonly used?

   Answer – To remove any contaminants from the compressor section and improve engine performance. The fluid wash and abrasive grit wash are commonly used. (Page Reference: JSPT 4-10)

2. How can you tell if a turbofan or turbojet engine is out of trim?

   Answer – There will be a high exhaust gas temperature at the target engine pressure ratio for takeoff power. (Page Reference: JSPT 4-10)

3. Name the different types of compressor blade damage that may be found during inspection.

   Answer – Dents, cracks, galling, pitting, scratches, burrs, burns, gouges. (Page Reference: JSPT 4-23)

4. What kind of markers can be used to mark the parts in hot and cold sections during repair?

   Answer – Layout dye, felt tip marker, chalk. (Page Reference: JSPT 4-27)

5. How does relative humidity affect turbine engines?

   Answer – Negligible effect. (Page Reference: JSPT 4-7)

6. What criteria determines replacement of life limited turbine engine components?

   Answer – Cycles, hours and/or calendar time. (Page Reference: JSPT 4-18)

7. If turbine blades are removed from a turbine disc, why should they be re-installed in the same location?

   Answer – To maintain the balance of the turbine wheel. (Page Reference: JSPT 4-26)

8. How are gas turbine engine tachometers calibrated?

   Answer – They are calibrated in percent r.p.m. (Page Reference: JSPT 4-3)

9. On a turbine engine, what is the engine pressure ratio and what does it indicate?

   Answer – It is the ratio between the total inlet pressure and total turbine exhaust pressure and is used to indicate the thrust developed by the engine. (Page Reference: JSPT 4-3)

10. On a turbine engine, what does exhaust gas temperature (EGT) indicate and how is it obtained?

    Answer – EGT is the average temperature of the turbine discharge gasses and is obtained by thermocouples placed near the turbine exit. (Page Reference: JSPT 4-5)

11. Can the EGT system on a turbine engine be checked without running the engine?

    Answer – Yes, by checking the resistance of the thermocouples and circuits. (Page Reference: JSPT 4-13)

PRACTICAL TEST

1. Project: Measure turbine engine rotor blade clearance. (Level 3)

   Given: A turbine engine, tools, and reference materials.

   Performance Standard: The applicant will measure the axial and radial clearances of turbine blades.

2. Project: Blend out damage on a stator or rotor blade. (Level 3)

   Given: A blade with minor damage, tools, and reference material.

   Performance Standard: The applicant will blend out minor damage according to the manufacturer's instructions.

3. Project: Inspect a combustion liner. (Level 3)

   Given: A turbine engine combustion liner, inspection equipment, and reference materials.

   Performance Standard: The applicant will inspect a combustion liner, and identify and record any defects.

4. Project: Remove and install a combustion case and liner. (Level 3)

   Given: A turbine engine, tools, and reference material.

   Performance Standard: The applicant will remove and install a combustion case and liner.

5. Project: Remove and install a fuel nozzle in a turbine engine. (Level 3)

   Given: A turbine engine, tools, and reference materials.

   Performance Standard: The applicant will remove and install a fuel nozzle.

6. Project: Remove and install a turbine engine r.p.m. tachometer generator. (Level 3)

   Given: A turbine engine, tools, and reference materials.

   Performance Standard: The applicant will remove and install a turbine engine r.p.m. tachometer generator.

7. Project: Perform a hot start inspection. (Level 3)

   Given: A turbine engine, any necessary tools and equipment, and reference materials.

   Performance Standard: The applicant will perform a turbine engine hot start inspection in accordance with the manufacturer's instructions.

8. Project: Perform a turbine engine inlet guide vane and compressor blade inspection. (Level 3)

   Given: A turbine engine, tools, and reference materials.

   Performance Standard: The applicant will inspect inlet guide vanes and the first rows of compressor blades for damage to determine if they meet the manufacturer's specifications.

9. Project: Determine the repairability of a turbine engine rotor or stator blade. (Level 2)

   Given: A damaged rotor or stator blade, any necessary tools, and reference materials.

   Performance Standard: The applicant will assess the extent, nature, and location of damage and determine, according to the manufacturer's instructions, whether repair or replacement is appropriate.

10. Project: Identify damaged turbine blades. (Level 2)

    Given: Sample turbine blades, tools, and reference materials.

    Performance Standard: The applicant will identify damaged turbine blades, and assess the damage to each.

11. Project: Identify causes for engine performance loss. (Level 2)

    Given: A list of items identifying causes for determining engine performance loss related indications.

    Performance Standard: The applicant will match the turbine engine indication malfunction with the possible causes of the malfunctions.

12. Project: Remove and install one or more compressor rotor disk blades. (Level 3)

    Given: A disk, blades, tools, and reference materials.

    Performance Standard: The applicant will remove and install one or more compressor rotor disk blades in accordance with the manufacturer's instructions.

13. Project: Identify damaged nozzle guide vanes. (Level 3)

    Given: Turbine nozzle guide vanes, tools, and reference materials.

    Performance Standard: The applicant will inspect nozzle guide vanes, and identify damage by marking with an approved marking tool.

14. Project: Demonstrate turbine engine field cleaning procedures. (Level 3)

    Given: A turbine engine, tools, equipment, and reference materials.

    Performance Standard: The applicant will demonstrate proper procedures anduse of equipment in performing engine field cleaning.

15. Project: Perform some of the steps involved in removing a turbine engine. (Level 3)

    Given: An aircraft or mockup with a turbine engine installed (partially or completely), tools, equipment, and reference materials.

    Performance Standard: The applicant will perform some of the steps involved inr emoving a turbine engine in accordance with the manufacturer's instructions.

16. Project: Perform some of the steps involved in installing a turbine engine. (Level 3)

    Given: An aircraft or mockup, a turbine engine, tools, equipment, and reference materials.

    Performance Standard: The applicant will perform some of the steps involved in installing a turbine engine in accordance with the manufacturer's instructions.

17. Project: Inspect an engine inlet area for defects. (Level 3)

    Given: An aircraft engine, any necessary tools, and reference materials.

    Performance Standard: The applicant will inspect an engine inlet area for defects, including foreign object damage (FOD), in accordance with the manufacturer's instructions.

18. Project: Inspect an engine exhaust area for defects. (Level 3)

    Given: An aircraft engine, any necessary tools, and reference materials.

    Performance Standard: The applicant will inspect the exhaust area in accordance with the manufacturer's instructions.

19. Project: Determine the appropriate repair for a compressor blade with foreign object damage (FOD). (Level 2)

    Given: A turbine engine compressor blade, any necessary tools, and reference materials.

    Performance Standard: The applicant will assess the damage and determine the appropriate repair in accordance with the manufacturer's instructions.

20. Project: Determine the appropriate repair for a defect in a turbine engine exhaust area. (Level 2)

    Given: An aircraft engine, any necessary tools, and reference materials.

    Performance Standard: The applicant will assess the defect and determine the appropriate repair in accordance with the manufacturer's instructions.

21. Project: Prepare an oil sample for an oil analysis inspection on a turbine or turboprop engine. (Level 3)

    Given: A turbine or turboprop engine, tools, sample bottle and reference materials.

    Performance Standard: The applicant will take a sample of engine oil and prepare itfor an analysis inspection in accordance with the manufacturer's instructions.

22. Project: Troubleshoot a turbine engine EPR system. (Level 3)

    Given: Pilot reports, drawings of an EPR system, and reference materials.

    Performance Standard: The applicant will review the pilot reports and EPR system drawings, and determine the possible causes of the malfunction.

23. Project: Troubleshoot an EGT indicating system. (Level 3)

    Given: Pilot reports, schematics of an EGT system, and reference materials.

    Performance Standard: The applicant will analyze the pilot reports, and determine the possible cause or causes of the system malfunction(s).

24. Project: Inspect a turbine engine EGT harness. (Level 3)

     Given: A turbine engine or mockup, any necessary tools and equipment, and reference materials.

     Performance Standard: The applicant will inspect a turbine engine EGT harness.

25. Project: Remove and replace an EGT gauge. (Level 3)

     Given: An aircraft or mockup and reference material.

     Performance Standard: The applicant will remove, inspect, and reinstall an EGT gauge in accordance with the manufacturer's instructions.

26. Project: Inspect EGT probes installed on a turbine or reciprocating-engine installation. (Level 3)

     Given: A turbine or reciprocating-engine EGT system, inspection equipment, and reference materials.

     Performance Standard: The applicant will review the reference materials, inspect the EGT probes, and list any defects.

27. Project: Repair an EPR system. (Level 3)

     Given: Access to a turbine engine with a loose line in the EPR system, tools, and reference materials.

     Performance Standard: The applicant will troubleshoot and repair the turbine EPR system.

28. Project: Check the operation of an APU air intake door system. (Level 3)

     Given: An aircraft with an APU or mockup, any necessary tools and equipment, and reference materials.

     Performance Standard: The applicant will test the operation, travel, and condition of the APU air intake door system in accordance with the reference materials.

29. Project: Inspect an APU for security, proper installation, and leaks. (Level 3)

     Given: An aircraft with an APU or mockup, any necessary tools and equipment, and reference materials.

     Performance Standard: The applicant will inspect the APU for security, proper installation, and leaks in accordance with the reference materials.

30. Project: Inspect an APU's oil level. (Level 3)

     Given: An APU, a selection of lubricating oils, any necessary tools and equipment, and reference materials.

     Performance Standard: The applicant will inspect an APU's oil level, select the proper oil, and service the APU as necessary.

31. Project: Change the oil in an APU. (Level 3)

     Given: An APU, a selection of lubricating oils, tools, and reference materials.

     Performance Standard: The applicant will drain the APU's oil, select the proper oil, and service with fresh oil in accordance with the reference materials.

32. Project: Remove, inspect, and install an APU oil filter or screen. (Level 3)

     Given: An APU, tools, and reference materials.

     Performance Standard: The applicant will install an APU oil filter as prescribed by the reference materials.

33. Project: Start and operate an APU. (Level 3)

     Given: An operable APU system and reference materials.

     Performance Standard: The applicant will start and operate the APU, and shut down the APU in accordance with the reference material.

34. Project: Check the operation of an APU generator system. (Level 3)

   Given: An operable APU system and reference materials.

   Performance Standard: The applicant will check the operation of the generator system in accordance with the reference materials.

35. Project: Check the operation of an APU pneumatic system. (Level 3)

   Given: An operable APU system and reference materials.

   Performance Standard: The applicant will check the operation of the pneumatic system in accordance with the reference materials.

36. Project: Check the operation of an APU fire warning system. (Level 3)

   Given: An operable APU system and reference materials.

   Performance Standard: The applicant will check the operation of the APU firewarning system in accordance with the reference materials.

37. Project: Inspect an APU tailpipe area. (Level 3)

   Given: An APU system, any necessary tools and equipment, and reference materials.

   Performance Standard: The applicant will inspect the APU tailpipe area in accordance with the reference materials.

38. Project: Locate servicing information for an APU. (Level 1)

   Given: Wiring materials and access to reference materials.

   Performance Standard: The applicant will locate and outline servicing information for an APU.

39. Project: Remove and inspect an APU fuel nozzle. (Level 3)

   Given: An APU, tools, and reference materials.

   Performance Standard: The applicant will remove, clean, and inspect an APU fuel nozzle.

40. Project: Remove and install an APU igniter plug. (Level 3)

   Given: An APU, tools, and reference materials.

   Performance Standard: The applicant will remove and install an igniter plug.

41. Project: Inspect an APU compressor and exhaust area. (Level 3)

   Given: An APU, any necessary tools and equipment, and reference materials.

   Performance Standard: The applicant will inspect the compressor and exhaust area in accordance with the reference materials.

42. Project: Read an APU hour meter. (Level 1)

   Given: An APU and reference materials.

   Performance Standard: The applicant will locate and read the APU hour meter.

43. Project: Remove and install an APU thermocouple. (Level 3)

   Given: An APU, tools, and reference materials.

   Performance Standard: The applicant will remove, inspect, and install a thermocouple.

CHAPTER 5 — INDUCTION SYSTEMS

ORAL QUESTIONS

1. Name the three components on the induction system of a reciprocating engine.

    Answer – The air scoop, carburetor or fuel control, and the intake manifold. (Page Reference: JSPT 5-2)

2. What could happen if the induction system becomes obstructed?

    Answer – The engine may not be able to produce its rated power or It may not run at all. This may also be an indication of a dirty air inlet filter. (Page Reference: JSPT 5-3)

3. How does induction icing affect engine performance?

    Answer – It causes a reduction in power and possible erratic operation. (Page Reference: JSPT 5-3)

4. How is induction icing categorized?

    Answer – As impact ice, fuel evaporation ice, and throttle ice. (Page Reference: JSPT 5-3)

5. What is the common method used to prevent induction system ice in a reciprocating engine?

    Answer – Raise the temperature of induction air with a preheater. (Page Reference: JSPT 5-4)

6. What causes fuel evaporation ice?

    Answer – Fuel evaporation ice is formed because of the decrease in air temperature resulting from evaporation of the fuel after it is introduced into the air stream. (Page Reference: JSPT 5-3)

7. Is carburetor throttle ice more likely to occur at a higher or lower power setting? Why?

    Answer – At a lower power setting because the throttle is partly closed, offering a larger surface area for ice accumulation. (Page Reference: JSPT 5-3)

8. What may be the indication of leaking intake pipes?

    Answer – The engine runs rough at low r.p.m. (Page Reference: JSPT 14-11)

9. What happens to engine power when the carburetor heat is applied?

    Answer – There is a noticeable drop in power. (Page Reference: JSPT 5-4)

10. What could happen if carburetor heat is applied at high engine power settings?

    Answer – Detonation. (Page Reference: JSPT 5-5)

11. What are two types of supercharged induction systems?

    Answer – Internally driven and externally driven. (Page Reference: JSPT 5-6)

12. How and at what point does an internally driven supercharger boost air pressure?

    Answer – An (engine-driven) impeller compresses the fuel/air mixture after it leaves the carburetor. (Page Reference: JSPT 5-6)

13. What is used to power a turbocharger?

    Answer – Engine exhaust gas directed onto the turbocharger turbine. (Page Reference: JSPT 5-7)

14. What could result if the waste gate on a turbocharger system does not close fully?

    Answer – The engine may not be able to produce its rated power at certain altitudes, and the aircraft may not be capable of reaching critical altitude. (Page Reference: JSPT 5-10)

15. What function does a turbocharger waste gate perform?

    Answer – It controls the amount of exhaust gas either into or around the turbocharger, thus controlling the boot pressure of the turbocharger. (Page Reference: JSPT 5-10)

16. What could cause a turbocharged engine to surge?

    Answer – There could be a waste gate or controller malfunction. (Page Reference: JSPT 5-10)

17. What are the most common ways to control a waste gate?

    Answer – Either mechanically with linkages to the throttle or a separate control, or by an actuator that is driven by oil pressure. (Page Reference: JSPT 5-10)

18. In a pressurized reciprocating aircraft, what component in the turbocharger system is used to limit the amount of turbocharger airflow used for cabin pressurization?

    Answer – The sonic venturi. (Page Reference: JSPT 5-13)

19. What is the function of a divergent-shaped jet engine inlet during subsonic flight?

    Answer – It causes the air velocity to decrease with a subsequent increase in air pressure. (Page Reference: JSPT 5-21)

20. Where are bellmouth inlet ducts typically found?

    Answer – On helicopter engines. (Page Reference: JSPT 5-24)

21. How do venturi-type particle separators, found on many turbine powered helicopters, function?

    Answer – A venturi is used to accelerate the flow of incoming air and debris through a curved intake. The debris gains too much inertia to allow it to follow the curved intake towards the engine, and is channeled away from the compressor. (Page Reference: JSPT 5-25)

22. What are the most common methods used for anti-icing of turbine engine inlet ducts?

    Answer – Engine bleed air and electric heating elements. (Page Reference: JSPT 5-26)

PRACTICAL TEST

1. Project: Inspect a carburetor heat system. (Level 3)

    Given: An engine or mockup with a heat system, tools, and reference materials.

    Performance Standard: The applicant will inspect a heater muff, ducts, heater box, and air valve, and determine if repairs are needed.

2. Project: Check a carburetor heat valve for full travel. (Level 2)

    Given: An engine with carburetor heat, tools, and reference materials.

    Performance Standard: The applicant will verify the travel of a carburetor heat shutter as prescribed by the reference material.

3. Project: Check carburetor heat. (Level 3)

    Given: An operable engine with carburetor heat and reference materials.

    Performance Standard: The applicant will run an engine, operate the carburetor heat, and determine if the system operation is normal.

4. Project: Identify the probable location of induction ice. (Level 2)

    Given: Drawings of a carburetor system and reference materials.

    Performance Standard: The applicant will identify the location of probable icing in a carburetor.

5. Project: Identify turbine engine air intake ice protected areas. (Level 2)

    Given: Drawings of turbine engine air intake systems and reference materials.

    Performance Standard: The applicant will identify the areas of turbine engine air intake systems that have ice protection.

6. Project: Service an induction air filter. (Level 3)

    Given: An engine with an induction air filter, tools, and reference materials.

    Performance Standard: The applicant will remove, clean, inspect, and install an air filter as prescribed by the reference materials.

7. Project: Inspect a turbocharger for evidence of exhaust leaks and security. (Level 3)

    Given: An engine with a turbocharger, tools, and reference materials.

    Performance Standard: The applicant will inspect a turbocharger, exhaust pipes, and connections for general condition, evidence of leaks and cracks, and list any defects.

8. Project: Check a turbocharger for operation. (Level 3)

    Given: An operable engine with a turbocharger and reference material.

    Performance Standard: The applicant will operate the engine, and determine if the turbocharger is operating properly.

9. Project: Inspect an induction system for an obstruction. (Level 3)

    Given: An induction system with an obstruction and reference materials.

    Performance Standard: The applicant will inspect an induction system and remove any obstructions.

10. Project: Service an air intake pipe. (Level 3)

    Given: An engine, tools, packing seals or gaskets, and reference material.

    Performance Standard: The applicant will install new packing seals or gaskets in an intake air pipe.

11. Project: Inspect an air intake manifold for defects. (Level 3)

    Given: An engine and reference materials.

    Performance Standard: The applicant will inspect the engine air intake manifold, and list any defects.

12. Project: Troubleshoot an engine that idles improperly. (Level 3)

    Given: Pilot reports, an operable engine with air induction problems, and reference materials.

    Performance Standard: The applicant will analyze the pilot reports, and repair air induction items to make the engine idle properly.

13. Project: Troubleshoot an engine that will not reach critical altitude. (Level 2)

    Given: Pilot reports, a list of turbocharger malfunctions, and reference materials.

    Performance Standard: The applicant will analyze the pilot reports, and list the possible causes of the turbocharger malfunction.

14. Project: Troubleshoot an engine that fails to start. (Level 3)

    Given: Pilot reports, a list of air induction problems, and reference materials.

    Performance Standard: The applicant will analyze the pilot reports, and identify air induction items that may be a possible cause of the engine's failure to start.

15. Project: Identify components of a turbocharger induction system. (Level 3)

    Given: An aircraft or mockup of a turbocharger induction system and reference material.

    Performance Standard: The applicant will point out turbocharger components.

16. Project: Troubleshoot a carburetor heat system. (Level 2)

    Given: Pilot reports, drawings of a carburetor heat system, and reference materials.

    Performance Standard: The applicant will analyze the pilot reports, and list the possible cause of the carburetor heat malfunction.

17. Project: Troubleshoot a turbine engine air inlet ice protection system. (Level 3)

    Given: Pilot reports, a turbine engine with an air inlet ice protection system, and reference materials.

    Performance Standard: The applicant will analyze the pilot reports, and determine the possible cause of the malfunction.

18. Project: Identify turboprop engine ice and rain protection system components. (Level 2)

   Given: A turboprop ice and rain protection system, and reference material.

   Performance Standard: The applicant will remove cowling as necessary and point out ice and rain protection system components.

19. Project: Remove, inspect, and install a turbocharger. (Level 3)

   Given: An engine with a turbocharger, tools, and reference materials.

   Performance Standard: The applicant will remove, inspect, and install a turbocharger as detailed in the reference materials.

20. Project: Inspect a carburetor air inlet duct attachment. (Level 3)

   Given: An engine, tools, and reference materials.

   Performance Standard: The applicant will determine if the air inlet duct is properly secured to the carburetor.

21. Project: Check an aircraft manifold pressure gauge for proper operation. (Level 3)

   Given: An aircraft or mockup with an operable manifold pressure system, and reference materials.
   Performance Standard: The applicant will check the static reading of a manifold pressure gauge against barometric pressure, and note any differences.

22. Project: Repair a leaking manifold pressure system. (Level 3)

   Given: Access to a manifold pressure system with a loose line, tools, and reference materials.

   Performance Standard: The applicant will locate and repair any line found loose.

CHAPTER 6 — EXHAUST SYSTEMS

ORAL QUESTIONS

1. What is the purpose of the exhaust system?

    Answer – To remove high temperature noxious gases. (Page Reference: JSPT 6-2)

2. Name two types of reciprocating engine exhaust systems.

    Answer – The short stack and the collector system. (Page Reference: JSPT 6-2)

3. What drawback in using collector-type exhaust systems is more than offset when used on turbocharged engines?

    Answer – The loss of horsepower due to exhaust system back pressure. (Page Reference: JSPT 6-2)

4. What could result if the internal baffles or diffusers in an exhaust system fail?

    Answer – The flow of the exhaust gasses could be restricted, resulting in a loss of engine power. (Page Reference: JSPT 6-6)

5. What type of exhaust system is used on turbocharged engines?

    Answer – The collector system. (Page Reference: JSPT 6-2)

6. What kind of material is normally used to make the muffler shrouds found in the exhaust system?

    Answer – Stainless steel. (Page Reference: JSPT 6-4)

7. How do you inspect the internal baffles and diffusers of an exhaust system?

    Answer – By disassembling the exhaust system as necessary and visually inspecting the components. (Page Reference: JSPT 6-4)

8. Why is an exhaust system failure considered a severe hazard?

    Answer – It can result in carbon monoxide poisoning, loss of engine power, or fire. (Page Reference: JSPT 6-5)

9. What could happen if lead, zinc, or galvanized marks are made on an exhaust system?

    Answer – They cause a change in molecular structure, which could result in cracks when heated. (Page Reference: JSPT 6-4)

10. What happens if the heat exchanger leaks exhaust gasses into the induction system?

    Answer – There is a loss of engine power. (Page Reference: JSPT 6-5)

11. What is an indication of an exhaust gas leak?

    Answer – A flat gray or sooty black deposit in the area of the leak. (Page Reference: JSPT 6-6)

12. Where are the most common places to find cracks in an exhaust system?

    Answer – At welded or clamped areas and at the flanges. (Page Reference: JSPT 6-6)

13. What is a common cause of turbocharger waste gate sticking?

    Answer – Coke deposits or carbon buildup. (Page Reference: JSPT 6-7)

14. Why are turbocharged exhaust system leaks very damaging at high altitudes?

    Answer – Pressure differential will cause the leak to escape with torch-like intensity. (Page Reference: JSPT 6-7)

15. What are exhaust system coke deposits?

    Answer – Excessive carbon buildup. (Page Reference: JSPT 6-7)

16. What is the result of changing the exhaust nozzle area of a turbine engine?

    Answer – The engine's performance and exhaust gas temperature change. (Page Reference: JSPT 6-9)

17. Name the components of a typical turbine exhaust nozzle.

    Answer – The tail cone, exhaust ducts and support struts. (Page Reference: JSPT 6-9)

18. What is the purpose of thrust reversers?

    Answer – They help decelerate an aircraft after landing. (Page Reference: JSPT 6-10)

19. How does a noise suppressor found on older turbojet engines work?

    Answer – It converts low frequency sound, which is audible over great distance, into high frequency sound, thus reducing the sound footprint. (Page Reference: JSPT 6-11)

20. What are the two most commonly used types of thrust reversers?

    Answer – The clamshell (or mechanically blocked) and the Cascade (or aerodynamically blocked). (Page Reference: JSPT 6-10)

21. How much thrust do the thrust reversers produce compared to the engine's full forward thrust?

    Answer – Substantially less. (Page Reference: JSPT 6-10)

22. What are the hazards of operating some thrust reversers at low ground speeds?

    Answer – Ingestion of foreign objects stirred up by the exhaust gasses and re-ingestion of hot exhaust gasses. (Page Reference: JSPT 6-10)

PRACTICAL TEST

1. Project: Identify exhaust system components. (Level 2)

    Given: An engine exhaust system and reference materials.

    Performance Standard: The applicant will remove cowling, as necessary, and identify exhaust system components.

2. Project: Inspect damaged exhaust system components. (Level 3)

    Given: Damaged exhaust system parts and reference materials.

    Performance Standard: The applicant will inspect exhaust system components,and determine repairability.

3. Project: Repair or replace exhaust system components. (Level 3)

    Given: Damaged exhaust system components, and reference materials.

    Performance Standard: The applicant will repair or replace one or more exhaust system components.

4. Project: Clean an exhaust system component. (Level 3)

    Given: An exhaust system component with carbon deposits, necessary equipment,and reference materials.

    Performance Standard: The applicant will clean an exhaust system component as prescribed by the reference material.

5. Project: Inspect a reciprocating engine exhaust system. (Level 3)

    Given: An engine with an exhaust system, and reference materials.

    Performance Standard: The applicant will inspect an exhaust system as prescribed by the reference material, and list any defects.

6. Project: Inspect exhaust system internal baffles or diffusers. (Level 3)

    Given: Exhaust components with internal baffles or diffusers.

    Performance Standard: The applicant will inspect exhaust ducts, and list any damage.

7. Project: Remove and install exhaust ducts. (Level 3)

    Given: An engine with an exhaust system, tools, and reference materials.

Performance Standard: The applicant will remove and install exhaust system ducts and components as prescribed by the reference materials.

8. Project: Inspect an exhaust heat exchanger. (Level 3)

    Given: An exhaust heat exchanger, tools, and reference materials.

    Performance Standard: The applicant will inspect an exhaust heat exchanger and list any cracks or damage as prescribed by the reference materials.

9. Project: Remove and install a heat exchanger collector tube. (Level 3)

    Given: An engine with a heat exchanger, tools, and reference material.

    Performance Standard: The applicant will remove and install a heat exchanger collector.

10. Project: Perform a heat exchanger collector tube leak test. (Level 3)

    Given: A heat exchanger collector tube, tools and equipment, and reference materials.

    Performance Standard: The applicant will leak test a heat exchanger collector tube.

11. Project: Inspect a turbine engine exhaust nozzle. (Level 3)

    Given: A turbine engine and reference material.

    Performance Standard: The applicant will inspect an exhaust nozzle as prescribed by the reference material, and list any defects.

12. Project: Check a turbine engine thrust reverser system. (Level 3)

    Given: An operable turbine engine reverser system and reference material.

    Performance Standard: The applicant will check the operation of a turbine engine thrust reverser system in accordance with the reference material.

13. Project: Troubleshoot a thrust reverser system. (Level 3)

    Given: Pilot reports, a drawing of a thrust reverser system, and reference materials.

    Performance Standard: The applicant will analyze the pilot reports, and determine the possible cause of the malfunction.

14. Project: Troubleshoot an exhaust muffler heat exchanger. (Level 3)

    Given: Pilot reports, a drawing of an exhaust muffler heat exchanger, and reference materials.

    Performance Standard: The applicant will analyze the pilot reports, and determine the possible cause of the malfunction.

15. Project: Repair an exhaust system leak. (Level 3)

    Given: An engine with an exhaust system leak, tools, and reference materials.

    Performance Standard: The applicant will repair an exhaust system leak.

16. Project: Inspect a turbojet engine noise suppressor. (Level 3)

    Given: A turbojet engine noise suppressor and reference materials.

    Performance Standard: The applicant will inspect the noise suppressor in accordance with the reference materials.

17. Project: Inspect the rigging of a thrust reverser. (Level 3)

    Given: An aircraft or mockup of a thrust reverser system and reference materials.

    Performance Standard: The applicant will inspect the thrust reverser for proper rigging and record the findings.

18. Project: Visually inspect a thrust reverser for damage/deterioration. (Level 3)

    Given: A thrust reverser and reference materials.

    Performance Standard: The applicant will inspect the thrust reverser and list any defects.

CHAPTER 7 — ENGINE FUEL AND FUEL METERING

ORAL QUESTIONS

1. What are some of the sources used to heat the fuel in a turbine engine fuel system?

   Answer – Bleed air and engine lubricating oil. (Page Reference:JSPT 7-13)

2. What are the most common types of fuel metering systems used on small reciprocating engines?

   Answer – Float-type carburetors, pressure-injection carburetors and direct fuel injection systems. (Page Reference: JSPT 7-21)

3. What function does the mixture control perform?

   Answer – Controls the fuel/air mixture. (Page Reference: JSPT 7-24)

4. What generally causes spark plug fouling?

   Answer – Operating the engine with an excessively rich mixture at idle. (Page Reference: JSPT 7-28)

5. What is the purpose of an accelerating system?

   Answer – It provides an immediate but brief increase in fuel flow in the venturi to enrich the mixture. (Page Reference: JSPT 7-25)

6. What is a carburetor economizer system?

   Answer – It is a power enrichment system that provides a richer mixture at high power settings, where the excess fuel aids in engine cooling. This system functions at throttle settings above cruise power settings. (Page Reference: JSPT 7-26)

7. When the mixture is placed in the idle-cutoff position, a slight rise in r.p.m. is noted prior to the engine decelerating. What does this indicate?

   Answer – The idle mixture is set correctly. (Page Reference: JSPT 7-37)

8. Why should engine r.p.m. be accelerated periodically when making carburetor adjustments?

   Answer – To clear the engine. (Page Reference: JSPT 7-37)

9. What maintains the fuel pressure in a pressure-injection carburetor?

   Answer – An engine-driven fuel pump. (Page Reference: JSPT 7-32)

10. What happens if the manual mixture control of a pressure injection carburetor is moved to the idle cutoff position? **Answer** – The engine stops. (Page Reference: JSPT 7-37)

11. How does an automatic mixture control (AMC) function?

    Answer – A sealed brass bellows connected to the fuel metering system, expands and contracts with changes in pressure and temperature, adjusting the mixture accordingly. (Page Reference: JSPT 7-33)

12. What are some of the advantages of fuel injection systems over carburetor systems?

    Answer – Less danger of induction icing, better acceleration, better fuel distribution, better fuel economy, reduced overheating of individual cylinders. (Page Reference: JSPT 7-37)

13. What purpose do turbine engine fuel control units serve?

    Answer – They automatically meter fuel to the engine. (Page Reference: JSPT 7-57)

14. What are the two basic types of turbine engine fuel control units?

    Answer – Hydromechanical and electronic. (Page Reference: JSPT 7-57)

15. What are the engine variables detected by the fuel control unit?

    Answer – Power lever position, engine r.p.m., compressor inlet temperature, compressor inlet pressure, compressor discharge pressure, burner pressure. (Page Reference: JSPT 7-54)

16. What are the two major components of a supervisory electronics engine control?

    Answer – The electronic control unit (computer), and the hydromechanical fuel control. (Page Reference: JSPT 7-61)

17. What are some of the advantages of a full-authority digital engine control (FADEC) over a hydromechanical fuel control?

    Answer – Better fuel economy, improved starts, requires no engine trimming, provides engine limit protection, provides constant idle speeds regardless of atmospheric conditions or bleed air requirements, fully modulates the active clearance control, and allows more repeatable engine transients. (Page Reference: JSPT 7-61)

18. What do turbine engine fuel spray nozzles do?

    Answer – They inject fuel into the combustion area. (Page Reference: JSPT 7-62)

19. What are the different engine indications used for trimming a turbine engine?

    Answer – Either EPR or r.p.m. is used depending on the particular engine. (Page Reference: JSPT 7-65)

20. What maintenance adjustments are normally allowed on an installed hydromechanical fuel control?

    Answer – Specific gravity for fuel, idle r.p.m., and maximum r.p.m. (or maximum EPR). (Page Reference: JSPT 7-65)

21. What type of pump can vary the amount of fuel discharged regardless of speed?

    Answer – A variable displacement pump. (Page Reference: JSPT 7-8)

22. What is used to keep water, sediment, and foreign matter out of the carburetor?

    Answer – The main fuel strainer. (Page Reference: JSPT 7-6)

23. What is the purpose of a pressure relief valve in a constant displacement pump?

    Answer – It returns excess fuel that is not required by the engine to the inlet side of the pump. (Page Reference: JSPT 7-8)

24. What type of engine-driven fuel pump is widely used other than gear or piston pumps?

    Answer – A rotary vane type. (Page Reference: JSPT 7-6)

25. What function do fuel boost pumps perform?

    Answer – They supply pressurized fuel to the fuel pump, which helps prevent vapor lock and cavitation. (Page Reference: JSPT 7-8)

26. What is a commonly used type of fuel boost pump?

    Answer – The centrifugal type. (Page Reference: JSPT 7-9)

27. What causes vapor lock and why is it of concern?

    Answer – Vapor lock is caused by insufficient fuel pressure, high fuel temperatures and excessive fuel turbulence, which may completely block any fuel flow resulting in engine failure. (Page Reference: JSPT 7-9)

28. What function does the engine-driven pump on a turbine engine perform?

    Answer – It provides a continuous supply of fuel at the proper pressure while the engine is running. (Page Reference: JSPT 7-7)

29. Name the two categories of turbine engine pumps.

    Answer – Constant and variable displacement. (Page Reference: JSPT 7-8)

30. What category is a gear-type pump classified in?

    Answer – Constant displacement. (Page Reference: JSPT 7-8)

31. When performing an external inspection of an engine-driven fuel pump, what should you look for?

    Answer – Leaks and security of mounting. (Page Reference: JSPT 14-9)

32. What is the purpose of a shear section of the driveshaft in a dual element constant displacement pump?

    Answer – If one element seizes, a portion of the driveshaft seizes, allowing the other element to continue to operate. (Page Reference: JSPT 7-8)

33. Where in a turbine engine fuel system is ice formation likely to occur and how is it prevented?

    Answer – The fuel filter is most susceptible to ice formation, so a fuel heater is used that consists of a heat exchanger using either engine oil or bleed air to warm the fuel. (Page Reference: JSPT 7-13)

34. What is the purpose of a bypass valve in an engine fuel system micron filter?

    Answer – It is a safety feature that allows fuel to flow to the engine if the filter becomes blocked.(Page Reference: JSPT 7-10)

35. What is the purpose of a duplex fuel nozzle?

    Answer – A duplex fuel nozzle discharges two different spray patterns. The spray pattern is wider during start up and acceleration and narrows when engine speed increases above idle. (Page Reference: JSPT 7-62)

36. What are the functions of the pressurizing and dump portions of a pressurizing and dump valve?

    Answer – The pressurizing portion provides primary and secondary fuel flow to dual-line duplex fuel nozzles, and the dump portion allows fuel to drain from the manifolds after engine shutdown. (Page Reference: JSPT 7-64)

37. What purpose do fuel selector valves serve?

    Answer – They allow tank and engine selection, and provide a means for shutting off fuel flow. (Page Reference: JSAT 7-3)

PRACTICAL TEST

1. Project: Remove, inspect, and install a turbine engine fuel nozzle. (Level 3)

    Given: A turbine engine or mockup, tools, and reference materials.

    Performance Standard: The applicant will remove, inspect, and install a fuel nozzle.

2. Project: Identify carburetor components. (Level 2)

    Given: A float-type carburetor and reference materials.

    Performance Standard: The applicant will point out major components (venturi,throttle valve, discharge nozzle, accelerator pump, etc.)

3. Project: Interpret charts showing fuel and airflow through a float-type carburetor. (Level 2)

    Given: Carburetor fuel and airflow charts, and reference material.

    Performance Standard: The applicant will trace fuel and airflow through the charts.

4. Project: Install a float needle valve and seat in a carburetor. (Level 3)

    Given: A carburetor and a float needle valve and seat assembly, tools, and reference materials.

    Performance Standard: The applicant will install a float needle valve and seat in accordance with the reference materials.

5. Project: Service a carburetor fuel inlet strainer. (Level 3)

    Given: A carburetor with a fuel inlet strainer, tools, and reference materials.

    Performance Standard: The applicant will remove the fuel inlet screen, inspect it for foreign matter, clean, and install it as prescribed by reference materials.

6. Project: Identify a carburetor air bleed system. (Level 2)

    Given: A float-type carburetor, tools, and reference materials.

    Performance Standard: The applicant will disassemble a float-type carburetor to the point of being able to point out the air bleed system.

7. Project: Identify the main discharge nozzle in a pressure carburetor. (Level 2)

    Given: A pressure carburetor, tools, and reference materials.

    Performance Standard: The applicant will point out the main discharge nozzle in a pressure carburetor.

8. Project: Remove the accelerating pump in a float-type carburetor. (Level 2)

    Given: A float-type carburetor, tools, and reference materials.

    Performance Standard: The applicant will remove a float-type carburetor accelerator pump, and identify the components.

9. Project: Check the float level on a float-type carburetor. (Level 3)

    Given: A float-type carburetor, tools, and reference materials.

    Performance Standard: The applicant will measure the float level, and determine if the float level is within limits.

10. Project: Remove the mixture control system in a float-type carburetor. (Level 2)

    Given: A float-type carburetor, tools, and reference materials.

    Performance Standard: The applicant will remove a mixture control, identifying parts and passages.

11. Project: Inspect a carburetor float valve assembly. (Level 3)

    Given: A float-type carburetor, tools, and reference materials.

    Performance Standard: The applicant will remove the float valve assembly, and determine its serviceability.

12. Project: Identify, remove, and install a float-type carburetor. (Level 3)

    Given: An engine with a float-type carburetor, tools, and reference materials.

    Performance Standard: The applicant will remove a carburetor, identify major components, and reinstall.

13. Project: Check a throttle for proper operation. (Level 3)

    Given: An engine, tools, and reference materials.

    Performance Standard: The applicant will check the throttle for correct travel and inspect for defects and improper safety.

14. Project: Inspect a turbine engine fuel control unit. (Level 3)

    Given: A turbine engine or mockup, tools, and reference materials.

    Performance Standard: The applicant will inspect a fuel control unit for evidence of fuel leaks, security, and proper safety.

15. Project: Trim a turbine engine. (Level 3)

    Given: An operable turbine engine, tools, and reference materials.

    Performance Standard: The applicant will operate a turbine engine, check the idle and maximum r.p.m., and adjust the fuel control unit.

16. Project: Analyze a turbine engine r.p.m. overspeed. (Level 3)

   Given: Pilot reports, fuel control unit drawings, and reference materials.

   Performance Standard: The applicant will analyze the pilot reports, and determine the possible causes of the overspeed condition.

17. Project: Analyze a pressure carburetor engine with slow acceleration. (Level 3)

   Given: Pilot reports, carburetor drawings, and reference materials.

   Performance Standard: The applicant will analyze pilot reports, and determine the possible causes of the slow acceleration.

18. Project: Analyze a malfunction in a pressure injection carburetor fuel regulator unit. (Level 3)

   Given: A drawing of a regulator unit, a malfunction (boost venturi plugged, fuel diaphragm leaking, air diaphragm or vent chamber plugged), and reference materials.

   Performance Standard: The applicant will analyze one of the malfunctions and list the operational indications.

19. Project: Replace a direct injection fuel nozzle. (Level 3)

   Given: A direct injection engine or mockup, tools, and reference material.

   Performance Standard: The applicant will remove, inspect, clean, and install a fuel nozzle.

20. Project: Set or position cockpit controls for engine start. (Level 2)

   Given: An aircraft with engine or mockup and reference materials.

   Performance Standard: The applicant will position the cockpit controls for engine start.

21. Project: Determine fuel control unit adjustment. (Level 3)

   Given: Adjust a turbine engine idle r.p.m.

   Performance Standard: The applicant will determine what fuel control unit adjustment is required.

22. Project: Adjust a turbine engine idle r.p.m. (Level 3)

   Given: An operable engine, tools, and reference materials.

   Performance Standard: The applicant will adjust turbine engine idle r.p.m.according to the reference material.

23. Project: Adjust a turbine engine maximum takeoff thrust or r.p.m. (Level 3)

   Given: An operable engine, tools, and reference materials.

   Performance Standard: The applicant will adjust turbine engine maximum thrustor r.p.m. according to the specifications in the reference material.

24. Project: Remove, inspect, and install a fuel flow gauge. (Level 3)

   Given: An aircraft engine or mockup, tools, and reference material.

   Performance Standard: The applicant will remove, inspect, and install a fuel flow gauge.

25. Project: Remove, inspect, and install a fuel flow transmitter. (Level 3)

   Given: An aircraft engine or mockup, tools, and reference material.

   Performance Standard: The applicant will remove, inspect, and install a fuel flow transmitter.

26. Project: Locate and inspect fuel flow components on an engine. (Level 3)

   Given: An aircraft engine or mockup and reference material.

   Performance Standard: The applicant will locate engine fuel flow components (transmitter, fuel lines, electrical wires, and brackets), and inspect for visible defects and security.

27. Project: Check a fuel flow transmitter power supply. (Level 3)

    Given: An aircraft or mockup with components, tools, and reference material.

    Performance Standard: The applicant will measure and determine if the electrical power supplied to a fuel flow transmitter is correct.

28. Project: Troubleshoot a fuel flow system. (Level 3)

    Given: Pilot reports (actual or simulated), a diagram of a fuel flow system, and reference material.

    Performance Standard: The applicant will review the pilot reports, and list the possible cause or causes of the malfunction(s).

29. Project: Locate and inspect engine low fuel pressure warning system components. (Level 3)

    Given: An aircraft engine or mockup and reference material.

    Performance Standard: The applicant will locate and inspect the low fuel pressure warning system components.

30. Project: Remove, inspect, and install an engine-driven fuel pump. (Level 3)

    Given: An engine with an engine-driven fuel pump, tools, and reference materials.

    Performance Standard: The applicant will remove, inspect, and install the pump.

31. Project: Check a remotely operated fuel valve. (Level 3)

    Given: An aircraft with a remotely operated fuel valve, tools, and reference materials.

    Performance Standard: The applicant will establish the engine fuel supply from sources controlled by a remote fuel valve, and determine if the fuel valve operates properly.

32. Project: Remove and install a remotely operated fuel valve. (Level 3)

    Given: An aircraft with a remotely operated fuel valve, tools, and reference materials.

    Performance Standard: The applicant will remove, inspect, and install a fuel valve as prescribed in the reference material.

33. Project: Inspect a main fuel filter assembly for leaks. (Level 3)

    Given: An aircraft engine fuel system and reference material.

    Performance Standard: The applicant will pressurize a fuel system, and observe for fuel leaks in the fuel filter area.

34. Project: Check fuel boost pumps for correct pressure. (Level 3)

    Given: Aircraft boost pumps and reference materials.

    Performance Standard: The applicant will check the boost pumps for correct output pressure.

35. Project: Remove, inspect, and install a fuel boost pump. (Level 3)

    Given: An aircraft with a fuel boost pump, tools, and reference materials.

    Performance Standard: The applicant will remove, inspect, and install a fuel boost pump.

36. Project: Locate and identify a turbine engine fuel heater. (Level 3)

    Given: A turbine engine with fuel heater and reference material.

    Performance Standard: The applicant will point out a fuel heater, and identify the inlet and outlet fuel, oil, or bleed air ports.

37. Project: Check a fuel pressure warning light function. (Level 3)

    Given: An aircraft or mockup with a fuel system warning light, tools, and reference materials.

    Performance Standard: The applicant will check a fuel pressure warning light, and determine if the light operates within the limits prescribed in the reference materials.

38. Project: Adjust fuel pump pressure. (Level 3)

   Given: An aircraft or mockup with an adjustable fuel pump, tools, and reference materials.

   Performance Standard: The applicant will check and adjust the fuel pump pressure to the limits prescribed in the reference material.

39. Project: Inspect engine fuel system components. (Level 3)

   Given: An aircraft or engine and reference material.

   Performance Standard: The applicant will inspect engine fuel system components for security of attachment and evidence of fuel leaks.

40. Project: Determine the reason for low fuel pressure. (Level 3)

   Given: A drawing of an engine fuel system, pilot reports, and reference materials.

   Performance Standard: The applicant will determine the cause of the low fuel pressure.

41. Project: Troubleshoot the cause of a high fuel pressure. (Level 3)

   Given: A drawing of a fuel system, pilot reports, and reference materials.

   Performance Standard: The applicant will analyze pilot reports, and reference material.

42. Project: Troubleshoot a turbine engine fuel heater system. (Level 3)

   Given: Pilot reports, system schematics, and reference materials.

   Performance Standard: The applicant will analyze pilot reports, and determine the possible cause of the malfunction.

43. Project: Remove, clean, and reinstall an engine fuel strainer. (Level 3)

   Given: An engine with a fuel strainer, tools, and reference materials.

   Performance Standard: The applicant will remove, clean, and replace an engine fuel strainer.

44. Project: Troubleshoot an engine fuel pressure fluctuation. (Level 3)

   Given: Pilot reports, system schematics, and reference materials.

   Performance Standard: The applicant will analyze the pilot reports, and determine the possible cause of the system malfunction.

45. Project: Inspect a fuel selector valve. (Level 3)

   Given: An aircraft or mockup and reference materials.

   Performance Standard: The applicant will inspect the fuel selector valve for leaks,operation, security, placards, and detents.

46. Project: Determine correct fuel nozzle spray pattern. (Level 3)

   Given: A fuel nozzle test stand, fuel nozzles, and reference materials.

   Performance Standard: The applicant will operate a test stand, and determine which nozzles have correct spray patterns.

47. Project: Locate the requirements for fuel selector placards. (Level 1)

   Given: Reference materials.

   Performance Standard: The applicant will locate and identify the required fuelselector placards for a specific aircraft.

48. Project: Locate, identify, and inspect engine fuel lines. (Level 2)

    Given: An engine and reference materials.

    Performance Standard: The applicant will locate, identify, and inspect engine fuel lines for routing, security, and condition in accordance with the reference materials.

49. Project: Adjust a fuel control unit to meet the engine acceleration or fuel density specifications. (Level 2)

    Given: Turbine engine reference materials.

    Performance Standard: The applicant will locate the field adjustment procedures for a turbine engine fuel control unit and list them.

CHAPTER 8 — ELECTRICAL, STARTING, AND IGNITION SYSTEMS

ORAL QUESTIONS

1. How can the remaining service life of starter-generator brushes be determined?

    Answer – By visually inspecting the amount of wear groove remaining on the brushes. (Page Reference: JSPT 8-17)

2. What components of the starter-generator require periodic inspection?

    Answer – Both commutator and brushes should be inspected for wear beyond operational limits. (Page Reference: JSPT 8-17)

3. Between field and armature windings in starter-generators, which ordinarily receive current for operation in the start mode?

    Answer – Generally, both field and armature receive current for operation in the start mode? (Page Reference: JSPT 8-12)

4. What are possible sources of low pressure compressed air used for starting jet transport aircraft equipped with air turbine starters?

    Answer – A ground power unit, (GPU), an on-board auxiliary power unit (APU), compressed bleed air form an already running engine. (Page Reference: JSPT 8-30)

5. When should ignition ideally occur?

    Answer – A specific number of degrees (as determined by the manufacturer) before the piston reaches top dead center on the compression stroke. (Page Reference: JSPT 1-39)

6. Why are dual magnetos used in the engine ignition system?

    Answer – To improve combustion efficiency, and provide redundancy for safety. (Page Reference: JSPT 8-77)

7. Why is magneto timing so important?

    Answer – For an engine to run properly, the spark plug in a cylinder has to fire at a specific time. To produce the required energy for the spark at the required time, the magneto must be in the E-gap position, the breaker points must start to open, and the distributor must be electrically aligned with the particular cylinder. If any of these requirements are not correctly adjusted, the engine will run rough or may not run at all. When preparing a magneto for installation, first the internal timing must be correctly adjusted, then the magneto-to-engine timing is adjusted. (Page Reference: JSPT 8-89)

8. What function does a magneto perform?

    Answer – It produces a high voltage that forces a spark to arc across a spark plug gap. (Page Reference: JSPT 8-78)

9. Name the components of a high tension magneto system.

    Answer – A permanent multipole rotating magnet, soft iron core, and pole shoes. (Page Reference: JSPT 8-78)

10. Name the three main circuits of a high tension magneto system.

    Answer – Magnetic, primary and secondary. (Page Reference: JSPT 8-80)

11. What is an E-gap angle?

    Answer – It is a point a few degrees beyond the neutral position of a rotating magnet where maximum magnetic field stress exists. (Page Reference: JSPT 8-82)

12. What reduces arcing in the points and also aids the collapsing of the magnetic field in a magneto?

    Answer – A capacitor. (Page Reference: JSPT 8-82)

13. How does a magneto produce the high voltage required to fire a spark plug?

Answer – In the rotation cycle, when the magnetic rotor is in the E-gap position, the primary points open, which interrupts the current flow in the primary circuit causing a high rate of flux change in the core, and inducing a pulse of high voltage in the secondary coil. (Page Reference: JSPT 8-82)

14. What is the P-lead and how does it function?

Answer – The P-lead connects the ignition switch to the primary circuit of the magneto. When the ignition switch is turned off, the P-leads on both magnetos are grounded. When the ignition switch is turned to the "LEFT" position, the right magneto is grounded, so that only the left magneto operates, and visa versa. (Page Reference: JSPT 8-87)

15. What is a magneto timing light used for, and what does it indicate?

Answer – It is used for both internal magneto timing and magneto-to-engine timing, and indicates the exact instant the magneto points open. (Page Reference: JSPT 8-90)

16. Why are turbine engine igniters generally not susceptible to carbon fouling?

Answer – Because the high energy sparks they produce clean off any deposits on the firing end. (Page Reference: JSPT 8-115)

17. What is the function of a duty cycle in relation to a turbine engine ignition system?

Answer – A duty cycle allows the operation of the ignition system for a given amount of time, and is then followed by a minimum specified cooling down period. (Page Reference: JSPT 8-115)

18. What are the three main components of a turbine engine ignition system?

Answer – Ignition exciters, high tension leads, igniters. (Page Reference: JSPT 8-115)

19. When the engine is operating, what does an ammeter / loadmeter indicate when connected to: 1. Battery positive lead? 2. Generator output lead?

Answer – When connected to the battery positive lead, the ammeter indicates whether the battery is charging or discharging. When connected to the generator output lead, it indicates the current produced by the generator, or electrical system load. (Page Reference: JSAT 7-43)

20. What is done to ensure that each generator shares the load in a multiple generator system?

Answer – The generators are paralleled. (Page Reference: JSAT 7-51)

21. Where would you find generator rating and performance data?

Answer – On the data plate attached to the generator. (Page Reference: JSPT 8-11)

22. How is the voltage of a DC generator controlled?

Answer – By varying the field current strength. (Page Reference: JSPT 8-12)

23. What is the most common type of alternator used in most aircraft AC systems?

Answer – The three phase alternator. (Page Reference: JSPT 8-21)

24. How does a voltage regulator control the voltage of an alternator?

Answer – By regulating the voltage output of the DC exciter. (Page Reference: JSPT 8-23)

25. What does the speed of rotation and number of poles of an alternator determine?

Answer – The frequency of the alternator output. (Page Reference: JSPT 8-27)

26. What are some of the methods used to maintain 400 Hertz alternator output frequency on large turbojet or turbofan engines?

Answer – Constant speed drives, integrated drive generators, and variable-speed constant frequency (VSCF) power systems. (Page Reference: JSPT 8-27)

27. Name the major parts of a DC motor.

Answer – The armature, field, brushes and frame assembly. (Page Reference: JSPT 8-42)

28. Name the components of a direct cranking electric starter system.

    Answer – An electric motor, reduction gears, and an automatic engaging and disengaging mechanism. (Page Reference: JSPT 8-35)

29. Name three types of DC motors.

    Answer – Series, shunt and compound. (Page Reference: JSPT 8-36)

30. What type of DC motor is commonly used for a reciprocating engine starter and why?

    Answer – A series wound motor is commonly used because it has a high starting torque under heavy load conditions. (Page Reference: JSPT 8-36)

31. What are the operating modes of a turbine engine starter generator?

    Answer – It operates first as a starter, then as a generator once the engine is running. (Page Reference: JSPT 8-46)

32. What is a possible indication when a starter drags?

    Answer – A dirty or worn starter commutator. (Page Reference: JSPT 8-32)

33. Where would wire with high temperature insulation material be used?

    Answer – When they run close to high temperature areas such as exhaust stacks or heating ducts. (Page Reference: JSPT 8-57)

34. What is the size standard for electrical wire used in US manufactured aircraft?

    Answer – The American Wire Gauge (AWG). (Page Reference: JSPT 8-57)

35. How are wire sizes represented?

    Answer – By a numbered gauge size. The smaller wires are represented by larger numbers. The smallest size wire normally used in aircraft is 22-gauge. (Page Reference: JSPT 8-57)

36. What is the maximum slack allowed between the supports of a single wire or bundle installation?

    Answer – Not over ½ inch. (Page Reference: JSPT 8-62)

37. Why are wires bonded on powerplant installations?

    Answer – To provide a current return path for electrical accessories, and to prevent static discharge. (Page Reference: JSPT 8-69)

PRACTICAL TEST

1. Project: Disassemble, identify components, and reassemble a magneto. (Level 3)

    Given: Magneto, tools, and reference material.

    Performance Standard: The applicant will disassemble a magneto, identify the major parts, and reassemble.

2. Project: Inspect magneto breaker points. (Level 3)

    Given: Samples of breaker points, tools, and reference materials.

    Performance Standard: The applicant will inspect breaker point assemblies, and determine serviceable from non-serviceable assemblies.

3. Project: Time a magneto. (Level 3)

    Given: A magneto, tools, and reference materials.

    Performance Standard: The applicant will internally time a magneto and explain E-gap, point opening, and distributor gear position.

4. Project: Test high-tension leads. (Level 3)

    Given: An ignition harness, tools, and reference materials.

    Performance Standard: The applicant will use test equipment to determine serviceability of ignition wiring.

5. Project: Remove and install an ignition harness. (Level 3)

    Given: An engine with ignition harness installed, tools, and reference materials.

    Performance Standard: The applicant will remove and install an engine ignition harness.

6. Project: Check a magneto on a test bench. (Level 3)

    Given: A magneto, a test bench, tools, and reference materials.

    Performance Standard: The applicant will test a magneto, and determine its serviceability.

7. Project: Test the serviceability of a capacitor. (Level 3)

    Given: A capacitor, capacitor tester, and reference material.

    Performance Standard: The applicant will test the capacitor, and determine its serviceability.

8. Project: Check ignition coils. (Level 3)

    Given: Samples of coils, any necessary tools, test equipment, and reference materials.

    Performance Standard: The applicant will test the coils, and determine their serviceability.

9. Project: Test an ignition harness. (Level 3)

    Given: An ignition harness, test equipment, and reference materials.

    Performance Standard: The applicant will test the ignition leads in accordance with the reference materials.

10. Project: Troubleshoot an ignition switch circuit. (Level 3)

    Given: A faulty ignition switch circuit, any necessary tools and test equipment, and reference materials.

    Performance Standard: The applicant will troubleshoot the ignition switch circuit.

11. Project: Service spark plugs. (Level 3)

    Given: Spark plugs, tools, and reference material.

    Performance Standard: The applicant will service the spark plugs, and determine serviceability.

12. Project: Replace spark plugs. (Level 3)

    Given: An engine, spark plugs, tools, and reference materials.

    Performance Standard: The applicant will select the proper spark plugs, and install them in the engine.

13. Project: Troubleshoot a reciprocating-engine ignition system. (Level 3)

    Given: An engine with a dual magneto ignition system and one inoperative spark plug, tools, and reference materials.

    Performance Standard: The applicant will analyze the ignition system, and determine which plug is inoperative.

14. Project: Install a magneto on an engine. (Level 3)

    Given: An engine, magneto, tools, equipment, and reference materials.

    Performance Standard: The applicant will install and time a magneto.

15. Project: Verify magneto-to-engine timing. (Level 3)

    Given: An aircraft engine, tools, and reference material.

    Performance Standard: The applicant will inspect the oil system lines for leaks.

16. Project: Install turbine engine igniter plugs. (Level 3)

    Given: A turbine engine, tools, igniter plugs, and reference materials.

    Performance Standard: The applicant will install the igniter plugs in accordance with the reference materials.

17. Project: Check the operation of turbine engine igniters. (Level 3)

    Given: A turbine engine, tools, and reference materials.

    Performance Standard: The applicant will check the operation of the ignition system without starting the engine.

18. Project: Inspect a turbine engine ignition system. (Level 3)

    Given: A turbine engine and ignition system.

    Performance Standard: The applicant will inspect ignition system components.

19. Project: Inspect turbine engine igniter wear. (Level 3)

    Given: Turbine engine igniter(s), tools, and reference materials.

    Performance Standard: The applicant will inspect igniter electrode wear and determine its serviceability.

20. Project: Troubleshoot a turbine engine autoignition system. (Level 3)

    Given: Drawings of turbine engine ignition system, pilot reports, and reference materials.

    Performance Standard: The applicant will review a pilot report, analyze the ignition system drawings, and list possible causes of the malfunction.

21. Project: Use the engine electrical portion(s) of a manufacturer's maintenance manual. (Level 1)

    Given: Manufacturer's maintenance manuals and written instructions.

    Performance Standard: The applicant will locate several areas of the manuals that would be required reference for different electrical system component repairs listed in written instructions.

22. Project: Locate and list engine electrical components. (Level 2)

    Given: A manufacturer's parts catalog and written instructions.

    Performance Standard: The applicant will use a manufacturer's parts catalog to locate and list electrical components for a particular engine, applying usable codes as necessary.

23. Project: Replace an engine-driven generator. (Level 3)

    Given: An aircraft engine with a generator installed, written instructions, and reference materials.

    Performance Standard: The applicant will remove and install an engine-driven generator in accordance with the reference material.

24. Project: Check an engine-driven generator. (Level 3)

    Given: An operable engine with a DC generator installed, written instructions, and reference materials.

    Performance Standard: The applicant will check a DC generator by running the engine and determine whether the generator operates within the manufacturer's limits.

25. Project: Service an engine-driven generator. (Level 3)

    Given: A generator, a set of generator brushes, tools, and reference materials.

    Performance Standard: The applicant will determine if the brushes are within wear limits, and if not, replace the brushes.

26. Project: Parallel a dual generator electrical system. (Level 3)

    Given: An aircraft or mockup with dual generator system, tools, and reference materials.

    Performance Standard: The applicant will adjust dual generators for parallel operation in accordance with the manufacturer's instructions.

27. Project: Inspect an engine-driven generator. (Level 3)

    Given: An aircraft engine with a generator installed, tools, and reference materials.

    Performance Standard: The applicant will inspect the generator for general condition, security, and wire connections.

28. Project: Troubleshoot a voltage regulator in an aircraft electrical system. (Level 3)

    Given: An aircraft electrical generating system (aircraft or mockup), written instructions, tools, and reference materials.

    Performance Standard: The applicant will troubleshoot the voltage regulator and determine the malfunction(s).

29. Project: Repair a generator field circuit. (Level 3)

    Given: An aircraft or mockup generator field circuit with an open wire, written instructions, tools, and reference materials.

    Performance Standard: The applicant will use test equipment, locate an open generator field circuit, and repair it.

30. Project: Inspect a direct drive electric starter. (Level 3)

    Given: An engine or mockup with a direct drive starter, written instructions, tools, and reference materials.

    Performance Standard: The applicant will remove, inspect, and install a direct-drive electric starter.

31. Project: Troubleshoot a direct-drive electric starter system. (Level 3)

    Given: An engine-driven, direct-drive electric starter system.

    Performance Standard: The applicant will locate and determine the cause of the malfunction.

32. Project: Fabricate an electrical system cable for a component. (Level 3)

    Given: Samples of cable, lugs, tools, reference materials, and a sample electrical component.

    Performance Standard: The applicant will select the properly sized cable, and install the properly sized lug after considering the current draw and voltage drop for the component.

33. Project: Determine wire size for an engine electrical system. (Level 2)

    Given: Cable size charts, electrical specifications for various engine electrical components, written instructions, and reference materials.

    Performance Standard: The applicant will select the proper wire size for the electrical system components.

34. Project: Repair a broken wire on an engine electrical system. (Level 3)

    Given: Samples of wire, written instructions, tools, and reference materials.

    Performance Standard: The applicant will splice different wire sizes in accordance with the reference materials.

35. Project: Replace wire bundle lacing. (Level 3)

    Given: A wire bundle without lacing, lacing cord, tie-wraps, tools, and reference materials.

    Performance Standard: The applicant will lace or tie-wrap a wire bundle.

36. Project: Demonstrate the use of an engine electrical wiring schematic. (Level 2)

    Given: An electrical schematic and reference materials.

    Performance Standard: The applicant will trace current flow through the schematic.

37. Project: Fabricate a bonding jumper. (Level 3)

    Given: Jumper materials, written instructions, tools, and reference materials.

    Performance Standard: The applicant will make a bonding jumper according to the reference materials.

38. Project: Inspect turbine engine electrical wiring. (Level 3)

   Given: An aircraft or mockup with an engine installed, any necessary tools and equipment, and reference materials.

   Performance Standard: The applicant will inspect engine electrical wiring in accordance with the reference materials.

39. Project: Fabricate solderless terminals. (Level 3)

   Given: Terminal materials, written instructions, and reference materials.

   Performance Standard: The applicant will select the appropriate materials, and fabricate one or more solderless terminals.

40. Project: Troubleshoot engine electrical connectors. (Level 3)

   Given: An engine electrical system with AN or MS connectors, one with a missing wire, written instructions, tools, and reference materials.

   Performance Standard: The applicant will use test equipment, and locate the missing connector wire.

CHAPTER 9 — LUBRICATION SYSTEMS

ORAL QUESTIONS

1. A reciprocating engine is found to have excessive oil consumption without evidence of any oil leaks. What is the likely cause?

   Answer – The piston rings are worn or broken. (Page Reference: JSPT 9-3)

2. What are the functions of lubricating oil in reciprocating engines?

   Answer – To reduce friction between moving parts and remove heat. (Page Reference: JSPT 9-2)

3. Name two important characteristics of aircraft engine oil.

   Answer – The oil must be light enough to circulate freely yet heavy enough to provide the proper oil film at engine operating temperatures. (Page Reference: JSPT 9-2)

4. What could happen to an oil that is too low in viscosity at normal engine operating temperatures?

   Answer – It may become so thin that the oil film between moving parts is easily broken, resulting in premature wear. (Page Reference: JSPT 9-3)

5. What are some of the factors that must be considered by an engine manufacturer in determining the proper grade of oil for a particular engine?

   Answer – The operating load and temperature as well as the rotational speed. (Page Reference: JSPT 9-3)

6. Why do aircraft reciprocating engines use a relatively high viscosity oil?

   Answer – Because they usually have large operating clearances, and operate at high temperatures and pressures. (Page Reference: JSPT 9-3)

7. Name some oil contaminants.

   Answer – Metal particles, dirt, carbon, moisture and acids. (Page Reference: JSPT 9-3)

8. What is a possible indication of low oil pressure together with high oil temperature?

   Answer – A low or inadequate oil supply. (Page Reference: JSPT 9-20)

9. In ashless dispersant (AD) oils, what function does the dispersant perform?

   Answer – The dispersant causes sludge-forming materials to repel each other and remain in suspension until they can be trapped by the oil filter or drained. This keeps the oil passages and ring grooves free of harmful deposits, and the inside of the engine clean. (Page Reference: JSPT 9-5)

10. Why do oil reservoirs have expansion space?

    Answer – To provide for oil foaming, thermal expansion, and air in the return oil. (Page Reference: JSPT 9-9)

11. What could cause oil foaming?

    Answer – Diluted oil, contaminated oil, and the oil level being too high. (Page Reference: JSPT 9-13)

12. What controls oil pressure in a gear-type oil pressure pump?

    Answer – An oil pressure relief valve. (Page Reference: JSPT 9-13)

13. What function does an oil cooler bypass valve perform?

    Answer – It directs the oil either through the cooler or around it in order to maintain proper operating oil temperatures. (Page Reference: JSPT 9-18)

14. What could be a possible indication if the oil cooler passage becomes obstructed?

    Answer – A high oil temperature. (Page Reference: JSPT 4-18)

15. Where is the oil temperature bulb usually located?

    Answer – At the engine oil inlet. (Page Reference: JSPT 9-20)

16. What does the presence of metal particles in an engine oil filter indicate?

    Answer – Depending on the type and size of the metal particles, this usually indicates abnormal wear and possible engine internal failure. (Page Reference: JSPT 9-21)

17. What should be done if metal particles are found in an engine oil filter?

    Answer – Follow engine manufacturer's maintenance instruction. (Page Reference: JSPT 9-21)

18. Where is the most critical point of lubrication in a gas turbine engine?

    Answer – At the turbine bearing. (Page Reference: JSPT 9-33)

19. What type of oil is used in a turbine engine oil system?

    Answer – Synthetic oil. (Page Reference: JSPT 9-27)

20. Where are oil screens or filters most likely located in a turbine engine oil system?

    Answer – At the oil pressure system (main filter), scavenge system, and at or just before the oil jet (last chance). (Page Reference: JSPT 9-31)

21. Name two types of turbine engine oil coolers.

    Answer – Air cooled and fuel cooled. (Page Reference: JSPT 9-33)

22. What could happen to an oil that is too low in viscosity at normal engine operating temperatures?

    Answer – It may become so thin that the oil film between moving parts is easily broken resulting in premature wear. (Page Reference: JSPT 9-3)

PRACTICAL TEST

1. Project: Select approved engine oils. (Level 1)

   Given: A list of oils and reference materials.

   Performance Standard: The applicant will review the reference materials and list the proper oils for one or more specific engines.

2. Project: Determine the oil to use for different climatic temperatures. (Level 2)

   Given: Climatic temperature conditions, and reference materials.

   Performance Standard: The applicant will review the reference material and select an oil to be used in each climatic condition.

3. Project: Change the oil and filter in a reciprocating engine. (Level 3)

   Given: An engine, filter, oil, tools, and reference materials.

   Performance Standard: The applicant will change the oil and filter in accordance with the reference material.

4. Project: Inspect an oil filter. (Level 3)

   Given: An engine, filter, oil, tools, and reference materials.

   Performance Standard: The applicant will open and examine the oil filter in accordance with the manufacturer's procedures.

5. Project: Remove, inspect, and install a disk-type oil filter. (Level 3)

   Given: The applicant will open and examine the oil filter in accordance with the manufacturer's procedures.

   Performance Standard: The applicant will remove, disassemble, inspect, reassemble, and reinstall a disk-type oil filter in accordance with the manufacturer's instructions.

6. Project: Identify a turbine engine oil bypass indicator. (Level 2)

    Given: An oil filter with a bypass indicator.

    Performance Standard: A turbine engine, tools, and reference materials.

7. Project: Inspect a turbine engine's oil level and service as necessary. (Level 3)

    Given: The applicant will locate and describe the function of the bypass indicator.

    Performance Standard: The applicant will inspect the oil level of a turbine engine,and service as necessary, according to the reference materials.

8. Project: Inspect an oil cooler for leaks. (Level 3)

    Given: An aircraft engine with an oil cooler and reference materials.

    Performance Standard: The applicant will inspect an engine oil cooler for leaks.

9. Project: Inspect an oil screen. (Level 3)

    Given: A used oil screen, tools, and reference materials.

    Performance Standard: The applicant will examine the oil screen and identify materials.

10. Project: Check engine oil pressure. (Level 3)

    Given: The applicant will examine the oil screen and identify materials.

    Performance Standard: The applicant will operate the engine, and determine if oil pressure is within limits.

11. Project: Perform oil pressure adjustment. (Level 3)

    Given: An operable aircraft engine, tools, and reference materials.

    Performance Standard: The applicant will adjust the engine oil pressure relief or pressure regulator to the limits prescribed by the manufacturer.

12. Project: Identify oil system components. (Level 2)

    Given: An oil system and reference materials.

    Performance Standard: The applicant will identify each oil system component.

13. Project: Install an oil tank. (Level 3)

    Given: An aircraft or mockup, oil tank, tools, and reference materials.

    Performance Standard: The applicant will secure an oil tank according to the reference material.

14. Project: Identify oil system flow. (Level 2)

    Given: A drawing of an oil system and reference material.

    Performance Standard: The applicant will draw arrows in the direction of oil flow, throughout the system.

15. Project: Locate and service an oil filter screen on a turbine engine. (Level 3)

    Given: A turbine engine and reference materials.

    Performance Standard: The applicant will locate an oil filter screen and service itin accordance with the manufacturer's instructions.

16. Project: Drain and service an oil tank. (Level 3)

    Given: An oil tank, tools, and reference materials.

    Performance Standard: The applicant will drain and service an oil tank in accordance with the manufacturer's instructions.

17. Project: Inspect oil lines for leaks. (Level 3)

    Given: An aircraft engine, tools, and reference materials.

    Performance Standard: The applicant will inspect the oil system lines for leaks.

18. Project: Perform an engine preoil operation. (Level 3)

   Given: An aircraft engine, tools, and reference materials.

   Performance Standard: The applicant will preoil an engine as directed by reference materials.

19. Project: Troubleshoot an engine oil pressure malfunction. (Level 3)

   Given: Pilot reports and reference materials.

   Performance Standard: The applicant will analyze the pilot reports and list the possible causes of low or high oil pressure malfunctions.

20. Project: Troubleshoot an engine oil temperature system. (Level 3)

   Given: Pilot reports and reference materials.

   Performance Standard: The applicant will analyze the pilot reports and list the possible causes of low or high oil temperature malfunctions.

21. Project: Repair a low oil pressure warning system. (Level 3)

   Given: Access to an engine low oil pressure warning system with a loose electrical wire, tools, and reference materials.

   Performance Standard: The applicant will troubleshoot and repair the low oil pressure warning system.

CHAPTER 10 — COOLING SYSTEMS

ORAL QUESTIONS

1. What effect does excessive heat have on reciprocating engines?

    Answer – It shortens the life of the engine parts, changes the behavior of combustion, and impairs lubrication. (Page Reference: JSPT 10-2)

2. What is the purpose of cooling fins?

    Answer – They provide a larger cooling surface area for removing heat from cylinder heads of air-cooled reciprocating engines. Airflow around the cooling fins transfers the heat from the cylinder heads to the air. (Page Reference: JSPT 10-2)

3. What are the reasons for using engine cowlings, baffles and cowl air seals?

    Answer – The cowling performs two main functions: it streamlines the engine area to reduce drag, and is used together with the baffles and cowl air seals to direct airflow over the cylinders for cooling. (Page Reference: JSPT 10-2)

4. What is the purpose of cowl flaps and how are they operated?

    Answer – They are used to control the amount of airflow through the cowling. They are either mechanically, electrically or hydraulically operated. (Page Reference: JSPT 10-3)

5. How does an augmenter cooling system work?

    Answer – An outer tube placed over the exiting exhaust gas creates a venturi effect that draws more airflow over the engine, thus providing additional cooling. (Page Reference: JSPT 10-4)

6. Where should cowl flaps be positioned for ground operations?

    Answer – Fully open. (Page Reference: JSPT 10-3)

7. What type of power is used to operate cowl flaps?

    Answer – Manual, hydraulic, or electrical. (Page Reference: JSPT 10-3)

8. What should be done when cooling fin damage is discovered?

    Answer – Depending on the scope of damage, some cooling fins may be repaired subject to the manufacturer's overhaul and repair limitations. If an excessive amount of the cooling fin is broken off, the cylinder should be replaced. (Page Reference: JSPT 10-7)

9. Why is cowl flap adjustment important?

    Answer – The movement must be within tolerances to keep cylinder head temperatures within allowable limits. (Page Reference: JSPT 10-7)

10. How are turbine engines cooled?

    Answer – They are cooled by air passing through the engine. About 75% of the air passing through the engine is used for cooling which leaves only about 25% for combustion. This air is used to cool the combustion chamber and turbine. (Page Reference: JSPT 10-10)

11. In a turbine engine, where does bleed air come from that is used to cool bearings and other parts?

    Answer – The engine compressor. (Page Reference: JSPT 10-10)

12. What is the relationship between turbine engine upper temperature limits and power produced?

    Answer – The higher the combustion temperatures that an engine can withstand without damage, the more power it is capable of producing. (Page Reference: JSPT 10-10)

13. What is the approximate percentage of air passing through a turbine engine that is used for cooling rather than combustion?

    Answer – Approximately 75% (Page Reference: JSPT 10-10)

14. What can be done to effectively allow higher gas temperatures in the turbine section of some engines?

> **Answer** – Compressor bleed air ducted through hollow sections in the turbine inlet guide vanes and first stage rotor blades can lower temperatures enough to prevent heat damage. (Page Reference: JSPT 10-11)

PRACTICAL TEST

1. Project: Repair a cylinder head baffle. (Level 3)

   Given: A baffle plate, tools, and reference materials.

   Performance Standard: The applicant will select and repair a damaged baffle plate.

2. Project: Inspect cylinder head baffles. (Level 3)

   Given: An engine, tools, and reference materials.

   Performance Standard: The applicant will remove, inspect, and install cylinder baffles.

3. Project: Check cowl flap travel. (Level 3)

   Given: An engine with cowl flaps, tools, and reference materials.

   Performance Standard: The applicant will measure cowl flap travel, and determine if the open and close positions are within limits.

4. Project: Inspect cylinder cooling fins. (Level 3)

   Given: Samples of cylinders with damaged cooling fins and reference materials.

   Performance Standard: The applicant will review reference material, and select repairable cooling fins.

5. Project: Repair a cylinder cooling fin. (Level 3)

   Given: A cylinder with a damaged but repairable cooling fin, tools, and reference material.

   Performance Standard: The applicant will re-profile a damaged cylinder cooling fin as prescribed by the reference material.

6. Project: Identify the area of a turbine engine where the operating temperature is the highest. (Level 2)

   Given: Drawings of a turbine engine and reference material.

   Performance Standard: The applicant will point out the location of the highest operating temperatures and what major internal components are most exposed to high temperature stress.

7. Project: Identify turbine engine cooling airflow. (Level 2)

   Given: A drawing of a turbine engine and reference material.

   Performance Standard:

8. Project: Troubleshoot a cowl flap system. (Level 2)

   Given: Pilot reports, a drawing of a cowl flap system, and reference materials.

   Performance Standard: The applicant will analyze the pilot reports, and determine the possible cause of the cowl flap malfunction.

9. Project: Troubleshoot an engine cooling system. (Level 3)

   Given: Pilot discrepancy reports, a drawing of a cowl cooling system, and reference materials.

   Performance Standard: The applicant will analyze the pilot reports, and list the possible causes of the discrepancy.

10. Project: Identify exhaust augmentor cooling system components. (Level 2)

    Given: An augmentor cooling system or mockup and reference materials.

Performance Standard: The applicant will remove cowling, as necessary, and point out augmentor cooling components.

11. Project: Inspect for and identify heat damage to hot section components of a turbine engine. (Level 3)

 Given: Heat damaged and undamaged hot section components, or access to a turbine engine hot section and reference materials.

 Performance Standard: The applicant will inspect for and identify any heat related damage in turbine engine hot section components.

12. Project: Identify rotorcraft engine cooling components. (Level 2)

 Given: A rotorcraft with an engine cooling fan and reference materials.

 Performance Standard: The applicant will point out the rotorcraft cooling fan and associated components.

13. Project: Troubleshoot a rotorcraft engine cooling system. (Level 3)

 Given: Pilot discrepancy reports, system schematics, and reference materials.

 Performance Standard: The applicant will analyze the pilot reports, and determine the possible cause of the cooling system malfunction.

14. Project: Inspect a rotorcraft engine cooling system. (Level 3)

 Given: A rotorcraft with an engine cooling fan and reference materials.

 Performance Standard: The applicant will inspect a rotorcraft engine cooling fan system, and determine serviceability.

15. Project: Inspect an engine exhaust augmentor cooling system. (Level 3)

 Given: An engine with an augmentor-type cooling system and reference materials.

 Performance Standard: The applicant will inspect the engine cooling system in accordance with the reference materials.

16. Project: Inspect a liquid cooled engine's cooling system. (Level 3)

 Given: A liquid cooled engine with coolant, any necessary tools, and reference materials.

 Performance Standard: The applicant will inspect the system for leaks and component deterioration or damage in accordance with the reference materials.

17. Project: Inspect/test a liquid cooled engine's coolant. (Level 3)

 Given: A liquid cooled engine with coolant, any necessary tools and test equipment, and reference materials.

 Performance Standard: The applicant will inspect and test the coolant for condition/contamination and serviceability in accordance with the reference materials.

18. Project: Inspect cowling. (Level 2)

 Given: An aircraft or mockup with cowling and reference materials.

 Performance Standard: The applicant will inspect the cowling and test the coolant for condition/contamination and serviceability in accordance with the reference materials.

19. Project: Install an air seal for a reciprocating engine cooling system. (Level 3)

 Given: An aircraft or cooling system mockup, seal, fasteners, any necessary tools and equipment, and reference materials.

 Performance Standard: The applicant will install the air seal in accordance with the reference materials.

CHAPTER 11 — ENGINE FIRE PROTECTION

ORAL QUESTIONS

1. What types of fire detector systems are used for engine fire detection?

    Answer – Overheat, rate of rise, and flame detectors. (Page Reference: JSPT 11-2)

2. How does a thermal switch fire protection system operate?

    Answer – When heated past a predetermined temperature, the switch closes causing the warning devices in the cockpit to activate. (Page Reference: JSPT 11-2)

3. How many thermal switches are needed in a thermal switch fire protection system?

    Answer – At least one. (Page Reference: JSPT 11-2)

4. What kind of fire detection system allows more complete coverage than a spot-type system?

    Answer – A continuous loop system. (Page Reference: JSPT 11-2)

5. What happens if an engine equipped with a thermocouple fire warning systemoverheats slowly?

    Answer – Nothing, because a fast temperature rise or rapid heating is required for this type of fire system to operate. (Page Reference: JSPT 11-4)

6. What electrical power is required for a thermocouple fire protection system to operate?

    Answer – Both the thermocouple-produced power and the aircraft electrical system are required for this type of fire protection system to operate. (Page Reference: JSPT 11-4)

7. What is the likely cause of a false fire warning?

    Answer – The engine fire sensing loop is bent or kinked excessively. (Page Reference: JSPT 11-10)

8. What are fire extinguishing systems designed to do?

    Answer – They are designed to dilute the oxygen levels around the engine to a point that does not allow combustion, or to reduce temperatures below the ignition point. (Page Reference: JSPT 11-13)

9. Describe how a Kidde and Fenwal continuous loop fire protection system functions.

    Answer – A Kidde system has a sensing element consisting of a sealed Inconel® tube containing two conductors that are embedded in a thermistor material. One wire is electrically grounded to the outer tube at each end and acts as an internal ground, and the other is a positive lead. When a fire or overheat occurs, the resistance of the thermistor material drops, allowing current to flow between the two wires to activate an alarm. A Fenwal system uses a sensing element consisting of a small diameter flexible Inconel tube containing a single wire electrode surrounded by ceramic beads. These ceramic beads prevent the electrode and tube from touching each other. Current is applied to the electrode while the outer tube is grounded to the aircraft structure. When a fire or overheat occurs, the core resistance of the ceramic beads drops, allowing current to flow between the center electrode and ground, energizing the alarm system. (Page Reference: JSPT 11-4)

10. What elements must be present for a fire to occur?

    Answer – An ignition source such as heat or a spark, fuel and oxygen. (Page Reference: JSPT 11-13)

11. What group of fire extinguishing agents are no longer manufactured because of environmental concerns?

    Answer – Halons (or Freon® or chlorofluorocarbons [CFCs]) were no longer manufactured after 1995. However existing stocks of CFC may still be used and are subject to strict handling and disposal regulations. (Page Reference: JSPT 11-14)

12. How are fire extinguishing agents distributed?

    Answer – Through perforated tubing and/or discharge nozzles. (Page Reference: JSPT 11-15)

13. What is the purpose of the discharge cartridge and how is it activated?

    Answer – The discharge cartridge, or squib, which is electrically ignited, fires a projectile into the frangible disk, thereby releasing fire extinguishing agent. (Page Reference: JSPT 11-16)

14. How is a fire extinguisher system with a high rate of discharge classified?

    Answer – As an HRD fire extinguisher system. (Page Reference: JSPT 11-16)

15. What do the red and yellow discs in a fire extinguishing system indicate?

    Answer – A yellow disc indicates a normal discharge. A red disc indicates a thermal discharge. (Page Reference: JSPT 11-16)

16. How is the fire extinguishing agent in an HRD system distributed, and how long does it take to discharge?

    Answer – The agent is distributed through a series of high pressure tubes and takes one to two seconds to discharge. (Page Reference: JSPT 11-17)

17. What is the purpose of a pressure gauge in a fire extinguishing system?

    Answer – Indicates pressure within the container. To check if the pressure is within limits, a pressure-temperature chart is used. (Page Reference: JSPT 11-17)

PRACTICAL TEST

1. Project: Identify fire detection sensing units. (Level 2)

    Given: Sample fire detection units and reference materials.

    Performance Standard: The applicant will identify different types of sensing units.

2. Project: Identify continuous loop fire detection system components. (Level 2)

    Given: One or more continuous loop fire detection systems or mockups and reference materials.

    Performance Standard: The applicant will identify components of a Kidde-type(two wire), Fenwal-type (single wire), or inert gas pressure-type system.

3. Project: Inspect a fire detection continuous-loop system for visible defects. (Level 3)

    Given: A section of damaged continuous-loop, necessary tools and equipment, and reference materials.

    Performance Standard: The applicant will inspect the fire detection continuous-loop system, and point out the damaged area.

4. Project: Check a fire detection warning system. (Level 3)

    Given: An aircraft or mockup of a fire detection warning system, and reference materials.

    Performance Standard: The applicant will utilize the test feature and determine if the fire detection and warning system operates properly.

5. Project: Inspect a continuous-loop fire detection system installation. (Level 3)

    Given: An aircraft fire detection and warning system, and reference materials.

    Performance Standard: The applicant will inspect a continuous-loop fire detection system for proper routing and installation.

6. Project: Locate faults in a fire detection system. (Level 3)

    Given: A fire detection system with faults, any necessary tools and equipment, and reference materials.

    Performance Standard: The applicant will use test equipment to locate faults in a fire detection system.

7. Project: Troubleshoot a fire detection system. (Level 3)

   Given: The applicant will inspect the fire detection continuous-loop system, and point out the damaged area.

   Performance Standard: The applicant will analyze a fire detection system, and identify the malfunction(s).

8. Project: Inspect an engine fire detection system. (Level 3)

   Given: The applicant will analyze a fire detection system, and identify the malfunction(s).

   Performance Standard: The applicant will inspect the engine fire detection system components, and list any defects found.

9. Project: Inspect engine fire extinguisher system blowout disks. (Level 3)

   Given: An aircraft with an engine fire extinguisher system, and reference materials.

   Performance Standard: The applicant will inspect the fire extinguisher system disks to determine their condition and proper installation.

10. Project: Inspect the fire extinguishing agent container's pressure on a turbine engine system. (Level 3)

    Given: The applicant will inspect the fire extinguisher system disks to determine their condition and proper installation.

    Performance Standard: The applicant will inspect a fire extinguisher agent container and determine if the pressure is acceptable.

11. Project: Check a fire extinguisher discharge circuit. (Level 3)

    Given: The applicant will inspect a fire extinguisher agent container and determine if the pressure is acceptable.

    Performance Standard: The applicant will check a fire extinguisher discharge circuit with a multimeter in accordance with the reference materials.

12. Project: Troubleshoot a fire protection system. (Level 3)

    Given: Pilot reports, a diagram of a fire protection system, and reference materials.

    Performance Standard: The applicant will review pilot reports, and references to list the possible causes of the malfunction(s).

13. Project: Determine fire extinguisher carbon dioxide bottle serviceability. (Level 3)

    Given: A fire extinguisher carbon dioxide bottle, tools, and reference materials.

    Performance Standard: The applicant will determine the carbon dioxide extinguisher bottle's serviceability according to the reference materials.

14. Project: Install support clamps on a fire detector heat sensing loop. (Level 3)

    Given: An engine or mockup with a heat sensing loop, support clamps, tools, and reference materials.

    Performance Standard: The applicant will remove and install or replace heat sensing loop clamps.

15. Project: Inspect a fire extinguisher container discharge cartridge. (Level 3)

    Given: The applicant will determine the carbon dioxide extinguisher bottle's serviceability according to the reference materials.

    Performance Standard: The applicant will inspect a discharge cartridge for service life, and determine its serviceability.

16. Project: Check a manually operated fire extinguisher discharge handle. (Level 3)

    Given: The applicant will inspect a discharge cartridge for service life, and determine its serviceability.

    Performance Standard: The applicant will check a fire extinguishing discharge handle for proper operation without discharging the agent.

17. Project: Inspect a fire extinguisher system for hydrostatic test requirements. (Level 3)

    Given: A fire extinguisher system and reference material.

    Performance Standard: The applicant will determine if the system is approved, determine its test intervals, verify that last hydrostatic test date, and determine if the required interval has been exceeded.

18. Project: Check flame detectors for operation. (Level 3)

    Given: The applicant will determine if the system is approved, determine its test intervals, verify that last hydrostatic test date, and determine if the required interval has been exceeded.

    Performance Standard: The applicant will perform operation tests of flame detectors.

19. Project: Check the operation of firewall shutoff valves. (Level 3)

    Given: An aircraft or mockup and reference material.

    Performance Standard: The applicant will check the operation of the shutoff valves.

20. Project: Check the operation of a master caution press to test. (Level 3)

    Given: A fire detection system and references.

    Performance Standard: The applicant will check the operation of the master caution press to test, and identify any faults.

CHAPTER 12 — PROPELLERS

ORAL QUESTIONS

1. What is the function of a propeller?

    Answer – The propeller blades create thrust to pull or push an airplane through the air. (Page Reference: JSPT 12-2)

2. What is the difference between a fixed pitch propeller and a controllable pitch propeller?

    Answer – A fixed pitch propeller is one that has a built-in blade angle that cannot be changed by the pilot. These propellers can have the blade angle changed by the manufacturer or an approved repair station to optimize performance. A controllable pitch propeller is one that can be changed by the pilot and is usually controlled by a governor that maintains a constant speed. Some controllable propellers also provide reverse pitch and feathering. (Page Reference: JSPT 12-8)

3. How are some wooden propeller blades protected from wear and damage?

    Answer – By metal tipping fastened to the leading edge and tip. (Page Reference: JSPT 12-13)

4. What happens to the blade angle of a constant speed propeller during a constant power dive?

    Answer – The blade angle increases to prevent an overspeed. (Page Reference: JSPT 12-19)

5. What are the functions of a constant speed propeller governor?

    Answer – It boosts engine oil pressure before it enters the propeller hub, it senses rotational speed of the propeller, and then adjusts the oil flow to the propeller hub to change pitch and, therefore, speed of the propeller. (Page Reference: JSPT 12-19)

6. What is the purpose of propeller counterweights?

    Answer – Centrifugal force acting on the counterweights causes the blade angle to increase. (Page Reference: JSPT 12-20)

7. What is meant when a propeller governor is in an "on-speed" condition?

    Answer – The governor is not accelerating or decelerating and the speeder spring and flyweight forces are in balance. (Page Reference: JSPT 12-20)

8. How is a constant speed feathering propeller feathered?

    Answer – By releasing oil pressure in the governor, the counterweights and feathering spring move the propeller into feather. This happens automatically if the governor oil pressure drops to zero (following an engine failure in most turboprops), or can be manually controlled by the pilot by moving the propeller control into the feathering detent. (Page Reference: JSPT 12-27)

9. What is an unfeathering accumulator?

    Answer – It is an oil accumulator used to provide oil pressure to unfeather a propeller. (Page Reference: JSPT 12-28)

10. What is "alpha range" and "beta range" and where are they found?

    Answer – The alpha and beta ranges pertain to the operating modes of turboprop reversible-pitch propellers. In the alpha range, the propeller is operating in the standard, constant speed mode, which is usually in flight. In the beta range, the propeller is operating in the zero or minimum thrust range and negative thrust or reverse thrust mode, which is usually on the ground. (Page Reference: JSPT 12-37)

11. What systems are commonly used for propeller ice control?

    Answer – Fluid (alcohol) and electrical heat applied to the propeller blade root. (Page Reference: JSPT 12-51)

12. What propeller repairs can be performed by a certified mechanic with a powerplant rating?

    Answer – Only minor repairs and alterations can be performed by a certified mechanic with a powerplant rating. Major repairs must be performed by the manufacturer or a certified repair station. The propeller manufacturer's maintenance manual outlines the scope of repairs. (Page Reference: JSPT 12-57)

13. How are wooden propellers generally cleaned?

    Answer – With a brush or cloth and warm water with mild soap. (Page Reference: JSPT 12-58)

14. Where would you find the correct method and technique for cleaning an aluminum propeller and hub?

    Answer – The propeller manufacturer's maintenance instructions. (Page Reference: JSPT 12-59)

15. What type of nondestructive testing should be accomplished to a propeller after blending?

    Answer – The procedures recommended by the manufacturer. (Page Reference: JSPT 12-59)

16. What are the two criteria used by many manufacturers to determine the amount of bend damage that can be repaired by cold bending of aluminum propellers?

    Answer – The extent of the bend and its blade station location. (Page Reference: JSPT 12-60)

17. How can repair file marks be removed from an aluminum propeller?

    Answer – With very fine sandpaper. (Page Reference: JSPT 12-59)

18. When performing a static balance on a two bladed propeller, what positions must the propeller be placed in when measurements are taken?

    Answer – Vertical and horizontal positions. (Page Reference: JSPT 12-63)

19. What is a propeller protractor used for?

    Answer – It is used to measure propeller blade angle. (Page Reference: JSPT 12-64)

20. What blade conditions can cause engine vibration?

    Answer – Vibration can be caused by a propeller being out of track and/or balance, as well as incorrect blade angle setting. (Page Reference: JSPT 12-67)

21. What is blade tracking?

    Answer – Blade tracking is a procedure that compares the position of the propeller blade tips relative to each other. (Page Reference: JSPT 12-68)

22. What controls both manifold pressure and r.p.m. on an engine equipped with a fixed pitch propeller?

    Answer – The throttle. (Page Reference: JSPT 12-19)

PRACTICAL TEST

1. Project: Locate propeller ice control inspection procedures. (Level 1)

    Given: Reference materials.

    Performance Standard: The applicant will locate inspection procedures for propeller ice control.

2. Project: Perform propeller lubrication. (Level 3)

    Given: A propeller, a selection of lubricants, and reference materials.

    Performance Standard: The applicant will select the proper lubricant and lubricate a propeller as prescribed in the reference materials.

3. Project: Determine the procedure for balancing a fixed pitch propeller. (Level 2)

   Given: Access to reference material for balancing a fixed pitch propeller.

   Performance Standard: The applicant will use reference materials to determine the procedure for balancing a fixed pitch propeller.

4. Project: Remove, inspect, and install a propeller governor. (Level 3)

   Given: An engine with propeller governor, tools, and reference materials.

   Performance Standard: The applicant will remove, inspect, and install a propeller governor.

5. Project: Install a fixed pitch propeller. (Level 3)

   Given: An engine and a fixed pitch propeller, tools, and reference materials.

   Performance Standard: The applicant will install a propeller as prescribed by the reference materials.

6. Project: Check the track of a propeller. (Level 3)

   Given: An engine with a propeller, tools, and reference materials.

   Performance Standard: The applicant will determine if the propeller is within track limits as prescribed by the reference material.

7. Project: Adjust a propeller governor. (Level 3)

   Given: An operable engine with a controllable pitch propeller, tools, and reference materials.

   Performance Standard: The applicant will adjust the propeller governor.

8. Project: Describe the operation of a controllable pitch propeller. (Level 2)

   Given: Drawings and reference materials.

   Performance Standard: Utilizing drawings and reference materials, the applicant will describe the operation of a controllable pitch propeller.

9. Project: Determine propeller blade pitch angle. (Level 3)

   Given: A propeller, measuring equipment, and reference materials.

   Performance Standard: The applicant will use the measuring equipment, and determine the propeller blade pitch angle.

10. Project: Determine propeller critical range of operation. (Level 2)

    Given: The applicant will use the measuring equipment, and determine the propeller blade pitch angle.

    Performance Standard: The applicant will review the reference materials, and list the critical range of operation.

11. Project: Describe the operation of a counterweight propeller. (Level 2)

    Given: The applicant will review the reference materials, and list the critical range of operation.

    Performance Standard: The applicant will describe the operation of a counterweight propeller.

12. Project: Inspect a wooden propeller metal tipping. (Level 3)

    Given: A wooden propeller and reference materials.

    Performance Standard: The applicant will inspect a wooden propeller metal tipping, and list any defects.

13. Project: Check propeller blade feather angle. (Level 3)

    Given: A propeller feathering system, blade angle measuring equipment, and reference materials.

    Performance Standard: The applicant will check the feather angle of a propeller, and determine if it is correct according to the reference material.

14. Project: Repair a metal propeller leading edge and trailing edge or tip that has a minor nick, scratch, or cut. (Level 3)

   Given: A propeller blade with minor damage, tools, and reference materials.

   Performance Standard: The applicant will perform a minor repair of a propeller blade as prescribed in the reference material.

15. Project: Clean an aluminum alloy propeller. (Level 3)

   Given: An aluminum alloy propeller, cleaning materials, and reference materials.

   Performance Standard: The applicant will select approved cleaning materials,clean a propeller, and apply an approved protective coating.

16. Project: Determine the correct propeller installation for an aircraft. (Level 2)

   Given: The applicant will perform a minor repair of a propeller blade as prescribed in the reference material.

   Performance Standard: The applicant will determine if the correct propeller is installed on the aircraft.

17. Project: Inspect a turboprop propeller system. (Level 3)

   Given: A turbopropeller system and reference materials.

   Performance Standard: The applicant will identify and inspect the components ofa turbopropeller system.

18. Project: Perform the 100-hour inspection requirements of part 43, appendix D, on a constant speed propeller. (Level 3)

   Given: An engine with a constant speed propeller, tools, and reference materials.

   Performance Standard: The applicant will perform a 100-hour inspection on a propeller and list any discrepancies.

19. Project: Troubleshoot a turbopropeller system. (Level 3)

   Given: A drawing of a turboprop system, pilot reports, and reference materials.

   Performance Standard: The applicant will analyze the pilot reports, and determine the possible cause of the malfunction.

20. Project: Determine constant speed propeller oil flow path. (Level 2)

   Given: The applicant will analyze the pilot reports, and determine the possible cause of the malfunction.

   Performance Standard: The applicant will determine the propeller oil flow path.

CHAPTER 13 — POWERPLANT AND PROPELLER AIRWORTHINESS INSPECTIONS

ORAL QUESTIONS

1. What publications can be used as a guide for 100-hour inspections on aircraft engines?

    Answer – Manufacturers maintenance manuals and FAR part 43, Appendix D. (Page Reference: JSPT 13-9)

2. How do you identify the engine serial number?

    Answer – It is on the engine data plate. (Page Reference: JSPT 13-12)

3. Prior to returning a reciprocating engine to service after a 100-hour inspection, what operational checks must be performed?

    Answer – Check the power output (static and idle r.p.m.), check magnetos, fuel and oil pressure check, cylinder and oil temperature check. (Page Reference: JSPT 13-19)

4. Where are life-limited parts of an engine listed?

    Answer – Engine maintenance manuals, Type Certificate Data Sheet, and the Airworthiness Limitations section of the instructions for continued airworthiness. (Page Reference: JSPT 13-12)

5. Where can engine operating limits be found?

    Answer – Engine manual, engine specification, type certificate data sheet, and aircraft manufacturer's maintenance manual. (Page Reference: JSPT 13-12)

6. Why are hot section inspections performed on turbine engines?

    Answer – To determine the integrity and wear of the hot section components. (Page Reference: JSPT 13-15)

7. What inspections must be performed following a turbine engine overspeed?

    Answer – Refer to the engine manufacturer's maintenance manual for the required procedures. (Page Reference: JSPT 13-36)

8. What inspections must be performed on a turbine engine if the exhaust gas temperature exceeds limitations?

    Answer – A hot section inspection. (Page Reference: JSPT 13-35)

9. What FAA approvals are required when installing an engine that is not on the aircraft type certificate?

    Answer – An STC (supplemental type certificate) or an FAA field approval. (Page Reference: JSGT 13-4)

10. Under what conditions is compliance with an engine service bulletin mandatory?

    Answer – When an airworthiness directive references the service bulletin or when compliance is part of the approved operating specifications for a commercial or air carrier operator. When engine or component overhaul procedures require compliance at time of overhaul. (Page Reference: JSGT 13-8)

PRACTICAL TEST

1. Project: Inspect an engine appliance for compliance with ADs. (Level 3)

    Given: An aircraft engine, AD file, and maintenance record.

    Performance Standard: The applicant will review engine maintenance records and ADs, and determine if compliance with the required ADs has been accomplished.

2. Project: Inspect an aircraft engine for specific AD compliance. (Level 3)

    Given: The applicant will review engine maintenance records and ADs, and determine if compliance with the required ADs has been accomplished.

    Performance Standard: The applicant will determine compliance with a specific AD and enter a sample maintenance record entry showing AD compliance.

3. Project: Determine engine conformity with engine specifications or type certificate data sheet. (Level 2)

    Given: An aircraft engine, engine specifications or type certificate data sheet.

    Performance Standard: The applicant will inspect an engine, and determine conformity with engine specifications or type certificate data sheet.

4. Project: Construct a checklist for the engine portion of a 100-hour inspection. (Level 2)

    Given: An aircraft engine and 14 CFR part 43.

    Performance Standard: The applicant will make a checklist for the engine portion of a 100-hour inspection on a particular engine that covers the scope and detail in14 CFR part 43, Appendix D.

5. Project: Perform the engine portion of a 100-hour inspection. (Level 3)

    Given: An aircraft engine, 100-hour checklist, and reference materials.

    Performance Standard: The applicant will conduct the engine portion of a 100-hour inspection, or assigned portion thereof, and list any discrepancies found.

6. Project: Inspect one or more aircraft engine accessories for conformity. (Level 3)

    Given: An aircraft engine and engine specifications or type certificate data sheet.

    Performance Standard: The applicant will inspect one or more aircraft engine accessories for conformity.

7. Project: Inspect an aircraft engine for compliance with a service bulletin. (Level 3)

    Given: An aircraft engine, service bulletin, and reference materials.

    Performance Standard: The applicant will inspect for compliance by reviewing the service bulletin and inspecting the engine.

8. Project: List the life limited parts for a turbine engine. (Level 3)

    Given: Reference material for a specific engine.

    Performance Standard: The applicant will determine which parts of an engine are life limited.

9. Project: Determine if an overtemperature inspection is required. (Level 2)

    Given: Hypothetical engine conditions and reference materials.

    Performance Standard: The applicant will determine if an inspection is required, and if so, to what extent.

10. Project: Determine if an overtorque inspection is required. (Level 2)

    Given: Hypothetical turbopropeller engine conditions and reference materials.

    Performance Standard: The applicant will determine if an inspection is required,and if so, to what extent.

11. Project: Determine if an aircraft engine overspeed inspection is required. (Level 2)

    Given: Hypothetical engine conditions and reference materials.

    Performance Standard: The applicant will determine if an overspeed inspection is required, and if so, to what extent.

12. Project: Perform a conformity inspection on an aircraft engine to determine if correct spark plugs or igniters are installed. (Level 3)

   Given: An aircraft engine and reference materials.

   Performance Standard: The applicant will determine if the proper spark plugs or igniters are installed.

13. Project: Locate the recommended time between overhaul (TBO) for an APU. (Level 1)

   Given: Access to reference materials.

   Performance Standard: The applicant will locate the recommended TBO for an APU.

CHAPTER 14 — POWERPLANT TROUBESHOOTING

ORAL QUESTIONS

1. What are the possible causes for a turbojet or turbofan engine having high exhaust gas temperatures, low r.p.m., and high fuel flow at all engine pressure ratios?

    Answer – Turbine damage or loss of turbine efficiency due to wear. (Page Reference: JSPT 14-38)

PRACTICAL TEST

1. Project: Troubleshoot a turbine engine malfunction. (Level 3)

    Given: A turbine engine, an actual or simulated engine malfunction or condition, any necessary tools and equipment, and reference materials.

    Performance Standard: The applicant will troubleshoot the malfunction and determine the probable cause or causes.